D0376173

The North Pole: A Narrative History

The North Pole:
A Narrative History

*

EDITED BY ANTHONY BRANDT

National Geographic
Adventure Classics

Washington, D.C.

Library of Congress Cataloging-in-Publication Data

The North Pole: A Narrative History/ edited by Anthony Brandt
          p.cm
     Includes bibliographical references.
     ISBN 079224113
          1. North Pole—Discovery and exploration. 2. Arctic Regions—Discovery and
exploration. I. Brandt, Anthony.

G620.N67 2005
910'.9163'2—dc22   2204063237

One of the world's largest nonprofit scientific and educational organizations, the National Geographic Society was founded in 1888 "for the increase and diffusion of geographic knowledge." Fulfilling this mission, the Society educates and inspires millions every day through its magazines, books, television programs, videos, maps and atlases, research grants, the National Geographic Bee, teacher workshops, and innovative classroom materials. The Society is supported through membership dues, charitable gifts, and income from the sale of its educational products. This support is vital to National Geographic's mission to increase global understanding and promote conservation of our planet through exploration, research, and education.

For more information, please call 1-800-NGS LINE (647-5463) or write to the following address:

National Geographic Society
1145 17th Street N.W.
Washington, D.C. 20036-4688 U.S.A.

Visit the Society's Web site at www.nationalgeographic.com.

Contents

For Lisa Thomas, friend, co-worker, and the guiding spirit behind the Adventure Classics series

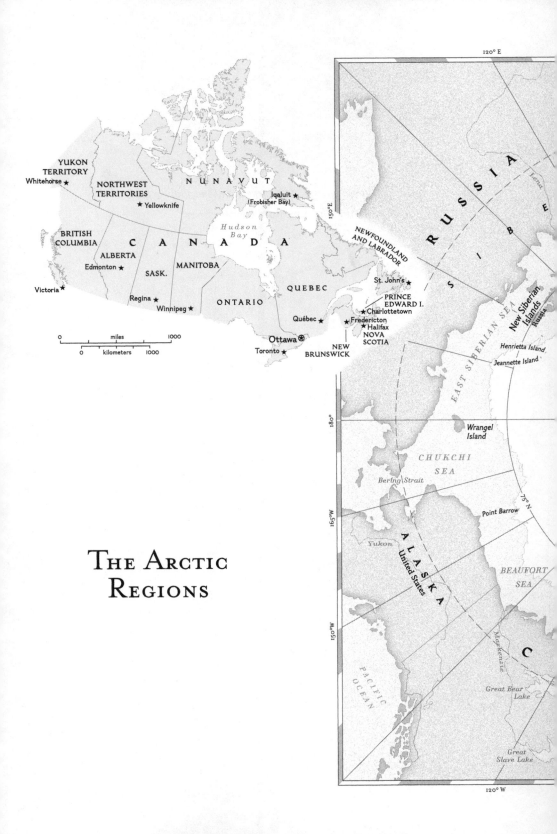

THE ARCTIC
REGIONS

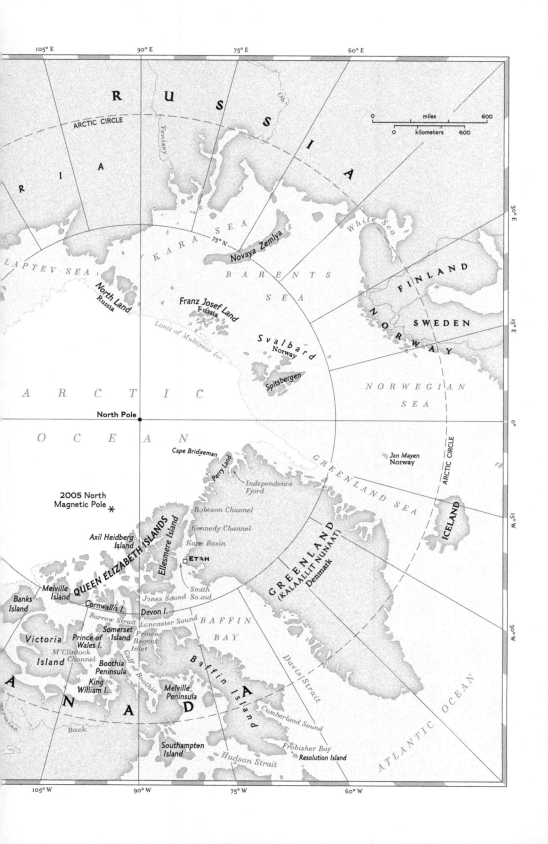

INTRODUCTION

BY ANTHONY BRANDT

"I TRY IN VAIN TO BE PERSUADED THAT THE POLE IS THE SEAT OF FROST and desolation," writes explorer Robert Walton to his sister, Mrs. Saville; "it ever presents itself to my imagination as the region of beauty and delight. There, Margaret, the sun is for ever visible; its broad disk just skirting the horizon, and diffusing a perpetual splendour. There—for with your leave, my sister, I will put some trust in preceding navigators—there snow and frost are banished; and, sailing over a calm sea, we may be wafted to a land surpassing in wonders and in beauty every region hitherto discovered on the habitable globe."

So begins Mary Shelley's novel *Frankenstein*. It seems odd at first that she should frame her story about scientific hubris in the Swiss Alps, where Dr. Victor Frankenstein assembles and quickens a living human being, if that's what it is, out of dead body parts, with a story about an English explorer in the Arctic. But it makes a certain kind of sense. What Robert Walton finds (besides Dr. Frankenstein himself, pursuing his monster across the icy wastes) when he sets sail for the North is not wonders and beauty but precisely frost and desolation, and the Arctic becomes for Walton not a stage for the glory he seeks but a scene of despair. "I am surrounded by mountains of ice, which admit of no escape, but threaten every moment to crush my vessel," he writes his sister at the end of the book. Like Dr. Frankenstein, who tells him his story, he has gone too far. He has overreached. He has tried to do what cannot be done.

The novel, furthermore, proved eerily predictive. Hundreds of Arctic explorers afterwards came to the same end: the frustration of their hopes; the destruction of their illusions,horror and often death. In the history of mankind the Arctic became one of the great theaters of disillusionment and tragedy, of heroic effort expended to no end. Only the realistic, the practical, the hard-hearted survived the Arctic, men like John Rae, who learned to hunt, eat, dress, and travel light, all like an Eskimo, or the obsessed Robert Peary, who kept going back for more despite the loss of nine toes to frostbite, or Dr. John Richardson, who preemptively shot the man who had already killed and eaten two of his companions and was planning to do the same to him.

Robert Walton returned from the Arctic a much wiser man. So have so many others who tried to conquer it.

But in 1818, when Mary Shelley wrote *Frankenstein*, Robert Walton could entertain hopes and dreams about calm open seas and the splendor of the Arctic landscape because so little was known about the Arctic. An influential geographic theory of the time in fact held that while the Arctic Ocean did seem to be frozen, that was true only at its edges. North of the ice pack lay open ocean (assuming it was ocean, and not undiscovered land), navigable its entire breadth. One had only to penetrate the wall of ice guarding this placid ocean.

There were other theories, too. No one had been to the top of Greenland, so no one knew that it did not extend to the north all the way to the Pole, or perhaps all the way to Alaska. Some maps showed Greenland doing exactly that. Other maps were less speculative and showed the Arctic as a vast blank west and north of Baffin Island. The only chart of Baffin Bay in the early 1800s was the one made by William Baffin himself in the early 1600s, and it was little more than a sketch (which proved, as it happens, to be remarkably accurate). No one had been back since. If there were a Northwest Passage, it would have to begin in Baffin Bay, for by then it was clear that Hudson Bay had no exit to the west. The landscape beyond Baffin Bay was totally unknown. No one except the natives who lived there had been anywhere close to the complicated archipelago of the Canadian Far North. Was there land at the North Pole? Unknown. Alexander McKenzie and Samuel Hearne had penetrated to the northern coast of North America at the mouths, respectively, of the McKenzie River and the Coppermine, but on the map these were isolated spots of known land. Everything in between them was terra incognita.

Yet at the same time the Arctic seemed close by, almost familiar. Walk far enough north through Europe, as Victor Frankenstein's articulate monster had done, and somewhere along the way you came upon it, sidled into it, as it were, without knowing exactly where it began. News of it sometimes filtered south. The Greeks gave it its name, Arktos, the bear, after the constellation we know by the Latin name Ursa major, the great bear, and had their own theories about the Hyperboreans who lived there, and what kind of land it was that they inhabited—something of a paradise in their view. In the sixth century B.C. the Greek philosopher Pythagoras studied, it was said, with a sage from the far north, where the sun did not set for six months. A Greek merchant named Pytheas sailed north in the fourth century B.C., probably as far as Iceland, sailed to the edge of the frozen sea and found that the sun in the summer did not, indeed, dip below the horizon.

A millennium later the Vikings got to Greenland, which they colonized, and then to North America. The Vikings lived in Greenland under Arctic conditions for hundreds of years, and news of their occupation of this icy land similarly filtered south.

It gives the Arctic from the beginning a human dimension, a place in human history, that Antarctica notably lacks. Not only does the Arctic merge imperceptibly throughout most of its domain with the continental land masses that surround it, making its borders more a matter of climate than geography, it is also inhabited, and has been for thousands of years, not by the legendary Hyperboreans but by native tribes who long ago mastered the difficulties of Arctic life. The history of the Arctic thereby becomes a history of interaction, of cultural contact, as much as a history of exploration. Quite often explorers suffer and die right beside people who understand quite well how to find food and survive and stay relatively warm in temperatures that fall forty or fifty degrees or more below zero.

The Arctic is not as cold as Antarctica, but it is certainly cold enough to kill. It is a deadly place in many ways, even small ways. Mosquitoes and black flies, for example. The cold has permanently frozen the earth that abuts the Arctic Ocean to depths of as much as 1,500 feet. Because this subsoil never melts, water that falls upon it cannot seep into the ground but must stay on the surface, where it freezes in winter and melts in summer and creates a kind of slush underfoot nearly everywhere you walk. This water makes perfect breeding grounds for swarms of black flies and mosquitoes so numerous that they can suck enough blood out of a reindeer—not to mention a human being—to destroy it.

Agriculture, needless to add, is not possible in the Arctic climate. People must live on animal protein: seals, whales, musk oxen, fish, reindeer, polar bears, birds, hares, foxes, dogs. The people of the Far North are adapted to this diet, but for those from more temperate climates it has been historically hard to get used to, and most explorers have brought their own food with them, often to their great cost. Until the problem of scurvy was solved (for practical purposes, at any rate) in the nineteenth century, when sea captains began to understand that only fresh food, especially fresh fruit and vegetables, could prevent it, thousands of explorers and the sailors who sailed with them died of scurvy or suffered terribly from it. But the people of the Far North never suffered from scurvy. Fresh meat is also an excellent source of vitamin C, the lack of which is the cause of scurvy, and they lived on fresh meat, which they were perfectly capable of eating raw if they lacked the means to cook it. But almost none of the explorers who penetrated the Arctic, at least until the late nineteenth century, followed their example. Instead they dragged huge quantities of food with them on their sledges wherever they went, making Arctic travel a labor not to be endured. Yet they died regardless if this food was not fresh.

Knowing where you are in the Arctic, at least until global positioning devices became common, has also been difficult. In the Arctic summer the sun takes a long low trip around the horizon in which its noons and midnights, when navigational sun sights are taken, are hard to distinguish. You cannot steer by the stars because you never see the stars. The north magnetic pole wanders; near the geographic pole magnets, therefore, are close to useless. To reach that pole, furthermore, requires that you walk on water, frozen to an average depth (these days; global warming has affected it significantly) of about eight feet. The pack is thick. Scientists set up drift stations on it that survive for years. But it is unstable. It drifts. You may be walking across it toward the pole at eight or nine miles a day, dragging your sledge behind you, but the pack may be drifting south at fifteen miles a day or more.

Not only does the pack drift, it wrinkles. Winds and currents drive floes apart, creating leads of open water. North of Greenland something like a permanent lead, in some places several miles across—the Big Lead, explorers called it—separates the ice that's frozen fast to northern Greenland from the permanent pack to the north, at about where the continental shelf ends. This Big Lead was a barrier early venturers to the North Pole had to cross. And when leads close, floes can ride over each other or tip up perpendicular to the surface, creating ridges that can stand forty feet high or more. Whether with dogsleds or snowmobiles, these can be extremely difficult and time-consuming to cross. Ridges occur about four in a mile. In addition to ridges the pack is often covered with hummocks, the eroded remains of ridges. The surface of the pack, in short, is rarely smooth. Rarely could you make haste crossing it. You had to feed yourself and also your dogs. The weight of food alone was formidable. Polar bears might appear anywhere on the pack, which they range all summer. The list of explorers lost to bears is a long one.

When ships try to navigate leads and work their way through the ice, it is worth adding, they run the constant danger of a "nip"—the leads vanishing, the floes closing in on them, crushing them to splinters. Even ships frozen solidly into the pack may suffer this fate as the pack moves and shifts, always unpredictably. Leopold McClintock, in *The Voyage of the Fox*, his account of his search for Sir John Franklin's remains, tells the story of Captain Deuchars and his ship, the *Princess Charlotte*. "It was a beautiful morning," he writes; "they had almost reached the North Water, and were anticipating a very successful voyage; the steward had just reported breakfast ready, when Captain Deuchars, seeing the floes closing together ahead of the ship, remained on deck to see her pass safely between them, but they closed too quickly; the vessel was almost through, when the points of ice caught her sides abreast of the misenmast, and, passing through, held the wreck up for a few minutes, barely long enough for the crew to escape and save their boats." The ship sank in ten minutes. Among the great Arctic explorers only Fridtjof Nansen had the wit to design a ship (the *Fram*) whose rounded hull rode up onto the ice when it was frozen in.

The Arctic is a Gothic scene. It is no accident that Mary Shelley found it an appropriate place to set the stage for her own Gothic tale, or that so many Arctic exploration stories involve starvation, madness, murder, cannibalism, reading like something out of Edgar Allan Poe. In this the Arctic differs significantly from the Antarctic. The Antarctic, all ice and emptiness, seemed to instill a nobility in its explorers that stands out even now. Scott died with a stoicism that inspired an entire generation of Englishmen to die in the trenches of World War I with equal panache. Shackleton took a little whale-boat across 800 miles of the stormiest seas in the world, and then climbed the dangerous cliffs of South Georgia, to rescue his men, and did rescue them, and not a single man died. Mawson pulled himself out of his crevasse with the last ounce of his energy, reciting some verses from Robert Service to give himself the heart to survive. The stories are deeply moving. But the Arctic stories are dark. Starving men steal crumbs from each other. Men kill and eat other men. They abandon their companions on ice floes. The first three men who claimed to reach the North Pole, two on the surface, one in the air, all apparently lied about it.

Yet they all loved the place. It is, in its own way, awesomely beautiful, a place of unforgettable sunsets and hypnotizing phenomena, refraction throwing scenery into the sky from hundreds of miles away, the aurora borealis putting on its shows, wind and tide sculpting icebergs into the most fantastical shapes. Frederick Edwin Church, the American landscape painter, sailed to the coast of Labrador just to paint icebergs. Men would come home from the Arctic drained, scarred, sick, pieces of their bodies lost to frost-bite, then scheme to find ways to go back. Charles Francis Hall lived with the Eskimos for five years, then came home to persuade rich men to send him back, this time in charge of his own expedition. Men developed an appetite for the ice, the cold, the hardship. They wrote endlessly about their adventures, and their writings always sold. When the explorers went back to the Arctic, they almost always took accounts of other Arctic explorers with them, to read in the months-long winters. They were heroes, these men, lionized in their time. Emily Brontë, when a child, took Parry as her adopted surname, after William Edward Parry, who found the door to the Northwest Passage in 1819. Charles Dickens and Wilkie Collins co-wrote a play, *The Frozen Sea*, to celebrate the ordeal of Sir John Franklin.

The place retains its appeal to this day. Men and women are still trekking over the ice to reach the North Pole, the Big Nail, as the Eskimos came to call it when the explorers explained to them what they were seeking. Obsessed seekers are still looking for the remains of Sir John Franklin's ships on the bottom of the channels that lace through the Canadian Archipelago. It is as if the ice held a secret about us, and we are bound to find it. The Hyperboreans, the Greeks believed, lived in a golden age that never ended, in white purity and peace. The god Apollo returned there every fall to live among them and replenish his powers. The Arctic, that is, has an air of divinity about it, of the sublime, which men find somewhere between their terror and their exaltation.

*

I have tried in this anthology to find selections that capture both the beauty and the terror, and of course the history, of this amazing area of the globe. Because its history is so complicated and so long, going back as far as the ancients, no anthology can do it the justice it deserves. The area cries out for fuller historical treatment. The only recent broad-brush history of Arctic exploration we have is Charles Officer's and Jake Page's brief A Fabulous Kingdom, which I have used as one of my guides. More limited in scope is Pierre Berton's Arctic Grail, which covers only the nineteenth century, although it's an excellent book, beautifully researched and more or less definitive in the area it does cover. Two recent books by Fergus Fleming, Barrow's Boys and Ninety Degrees North, are also quite good. I would recommend any of these books to those readers who want more information.

But otherwise the history of Arctic exploration has not been given the kind of scrutiny that other areas of the globe have received, and the original texts written by the explorers themselves are hard to find and expensive to acquire. Many of the sources reprinted here come from rare books. Perhaps this anthology can spark an interest among historians in these strange obsessions with the Arctic and its vast unknowns. This anthology is only an introduction to the Arctic and an outline of its past. My hope for it is that it will inspire readers to look further into this extraordinary place and its history.

I should add that throughout most of the text I refer to native peoples as Eskimos, which is well-known as a name given to them by Indians living to the south of them in Canada. The word means "people who eat meat raw." It is not a name they use themselves. They use different names for themselves in different areas—Samoyeds in northern Russia, Aleut or Yupik in central Alaska, in eastern Canada Inuit, in western Canada Inupiaq, the Chukchi in Siberia, and so on. Nearly every text excerpted or cited in this anthology, however, uses the word Eskimo, and it would have been foolish to try either to change the texts to the correct usage or to explain at every turn what name they actually used of themselves. Most recent histories of this period make the same choice and use the word Eskimo for people who were called Eskimo until the twentieth century. Where the texts I am quoting use the word Eskimo, therefore, I follow their practice.

*

PART ONE

LOOKING NORTH

*

LOOKING NORTH

ONE OF THE LURES THAT DREW EARLY EXPLORERS INTO THE ARCTIC *even into the nineteenth century, and that separates the history of Arctic exploration from that of Antarctica, was commerce. Exploration in Antarctic has always been essentially scientific in nature. Antarctica is barren, a crystal desert, and has no resources to offer except knowledge.*

But the Arctic was in range of European ships even in the time of the Greeks and the Greeks knew that the North was a source of tin, amber, and gold, which moved into Mediterranean Europe down local trade routes, tribe to tribe. From the first, then, the exploration of the Arctic was driven by mixed motives. Part of it was scientific in nature, a function of Western curiosity about what might lie over the horizon. But the other, and the initial, motive was commercial: trade. If it was not trade for amber and tin, it was trade with China. Men spent three centuries, from the middle 1500s to the middle 1800s, trying to penetrate the Arctic in search of a northwest passage around the unbroken barrier that North and South America proved to be, all for trade with China and the rest of the Orient. It was a measure of how valuable that trade was thought to be.

The first voyage to the Far North we know about was just this kind of voyage, driven by curiosity about what lay across the North Sea but made by a merchant, the Greek named Pytheas from the Greek colony of Massalia (now Marseille), interested in finding the sources of the commodities mentioned above. He made his voyage sometime between 330-320 B.C. and seems to have gotten as far as Iceland, which touches the Arctic Circle at its northernmost point. He was the first European we know about to have seen the Arctic ice pack.

By the eighth century A.D. Irish monks were actually living in Iceland, having reached it in their remarkable coracles, boats made of animal skins. The Norse drove the Irish out in the ninth century and settled it permanently. They went on to settle in Greenland as well, and to stay there for more than four centuries. Attempts to find a route west of Greenland into and through the Arctic Ocean began in the sixteenth century and were renewed on a large scale in the nineteenth. These attempts, again, had an element of the scientific in them, as no one went to the Arctic without adding to the map, but the real object was to discover a Northwest Passage (or, failing that, a Northeast) to the Orient that would be shorter and easier than the known routes around the Cape of Good Hope or through the Straits of Magellan.

Shorter, yes—but it was never going to be easier. The repeated quests for the Northwest Passage neatly fit Samuel Johnson's well-known definition of a second marriage: the triumph of hope over experience. The experience was routinely disastrous. But men pursued it again and again and yet again, regardless of previous failures, testifying both to the importance of the goal and the familiar double nature of human heroism, its two faces: courage and folly. It took hundreds of years and hundreds of lives just to discover that there was, in fact, a Northwest Passage. It was not sailed until the early twentieth century, when Roald Amundsen piloted a small converted herring schooner through it over the course of three years, 1903-06. Not until 1944 did someone make the trip in a single season.

＊

WE WOULD BEGIN THIS COLLECTION WITH A SELECTION FROM PYTHEAS if we could, but the book he wrote about his journey, On the Ocean, has not survived. We know what we know about it through quotations from it and discussions of it in ancient sources that have survived. The best recent scholarship on his voyage argues that he made his trip not in a ship of his own but locally, in stages, along the French and British coastlines, using local shipping. Tin, a key ingredient in bronze, came mostly from sources in the west country of Britain, in Devon and Cornwall, which also contained small quantities of gold. Amber was found along the southern shores of the Baltic. Pytheas appears to have visited both places. We know that he probably got as far as Iceland because he describes a day that lasts six months and a night equally long. He says that Thule, the name he gives what is probably Iceland, lies six days' sail north of Britain, which is about right if sailed in a coracle in favorable conditions. He speaks of a "congealed sea," i.e. the frozen seas of the North. He describes the North with enough detail to persuade us, in short, that he was there.

The information Pytheas provided about the north was not very successful, however, in running the gauntlet of history. Later writers and geographers often did not believe him even while they described what he had to say. Much of what we know about his discoveries comes from sources calling him a liar. And nobody in the classical world followed him north. The Romans were conquerors, not explorers. The phrase "ultima Thule," which has had a certain resonance in history as representing the last place on earth, comes from the Roman philosopher and playwright Seneca, who in Medea puts into the mouth of one of his characters this prophecy: that at some point in the future, "when the earth is older," explorers will find new continents. "Then Thule will no longer be the last land." But no Roman showed any interest in going to this Thule that Pytheas had discovered. When the Romans got to Britain they stopped short of Scotland and built a wall, to keep the barbarians out. They had gone far enough north.

After the collapse of the Roman Empire travel largely ceased and knowledge of the North, such as it was, fell back into monastery libraries. The Late Classical encyclopedias that kept fragments of ancient learning alive have little to say about the North. The fact that toward the Poles day and night each lasts for months at a time did survive, but the men who compiled these encyclopedias showed little interest in the matter, and one learned thirteenth-century churchman, Robert Grosseteste, argued that because the sun did shine in the North for such long periods of time it must generate intense heat, which must mean in turn that no animal or plant life could survive there. Grosseteste was wrong, of course, and his argument was unique. The standard Medieval theory of the polar regions held that they were uninhabitable precisely because of the intense cold.

Otherwise the north polar regions belonged as much to legend as to fact. In 1598 Richard Hakluyt's great collection of exploration narratives, the Principall Navigations, repeats the fictional twelfth-century account by Geoffrey of Monmouth of King Arthur's voyages to the North, including Iceland, as well as a later Medieval account that extends Arthur's conquests from Iceland to Greenland and Norway "and many other islands beyond Norway, even under the North Pole." No one believes now that King Arthur, whoever he might have been, made such voyages. Hakluyt goes on to remark that "all evil comes from the north." He doesn't make clear whether he was talking about the weather, or Norse invaders, or some metaphysical concept about the location of the Gates of Hell. Sir Francis Bacon, generally thought to be a rational man, believed that Gog and Magog, the giants in the Old Testament, lived in the Far North and that it ought to be a project of mankind to go north and build a wall that would confine them forever to their icy domain.

Maybe he was thinking of the Norse. While the rest of Europe stayed home the Norse sailed forth over much of the known world and into the unknown as well. Besides King Arthur's voyages Hakluyt also describes Ottar (or Othere; the spelling is various) the Norseman's historic voyage around the year 890 up the coast of Norway and east along the shores of Lapland to the White Sea, which is north of Russia. No one doubts that he made this voyage. Subsequent Viking voyages penetrated from the White Sea down Russian rivers into the heart of Russia, and then beyond into the Middle East, where Viking coins have been found. The Vikings reached Greenland late in the tenth century, and North America shortly thereafter. The Vikings knew that the Siberian shore of the Arctic Ocean was inhabited, as was Greenland. Viking sailors had seen glaciers and icebergs and the Arctic ice pack; they had encountered polar bears and narwhals.

How much of the knowledge they acquired made its way to the rest of Europe, however, remains an open question. Ottar personally told his story to King Alfred the Great of England in the ninth century, and Alfred incorporated it into his translation into Anglo-Saxon of the General History written by Orosius, a Christian writer of the fifth century, which includes chapters on geography. A little earlier a monk named Dicuil reported, in his Liber de Mensura Orbis Terrae, what Irish friends had told him about their visit to Iceland, probably in 795, that around the time of the summer solstice the sun hardly went down below the horizon at all, "there was no darkness, and you could engage in whatever occupation you wished, even picking the lice from your shirt." The later saga literature of the Vikings is full of their voyages, which is full of geographical information. This literature was not translated into other European languages, however, for hundreds of years. If Norse voyages did have any influence on subsequent exploration, it was not large. There is evidence that Prince Henry the Navigator knew about them and that later kings of Portugal were aware of Danish pirate activity in the area between Norway and Greenland. Knowledge of Greenland was never really lost, even after the Norse colonists had blended into its native population and ships had stopped making the journey there. The Vatican certainly knew about it. However symbolic the gesture, since the bishops in question made no attempt to reach it, the Vatican continued to assign bishops to Greenland through the early 1500s.

With Prince Henry we enter the great age of European exploration, which began with the Portuguese voyages he sponsored down the west coast of Africa in the 1430s. The goal was to reach the legendary markets and wonders of Asia. The land routes were blocked by unfriendly Muslim kingdoms in the Middle East. Only by sea could the West trade with Asia. A century and a half later European ships had opened up the world. The Portuguese had not only reached India, they had founded colonies there. Two huge continents had been discovered. Magellan and Drake had circumnavigated the earth. Trade routes to the Far East were well established. Spain was building an empire in South and Central America, vast and incredibly rich, and in the Philippines as well.

Only the English, among the maritime nations, had failed to join this rush to make the unknown known. By the time the English began to generate a little interest in the opportunities exploration provided, the Spanish and the Portuguese owned the world, or at least its sea lanes, a division that the Papal Bull of 1493 ratified when Pope Alexander VI (a Spaniard, by the way) drew a north-south line 370 leagues (call it a thousand miles) west of the Azores and gave Spain everything to the west of the line and Portugal everything to the east of it. That division explains why Brazil speaks Portuguese and the rest of South America speaks Spanish.

In the 1490s King Henry VII of England had licensed a voyage by John Cabot to the west and he discovered what historians believe was Newfoundland, but whatever maps and documents he brought back were lost long ago. We know little more about the Cabot voyage than that it happened. Sebastian Cabot, his son, claimed to have made a voyage toward the North Pole in 1508, but no records of this voyage, if it ever took place, have survived, and most historians believe that it never did take place. More to the point, the English did not follow John Cabot's efforts up and this late start had a profound impact on the history of the world. When the English did come to explore and colonize, the newfound lands to the south were more or less taken. They turned north because that was what was left to them. They turned to the far north because there lay the only remaining route to the Orient, or so they believed. Until Americans became involved in the second half of the nineteenth century, most exploration of the Arctic was British.

But it was slow to develop. During the reign of Henry VIII sporadic attempts were made to explore toward the Northwest Atlantic, but we know very little about them and they were unsuccessful in any case. In 1527 an English merchant named Robert Thorne wrote to the King, pointing out that "of the four parts of the world, it seems three parts are discovered by other Princes." All that remains are the "North parts, the which it seems to me is only your charge and duty." England, he notes, is the "nearest and aptest" to the North, and after one gets past the cold regions "it is clear, that from thenceforth the seas and lands are as temperate as in these parts." Where he got that idea he doesn't say.

In a later publication Thorne argued that if one sailed northeast from the Spice Islands just 1700 or 1800 leagues one would come to the backside, as it were, of the "new found islands that we discovered"—to wit, Newfoundland. No one yet knew the size of North America or its extent, and Spanish charts of the time showed the area around the North Pole to be open sea. Thorne proposed that English ships sail north from the "new found lands" past the North Pole and descend to the Equator, thereby cutting 2000 leagues (about 6,000 miles) from the trip via the Straits of Magellan. Thorne knew that the northern seas were supposed to be frozen, but, ignoring his own conjectures about where Newfoundland lay in relation to the Pacific Ocean, he points out that formerly cosmographers held that no one could live in the equatorial zones because of the extreme heat, and the equatorial zones were inhabited. With a breathtaking leap of logic he concludes from this that "there is no land unhabitable nor sea unnavigable." This doctrine would govern British attempts to find the Northwest Passage for the next three hundred years.

In the meantime, however, Thorne's enthusiasm for northern exploration fell largely on deaf ears. Bristol fishermen did some exploring on their own and the Grand Banks off Newfoundland became what they remain to this day, a fishing mecca, not just for the Bristol men but for Portuguese and other fishermen as well. They left no records behind, however, and no maps. Even then men may have been penetrating into Davis Strait farther north, but without a record of their travels, these voyages remain in the realm of conjecture. A Portuguese sailor named Gaspar Cortereal had "rediscovered" Greenland in 1500. He vanished on his next voyage north (not an uncommon event in the Arctic). When his brother sailed in search of him, he, too, vanished. But while the Spanish were sacking the Aztec and Incan kingdoms and making themselves criminally rich, the English were sitting on their thumbs. The most daring maritime nation in history had yet to grow into its role.

There were, however, other Englishmen like Robert Thorne interested in exploration and they kept up with what was happening elsewhere in the world as well as they could. In 1553 a group of them formed what would become the Muscovy Company and sponsored an expedition over the top of Norway in search of a passage to Asia by the Northeast. Three ships under the overall command of Sir Hugh Willoughby, a soldier of some small renown but no sailor, headed north. By the end of July the ships had sailed against contrary winds halfway up the Norwegian coast when a storm separated two ships from the third, which then retreated down the coast to Denmark and a rendezvous point they had earlier agreed upon. The other two ships, however, with Willoughby in command, wandered lost in the seas above Norway and finally, in mid-September, came ashore they knew not where. It was Lapland. Willoughby sensibly decided to spend the winter there.

Richard Chancellor, unlike Willoughby an experienced sailor, was in charge of the third ship and after waiting a week in Denmark for his companions he sailed on over the top of Norway and into the White Sea, where he landed at Archangel. From Archangel he trekked south overland to Moscow and talked a receptive Ivan the Terrible into granting a license to trade with Russia by way of this northern route to the merchants who had sponsored Willoughby's voyage. At the time the Hanseatic League, an international trading consortium that controlled all trade in the Baltic Sea, was the only European organization that was trading with Russia, and relations between Russia and the League had broken off. The Russians were eager for European goods, especially English wool. The license Chancellor obtained became the foundation of the Muscovy Company (later the Russia Company) of England, and Chancellor's voyage remains one of the great early English expeditions.

Chancellor himself perished on a second voyage, however, and the Muscovy Company, despite the monopoly it held from the crown on trade with Russia, was never a thriving organization, partly because the voyage to the White Sea was an iffy proposition in the best of circumstances. The seas were stormy, the pack ice fickle. As for Sir Hugh Willoughby and his companions, they too perished, all 63 of them. Russian fishermen found them the following summer in their ships, dead, frozen in the strangest positions: some at tables with pen in hand, others in the arrested act of eating dinner, "like statues, as if they had been adjusted and placed in these attitudes," according to one report. They say that some of the dogs on board the ships displayed the same phenomena." Eleanora C. Gordon, a British medical historian, believes that they died of carbon monoxide poisoning when they burned sea coal—mineral coal, that is, which produces carbon monoxide in quantity—to stay warm and then stopped up all the portholes and other openings to keep the warmth in. Carbon monoxide poisoning almost killed Richard Byrd in a similar fashion when he wintered over alone in Antarctica in 1934 and ice blocked up his stovepipe.

After Willoughby's expedition and the establishment of the Russia Company's monopoly on Russian trade, English interest in penetrating the Northeast Passage beyond the White Sea faded away. It was the Dutch who, later in the century, took it up. The English turned back to the Northwest Passage. Geographers were by this time well aware that the eastern coasts of North and South America were unbroken and the general shape of South America was also known, but no one had sailed up the West Coast of North America and therefore no one knew what it was: merely a thin slice of land tending to the northeast from South America? A continent? In the dark on the facts, geographers speculated and hoped. When the French sent out Giovanni da Verrazano in 1523—the French, too, hoped for a northwest passage—he coasted North America, came to the Outer Banks off North Carolina, and decided that the large body of water he saw inland of them, what we know as Pamlico Sound, was the Pacific. For years afterwards maps showed North America this way, as having, at that one point, only the slimmest of barriers between the Atlantic and the Pacific.

Later maps relied on equally tenuous information, some of it completely fraudulent. A map in Sebastian Munster's edition of Ptolemy's Geographia of 1540 showed a passage above the "Novus Orbis," the new world, as a wide strait, with India, i.e. the Far East, on the northwest side of it. This became known as the Strait of Anian. Mariners searched for it well into the eighteenth century. It was pure fiction. In 1545 a map by Apianus has this same strait while North America is hardly more than a long finger of land stretching to the northeast from South America. By 1570, when the world map of Abraham Ortelius appeared, North America looks continental; indeed, it has the same shape, roughly, as it has in fact. But Ortelius still shows a northwest passage above the North American continent as a strait between two large bodies of land. So does the influential world map of Gerhard Mercator, published a year earlier. With his map Mercator printed a separate projection of the North Pole area, as if looking down on it from above. At the North Pole itself, as Mercator has it, stood a huge mountain made of iron, or lodestone. This would explain the magnetic attraction to it exhibited by compasses. A small ocean surrounds this mountain, and then on four sides, separated by wide rivers, lie four roughly symmetrical bodies of land. Below them lie the straits, all, apparently, navigable.

Mercator, like all the other mapmakers, relied on bad information and bad reasoning to construct this picture, but he was a great authority, so the passage had to exist. In 1567 a promoter named Humphrey Gilbert wrote a treatise arguing that it had to exist, and tried unsuccessfully to obtain a license from the crown to send an expedition to find it. Finally, in 1576, a group of backers, many of them members of the Russia Company and led by a fellow member, a merchant named Michael Lok, put together an expedition consisting of two small barks and a pinnace of four tons (no more than what we would call a modest little yacht), under the overall command of a sailor named Martin Frobisher, and they sailed for North America. Thus was begun the search for the Northwest Passage.

Frobisher made three voyages in three successive years, 1576, '77, and '78. All of them generated multiple accounts of what happened, although all the accounts are relatively short. We print here an account of the second voyage written by one Dionyse Settle, a gentleman-soldier about whom we otherwise know very little. The first voyage was from beginning to end a near-disaster. The pinnace, with four men aboard, vanished in a storm somewhere west of Greenland. One of the other two ships turned back in the same storm and returned to England. Only Frobisher's ship remained. He crossed what would become known as Davis Strait and coasted Baffin Island, looking for a way west, then "found" it—a large open sea route into the land. Although he would never discover the fact, despite having sailed into it three times, it is in fact a bay, now named after him. There he encountered some Inuit (not yet known as Eskimos), traded with them, then sent five men ashore in the ship's boat to investigate them some more. The men rounded a point and were never seen again. A search the next day failed to turn up either Inuit or the five Englishmen. His crew, suddenly, was down from eighteen men to thirteen. He took an Inuit captive and sailed home with him. The Inuit died within days of reaching London. Frobisher had accomplished none of his goals.

Nevertheless he returned a hero, a phenomenon that would become common in Arctic history. Failures always got far more credit than they deserved. Frobisher also brought back a piece of rock one of his sailors had picked up on a small island. The rock glittered. It shone yellow in the light.

The second voyage grew out of that piece of rock, which Frobisher's now desperate backer, the merchant Michael Lok, was able, with the help of a Venetian goldsmith who had his own interests to further, to persuade himself contained gold. Word spread rapidly and within months of the assay a number of important people, including the Queen of England, wanted to climb aboard this project. Gold, of course, changed everything. The object was no longer a northwest passage; it was the world's most precious metal. Many investors were skeptical, but enough backing was found to send three ships (and a company of miners) back to Baffin Island to look and dig for ore. The following comes from Dionyse Settle's account of the voyage, printed in 1577. For ease of reading we have modernized the spelling and smoothed out the language enough to make the text accessible to modern readers.

DIONYSE SETTLE

A True Report of Captain Frobisher, His Last Voyage into the West and Northwest Regions, 1577

ON WHITSUNDAY LAST PAST, BEING THE 26 OF MAY, IN THIS PRESENT year of our Lord God 1577, Captain Frobisher departed from Blackwall with one of the Queen's Majesty's ships, called *The Ayde*, of nine score tons, or thereabouts, and two other little barks likewise, the one called *The Gabriel*, whereof Master Fenton, a gentleman of my Lord of Warwick's, was captain; and the other, *The Michael*, whereof Master York, a gentleman of my Lord Admiral's was captain; accompanied with seven score gentlemen, soldiers and sailors, well furnished with victuals and other provision necessary for one half year, on this his second voyage for the further discovering of the passage to Cathay, and other countries thereunto adjacent, by West and Northwest navigations. Which passage, or way, is supposed to be on the North and Northwest parts of America, and the said America to be an island environed with the sea, through which our merchants might have course and recourse with their merchandise, from these our northernmost parts of Europe, to those oriental coasts of Asia, in much shorter time, and with greater benefit than any others, to their no little commodity and profit that do traffic the same.

Settle then goes on to describe a brief stay in the Orkney Islands to put on fresh water. They left the Orkneys on June 8 and sailed west and northwest until July 4:

All which time we had no night, but that easily, and without any impediment, we had when we were so disposed the fruition of our books and other pleasure to pass away the time, a thing of no small moment to such as wander in unknown seas and long navigations, especially when both the winds and raging surges do pass their common and wonted course. This benefit endures in those parts not six weeks, while the sun is near the Tropic of Cancer, but where the Pole is raised to 70 or 80 degrees it continues the longer.

All along these seas, after we were six days sailing from Orkney, we met, floating in the sea, great fir trees, which as we judged were with the fury of great floods rooted up and so driven into the sea. Iceland has almost no other wood nor fuel but such as they take up upon their coasts. It seems that these trees are driven from some part of the newfound land, with the current that sets from the west to the east.

The fourth of July we came within the making of Friesland [*Friesland was a mythical island put on the charts by the Zeno brothers a century before from a voyage that never actually took place, but that confused mapmakers for a long time; the land in question was actually Greenland*]. From this shore ten or twelve leagues we met great islands of ice [*a league was roughly three miles*] of half a mile, some more, some less in compass, showing above the sea 30 or 40 fathoms and, as we supposed, fast on ground where, with our lead, we could scarce sound the bottom for depth.

Here in place of odoriferous and fragrant smells of sweet gums and pleasant notes of musical birds, which other countries in more temperate zones do yield, we tasted the most boisterous boreal blasts, mixed with snow and hail, in the month of June and July, nothing inferior to our intemperate winter. [*It was*] a sudden alteration, and especially in a place or parallel where the Pole is not elevated above 61 degrees, at which height [*i.e., at which parallel of latitude*] other countries more to the north, yea unto 70 degrees, show themselves more temperate than this.

All along this coast ice lies, as a continual bulwark, and so defends the country that those who would land there incur great danger. Our general three days together attempted with the ship's boat to have gone on shore, which, because he could not accomplish it without great danger, he deferred until a more convenient time. All along the coast lie very high mountains covered with snow, except in such places where, through the steepness of the mountains, of force it must needs fall.

Four days coasting along this land we found no sign of habitation. Little birds, which we judged to have lost the shore, by reason of thick fogs, which that country is much subject to, came fleeing to our ships, which caused us to suppose that the country is both more tolerable, and also habitable within, than the outward shore makes show.

From hence we departed the eighth of July and the sixteenth of the same we came within the making of land, which our General the year before had named the Queen's Foreland, being an island, as we judge, lying near the supposed continent with America. And on the other side, opposite to the same, one other island called Hall's Isle, after the name of the master of our ship, near adjacent to the firm land, the supposed continent of Asia. Between the two islands there is a large entrance or strait, called Frobisher's Strait, after the name of our general, the first finder thereof. This said Strait is supposed to have passage into the Sea of Sur [*i.e. the Pacific, or the South Sea, "Sur" being the Spanish word for south*], which I leave unknown as yet....

At our first coming the Straits seemed to be shut up with a long wall of ice, which gave no little cause of discomfort to us all, but our General (to whose diligence imminent dangers and difficult attempts seemed nothing, in respect of his willing mind, for the commodity of his Prince and country) with two little pinnaces prepared for the purpose passed twice through them to the east shore, and the adjacent islands, while the ship, with the two barks, lay off and on something further into the sea from the danger of the ice.

While he was searching the country near the shore some of the people of the country showed themselves, leaping and dancing, with strange shrieks and cries, which gave no little admiration to our men. Our General desirous to allure them to him by fair means caused knives and other things to be offered them, which they would not take at our hands. But being laid on the ground and the party going away, they came and took them up, leaving something of theirs to countervail the same. At length, two of them leaving their weapons came down to our General and master, who did the like to them, commanding the company to stay, and went unto them, who, after certain dumb signs and mute congratulations, began to lay hands upon them, but they escaped and ran to their bows and arrows and came fiercely upon them, not respecting the rest of our company, which were ready for their defense, but with their arrows hurt diverse of them. We took the one, and the other escaped.

While our General was busy searching the country and those islands adjacent on the east shore, the ship and barks took great care not to put far into the sea from him, for he had a small store of victuals; but they were forced to abide in a cruel tempest, chancing in the night, among and in the thickest of the ice, which was so monstrous that even the least of a thousand had been of force sufficient to have shivered our ship and barks into small portions, if God ... had not provided for this our extremity a sufficient remedy, through the light of the night, whereby we might well discern to flee from such imminent dangers which we avoided with 14 bourds [*these would be tacks, or changes of direction*] in one watch, the space of four hours. If we had not incurred this danger among these monstrous islands of ice, we should have lost our General and master, and the most of our best sailors, which were on shore destitute of victuals. But by the valor of our master gunner, being expert both in navigation and other good qualities, we were all content to incur the dangers before we would, for our own safety, run into the seas, to the destruction of our General and his company.

The day following, being the 19th of July, our captain returned to the ship with good news of great riches, which showed itself in the bowels of those barren mountains, wherewith we were all satisfied. A sudden mutation: The one part of us being almost swallowed up the night before with cruel Neptune's force, and the rest on shore, taking thought for their greedy paunches, how to find the way to New found land—at one moment we were all rapt with joy, forgetting both where we were and what we had suffered. Behold the glory of man, tonight condemning riches, and rather looking for death than otherwise—and tomorrow devising how to satisfy his greedy appetite with gold.

Within four days after we had been at the entrance of the Strait, the northwest and west winds dispersed the ice into the sea, and made us a large entrance into the Strait, so that without any impediment, on the 19 of July we entered them, and the 20th our General and master, with great diligence, sought out and sounded the west shore, and found out a fair harbor for the ship and barks to ride in, and named it after our master's mate, Jackman's Sound, and brought the ship, barks, and all their company to safe anchor, except one man, who died by God's visitation.

We were forced sundry times, while the ship rode here at anchor, to have continual watch, with boats and men ready with hawsers, to knit fast unto such ice, which with the ebb and flood tides were tossed to and fro in the harbor, and with force of oars to haul them away, for endangering the ship.

Our General, certain days searched this supposed continent with America, and not finding the commodity to answer his expectation, after he had made trial thereof, he departed thence with two little barks and men sufficient to the east shore, being the supposed continent of Asia, and left the ship with most of the gentlemen, soldiers, and sailors, until such time as he either thought good to send or come for them.

The stones of this supposed continent with America be altogether sparkly and glitter in the sun like gold. So likewise does the sand in the bright water. Yet they verify the old proverb, all is not gold that glitters.

On this west shore we found a dead fish floating which had in his nose a horn straight and torqued [*i.e., spiraled*], of length two yards lacking two inches, being broken in the top, where we might perceive it hollow, into which some of our sailors putting spiders, they presently died. I saw not the trial thereof, but it was reported to me of a truth, by the virtue whereof, we supposed it to be the sea unicorn. [It *was a narwhal, the horn of which was once believed to be poisonous.*]

After our General had found out good harbor for the ship and barks to anchor in, and also such store of gold ore as he thought himself satisfied with, he sent back our master with one of the barks to conduct the great ship to him, who, coasting along the west shore, perceived a fair harbor, and willing to sound the same, at the entrance thereof they espied two tents of seal skins.

At the sight of our men the people fled into the mountains. Nevertheless our said master went to their tents, and left some of our trifles, as knives, bells, and glasses, and departed, not taking anything of theirs except one dog to our ship.

On the same day, after consultation, we determined to see if by fair means we could either allure them to familiarity or otherwise take some of them and so attain to some knowledge of those men, whom our General lost the year before [*the five men taken by the natives*].

At our coming back again to the place where their tents were before, they had removed their tents further into the bay or sound, where they might, if they were driven from the land, flee with their boats into the sea. We parting ourselves into two companies, and compassing a mountain, came suddenly upon them by land, who espying us, without any tarrying fled to their boats, leaving the most part of their oars behind them for hast, and rowed down the bay, where our two pinnaces met them and drove them to shore.

If they had had all their oars, so swift are they in rowing, it had been lost time to have chased them.

When they were landed they fiercely assaulted our men with their bows and arrows, who wounded three of them with our arrows. Perceiving themselves thus hurt, they desperately leapt off the rocks into the sea and drowned themselves. Which if they had not done, but had submitted themselves ... we would both have saved them and also have sought remedy to cure their wounds received at our hands. But they, altogether void of humanity, and ignorant what mercy means, in extremities look for no other than death. Perceiving they should fall into our hands, thus miserably by drowning rather desired death, than otherwise to be saved by us. The rest, perceiving their fellows in this distress, fled into the high mountains. Two women, not being so apt to escape as the men were, the one for her age, and the other being encumbered with a child, we took. The old wretch, whom divers of our sailors supposed to be either a devil or a witch, plucked off her buskins, to see if she were cloven-footed, and for her ugly hew and deformity we let her go. The young woman and child we brought away. We named the place where they were slain Bloody Point, and the bay or harbor, York Sound, after the name of one of the captains of the two barks.

Having this knowledge both of their fierceness and cruelty, and perceiving that fair means, as yet, are not able to allure them to familiarity, we disposed ourselves, contrary to our inclination, something to be cruel, returned to their tents, and made a spoil of the same. Their riches are neither gold, silver, or precious drapery, but their tents and boats, made of the skins of red deer and seal, also dogs like unto wolves, but for the most part black, with other trifles, more to be wondered at for their strangeness, than for any other commodity needful for our use.

Three more times over the next several days, on the east (or supposed Asian) side of the Bay, Inuits tried to entice Frobisher and some of his men to shore, and there were more encounters like this but no more deaths. During this time Frobisher was loading up with what he hoped was gold ore, 200 tons of it, according to Settle. Settle's description of the natives is worth quoting at length:

They are men of a large corporature [*he means their trunks are large*], and good proportion. Their color is not much unlike the sunburnt countryman, who labors daily in the sun for his living.

They wear their hair something long, and cut before, either with stone or knife, very disorderly. Their women wear their hair long, and knit up with two loops, showing forth on either side of their faces, the rest drawn up in a knot....

They eat their meat all raw, both flesh, fish, and fowl, or sometimes parboiled with blood and a little water, which they drink. For lack of water they will eat ice that is hard frozen as pleasantly as we do sugar candy, or other sugar.

If they, for necessity's sake, stand in need of the premises, such grass as the country yields they pluck up and eat, not daintily or salad-wise, to allure their stomachs to appetite; but for necessity's sake, without either salt, oils, or washing, like brute beasts they devour the same. They neither use table, stool, or table cloth for comeliness. But when they are imbrued with blood, knuckle deep, and their knives in like sort, they use their tongues as apt instruments to lick them clean. In doing so, they are assured to lose none of their victuals.

They keep certain dogs not much unlike wolves, which they yoke together, as we do oxen and horses, to a sled or train, and so carry their necessaries over the ice and snow from place to place, as the captive, whom we have, made perfect signs. When those dogs are not apt for the same use, or when with hunger they are constrained, for lack of other victuals, they eat them, so that they are as needful for them, in respect of their bigness, as our oxen are for us.

They apparel themselves in the skins of such beasts as they kill, sewed together with the sinews of them. All the fowl they kill they skin, and make thereof one kind of garment or another, to defend them from the cold.

They make their apparel with hoods and tails, which tails they give when they think to gratify any friendship showed to them—a great sign of friendship with them. The men and women wear their hose close to their legs, from the waist to the knee, without any opening before, as well the one kind as the other. Upon their legs they wear hose of leather, with the fur side inward, two or three pair on at once, and especially the women. In those hose they put their knives, needles, and other things needful to bear about. They put a bone within their hose, which reaches from the foot to the knee, whereupon they draw their hose, and so in places of garters, they are held from falling down around their feet.

They dress their skins very soft and supple with the hair on. In cold weather or winter they wear the fur side inward, and in summer outward. Other apparel they have none, except the skins.

Those beasts, flesh, fishes, and fowls they kill, they are both meat, drink, apparel, houses, bedding, hose, shoes, thread, sail for their boats, with many other necessaries whereof they stand in need, and almost all their riches.

Their houses are tents made of seal skins, pitched with four fir quarters, four square, meeting at the top, and the skins sewn together with sinews and laid thereon. So pitched are they that the entrance into them is always south, or against the sun....

Their weapons are bows, arrows, darts and slings. Their bows are of a yard long of wood, sinewed on the back with strong vines, not glued, too, but fast girded and tied on. Their bowstrings are likewise sinews. Their arrows are three pieces, nocked with bone, and ended with bone; with those two ends, and the wood in the middle, they pass not in length half a yard or little more. They are feathered with two feathers, the pen end being cut away, and the feathers laid upon the arrow with the broad side to the wood, insomuch that they seem, when they are tied on, to have four feathers. They have likewise three sorts of heads to those arrows: one sort of stone or iron, proportioned like to a heart; the second sort of bone, with a hook on the same; the third sort of bone likewise, made sharp at both sides, and sharp pointed....

Their darts are made of two sorts: one with many forks of bone in the fore end, and likewise in the middle; their proportions are not unlike our toasting irons, but longer. These they cast out of an instrument of wood, very readily. The other sort is greater than the first, with a long bone made sharp on both sides, like a rapier, which I take to be their most hurtful weapon.

They have two sorts of boats, made of leather, set out on the inner side with quarters of wood, artificially tied together with thongs of the same. The great sort are not much unlike our wherrys, wherein sixteen or twenty men may fit. They have for a sail dressed the guts of such beasts as they kill very fine and thin, which they sew together. The other boat is but for one man to sit and row in, with one oar....

Settle goes on to speculate that they don't live there year-round because he can find no other signs of habitation that would withstand the cold; he has, however, already described—which we omit—their winter houses, which were made of stone and used skins for a roof. They did in all likelihood live there year round. He wonders also where they get the little iron they have. Settle thinks it must be through trade with some other people.

What knowledge they have of God, or what idol they adore, we have no perfect intelligence. I think them rather Anthropophagi, or devourers of men's flesh, than otherwise, for there is no flesh or fish which they find dead (smell it ever so filthy) but they will eat it, as they find it, without any other dressing. A loathsome spectacle, either to the beholders or hearers.

There is no manner of creeping beast hurtful except some spiders (which, as many affirm, are signs of great store of gold), and also certain stinging gnats, which bite so fiercely that the place where they bite shortly after swells, and itches very sore.

They make signs of certain people that wear bright plates of gold in their foreheads and other places on their bodies.

Settle then describes the countryside, with its mountains and snows, and the scarcity of anything growing except grass and mosses; "to be brief," he writes, "there is nothing fit or profitable for the use of man, which that country yields or brings forth"— except, of course, gold. On August 24, having filled the ships with what they hoped was precisely that, gold, Frobisher and his little fleet retired and returned to England. Settle's account is the first lengthy ethnographical description we have of the Inuit of this or any other area in the Arctic. The misunderstandings between the two groups of people are obvious; the contempt in which the English held the Inuit is plain. These misunderstandings would last well into the twentieth century.

FROBISHER MADE ANOTHER VOYAGE THE FOLLOWING YEAR, 1578, THIS time with ten ships officially, more unofficially, with intentions to found a colony on the coast of "Asia" and mine gold in much larger quantities than the 200 tons brought back in 1577. In a rational world it would have been clear by that time that there was no gold in that ore, but the assayers assigned to test the ore had disagreed, and continued to disagree, about its content, with expert assayers who happened to be English, in London, unable to find gold in it, and German assayers, in Bristol, finding it to the value of 24 English pounds per ton. Since the German assayers had the reputation, they were believed. The English assayers did not have the reputation, and were not believed. The fleet sailed.

They never did found a colony, no doubt preventing thereby a great loss of life, but they did build a small house against the next expedition, which never came, to see how it would survive the winter. The foundation of this house is still there on the shore of Frobisher Bay. So are the trenches the miners dug to extract ore. The Spanish had secretly obtained a sample of the ore and determined that the "gold" it contained was actually marcasite. Not until 1581 did a final English assay determine the same. The ore was subsequently used to repair roads in the west of England.

The body of water that Martin Frobisher crossed between Greenland and Frobisher Bay was Davis Strait, a name it acquired from the next major English explorer to enter the area, John Davis. Davis was a different sort of person altogether from Frobisher. The latter had come out of obscure origins and made a living as a privateer who was none too discriminate about whose ship it was he relieved of its treasures. He had been brought to trial a number of times and had spent time in a Portuguese prison. At one point in his life he abandoned his wife and children. Only his fearlessness during the defeat of the Spanish Armada in 1588 salvaged his reputation.

Davis had grown up, on the other hand, as a friend of the Gilbert family, long interested in the Northwest Passage, and of Sir Walter Raleigh. If Frobisher was a hard case Davis was kindly and he had a sense of humor. He took four men on his second voyage—we print his account of it here—who played musical instruments and, as we shall see, they played for the Greenland Inuit, who danced to the music. Davis had scientific interests and invented a navigational instrument. Later in life he wrote a well-regarded navigational treatise.

He made three voyages all told to the Strait that bears his name, looking for the Passage, and on his third voyage sailed by, without recognizing it for what it was, Hudson Strait, which Henry Hudson would find some twenty years later. He never sailed far enough north into Baffin Bay to locate Lancaster Sound, which is the entrance to the actual Northwest Passage, but he did some first-rate exploring and he added to the map. His initial voyage, financed by merchants in the west of England and by Queen Elizabeth's Secretary of State, Francis Walsingham, was more a reconnaissance than anything else. He never wrote an account of the third voyage. We excerpt here from his second voyage, undertaken in 1586. Once again, we have modernized the spelling and made small changes in the text in the interests of accessibility.

JOHN DAVIS

The Second Voyage Attempted by
Master John Davis, 1586

THE SEVENTH DAY OF MAY I DEPARTED FROM THE PORT OF DARTMOUTH for the discovery of the Northwest Passage, with a ship of a hundred and twenty tons named the Mermaid, a bark of 60 tons named the Sunshine, a bark of 35 tons named the Moonlight, and a pinnace of ten tons named the North Star.

And the 15 of June I discovered land in the latitude of 60 degrees, and in longitude from the meridian of London westward 47 degrees [this is probably Cape Farewell, the southernmost tip of Greenland], mightily pestered with ice and snow, so that there was no hope of landing. The ice lay in some places 10 leagues, in some 20, and in some 50 leagues off the shore, so that we were constrained to bear into 57 degrees [latitude] to double the same and to recover a free sea, which, through God's favorable mercy, we at length obtained. The nine and twentieth of June, after many tempestuous storms, we again discovered land, in longitude from the meridian of London 58 degrees 30 minutes, and in latitude 64, being east from us, into which course, since it pleased God, by contrary winds, to force us, I thought it very necessary to bear in with it, and there to set up our pinnace, provided in the Mermaid to be our scout for this discovery. And so much the rather, because the year before I had been in the same place [the west coast of Greenland], and found it very convenient for such a purpose, well stored with float wood, and possessed by a people of tractable conversation. So that the nine and twentieth of this month we arrived within the isles which lay before this land, lying north northwest, and south southeast, we know not how far. This land is very high and mountainous, having before it, on the west side, a mighty company of isles full of fair sounds and harbors. This land was very little troubled with snow, and the sea altogether void of ice.

The ships being within the sounds, we sent our boats to search for shoal water where we might anchor, which in this place is very hard to find. As the boat went sounding and searching, the people of the country having espied them, came in their canoes toward them with many shouts and cries; but after they had espied in that boat some of our company that were the year before here with us, they presently rowed to the boat and took hold on the oar and hung about the boat with such comfortable joy as would require a long discourse to utter. They came with the boats to our ships, making signs that they knew all those that the year before had been with them. After I perceived their joy, and small fear of us, myself with the merchants and others of the company went ashore, bearing with me twenty knives. I had no sooner landed but they leapt out of their canoes and came running to me and the rest, and embraced us with many signs of hearty welcome. At this present there were eighteen of them, and to each of them I gave a knife. They offered skins to me for reward, but I made signs that it was not sold, but given them of courtesy, and so dismissed them for that time, with signs that they should return again after certain hours.

The next day, with all possible speed, the pinnace was landed upon an isle there to be finished, to serve our purpose for the discovery, which isle was so convenient for that purpose, that we were very well able to defend ourselves against many enemies. During the time that the pinnace was there setting up, the people came continually unto us, sometimes a hundred canoes at a time, sometimes forty, fifty, more and less, as occasion served. They brought with them seal skins, stag skins, white hares, seal fish, salmon, small cod, dry caplin, with other fish and birds, such as the country did yield.

Myself, still desirous to have a farther search of this place, sent one of the ship's boats to one part of the land, and myself went to another part, to search for the habitation of this people, with straight commandment that there should be no injury offered to any of the people, neither any gun shot.

The boats that went from me found the tents of the people made with seal skins, set up upon timber, wherein they found great store of dried caplin, being a little fish no bigger than a pilchard. They found bags of train oil [*an obsolete word for whale oil*], many little images cut in wood, seal skins in tanning tubs, with many other such trifles, whereof they diminished [*i.e., took or stole*] nothing.

They also found, ten miles within the snowy mountains, a plain country, with earth and grass, such as our moor and waste grounds of England are. They went up into a river (which in the narrowest place is two leagues broad) about ten leagues, finding it still to continue they knew not how far. But I, with my company, took another river, which although at first it offered a large inlet, yet it proved but a deep bay, the end whereof in four hours I attained, and there leaving the boat well manned, went with the rest of my company three or four miles into the country, but found nothing, nor saw anything, save only gyrfalcons, ravens, and small birds, as lark and linnet.

The third of July I manned my boat and went, with fifty canoes attending upon me, up into another sound, where the people by signs willed me to go, hoping to find their habitation. At length they made signs that I should go into a warm place to sleep, at which place I went on shore and ascended the top of a high hill to see into the country, but perceiving my labor vain, I returned again to my boat, the people still following me and my company, very diligent to attend us, and to help us up the rocks, and likewise down. At length I was desirous to have our men leap with them, which was done, but our men did overleap them. From leaping they went to wrestling. We found them strong and nimble, and to have skill in wrestling, for they cast some of our men that were good wrestlers.

The fourth of July we launched our pinnace and had forty of the people to help us, which they did very willingly. At this time our men again wrestled with them and found them as before, strong and skillful. This fourth of July the Master of the *Mermaid* went to certain islands to store himself with wood, where he found a grave with divers [*diverse; i.e., a number of*] people buried in it, only covered with seal skins, having a cross laid over them. [*That cross has made a lot of historians wonder. By this time the Christianized Norsemen who once populated Greenland had died out or faded away, and what became of them is still at issue.*]

The people are of good stature, well in body proportioned, with small slender hands and feet, with broad visages and small eyes, wide mouths, the most part unbearded, great lips, and close toothed. Their custom is as often as they go from us, still at their return to make a new truce, in this sort: holding his hand up to the sun, with a loud voice cries *Ylyaoute*, and strikes his breast. With like signs being promised safety, he gives credit. These people are much given to bleed and therefore they stop their noses with deer hair. They are idolaters and have a great store of images, which they wear about them, and in their boats, which we suppose they worship. They are witches and have many kinds of enchantments, which they often used, but to small purpose, thanks be to God.

Being among them at shore the fourth of July, one of them making a long oration began to kindle a fire in this manner: he took a piece of a board wherein was a hole half through; into that hole he put the end of a round stick like a bed-staff, wetting the end thereof in train [oil], and in the fashion of a [wood] turner, with a piece of leather, by his violent motion very speedily produced fire....

These people are very simple in all their conversation but marvelously thievish, especially for iron, which they hold in great account. They began through our lenience to show their vile nature—they began to cut our cables; they cut away the *Moonlight's* boat from her stern; they cut our cloth where it lay to air, though we did carefully look unto it; they stole our oars; a caliver [*a small gun*], a boar spear, a sword, with divers other things, whereat the company and masters being grieved, for our better security desired me to dissolve this new friendship and to leave the company of these thievish miscreants. Whereupon there was a caliver shot among them, and immediately upon the same a falcon [*a small cannon; it would have been mounted on one of the ships*], which strange noise did sore amaze them, so that with speed they departed. Notwithstanding, their simplicity is such that within ten hours after they came to us again to entreat peace, which being promised, we again fell into a great league. They brought us seal skins and salmon, but seeing iron, they could in no wise forbear stealing, which when I perceived it did but minister unto me an occasion of laughter, to see their simplicity, and willed that in no case they should be any more hardly used, but that our own company should be the more vigilant to keep their things, supposing it to be very hard in so short a time to make them know their evils. They eat all their meat raw, they live most upon fish, they drink salt water, and eat grass and ice with delight. They are never out of the water but live in the nature of fishes, but only when dead sleep takes them, and then under a warm rock, laying his boat upon the land, he lies down to sleep....

Davis then sailed up the coast for a few days in the pinnace to explore the country, saw a whirlwind that lasted three hours, sailed into a river but discovered it to be a fjord, and on his way back to the ship came upon the dwelling place of the Inuit he had been dealing with. When he returned there had been more theft and his companions had had their fill of it. The Inuit had stolen an anchor, among other things, and slung stones at the ships. They kept one of the Inuit hostage to get the anchor back, and then, the wind coming up, set sail with him on board. What became of him subsequently Davis does not report. They were now crossing Davis Strait and they ran into ice.

The 17th of this month [July], being in the latitude of 63 degrees 8 minutes, we fell upon a most mighty and strange quantity of ice, in one entire mass, so big as that we knew not the limits thereof, and being withal so very high, in form of land, with bays and capes, and like high cliff land, as that we supposed it to be land, and therefore sent our pinnace off to discover it. But at her return we were certainly informed that it was only ice, which bred great admiration to us all, considering the huge quantity thereof, incredible to be reported in truth as it was....I think the like before was never seen, and in this place we have very strong currents.

We coasted this mighty mass of ice until the 30 of July, finding it a mighty bar to our purpose. The air in this time was so contagious [*he means injurious to human health or life*] and the sea so pestered with ice that all hope was banished of proceeding. The 24th of July all our shrouds, ropes, and sails were so frozen and compassed with ice, merely by a gross fog, as seemed to me more than strange, since the last year I found this sea free and navigable, without impediments.

At the behest of his men, who were becoming, he says, "sick and feeble," Davis turned the fleet around and returned to Greenland, where he transferred supplies from the larger Mermaid *to the smaller* Moonlight, *shuffled the crews, discovered the discomfiture attendant on a "fly" he called the "Musketa," and then, on August 12, left the* Mermaid *to make its own way home and proceeded to sail west in the* Moonlight *with a small crew. Davis struck Baffin Island in latitude 66 degrees 19 minutes.*

This fourteenth day, from nine o'clock at night till three o'clock in the morning, we anchored by an island of ice, twelve leagues off the shore, being moored to the ice.

The fifteenth day, at three o'clock in the morning, we departed from this land to the south, and the eighteenth of August we discovered land northwest from us in the morning, being a very fair promontory, in latitude 65 degrees, having no land on the south. Here we had great hope of a through passage. [*Davis is evidently at the entrance of Cumberland Sound, which he had discovered and explored the year before, although here he does not seem to recognize it.*]

This day, at three o'clock in the afternoon, we again discovered land southwest and south from us, where at night we were becalmed. The nineteenth of this month, at noon, by observation, we were in 64 degrees 20 minutes. From the eighteenth day, at noon, unto the nineteenth at noon, by precise ordinary care, we had sailed 15 leagues south and by west, yet by art and more exact observation, we found our course to be southwest, so that we plainly perceived a great current striking to the west. [*Davis had discovered the Labrador Current.*]

This land is nothing in sight but isles, which increases our hope. This nineteenth of August, at six o'clock in the afternoon, it began to snow, and so continued all night, with foul weather and much wind, so that we were constrained to lie at hull all night five leagues off shore. In the morning, being the twentieth of August, the fog and storm breaking up, we bore in with the land, and at nine o'clock in the morning we anchored in a very fair and safe road for all weathers.

Davis then went ashore and climbed a hill to check out the landscape, or seascape, and saw nothing but islands, which again gave him hope that this might be the Passage. It was probably the entrance to Hudson Strait, but Davis unaccountably did not turn into it. He continued sailing south now along the coast of Labrador, into September, and may have sailed as far south as Newfoundland. After a nasty ambush by Indians on an island off the coast, in which two of his men were killed outright and two others badly wounded, and after waiting out two storms, Davis sailed for England on September 11 and arrived without incident. It remains unexplained why he did not enter Hudson Strait, but he had done what Frobisher never even tried to do. He had coasted the west side of the strait that was subsequently named for him and had mapped what he found. He had also treated the Inuit he dealt with quite well, considering the standards of the time and the fact that they were stealing things off his ships.

Davis had a colorful career. He captained an English ship against the Spanish Armada and then was assigned another to harass what remained of the Spanish fleet, working as a privateer. He made enough money from this venture to try for the Northwest Passage once again, this time from the Pacific side, but his ship failed to round Cape Horn. He discovered the Falkland Islands on this voyage, however, which Richard Hawkins claimed for England two years later. He wrote two books, one a navigational guide called The Seaman's Secret, *the other a summary of what was known of the world's oceans. In 1598 he piloted a Dutch ship on the first Dutch voyage to the East Indies. He was killed by Malaysian pirates in 1605. He was never as celebrated as Drake or Hawkins, or even Frobisher, but he was as good a sailor as Elizabethan England produced.*

*

THE BATTLE WITH THE SPANISH ARMADA BEGAN AN ERA OF INTENSE *adventuring and privateering in what had been considered before to be Spanish waters, and it ended the search for the Northwest Passage for a number of years. In 1595 John Davis tried to revive it with an appeal to the Privy Council, but Francis Walsingham, his main sponsor in the government, was dead and no one else was interested. Not until 1609, with Henry Hudson, and under a different monarch, James I, would the search be revived. The Russia Company had not entirely given up on the Northeast Passage, meanwhile, and sent out a small expedition—two little ships with crews of ten and six men respectively—to try to get beyond the White Sea and Novaya Zemlya, the large island chain that juts out like a parenthesis from the Russian mainland and into the Kara Sea. One ship did make it a short distance into the Kara Sea, and then back to England. The other wintered in Norway and was lost the following year.*

The Dutch had their own ambitions to the Northeast, and our next excerpt comes out of it. They had been trading with Russia by way of the White Sea since the late 1570s, and it was inevitable that they, too, would be interested in carrying on past that point to the markets of China. In the 1590s they sent three expeditions over the top of Russia, all of them guided by the skillful, experienced Dutch navigator William Barents. The first of them set off in June 1594, with four ships, two of them under the overall command of Barents himself. Barents' role in the exploration was to find a way around Novaya Zemlya to the north. The other two ships were to make their way through the straits that divide Novaya Zemlya from the small island to the south of it, known now as Vaigac. Barents made it to the northern end of Novaya Zemlya only to be met with immense quantities of ice—the Arctic pack. For two weeks he struggled east, changing direction, according to his log, 81 times. Eventually the ice defeated him and he turned back.

The other half of this fleet, however, got as far east as the River Ob beyond Novaya Zemlya, and this achievement was encouraging enough for the Dutch to send out another fleet the following year. This was a much larger fleet of seven ships but for reasons that were never explained they left so late in the season, July 2, as to dash all hopes of success before they even started. They were nearly trapped by ice near Vaigac in late August and early September, and in mid-September they gave up yet again and returned home. Barents was one of a party who signed a formal protest against the decision. He would have liked to go on, or if that was impossible, to winter over and try his luck in the spring. But the admiral of the fleet ruled against him.

The fact that a polar bear had killed two men on September 6 did not seem to daunt Barents. It may be that nothing daunted him. Polar bears are, of course, the Arctic's most dangerous animal and the story of what happened to these two men is worth telling. Here it is in the words of Gerrit de Veer, the Dutchman who wrote the accounts of all three voyages to the northeast that Barents and his companions made.

GERRIT DE VEER

The True and Perfect Description of Three Voyages, So Strange and Wonderful, etc., 1609

THE 6TH OF SEPTEMBER, SOME OF OUR MEN WENT ON SHORE UPON THE firm land to seek for stones, which are a kind of diamond [*rock crystal*], whereof there are many...; and while they were seeking the stones, two of our men lying together in one place, a great lean white bear came suddenly stealing out, and caught one of them fast by the neck, who not knowing what it was that took him by the neck, cried out and said, "Who is it that pulls me so by the neck?"

Wherewith the other, that lay not far from him, lifted up his head to see who it was, and perceiving it to be a monstrous bear, cried and said, "Oh, mate, it is a bear!" and therewith presently rose up and ran away.

The bear at the first falling upon the man, bit his head in sunder and sucked out his blood, wherewith the rest of the men that were on land, being about 20 in number, ran presently thither, either to save the man, or else to drive the bear from the dead body; and having charged their pieces and lowered their pikes, set upon her, that was still devouring the man, but perceiving them to come towards her, fiercely and cruelly ran at them, and got another of them out from the company, which she tore in pieces, wherewith all the rest ran away.

We perceiving out of our ship and pinnace that our men ran to the seaside to save themselves, with all speed entered into our boats and rowed as fast as we could to the shore to relieve our men. Where being on land, we beheld the cruel spectacle of our two dead men, that had been so cruelly killed and torn in pieces by the bear. We seeing that, encouraged our men to go back again with us, and with pieces, axes, and half-pikes, to set upon the bear. But they would not all agree thereunto, some of them saying, "Our men are already dead, and we shall get the bear well enough, though we oppose not ourselves into so open danger. If we might save our fellows' lives, then we would make haste; but now we need not make such speed, but take her at an advantage, with most security for ourselves, for we have to do with a cruel, fierce and ravenous beast." Whereupon three of our men went forward, the bear still devouring her prey, not once fearing the number of our men, and yet they were thirty at the least. [*Two of the men shot three times at the bear and missed. A man named Hans van Nufflen then moved further forward and shot the bear between the eyes.*] And yet she held the man still fast by the neck, and lifted up her head, with the man in her mouth, but she began somewhat to stagger. Wherewith the purser and a Scottish man drew out their axes and struck at her so hard that their axes broke, and yet she would not leave the man. At last William Geyson went to them, and with all his might struck the bear upon the snout with his piece, at which time the bear fell to the ground, making a great noise, and William Geyson leaping upon her cut her throat. [*The next day they buried the two men, then skinned the bear and took its fleece back to Amsterdam.*]

THE DUTCH GOVERNMENT HAD HAD ENOUGH, BUT THEY WERE WILLING *to encourage private entrepreneurs to pursue the route if they wished, and the following year two more ships made the effort, with Barents on board one of them but not in charge. The voyagers wandered farther north than intended and discovered Spitzbergen (now Svalbard) and sailed all the way around it, but then the two ships parted company, Barents sailing southeast toward Russia, the other captain sailing back to Holland. When Barents reached the western coast of Novaya Zemlya he turned north and worked his way around the northern tip. But the ice stopped him once again—and this time there was no escape. Somewhere on the desolate coast of this barren island, Barents and his men settled in to spend the winter.*

    A ghastly, killing winter. The men built themselves a house out of the wood they could find washed up on the island and wood they took from the ship. They set traps for foxes, fought off polar bears, rationed their store of food, and began the long bitter night that is the Arctic winter. There were sixteen of them. They almost died in early December when they stopped up all the doors and the chimney to conserve heat when they were burning sea coal, and suddenly some of them started passing out: the same thing that evidently happened to Hugh Willoughby in Lapland in 1553. They were the first Europeans to winter over in the high Arctic. We pick up our excerpt in late December, at Christmas. Once again the spelling, and in small ways the language, have been modernized.

GERRIT DE VEER
The third voyage northward to the Kingdoms of Cathay and China, in Anno 1596.

The 24th of December, being Christmas Eve, it was fair weather. Then we opened our door again and saw much open water in the sea, for we had heard the ice crack and drive, and although there was no daylight yet we could see that far. Towards evening it blew hard out of the northeast, with great store of snow, so that all the passage that we had made open before was stopped up again.

The 25 of December, being Christmas Day, it was foul weather with a northwest wind, and yet, though it was foul weather, we heard the foxes run over our house [*the snow had mounted up to the roof by this time*], wherewith some of our men said it was an ill sign; and while we sat disputing why it should be an ill sign, some of our men said that it was an ill sign because we could not take them to put them into the pot to roast them, for that had been a very good sign for us.

The 26th of December it was foul weather, the wind northwest, and it was so cold that we could not warm ourselves, although we used all the means we could, with great fires, good store of clothes, and with hot stones laid upon our feet and our bodies as we lay in our cots. But notwithstanding all this, in the morning our cots were frozen, which made us behold one another with sad countenance. But yet we comforted ourselves again as well as we could, that the sun was then as low as it could go, and that it now began to come to us again, and we found it to be true, for the days beginning to lengthen the cold began to strengthen, but hope put us in good comfort and eased our pain.

The 27th of December it was still foul weather with a northwest wind, so that as then we had not been out in three days together, still we did not dare to thrust our heads outdoors. And within the house it was so extremely cold that as we sat before a great fire, and seemed to burn on the foreside, we froze behind our backs, and were all white, as the countrymen used to be when they came in at the gates of the town in Holland with their sleds, when they were gone all night.

The 28th of December it was still foul weather, with a west wind, but about evening it began to clear up. At which time one of our men made a hole open at one of our doors, and went out to see what news abroad, but found it so hard weather that he stayed not long, and told us that it had snowed so much that the snow lay higher than our house, and that if he had stayed out longer his ears would undoubtedly have been frozen off.

The 29th of December it was calm weather and a pleasant air, the wind being southward. That day he whose turn it was opened the door and dug a hole through the snow, where we went out of the house upon steps as if it had been out of a cellar, at least seven or eight steps high, each step a foot from the other. And then we cleaned our traps for the foxes, whereof for several days we had not taken any; and as we cleaned them one of our men found a dead fox in one of them that was frozen as hard as stone, which he brought into the house and thawed before the fire, and after flaying it some of our men ate it.

The 30th of December it was foul weather again, with a storm out of the west and great store of snow, so that all the labor and pain that we had taken the day before, to make steps to go out of our house and clean the traps, was all in vain, for it was all covered with snow again higher than it was before.

The 31 of December it was still foul weather with a storm out of the northwest whereby we were so fast shut up into the house as if we had been prisoners, and it was so extremely cold that the fire almost cast no heat. For as we put our feet to the fire we burned our hose [*stockings*] before we could feel the heat, so that we had work enough to do to patch our hose. If we had not sooner smelled them than felt them, we should have burned them away before we knew it.

After that, with great cold, danger, and hardship, we had brought the year to an end, we entered into the year of our Lord God 1597, the beginning of which was in the same manner as the end of anno 1596 had been; for the weather continued as cold, foul, and snowy as it was before, so that upon the first of January we were enclosed in the house, the wind then being west. At the same time we agreed to share our wine every man a small measure full, and that but once in two days. As we were in great care and fear that it would be long before we should get out from thence, and we sometimes having but small hope for it, some of us spared to drink wine as long as we could, so that if we should stay long there we might drink it at our need.

The 2nd of January it blew hard, with a west wind and a great storm, with both snow and frost, so that in four or five days we dared not put our head out of doors. As then by reason of the great cold we had almost burned all our wood in the house, yet we dared not go out to fetch more wood, because it froze so hard and there was no being outdoors. But seeking about we found some superfluous wood that lay over the door, which we clove [*split in half, or broke up*], and we clove the blocks whereon we used to beat our stock, and helped ourselves as well as we could.

The 3rd of January it was the same, and we had little wood to burn.

The 4th of January it was still stormy weather, with much snow and great cold, the wind southwest, and we were forced to keep in the house. To know where the wind blew we thrust a half pike out at the chimney with a little cloth or feather on it; but we had to look at it immediately the wind caught it, for as soon as we thrust it out it was presently frozen as hard as a piece of wood and could not go about or stir with the wind.

The 5th of January it was somewhat still and calm. Then we dug our door open again, that we might go out and carry out all the filth that had been made during the time of our being shut in the house, and made everything handsome, and fetched in wood. It was all our days work to further ourselves as much as we could, fearing lest we should be shut up again. As there were three doors in our portal, and because our house lay covered over with snow, we took the middle door away and dug a great hole in the snow that lay without the house, like to a side of a vault, wherein we might go to ease ourselves and cast other filth into it. When we had worked all day we remembered that it was Twelfth Night, and then we asked our skipper that we might be merry that night, and said that we were content to spend some of the wine that night which we had spared and which was our share every second day, and whereof for several days we had not drunk. So that night we made merry and drank to the three kings [*i.e, the Three Wise Men, whose visit Twelfth Night celebrates*]. Therewith we had two pounds of meal, whereof we made pancakes with oil, and every man had a white biscuit which we sopped in wine. So, supposing that we were in our own country and amongst our friends, it comforted us as well as if we had made a great banquet in our own house. We also made tickets [*this remark is unexplained*] and our gunner was king of Novaya Zemlya, which is at least two hundred miles long [*Dutch miles were four English miles, so Novaya Zemlya was eight hundred miles long*] and lies between two seas [*the Sea of Kara on the east and what would become known as the Barents Sea on the west*].

The 7th of January it was foul weather again, with a northwest wind and some snow, and very cold, which put us in great fear to be shut up in the house again.

The 8th of January it was fair weather again, the wind north. Then we made our traps ready to get more venison, which we longed for. And then we might see and mark daylight, which then began to increase, that the sun as then began to come towards us again which thought put us in no little comfort.

The 9th of January it was foul weather, with a northwest wind, but not so hard weather as it had been before, so that we might go out doors to clean our traps. But there was no need to bid us home again, for the cold taught us by experience not to stay out long, for it was not so warm to get any good by staying out in the air.

The 10th of January it was fair weather, with a north wind. Then seven of us went to our ship, well armed, which we found in the same state we left it in, and we saw many footsteps of bears, both great and small, whereby it seemed that there had been more than one or two bears therein. As we went under hatches we struck fire and lighted a candle, and found that the water was risen a foot higher in the ship.

The 11th of January it was fair weather, the wind northwest, and the cold began to be somewhat less, so that we were bold to go outdoors and went about a mile to a hill, from which we fetched some stones, which we laid in the fire, to warm us in our cots [*from contemporary drawings, these "cots" appear to have been little sleeping cubicles set against the walls*].

The 12th of January it was fair clear weather, the wind west. That evening it was very clear and the sky full of stars. We took the height of Occulus Tauri [*our Aldebaran*], which is a bright and well-known star.

This allowed them to calculate their latitude, which stood at about 75 degrees north. Most of their days were uneventful, as this diary indicates, an endless wait for the sun to return, and then enough warmth to melt the ice and allow them to sail home in the summer. They already suspected that the ship was a loss, nearly destroyed by the ice in August, and that they were going to have to use the ship's small boats to go home. We skip the next few days.

The 19th of January it was fair weather, with a north wind. Then our bread began to diminish, for some of our barrels were not full weight, and so the division was less and we were forced to make our allowance bigger with that which we had spared before. Then some of us went aboard the ship, where there was half a barrel of bread, which we thought to spare till the last, and there secretly each of them took a biscuit or two out of it.

The 20th of January the air was clear and the wind southwest. That day we stayed in the house and cut wood to burn, and broke some of our empty barrels and cast the iron hoops upon the top of the house.

The 21st of January it was fair, with a west wind. At that time the taking of foxes began to fail us, which was a sign that the bears would soon come again, as not long after we found to be true. For as long as the bears stayed away the foxes came abroad, and not much before the bears came abroad the foxes were but little seen.

The 22nd of January it was fair weather with a west wind. Then we went out again to cast the bullet [*this was a Dutch game with a ball; subsequent Arctic wintering parties also often played games outside to keep themselves fit*], and perceived that daylight began to appear, whereby some of us said that the sun would soon appear, too, but William Barents to the contrary said that it was yet two weeks too soon.

The 23rd of January it was fair calm weather, with a southwest wind. Then four of us went to the ship and comforted each other, giving God thanks that the hardest time of the winter was past, being in good hope that we should live to talk of these things at home in our own country. When we were in the ship we found that the water rose higher and higher in it, and so each of us taking a biscuit or two, we went home again.

The 24th of January it was fair clear weather, with a west wind. Then I and Jacob Hemskerck, and another with us, went to the seaside on the south side of Novaya Zemlya, where, contrary to our expectation, I first saw the edge of the sun, wherewith we went speedily home again, to tell William Barents and the rest of our companions that joyful news. But William Barents, being a wise and well experienced pilot, would not believe it, esteeming it to be about fourteen days too soon for the sun to shine in that part of the world. But we earnestly affirmed the contrary and said we had seen the sun, whereupon diverse wagers were laid.

The 25th and 26th of January it was misty and close weather so we could not see anything. Then they that laid the contrary wager with us thought that they had won; but upon the twenty-seventh day it was clear and then we saw the sun in his full roundness above the horizon, whereby it manifestly appeared that we had seen it upon the twenty-fourth day of January. As we were of diverse opinions touching the same, and that it was clean contrary to the opinions of all old and new writers, yea and contrary to the nature and roundness both of heaven and earth, some of us said, that seeing in long time there had been no day, that it might be that we had overslept ourselves, whereof we were better assured. But concerning the thing in itself, seeing God is wonderful in all his works, we will refer that to his almighty power, and leave it unto others to dispute of.... [*There follows a long disquisition on the question of the sun's appearance according to the table of Ephemerides they had with them, which there is no point reprinting here.*]

The 26th of January it was fair clear weather, but in the horizon there hung a cloud, whereby we could not see the sun; whereupon the rest of our companions said that we had mistaken ourselves upon the 24th day, and that the sun appeared not to us, and mocked us. But we were resolute in our affirmation that we had seen the sun, but not in the full roundness. That evening the sick man that was amongst us was very weak, and felt himself to be extremely sick, for he had lain sick a long time, and we comforted him as best we could, but he died not long after midnight.

The 27th of January it was fair clear weather, with a southwest wind. Then in the morning we dug a hole in the snow, hard by the house, but it was still so cold that we could not stay long at work, and so we dug by turns every man a little while, and then went to the fire, and another went and supplied his place, till at last we dug seven feet deep, where we went to bury the dead man. After that, when we had read some chapters and sung some psalms, we all went out and buried the man. Which done, we broke our fasts. And while we were at meat, and discoursed amongst ourselves touching the great quantity of snow that fell continually in that place, we said that if it fell out that our house should be closed up again with snow, we would find the means to climb out the chimney. Whereupon our master went to try if he could climb up through the chimney and so get out, and while he was climbing one of our men went forth out the door to see if the master were out or not, who, standing upon the snow, saw the

sun, and called us all out, and we all went forth and saw the sun in his full roundness a little above the horizon, and then it was without all doubt that we had
seen the sun upon the 24th of January, which made us all glad, and we gave God
hearty thanks for his grace unto us that that glorious light appeared unto us again.

They had, however, a long winter yet to endure, and it became more and more difficult as time went by. They were beginning to suffer the effects of scurvy and the
weather continued to be severe. In February they shot a bear but only took the grease
from it, to light their lamps; they did not eat the meat. If they had known that fresh
meat counteracted scurvy, they might have done better. They did eat foxes that they
trapped and that may be the only thing that kept them alive. One man lost a big toe
to frostbite. They were all weak. To obtain wood for their fire they had to go farther and
farther afield, away from the house, and it became a task almost beyond their endurance.
In April a bear tried to get into the house and tore at the chimney they had built.

As April wore on they began to see more and more open water in the area, but the
ship was locked fast into the ice. They were still maintaining a faint hope to sail away
in it, but in the end it was not possible. In early May they ran out of the salted beef that
had been sustaining them, and after that the small amount of bacon in store lasted only
three weeks. They had two small boats with them, an open boat probably the size of a
whaleboat, and a yawl that was smaller than the open boat. The bears continued to
be troublesome and the men never went anywhere alone, or unarmed. At the end of
May, while they were refitting the boats for the trip ahead of them, bears came near them
on three days running. They killed them and this time they did eat the liver of one, but
it made them all sick. Three men got very sick. "We verily thought we should have lost
them," de Veer wrote, "for all their skins came off from the foot to the head, but they recovered again, for which we gave God hearty thanks, for if as then we had lost these three
men, it was a hundred to one we should never have gotten away, because we should have
had too few men to draw and lift at our need."

Work continued preparing the boats well into June. On June 14 they finally left,
leaving a note in the chimney about their ordeal. Some of the men were sick, not from
the bear's liver but no doubt from scurvy, and William Barents was among them. Four
days out they were locked in the ice among shifting floes and only saved themselves by
fastening a rope to some ice frozen fast to the land and pulling the boats up on it. William
Barents died on the 20th of June; another man died shortly thereafter.

The boats continued to work their way down the coast of Novaya Zemlya.
When July came they found themselves locked in the ice once again, this time

amongst loose floes much driven about by the wind and the currents, and in great
danger. De Veer describes it:

The 1st of July it was indifferent fair weather, with a west-northwest wind,
and in the morning, the sun being east, there came a bear from the driving ice
and swam over the water to the fast ice whereon we lay. But when she heard
us she came no nearer, but ran away. And when the sun was southeast, the ice
came so fast in towards us that all the ice whereon we lay with our boats and
our goods broke and ran one piece upon another, whereby we were in no small
fear, for at that time most of our goods fell into the water. But we with great
diligence drew our boats further upon the ice towards the land, where we
thought to be better defended from the driving of the ice, and as we went to
fetch our goods we fell into the greatest trouble that ever we had before, for
we endured so great danger in the saving thereof, that as we laid hold upon one
piece thereof the rest sunk down with the ice, and many times the ice broke
under our own feet. We were wholly discomforted and in a manner clean out
of all hope, expecting no issue thereof, in such sort that our trouble at that time
surmounted all our former cares and impeachments. When we thought to draw
up our boats on the ice, the ice broke under us, and we were carried away, boat
and all, by the driving ice. When we thought to save the goods the ice broke
under our feet, and with that the boat broke in many places, especially where
we had mended it, as the mast, the mast plank, almost the whole boat, wherein
one of our men that was sick, and a chest of money, lay, which we with great
danger of our lives got out from it. As we were doing it, the ice that was under
our feet drove from us and slid upon other ice, whereby we were in danger to
break both our arms and legs. At which time, thinking we had lost our boat,
we beheld each other in pitiful manner, knowing not what we should do, our
lives depending thereon.

But God made so good provision for us, that the pieces of ice drove from each
other, wherewith we ran in great haste to the boat and drew it to us again in such
case as it was, and laid it upon the fast ice by the yawl, where it was in more security, which put us unto an exceeding and great and dangerous labor from the time
that the sun was southeast until it was west-southwest. In all that time we did not
rest, which made us extremely weary and wholly out of comfort, and it was much
more fearful to us than when William Barents died. For there we were almost
drowned, and that day we lost, sunk in the sea, two barrels of bread, a chest with linen

cloth, a trunk with the sailor's best clothes, our astrolabe [*the principal navigational instrument of the time*], a pack of scarlet cloth, a small barrel of oil, and some cheeses and wine, which were stove in by the ice so that there was not any thing saved.

They continued through July trying to get away from Novaya Zemlya. Not until August did they reach the coast of Russia, where they struggled to sail west under conditions that remained dangerous, and where they came close to starving. Once the two boats lost each other for a week. In September they happened, to their amazement, upon the same Dutch ship they had been separated from when they had discovered Spitzbergen the previous year. They sailed home in it, reaching Holland on November 1. Of the eighteen men who had set out in Barents' ship, twelve remained. Their ordeal is one of the great stories of Arctic survival, and it is too little known.

THE VOYAGES OF WILLIAM BARENTS DID NOT END EUROPEAN INTEREST in a northeast passage. A decade after Barents died English merchants sent Henry Hudson on the same track Barents had sailed, once in 1607 and again in 1608. We know almost nothing about Henry Hudson before 1607 except that he was a captain in the service of the Russia or Muscovy Company, which, incidentally, invented the ship's log, by which a daily record was kept of everything that happened in the navigation of the ship that day, plus other notable events. Almost everything we know about Hudson comes from these logs.

Hudson's own log of his first exploring voyage has been lost, but we have the log of someone else on the ship. He headed north by way of the Shetland Islands to the east coast of Greenland, and followed that coast to a latitude of 73 degrees, and then a little farther to the polar ice pack. He intended to cross the open polar sea that Mercator and Ortelius both postulated and sail directly to China. Following the edge of the pack he reached Spitzbergen, and then explored its shores. He claimed to have reached a latitude of 80 degrees north, although much doubt has been cast on this claim. He spent most of July in the Spitzbergen area, evidently attempting to find a break in the pack ice that would allow him to continue north. Eventually he gave up and sailed back to England.

In his next voyage, the following year, he gave up on the north and headed to the northeast instead, but he was no more successful than anyone else had been. When he returned the Dutch East India Company called him to Holland and proposed that he sail yet again to the northeast, under their patronage. He left Holland in April, 1609, with two ships, reached Novaya Zemlya in May, turned around when he could go no farther and returned to the Faroe Islands. From there he headed west, got to the coast of Nova Scotia in June, and sailed south, looking now for a northwest passage, or any likely passage, through the bulk of North America. On August 28 he arrived in Delaware Bay; on September 2, in the river we now call by his name, the Hudson.

This voyage was marked throughout by quarrels between the Dutch members of his crew, whom he had not chosen himself, and the English members. He stopped at Novaya Zemlya partly because his crew refused to go any farther into the ice. It was then that they decided to try North America. He sailed as far as Chesapeake Bay to the south, then doubled back. The idea Verrazano had proposed, that only a narrow isthmus stood between the Atlantic Ocean and the Pacific, was still current. This voyage did much to refute that idea.

It was only natural that, having explored much of the North American coast to the south, Hudson would want to extend his search to the north. He set out on his fourth and final voyage on April 17, 1610, reaching Iceland in May and Greenland at the beginning of June, and Resolution Island, at the mouth of what we now call Hudson Strait, on June 24. From there he wanted to sail north but "the wind would not suffer him" to sail in that direction, so he proceeded northwest into the unknown, his Strait, which was littered with icebergs. Abacuk Prickett, whose account of this voyage we are about to excerpt, writes that "in our going between the ice, we saw one of the great islands of ice overturn, which was a good warning to us, not to come near them nor within their reach." Icebergs do indeed flip over with no warning. Pack ice also littered the strait and Hudson was forced to dodge his way through it until he could dodge no more. At that time, early July, he called a meeting of his crew and gave them a choice: to go on, or to turn around and go home.

They chose to go on, zig-zagging through the ice, around ice-locked islands, naming features of the land as they proceeded. By the fourth of August they were sailing down the east coast of Hudson Bay and they continued to James Bay, at the southern end of Hudson Bay. By October, still in James Bay, they had no choice but to spend the winter.

That dissension marked this voyage there is no doubt, but we also don't have the whole story. Abacuk Prickett's account is self-serving, what survives of Hudson's log says little or nothing about the dissension, and other accounts are unreliable. History is written by the winners, and in this case the winners were mutineers, who needed to protect themselves as well as they could from English justice when they returned. The source of the trouble originally seemed to be Hudson's mate, Robert Juet, who had been plotting mutiny since at least Iceland and had, when they were "pestered in the ice, ... used words tending to mutiny, discouragement, and slander of the action, which easily took effect in those that were timorous." Hudson demoted Juet and appointed a man named Robert Bylot, who would distinguish himself on later voyages to the Arctic, to his place. We have not yet come to the time in the English Navy when mutinous talk like Juet's would have been dealt with much more harshly. These were not, indeed, naval voyages; they were commercial in nature, and a rough kind of democracy prevailed on board.

On November 1, having explored James Bay thoroughly, Hudson ran the ship aground somewhere near the southeast corner of James Bay to spend the winter. We turn now to Abacuk Prickett's account of what happened subsequently.

ABACUK PRICKETT

A Larger Discourse of the Same Voyage, 1611

WE WERE VICTUALED FOR SIX MONTHS IN GOOD PROPORTION, AND OF THAT
which was good. If our master would have had more, he might have had it at
home and in other places. Here we were now, and therefore it behooved us to
spend [*i.e., ration*], that we might have enough (when the time came) to bring
us to the capes where the fowls bred (*the capes at the northeast end of* Hudson Bay),
for that was all the hope we had to bring us home. Wherefore our master took
order, first for the spending of that we had, and then to increase it, by pro-
pounding a reward to them that killed either beast, fish, or fowl, as in his
journal you have seen. About the middle of this month of November died John
Williams, our gunner. God pardon the master's uncharitable dealing with
this man. Now that I am come to speak of him, out of whose ashes (as it were)
that unhappy deed grew which brought a scandal upon all that are returned
home, and upon the action itself, the multitude (like the dog) running after
the stone, but not at the caster: therefore, not to wrong the living nor slander
the dead, I will (by the leave of God) deliver the truth as near as I can.

You shall understand that our master kept (in his house at London) a
young man, named Henry Green, born in Kent, of worshipful parents, but by
his lewd life and conversation he had lost the good will of all his friends, and
had spent all that he had. This man our master would have to sea with him,
because he could write well. Our master gave him meat, and drink, and lodg-
ing, and by means of one Master Venson, with much ado got four pounds of

his mother to buy him clothes, wherewith Master Venson would not trust him, but saw it laid out himself (*i.e., he did not give him the money directly, but paid for the clothes instead*). This Henry Green was not set down in the owner's book, nor any wages made for him. He came first aboard at Gravesend (*at the mouth of the Thames*), and at Harwich should have gone into the field, with one Wilkinson. At Iceland the surgeon and he fell out in Dutch, and he beat him ashore in English, which set all the company in a rage, so that we had much ado to get the surgeon aboard. (*The nineteenth-century editor of this text does not explain what is going on here, but it's obvious that Green quarreled with the surgeon and may have struck him.*) I told the master of it, but he bade me let it alone, for, said he, the surgeon had a tongue that would wrong the best friend he had. But Robert Juet, the master's mate, would needs burn his finger in the embers, and told the carpenter a long tale (when he was drunk) that our master had brought in Green to crack his credit that should displease him. Which words came to the master's ears, who when he understood it, would have gone back to Iceland, when he was forty leagues from thence, to have sent home his mate Robert Juet in a fisherman. But, being otherwise persuaded, all was well. So Henry Green stood upright, and very inward with (*close to*) the master, and was a service-able man every way for manhood, but for religion he would say he was clean paper whereon he might write what he would. Now, when our gunner was dead, and, as the order is in these cases, if the company stand in need of anything that belonged to the man deceased, then is it brought to the main mast, and there sold to them that will give most for the same. This gunner had a gray cloth gown which Green prayed the master to friend him so much as to let him have it, paying for it as another would give. The master said he should, and there-upon he answered some that sought to have it that Green should have it, and none else, and so it rested.

Now out of season and time the master called the carpenter to go in hand with (*i.e., to build*) a house on shore, which at the beginning our master would not hear of, when it might have been done. The carpenter told him that the snow and frost were such as he neither could nor would go in hand with such work. Which when our master heard he ferreted him out of his cabin to strike him, calling him by many foul names, and threatening to hang him. The carpenter told him that he knew what belonged to his place better than him-self, and that he was no house carpenter. So this passed, and the house was after made with much labor, but to no end. The next day after the master and the carpenter fell out, the carpenter took his gun and Henry Green with him, for it was an order that none should go out alone, but one with a gun, the other with a pike. This did move the master so much the more against Henry Green that Robert Bylot his mate must have the gown and had it delivered to him. Which when Henry Green saw, he challenged the master's promise, but the master did so rail on Green, with so many words of disgrace, telling him that all his friends would not trust him with twenty shillings, and therefore why should he. As for wages he had none, nor none should have, if he did not please him well. Yet the master had promised him to make his wages as good as any man's in the ship, and to have him one of the prince's guard when we came home (*i.e., he would obtain a place for him in the King's Guards*). But you shall see how the devil out of this so wrought with Green, that he did the master what mischief he could in seeking to discredit him, and to thrust him and many other honest men out of the ship in the end. To speak of all our trouble in this time of winter (which was so cold, as it lamed the most of our company, and myself do yet feel it) would be too tedious.

But I must not forget to show how mercifully God dealt with us in this time. For the space of three months we had such store of fowl of one kind, which were partridges as white as milk, that we killed above a hundred dozen, besides others of sundry sorts, for all was fish that came to the net. The spring coming, this fowl left us, yet they were with us all the extreme cold. Then in their place came diverse sorts of other fowl, as swan, geese, duck, and teal, but hard to come by. Our master hoped they would have bred in those broken grounds, but they do not, but came from the south and flew to the north, further than we were this voyage. Yet if they be taken short with the wind at north, or northwest, or northeast, then they fall and stay till the wind serve them, and then fly to the north. Now in time these fowl are gone, and few or none to be seen. Then we went into the woods, hills, and valleys, for all things that had any show of substance in them, how vile soever: the moss of the ground, than which I take the powder of a post (*sawdust, in other words*) to be much better; and the frog in his engendering time, as loathsome as a toad, was not spared. But amongst the diverse sorts of buds, it pleased God that Thomas Woodhouse brought home a bud of a tree full of a turpentine substance. Of this our surgeon made a decoction to drink and applied the buds hot to them that were troubled with ache in any part of their bodies, and for my part I confess I received great and present ease of my pain.

About this time, when the ice began to break out of the bays, there came a savage to our ship, as it were to see and be seen, being the first that we had seen in all this time, whom our master entreated well, and made much of him, promising unto himself great matters by his means, and therefore would have all the knives and hatchets which any man had to his private use, but received none but from John King the carpenter, and myself. To this savage our master gave a knife, a looking glass (*a mirror*), and buttons, who received them thankfully, and made signs that after he had slept he would come again, which he did. When he came he brought with him a sled, which he drew after him, and upon it two deerskins and two beaver skins. He had a scrip under his arm, out of which he drew those things which the master had given him. He took the knife and laid it upon one of the beaver skins, and his glasses and buttons upon the other, and so gave them to the master, who received them. And the savage took those things which the master had given him, and put them up into his scrip again. Then the master showed him a hatchet, for which he would have given the master one of the deerskins, but our master would have them both, and so he had, although not willingly. After many signs of people to the north and to the south, and that after so many sleeps he would come again, he went his way, but never came more.

Now the ice being out of the sounds, so that our boat might go from one place unto another, a company of men were appointed by the master to go fishing with our net.... These men, the first day they went, caught five hundred fish, as big as good herrings, and some trout, which put us all in some hope to have our wants supplied, and our commons amended. But these were the most that ever they got in one day, for many days they got not a quarter so many. In this time of their fishing, Henry Green and William Wilson, with some others, plotted to take the net and the shallop, which the carpenter had now set up, and so to shift for themselves. But the shallop being ready, our master would go in it himself to the south and southwest, to see if he could meet with the people; for to that end was it set up, and we might see the woods set on fire by them. So the master took the seine and the shallop, and to the south he went. They that remained aboard were to take in water, wood, and ballast, and to have all things in readiness when he came back. But he set no time of his return, for he was persuaded that if he could meet with the people, he should have meat of them, and that good store. But he returned worse than he went forth. For he could by no means meet with the people, although they were near them, yet they would set the woods on fire in his sight.

Being returned, he fitted all things for his return, and first, delivered all the bread out of the bread room (which came to a pound apiece for every man's share) and delivered also a bill of return, willing them to have that to show, if it pleased God that they came home, and he wept when he gave it unto them. But to help us in this poor estate with some relief, the boat and seine went to work on Friday morning, and stayed till Sunday noon, at which time they came aboard, and brought fourscore small fish, a poor relief for so many hungry bellies. Then we weighed (*weighed anchor*) and stood out of our wintering place, and came to an anchor without, in the mouth of the bay, from whence we weighed and came to an anchor without in the sea, where our bread being gone, that store of cheese we had was to stop a gap, whereof there were five, whereat the company complained, because they made account of nine. But those that were left were equally divided by the master, although he had counsel to the contrary; for there were some who, having it, would make haste to be rid of it (*they would eat it too quickly, without rationing it*), because they could not govern it (*govern their hunger*). Henry Green gave half his bread, which he had for fourteen days, to one to keep, and prayed him not to let him have any until the next Monday; but before Wednesday night he never left till he had it again, having eaten up his first week's bread before. So Wilson the boatswain had eaten in one day his fortnight's bread, and had been two or three days sick for his labor. The cause that moved the master to deliver all the cheese was because they were not all of one goodness, and therefore they should see that they had no wrong done them; but every man should have alike the best and the worst together, which was three pounds and a half for seven days.

The wind serving, we weighed and stood to the northwest, and on Monday night (the eighteenth day of June) we fell into the ice, and the next day, the wind being at west, we lay there till Sunday in sight of land. Now being here, the master told Nicholas Simmes that there would be a breaking up of the chests and a search for bread, and willed him, if he had any, to bring it to him, which he did, and delivered to the master thirty cakes in a bag. [*Hudson was, in other words, going to go after private stashes of food in the seamen's chests. But the rest of this paragraph seems to refer not to that incident, but to the whole matter of the divisions amongst the crew.*] This deed of the master, if it be true, has made me marvel what should be the reason that he did not stop the breach in the beginning, but let it grow to that height, as that it overthrew himself and many other honest men. But "there are many devices in the heart of man, but the counsel of the Lord shall stand."

Being thus in the ice on Saturday, the one and twentieth of June, at night, Wilson the boatswain and Henry Green came to me lying in my cabin lame, and told me that they and the rest of their associates would shift the company, and turn the master and all the sick men into the shallop and let them shift for themselves. For there was not fourteen days victuals left for all the company, at that poor allowance they were at, and that there they lay, the master not caring to go one way or the other, and that they had not eaten anything these three days, and therefore were resolute, either to mend or end, and what they had begun they would go through with, or die. When I heard this, I told them I marveled to hear so much from them, considering that they were married men, and had wives and children, and that for their sakes they should not commit so foul a thing in the sight of God and man as that would be. For why should they banish themselves from their native country? Henry Green bade me hold my peace, for he knew the worst, which was to be hanged when he came home, and therefore of the two he would rather be hanged at home than starved abroad. And for the good will they bore me, they would have me stay in the ship. I gave them thanks, and told them that I came into her, not to forsake her, yet not to hurt myself and others by any such deed. Henry Green told me then that I must take my fortune in the shallop. If there be no remedy, said I, the will of God be done.

Away went Henry Green in a rage, swearing to cut his throat that went about to disturb them, and left Wilson by me, with whom I had some talk, but to no good. He was so persuaded that there was no remedy now but to go on while it was hot, lest their party should fail them and the mischief they had intended to others should light on themselves. Henry Green came again and demanded of him what I said. Wilson answered: He is in his old song, still patient. Then I spoke to Henry Green to stay three days, in which time I would so deal with the master that all should be well. I dealt with him to forbear but two days, nay twelve hours. There is no way then, said they, but out of hand (*i.e., immediately; they refused to delay executing their plan*). Then I told them, that if they would stay till Monday, I would join with them to share all the victuals in the ship, and would justify it when I came home; but this would not serve their turn. Wherefore I told them, it was some worse matter they had in hand than they made show of, and that it was blood and revenge he sought, or else he would not at such a time of night undertake such a deed. Henry Green with that took my Bible which lay before me, and swore that he would do no man harm, and what he did was for the good of the voyage, and for nothing else; and that all the rest should do the like. The like did Wilson swear.

Henry Green went his way, and presently came Juet, who, because he was an ancient man, I hoped to have found some reason in him. But he was worse than Henry Green, for he swore plainly that he would justify this deed when he came home. After him came John Thomas and Michael Perce as birds of one feather, but because they are not living, I will let them go, as then I did. Then came Moter and Bennet, of whom I demanded, if they were well advised what they had taken in hand. They answered, they were, and therefore came to take their oath.

Prickett's account here becomes very confused about who should go and who should stay in the ship. It was clear that Hudson, his son, John, and the sick men were to be put in the shallop and abandoned, but among the sick there were men who were friends of the plotters, so the question of who should stay and who go went back and forth all that time. The ship's carpenter was loyal to Hudson and had apparently stolen food, but ship's carpenters are useful and they were divided as to whether he should be put in the shallop. It is never clear why Prickett himself, who says he was himself lame, was spared. We pick up the narrative where Hudson is taken outside his cabin. "Cabin" here does not mean what we think of as a cabin; only the captain would have his own private cabin. Prickett is referring to the small cubby or sleeping shelf each man had to himself.

In the meantime Henry Green and another went to the carpenter and held him with a talk till the master came out of his cabin, which he soon did. Then came John Thomas and Bennet before him, while Wilson bound his arms behind him. He asked them what they meant. They told him he should know when he was in the shallop. Now Juet, while this was doing, came to John King into the hold, who was provided for him, for he had got a sword of his own, and kept him at bay, and might have killed him, but others came to help him, and so he came up to the master. The master called to the carpenter and told him that he was bound, but I heard no answer he made. Now Arnold Lodlo and Michael Bute railed at them, and told them their knavery would show itself.

Then was the shallop hauled up to the ship's side, and the poor, sick, and lame men were called upon to get out of their cabins into the shallop. The master called to me, who came out of my cabin as well as I could, to the hatchway to speak with him, where, on my knees, I besought them, for the love of God, to remember themselves, and to do as they would be done unto. They bade me keep myself well, and get into my cabin, not suffering the master to speak with me. But when I came into my cabin again he called to me at the horn which gave light into my cabin and told me that Juet would overthrow us all. Nay, said I, it is that villain Henry Green, and I spoke it not softly.

Now was the carpenter at liberty, who asked them if they would be hanged when they came home. As for himself, he said, he would not stay in the ship unless they would force him. They bade him go, then, for they would not stop him. I will, said he, so I may have my chest with me, and all that is in it. They said he should, and they put it into the shallop. Then he came down to me to take his leave of me, who tried to get him to stay, which if he did, he might so work that all should be well. He said, he did not think but they would be glad to take them in again. For he was so persuaded by the master, that there was not one in all the ship who could tell how to sail her home. But, said he, if we must part, which we will not willingly do, for they would follow the ship, he prayed me, if we came to the Capes (*he means the capes at the north end of* Hudson B*ay*) before them, that I would leave some token that we had been there, near to the place where the fowls bred, and he would do the like for us. So with tears we parted. Now were the sick men driven out of their cabins into the shallop....

In the meantime there were some of them that plied their work as if the ship had been entered by force and they had free leave to pillage, breaking up chests and rifling all places. One of them came by me and asked me what they should do. I answered he should make an end of what he had begun, for I saw him do nothing but shark up and down. Now were all the poor men in the shallop, whose names are as follows: Henry Hudson, John Hudson, Arnold Lodlo, Sidrack Faner, Phillip Staff, Thomas Woodhouse, Adam Moore, Henry King, Michael Bute. The carpenter got a gun from them, and powder and shot and some pikes, an iron pot, with some meal and other things. They stood out of the ice, the shallop being fast to the stern of the ship, and then, when they were nearly out, for I cannot say they were clean out, they cut her head fast from the stern of our ship (*i.e., they cut the rope*), then out with their topsails and towards the east they stood in a clear sea. In the end they took in their topsails, righted their helm, and lay under their foresail till they had ransacked and searched all places in the ship. In the hold they found one of the vessels of meal whole, and the other half spent, for we had but two. We found also two firkins (*a firkin was a small tub*) of butter, some twenty-seven pieces of pork, half a bushel of peas. But in the master's cabin we found two hundred of biscuit cakes, a peck of meal, beer to the quantity of a butt, one with another. Now it was said that the shallop was come within sight, they let fall the mainsail, and out with their topsails, and flew as if from an enemy.

Then I prayed them yet to remember themselves, but William Wilson, more than the rest, would hear of no such matter. Coming nigh the east shore they cast about, and stood to the west and came to an island, and anchored in sixteen or seventeen fathoms of water. So they sent the boat and the net ashore to see if they could have a draught (*presumably of fish*), but could not for rocks and great stones. Michael Perse killed two fowl, and here they found good store of that weed which we called cockle grass in our wintering place, whereof they gathered store, and came aboard again. Here we lay that night and the best part of the next day, in all which time we saw not the shallop, or ever after. Now Henry Green came to me and told me that it was the company's will that I should come up into the master's cabin and take charge thereof. I told him it was more fit for Robert Juet. He said he should not come in it, nor meddle with the master's card (*his card was his chart or map, and his record of the course he had kept*) or journals. So up I came, and Henry Green gave me the key of the master's chest, and told me then, that he had laid the master's best things together, which he would use himself when time did serve.

They then sailed to the northeast up the eastern shore of Hudson Bay. They were trapped in the ice for fourteen days on this route. Prickett's account is so vague about geographical details that historians have not been able to trace exactly where they went. Green, always treacherous, accused Prickett of taking thirty cakes of bread, when he himself had taken it, according to Prickett. Juet and Bylot argued as well about the course they should be following. They did not, in fact, know where they were. They did, however, recognize the capes at the head of Hudson Bay, and on July 27 anchored there and went in search of birds to kill and managed to shoot some thirty seagulls. This was the area they had identified the previous year as the place where "the fowls bred" and they were eager to find them, for they were starving. We take up the narrative again on July 28.

The eight and twentieth day the boat went to Digges Cape for fowl and made directly for the place where the fowl bred, and being near, they saw seven boats come about the eastern point toward them. When the savages saw our boat, they drew themselves together and drew their lesser boats into their bigger, and when they had done they came rowing to our boat and made signs to the west, but they made ready for all assays. The savages came to them, and by signs grew familiar one with another, so as our men took one of theirs into our boat, and they took one of ours into theirs. Then they carried our man to a cove where their tents stood towards the west of the place where the fowl bred. They carried him into their tents, where he remained till our men returned with theirs. Our boat went to the place where the fowl bred and were desirous to know how the savages killed their fowl. He showed them the manner how, which was thus: they take a long pole with a snare at the end, which they put about the fowl's neck, and so pluck them down. When our men knew that they had a better way of their own, they showed him the use of our guns, which at one shot would kill seven or eight. To be short, our boat returned to their cove for our man and to deliver theirs. When they came they made great joy, with dancing and leaping and striking of their breasts. They offered diverse things to our men, but they only took some morse's teeth (*whale's teeth*), which they gave them for a knife and two glass buttons. So receiving our man they came aboard, much rejoicing at this chance, as if they had met with the most simple and kind people of the world.

And Henry Green, more than the rest, was so confident that by no means we should take care to stand on our guard, God blinding him so, that where he made reckoning to receive great matters from these people, he received more than he looked for, and that suddenly, by being made a good example for all men that make no conscience of doing evil, and that we take heed of the savage people, how simple soever they seem to be.

The next day, the nine and twentieth of July, they made haste to be ashore, and because the ship rode too far off, they weighed and stood as near to the place where the fowl bred as they could. Because I was lame I was to go in the boat to carry such things as I had in the cabin, of everything somewhat (*he means trade goods*). With more haste than good speed, and not without swearing, away we went, Henry Green, William Wilson, John Thomas, Michael Perse, Andrew Moter, and myself. When we came near the shore, the people were on the hills dancing and leaping. To the cove we came where they had drawn up their boats. We brought our boat to the east side of the cove close to the rocks. Ashore they went and made fast the boat to a great stone on the shore. The people came, and everyone had something in his hand to barter. But Henry Green swore they should have nothing till he had venison, for they had so promised him by signs.

Now when we came they made signs to their dogs, whereof there were many like mongrels, as big as hounds, and pointed to their mountain and to the sun, clapping their hands. Then Henry Green, John Thomas, and William Wilson stood hard by the boat head, Michael Perse and Andrew Moter were got up upon the rock gathering sorrel. Not one of them had any weapon about him, not so much as a stick, save Henry Green only, who had a piece of a pike in his hand. Nor saw I anything that they had wherewith to hurt us. Henry Green and William Wilson had looking glasses, and Jews' harps, and bells, which they were showing the people. The savages standing round about them, one of them came into the boat's head to me to show me a bottle. I made signs to him to get him ashore, but he made as though he had not understood me, whereupon I stood up and pointed him ashore. In the meantime another stole behind me to the stern of the boat, and when I saw him ashore that was in the head of the boat I sat down again, but suddenly I saw the leg and foot of a man by me. Wherefore I cast up my head and saw the savage with his knife in his hand, who struck at my breast over my head. I cast up my right arm to save my breast. He wounded my arm and struck me into the body under my right breast. He struck a second blow, which I met with my left hand, and then he struck me into the right thigh, and had like to cut off my little finger of the left hand. Now I had got hold of the string of the knife, and had wound it about my left hand, he striving with both his hands to make an end of what he had begun. I found him but weak in the grip, God enabling me, and getting hold of the sleeve of his left arm, so bore him from me. His left side lay bare to me, which when I saw, I put his sleeve off his left arm into my left hand, holding the string of the knife fast in the same hand, and having got my right hand at liberty, I sought for something to strike him with, not remembering my dagger at my side, but looking down I saw it, and struck him into the body and the throat.

While I was thus assaulted in the boat, our men were set upon on the shore. John Thomas and William Wilson had their bowels cut, and Michael Perse and Henry Green, being mortally wounded, came tumbling into the boat together. When Andrew Moter saw this medley, he came running down the rocks and leapt into the sea, and so swam to the boat, hanging on the stern thereof, till Michael Perse took him in, who manfully made good the head of the boat against the savages, that pressed sore upon us. Now Michael Perse had got a hatchet, wherewith I saw him strike one of them, that he lay sprawling in the sea. Henry Green cried *courage*, and laid about him with his truncheon. I cried to them to clear the boat and Andrew Moter cried to be taken in. The savages betook them to their bows and arrows, which they sent amongst us, wherewith Henry Green was slain outright and Michael Perse received many wounds, and so did the rest. Michael Perse cleared the boat and put it from the shore and helped Andrew Moter in, but in turning of the boat I received a cruel wound in my back with an arrow. Michael Perse and Andrew Moter rowed the boat away, which, when the savages saw, they ran to their boats and I feared they would have launched them to have followed us, but they did not, and our ship was in the middle of the channel and could not see us.

Now, when they had rowed a good way from shore, Michael Perse fainted and could row no more. Then was Andrew Moter driven to stand in the boat head and wave to the ship, which at first saw us not, and when they did they could not tell what to make of us, but in the end they stood for us, and so took us up. Henry Green was thrown out of the boat into the sea, and the rest were had aboard, the savage being yet alive, but without sense (*he was unconscious, in other words*). But they died all there that day, William Wilson swearing and cursing in most fearful manner. Michael Perse lived two days after and then died. Thus you have heard the tragical end of Henry Green and his mates, whom they called captain, these four being the only lusty men (*he means healthy, capable of working*) in all the ship.

THE REMAINING MEN STAYED IN THE AREA, AT CONSIDERABLE DANGER *to themselves, to catch birds, and managed to gather in some three hundred. They then sailed east to the mouth of Hudson Strait, nearly running aground in dense fog. Prickett gives little sense of time but it was evident that they were starving; he remarks that after eating the birds they ate the skins, burning off the feathers, "and as for the garbage, it was not thrown away." Leaving Hudson Strait they set course for Ireland. They still had some birds left but not many. "Bennet, our cook," reports Prickett, "made a mess of meat of the bones of the fowl, frying them with candle grease till they were crisp, and with vinegar*

put to them, made a good dish of meat. Our vinegar was shared, and to every man a pound of candles delivered for a week, as a great dainty." Then Robert Juet, the mutinous mate, died "for mere want," of starvation, in other words, and the men were too weak for the most part to man the sails. They arrived finally on the southwest coast of Ireland, only to discover that nobody there had any spare food for them. Only when they sold their anchor to an English ship captain for cash could they obtain food.

What became of Hudson's mutineers? They were left to languish in prison until their trial in 1618, seven years after their return. None of them were hung, partly, perhaps, because of Prickett's account, which places the blame for the mutiny on men who were (conveniently) killed by the Inuit, and partly because they claimed to have discovered the Northwest Passage. An expedition under a man named Button sailed into Hudson Bay in 1613 to check out this so-called discovery, and incidentally to look for Henry Hudson, but no sign of Hudson has ever been found. Nor was this expedition able to find a way out of Hudson Bay to the west. In 1615 one of the mutineers, Robert Bylot, piloted another expedition back to Hudson Bay with William Baffin as the navigator. Baffin was a man like William Barents, an expert navigator and well able to handle a ship. On a subsequent expedition, again with Bylot as pilot, he sailed up Davis Strait into what we now know as Baffin Bay and then explored down the east coast of Baffin Island.

There is, of course, no way out of Hudson Bay to the west. Hudson Bay is a dead end. Two more notable expeditions, financed independently by groups of merchants, sailed into Hudson Bay in 1631-2. Both left names behind. One, led by Thomas James, sailed south and wintered over in the same area where Hudson had wintered, in the large bay at the south end of Hudson Bay. It now bears Thomas James' name. The other, led by Luke Foxe, sailed farther north into the Bay. Foxe Channel and Foxe Sound are named after Luke Foxe. Neither voyage had any other result. James and his men met with horrendous conditions and barely escaped with their lives. No other ship sailed into Hudson Bay until 1668, well after the end of the Civil War in England and the Restoration of Charles II. With the establishment of the Hudson's Bay Company in 1670, to carry on the fur trade, travel into Hudson Bay did become more common, and the English learned how to deal with the cold. The Company was not interested in looking for a northwest passage, however. The Company's forts were all established on the lower western shores of the Bay, where the winters were somewhat less severe. Supply ships came once a year, usually in August, and left as soon as they had unloaded their trade goods and taken on the year's supply of furs. After Thomas James left Hudson Bay in 1632 no English ship set out in search of the Northwest Passage for nearly a century.

✴

PART TWO

The Search for the
Northwest Passage Revived

✴

THE SEARCH FOR THE
NORTHWEST PASSAGE REVIVED

IT WAS A BUSY CENTURY, TO BE SURE. THE DEFEAT OF THE SPANISH Armada in 1588 had shown the English what they could do at sea and had brought to an end their fear of Spanish domination in the Pacific and the West Indies. The East India Company, chartered in 1600, began a trade with India and beyond that would end in the colonization of India in the 1700s. In the 1640s, even while civil war consumed the English people, English trade to the Far East continued to grow and England itself became a major maritime power. From 1686 until the end of the Napoleonic Wars in 1815, English tonnage in merchant ships rose from 340,000 to 2,477,000. English settlement of North America began in the early 1600s and by the end of the century English migration to the colonies had become a flood. The English, in short, were busy creating an empire.

But if the dream of a Northwest Passage faded away, it did not entirely die. Not until quite late in the eighteenth century did James Cook and George Vancouver establish exactly where the west coast of North America lay, and until that time it was still possible to speculate that somewhere north of California the coast strayed east by north and ended at a cape a short distance from the top of Hudson Bay. To modern eyes familiar with the globe and the shape of the continents it seems like a bizarre idea, but that part of the map was blank then. Vitus Bering had discovered the Aleutians and the Alaskan coast in the 1740s, but his findings were by no means extensive. He had not sailed the length of the Northwest Coast of the continent; he had only touched upon it. Who knew what lay to the south and north? Where there is ignorance, wishful thinking inevitably follows. The old Strait of Anian might exist after all. Men give up their dreams reluctantly.

The first voyage to pursue this particular dream set sail from England in 1719, under the command of James Knight, a former governor of the Hudson's Bay Company. In general the Company was not at all interested in exploration. It was a conservative organization happy to enjoy its monopoly of the fur trade in northern Canada, which was enormously profitable, and leave the excitement, and the risk, to others. Its "factories"(the word comes from "factor," i.e. the agent in charge of trade) at Fort Severn, Fort Albany, and York Fort on Hudson Bay were nothing more than trading posts where Indians from the interior brought their furs to exchange for blankets, guns, powder—the usual trade goods. Knight had been an officer in the Company for years, and he was not a young man. But there must have been enough romance left in him to want to explore. He had heard rumors in the past about a "yellow metal" somewhere in the interior. Glyn Williams, in Voyages of Delusion, his history of the search for the Northwest Passage in the eighteenth century, quotes an excited entry from Knight's journal in which he speaks of an Indian woman telling him "she has both seen [the yellow metal] taken and took it up out of the river herself as it has washed down out of the bank. It is very yellow, soft and heavy....They find lumps so big sometimes that they hammer it betwixt stones and make dishes of it." Think of it: dishes made of gold. It sounds like a king's dinner service.

The same Indians would tell Knight also about great bodies of water to the north and west and passages to them. It was all so tantalizing, and so in the mold of Martin Frobisher a century and a half earlier. In 1719, after much negotiation with the Company directors, Knight set sail for the northern Bay, where Company ships never ventured, with two small ships, contributing an eighth of the expedition's cost out of his own pocket. With him he had thirty-plus men, ten of them apparently miners.

Not until 1767 did Company whalers discover the remains of Knight's winter encampment on Marble Island, a couple of hundred miles north of Prince of Wales Fort (now Churchill), and the graves. A number of men seem to have survived the winter of 1719-20, according to Inuit testimony, but eventually they all died.

But Knight's fate did not stop people dreaming of a way out of Hudson Bay to the north. Outside Company circles, indeed, few people even knew about Knight's expedition, and those who did knew only that it had not come home. Inside the Company, to be sure, the failure confirmed the Company's disinterest in exploration, and for the next twenty years they made no serious effort to sail beyond the point Knight had reached with his two little ships. Any further efforts toward finding the Northwest Passage would not come from within the Hudson's Bay Company. It would come from an Irish Member of Parliament named Arthur Dobbs. In 1731 Dobbs published a Memorial on the

Northwest Passage *that advocated further exploration in Hudson Bay, and he continued to propagandize his idea with both the government and the Hudson's Bay Company for the next fifteen years. Dobbs' arguments sound exactly like the arguments of Humphrey Gilbert in the sixteenth century. A Northwest Passage would cut thousands of miles off voyages to the Pacific. It would be out of the way of Spanish shipping so that English privateers could descend upon the Spanish treasure galleons on the west coast of South America without warning. No longer would English ships have to brave the elements around Cape Horn, or endure the endless voyage around the Cape of Good Hope.*

Dobbs's *proposal met with official and unofficial indifference, but he was nothing if not persistent, and in 1740 the First Lord of the Admiralty mentioned the idea to the king, George II, who unexpectedly approved of it. That suddenly changed the prospect considerably. The following year two ships under the overall command of another ex-Company man, Christopher Middleton, set out for Hudson Bay to look for the passage once more. Middleton had left the Hudson's Bay Company to obtain a commission in the English Navy. This was the first time the Admiralty had manned an expedition whose only purpose was exploration.*

The Middleton voyage, like the Knight voyage before him, was a disaster, but not as great a disaster. The government had made it plain to the Company that they were to help Middleton and his crews in any way they could, and Middleton had the sense to winter over at a company fort rather than try to establish winter quarters on his own. Nevertheless ten of Middleton's men died of scurvy over the dreadful winter, while others lost fingers and toes to frostbite. In the spring the mosquitoes were so bad that, as Williams tells us in Voyages of Delusion, *"a bushel of mosquitoes might be swept off a hunter as he emerged from the woods, and they had to be shoveled off the ground before a door could be opened."*

The voyage north lasted through July and into August in 1742. Middleton coasted the western shore of the Bay, found Wager Inlet, which he did not sail far enough into to determine whether it was the Passage or not, and came to what he named, aptly, Repulse Bay, located under the base of the Melville Peninsula, which he did explore, thoroughly enough at any rate to determine that it had no exit except the way he had come in.

This voyage ought to have ended all speculation that the Northwest Passage had its origin in Hudson Bay. But it did not. Middleton returned to England to charges that he had not done enough, gone far enough, explored the coast south of Repulse Bay with enough diligence. Most of the criticism originated with Dobbs, who started a pamphlet war with Middleton that went on for years. On the sketchiest of evidence Dobbs insisted that the Northwest Passage could be found in Hudson Bay. He bribed men from Middleton's crew to support him. He brought charges against Middleton that Middleton was forced to answer before an Admiralty investigative board. Dobbs was interested now not just in the Northwest Passage, but in breaking the Hudson's Bay Company's monopoly of trade in the region. He was persuasive and influential. In 1745 his nonstop agitation against Middleton and the Company and on behalf of his imaginary Northwest Passage inspired Parliament to pass an act awarding L20,000 to the first explorer to find it.

The first to set out did so in 1746 under the financial sponsorship of Dobbs and a group of men known as the North West Committee, men prominent in trade and in the government willing to take a flyer on Dobbs's beliefs. Once more the men, under the joint command of William Moor and Francis Smith, wintered over at one of the Hudson's Bay Company's forts, to the discomfort of everyone involved. Once more the winter was brutal. One man, Glyn Williams reports, was carrying an open bottle of brandy to his tent and "used his finger as a stopper, only to find that his finger had frozen in the neck of the bottle and had to be amputated." Scurvy once again decimated the crews. The ships explored Wager Inlet this time, and found it to be a dead end. The ships returned to England in 1747 to the usual questions—why didn't they go up this inlet or that, how could they have failed to find what Dobbs was still sure was there—but their failure was the anti-climactic end to the search for the Northwest Passage in Hudson Bay. (For the time being, at least.) The net effect of all this effort was a somewhat more detailed map of the northern Bay, with more names on it—and a good many dead and crippled sailors. The Hudson's Bay Company retained its monopoly of the fur trade in northern Canada. Arthur Dobbs retired from the field.

The search for the Northwest Passage was not over by any means, however. While we may not hear from Arthur Dobbs any longer, others took his place. The Hudson's Bay Company, stung by widespread criticism of its conservatism and its disinterest in exploring its enormous territories, began in the second half of the eighteenth century to send small sloops north from its northernmost outpost, Prince of Wales Fort, toward Repulse Bay, with instructions to its captains not only to trade with the Inuit of the area but to explore the coastline and map it. In 1770 a Company man named Samuel Hearne made one of the greatest overland journeys in Canadian history when he left with a band of Chippewa Indians to find the Coppermine River and follow it to its mouth. The river rises north of Great Slave Lake and empties into the Arctic Ocean in the strait separating Victoria Island from the mainland. Hearne walked thousands of miles in the two years he was gone and endured amazing hardships. He crossed the Barrens, a treeless wasteland that froze as hard as iron in the winter and in spring and summer turned into an enormous bog. Williams quotes him on conditions in the winter of 1770: "Between seven and eight in the evening my dog, a valuable brute, was frozen to death; so that his sledge, which was a very heavy one, I was obliged to haul." And then: "For the last three days had not tasted a morsel of anything, except a pipe of tobacco and a drink of snow water; and as we walked daily from morning till night, and were all heavily laden, our strength began to fail. I must confess that I never spent so dull a Christmas." Hearne was nothing if not understated.

Hearne's journey, once again, ought to have settled forever the question of a Northwest Passage, a strait of some sort, originating in Hudson Bay, because he would have had to have crossed it to get to the Arctic Ocean. But it is in the nature of delusions that they persist, and Hearne's travels ended nothing. He had, for one thing, spotted open ocean at the mouth of the Coppermine—ocean not locked up in ice. Attention was now turning to the west coast of North America and the continuing speculations of European geographers about what might be found there, and whether the Strait of Anian or something like it might in fact exist. Speculation was encouraged by the appearance of various fraudulent accounts, with accompanying maps, of people who professed to have been there, found this Strait, sailed up it and emerged in Hudson Bay.

It was the kind of question that could only be settled by exploratory voyages. Interest in exploration was growing in England and the government was becoming increasingly involved in it. Merchant adventurers eager to find a new trade route to the Far East had been the primary sponsors of the voyages into Hudson Bay. Now, says Glyn Williams, "maritime exploration had become a matter of national policy," to be conducted largely by the Admiralty.

One of the principal promoters of this government enterprise was a member of the Royal Society named Daines Barrington, an Arthur Dobbs redux who believed not only in the Northwest Passage but also that salt water did not, could not, freeze, and that therefore the Arctic Ocean, once you got past the pack ice that had kept ships out of the Ocean in the past, was an open sea, which Hearne's sighting of the Arctic Ocean seemed to confirm. The pack ice? It no doubt came from the rivers that emptied into the Arctic ocean. Barrington and the Royal Society were behind the attempt in 1773 to sail to the North Pole and over it to the East Indies in two Royal Naval vessels under the command of Captain Constantine John Phipps. This would put the theory to the test. The two ships got as far as Spitzbergen, at latitude 80 N., before they ran into the pack. The voyage is most notable for an incident involving Horatio Nelson, then a fifteen-year-old midshipman, who found himself on the ice at one point racing back to his ship on foot just a few steps ahead of a polar bear. The incident became part of the Nelson legend.

But it was exploration in the North Pacific that would, presumably, settle the question of a Northwest Passage once and for all, and it was this area of the globe to which the Admiralty now turned—prodded, again, by Daines Barrington and the Royal Society, and by the prospect of that L20,000 reward, which Parliament renewed in an act of 1775 that opened the reward to Navy men and eliminated the specification that the Passage had to be found in Hudson Bay. It was this reward, and the glory that would inevitably attach to the person who found the Northwest Passage, that called Captain James Cook out of semiretirement and into his third great exploring voyage, when in 1776 the Admiralty sent him back to the Pacific to trace the west coast of North America north to wherever it ended and the Arctic Ocean began

Cook started late and did not reach North America until the spring of 1778, at what is now the coast of Oregon. He reached Vancouver Island, where he brought his ships ashore at Nootka Sound for repairs, without seeing the Strait of Juan de Fuca. From Vancouver Island he coasted north, following Russian charts which showed Alaska as a huge island, separated from North America by, what else, a strait: the Northwest Passage. Because of the fog and the generally bad weather the Northwest Coast is famous for, he could not keep close to the mainland and thereby missed some of the inlets and bays that mark the coast, leaving gaps in the record that could only lead to later speculation about what he might have missed.

But he did find that the coast did not trend straight north, as the Russian maps showed, but increasingly to the west. He stopped at Prince William Sound, thinking it might be the entry to the fabled Passage, only to find when the fog cleared that it was merely an inlet. He sailed into what is now known as Cook Inlet, past the location of what is now Anchorage, to find the same thing. He proceeded on, past Kodiak Island, unable to turn north until he reached Unalaska Island in the Aleutian chain. He then turned east again into the dead end of Bristol Bay, and from there north to Bering Strait. At what he himself named Icy Cape he saw the pack. The Arctic Ocean, he discovered, was frozen solid from the north coast of Alaska all the way to the north coast of Siberia. It seemed to be the singular destiny of James Cook to explode myths. The myth that salt water did not freeze died with this voyage. The edge of the pack, Cook noted, was in places ten to fifteen feet thick. The shallow rivers that flowed into the Arctic Ocean from both Asia and North America could never produce this much ice.

It would take the voyages of the Frenchman La Perouse in the 1780s, the Englishman George Vancouver in the 1790s, and a variety of Spanish voyages to fill in the blanks on Cook's charts. Vancouver's is perhaps the best known of these voyages, no doubt because he left his name on Vancouver Island. Slowly it became clear that, while there were plenty of sounds and inlets on the Northwest Coast of North America, none of them led deep into the interior. What happened at Lituya Bay is not atypical. La Perouse found Lituya Bay and sailed into it thinking it might be the entrance to the Passage, but it is, like all the others, a dead end. He lost 21 men when two small ships' boats capsized trying to get out of Lituya Bay in the deadly tidal rips at its entrance. Lituya Bay is, incidentally, the site of the largest wave ever recorded. Created the evening of July 9, 1958, when an earthquake shook loose an entire mountainside and a piece of one of the glaciers at the end of the bay and dropped them into the water, the resulting splash wave rode 1,740 feet up the sides of the mountains opposite, stripping them of all vegetation to that level.

Vancouver took three years to complete his enormously detailed survey of the coast, but it was worth the trouble, for he finally killed the idea that a passage ran in temperate latitudes between the Arctic Ocean and the North Pacific. It was now obvious that if a Northwest Passage existed it was to be found in the Arctic Ocean somewhere beyond Baffin Bay, and that it would have to round the great bulk of Alaska before it found warmer waters.

No one had explored Baffin Bay since William Baffin left it in 1616. Whalers were familiar with Davis Strait to the south, but even they knew little about Baffin Bay, which is choked with ice much of the Arctic summer. That, however, is where the search for the Northwest Passage was to resume after the Napoleonic Wars came to an end in 1815. That's where the great drama of Arctic exploration would continue through the nineteenth century.

WE BEGIN WITH THE WHALERS. THE BRITISH WHALING INDUSTRY HAD been moribund for most of the eighteenth century, but in the 1770s it began to revive and after the end of the American Revolution it positively throve. Some 200 ships a year sailed to Cape Farewell at the southern end of Greenland and up into Davis Strait. Among them, from the early 1800s on, was William Scoresby, Jr., himself the son of a whaler, who made his first trip when he was ten, in 1799, and became one of the best and most experienced Arctic sailors in England. He was also a highly intelligent and learned man. He had mastered Latin, French, German and Anglo-Saxon at school and had studied chemistry, anatomy, and other sciences. He made the first accurate charts of the east coast of Greenland. He retired from whaling in 1826 to become an Anglican clergyman. He also wrote a number of books, including the still authoritative An Account of the Arctic Region, with a History and a Description of the Northern Whale Fishery, published in two volumes in 1820. The illustrations in this book are all Scoresby's own, and they are handsome. He was, in the words of Richard Ellis, author of Men and Whales, "scientist, linguist, historian, clergyman, navigator, cartographer, illustrator, and above all, whalerman"—a truly remarkable man, one of the wonders of his age. One might add that he had the force of will, or personality, whatever it took, to tame polar bears. He brought them home from the Arctic and gave them as gifts to his friends.

But he was persona non grata to the British Admiralty, precisely because he was a whaler. In 1817, after returning from a whaling expedition, he contacted Sir Joseph Banks, the influential head of the Royal Society, to tell him that the ice that normally closed the wide straits between Greenland and Spitzbergen was gone. It was an opportune moment to reinaugurate the search for the Northwest Passage, which greatly interested Scoresby. He offered his services to Banks. The Admiralty turned him down. The English Navy had just won the Napoleonic Wars. They had no interest in using a mere whaler. They sent other men instead, as we shall see: Navy men. The Navy looked with open scorn upon all commercial voyagers. It would become one of the most fascinating and ironic notes in British Arctic exploration that the Navy never would learn from their supposed inferiors, no matter how expert they were, simply because they were, in Navy eyes, inferiors. They had the same attitude toward the Inuit, who had survived for thousands of years in Arctic conditions. The Navy refused to adopt any of their ways. Dozens of ships were lost and hundreds of men died as a result. This was a breed of men whose heroism was matched only by their arrogance.

We excerpt from Scoresby's account of the 1822 whaling voyage he made to the east of Greenland. He found precious few whales on this voyage and devoted it instead to mapping the east coast of Greenland, usually too beset by ice for ships to approach it closely. The text is shot through with Scoresby's scientific interests, and we excerpt here a description of some of the strange effects wrought by refraction in the Arctic atmosphere, as well as accounts of an incident with a polar bear and, from later on in the book, a tale illustrating the danger common to Arctic voyages: getting trapped in loose pack ice.

WILLIAM SCORESBY

A Voyage to the Whale Fishery, 1822

THE SOUTHERNMOST LAND HITHERTO SEEN, LYING THREE OR FOUR leagues, S by E., true, from Home's Foreland, was taken to be Bontekoe Island, a place laid down in some charts, though not within fifteen miles of the same latitude. It is high, precipitous land, and of a particularly dark appearance. Its longitude I found to be 20° 40' W., instead of 7° 5' W., the position given to it in the charts for the whale-fisheries.

About half a degree of longitude to the westward of Bontekoe Island, is a remarkable headland, which is probably the same that was discovered by Henry Hudson, in the year 1607, and named by him Hold-with-Hope. From thence the land trends more to the westward.

In the midst of my operations for the survey of this coast, it fortunately happened, that the moon, at a convenient distance from the sun, for determining the longitude, became visible. This was a circumstance of great importance to me, and was instantly embraced, for correcting the rate of my chronometer; it being impossible altogether to depend on the going of a single timepiece. The weather was uncommonly favourable, so as to enable me to take the distances with the greatest precision. From six sets of distances and altitudes, I obtained the mean longitude of 17° 54' 30" W., for the place of the ship on the 14th of June, and found the error of the chronometer to be nearly four minutes of time.[1]

---

[1] This lunar observation was afterwards proved, by comparing my chronometer with one of

These satisfactory observations for the longitude (established by many subsequent proofs), enabled me to ascertain the exact effect, in particular case, of the extraordinary refractive property of the atmosphere in the Arctic Seas, which, without such proofs, would scarcely have been credible. The coast that has just been described, is in general so bold, as to be distinctly visible in the ordinary state of the atmosphere, at the distance of sixty miles; but on my last voyage into these regions, one part of this coast was seen, when at more than double this distance. The particulars were these: —Towards the end of July 1821, being among the ice in latitude 74° 10', and longitude, by lunar observation and chronometer, (which agreed to twenty-two minutes of longitude, or within six geographical miles), 12° 30'15' W., land was seen from the mast-head to the westward, occasionally, for three successive days. It was so distinct and bold, that Captain Manby, who accompanied me on that voyage, and whose observations are already before the public, was enabled, at one time, to take a sketch of it from the deck, whilst I took a similar sketch from the mast-head, which is preserved in my journal of that year. The land at that time nearest to us was Wollaston Foreland, which, by my late surveys, proves to lie in latitude 74° 25' (the middle part of it), and longitude 19° 50': the distance, therefore, must have been at least 120 miles. But Home's Foreland, in 21° W. longitude, distinguished by two remarkable hummocks at its extremities, was also seen; its distance, by being calculation, founded on astronomical observations, being 140 geographical, or 160 English miles. In an ordinary state of the atmosphere (supposing the refraction to be one-twelfth of the distance), any land to have been visible from a ship's mast-head, an hundred feet high, at the distance of 140 miles, must have been at least two nautical miles, or 12,000 feet in elevation; but as the land in question is not more than 3500 feet in altitude, (by estimation), there must have been an extraordinary effect of refraction equal to 8,500 feet. Now, the angle corresponding with an altitude of 8,500 feet, and a distance of 140 miles, is 34' 47", the value of the extraordinary refraction, at the time the land was thus seen; or, calculating in the proportion of distance, which is the most usual manner of estimating the refraction, it amounted to

Captain Bennet's and by correcting its rate by subsequent observation. All the longitudes mentioned, therefore, in this narrative, are corrected longitudes, and not exactly those given by the chronometer, at its original rate, which proved to be nearly two seconds per day wrong.

one-fourth of the arch of distance, instead of one-twelfth, the mean quantity.

That land was seen under these circumstances there cannot be a doubt; for it was observed to be in the same position, and under a similar form, on the 18th, 23d, 24th, and 25th July 1821, when the ship was in longitude from 12° 30', to 11° 50' W., and on the 23d it remained visible for twenty-four hours together; and though often changing its appearance, by the varying influence of the refraction, it constantly preserved a uniformity of position, and general similarity of character. In my journal of this day, I find I have observed, that my doubts about the reality of the land were now entirely removed, since, with a telescope, from the mast-head "hills, dells, patches of snow, and masses of naked rock, could be satisfactorily traced, during four-and-twenty hours successively." This extraordinary effect of refraction, therefore, I conceive to be fully established.[2]

In the course of the night a bear was seen prowling about upon one of the adjoining sheets of ice, which, soon afterwards attempting to swim across an opening near the ship, was immediately pursued by one of our boats, and attacked by the harpooner commanding it, who wounded it with a lance, and, after it had bravely given battle for some time, eventually overcame it. It was a fine large specimen, the skin, which was very white, and well furred, measuring about eight feet in length.

We had expected to have seen very many of these animals on the coast of Greenland, as in a former voyage, on approaching the situation, we saw about

[2] I am not aware that this land was ever seen by any British navigator, (excepting Hudson, and two or three whale-fishers, who have, at different times, been forced to... when it was seen by myself, on the 29th of July, when the ship was in latitude 74° 0', longitude 10° 37' W. Its bearing being W by N. (true), the part of the coast in sight must have been Wollaston Foreland, at the distance of 152 miles. The apparent distance, however, being scarcely one-half of the true distance, I was led into an error respecting the longitude of the "West-Land:" the reason of which I take this opportunity of explaining. The supposed situation of this land was mentioned in a letter to the late Sir Joseph Banks; through whom it was inserted in some of the polar charts, in the longitude which I had attributed to it. But the distance I calculated from was merely conjecture; and from my ignorance at the time of the full effects of the unequal refractions of these parallels, my conjecture happened to be very wide of the truth. Had I not had full proof, in the instance noticed above, of the extraordinary extension of vision by refraction, I should now have believed, that, however confident I was at the time of its being the land that I saw, I must have been mistaken.

a hundred, of which more than twenty were killed, and four taken alive; but in this expectation we were quite disappointed, not more than three having yet been seen, and of these only one, the bear now captured, having given us a chance of attacking it, the other two prudently keeping on the middle of a large field of ice, where we had little encouragement to pursue them.

When the bear is found in the water, crossing from one sheet of ice to another, it may generally be attacked with advantage; but, when on the shore, or more especially when it is upon a large sheet of ice, covered with snow, — on which the bear supporting itself upon the surface, with its expended paws, can travel with twice the speed of a man, who, perhaps, sinks to the knees at every step, —it can seldom be assailed with either safety or success. Most of the fatal accidents that have occurred with bears, have been the result of encounters on the ice, or injudicious attacks made at such disadvantage.

A few years ago, when one of the Davis' Strait's whalers was closely beset among the ice at the "South-west," or on the coast of Labrador, a bear that had for some time been seen near the ship, at length became so bold, as to approach alongside, tempted probably by the offal of the provision that had been thrown over-board by the cook. At this time, the people were all at dinner, no one being required to keep the deck in the then immoveable state of the ship. A hardy fellow, who first looked out perceiving the bear so near, imprudently jumped upon the ice, armed only with a handspike, with a view, it is supposed, of securing all the honour of the exploit of capturing so fierce a visitor to himself. But the bear, regardless of such weapons, and sharpened probably by hunger, immediately, it should seem, disarmed his antagonist, and, seizing him by the back with his powerful jaws, carried him off with such celerity, that, on his dismayed comrades rising from their meal, and looking abroad, he was so far beyond their reach as to defy their pursuit.

A circumstance, communicated to me by Captain Munroe of the *Neptune*, of rather a humorous nature as to the result, arose out of an equally imprudent attack made on a bear in the Greenland fishery of 1820, by a seaman employed in one of the Hull whalers. The ship was moored to a field of ice, on which, at a considerable distance, a large bear was observed prowling about for prey. One of the ship's company, emboldened by an artificial courage, derived from the free use of his rum, which, in his economy, he had stored for special occasions, undertook to pursue and attack the bear that was within view. Armed only with a whale-lance, he resolutely, and against all persuasion, set out on his adventurous exploit. A fatiguing journey of about half a league, over a surface of yielding snow, and rugged hummocks, brought him within a few yards of the enemy, which, to his surprise, undauntedly faced him, and seemed to invite him to the combat. His courage being by this time greatly subdued, partly by the evaporation of the stimulus he had employed, and partly by the undismayed, and even threatening aspect of the bear, he levelled his lance in an attitude suited either for offensive or defensive action, and stopped. The bear also stood still. In vain the adventurer tried to rally courage to make the attack; his enemy was too formidable, and his appearance too imposing. In vain also he shouted,— advanced his lance,—and made feints of attack; the enemy either not understanding them, or despising such unmanliness, obstinately stood his ground. Already the limbs of the sailor began to shake,—the lance trembled in the rest,— and his gaze, which had hitherto been stedfast, began to quiver; but the fear of ridicule from his messmates still had its influence, and he yet scarcely dared to retreat. Bruin, however, possessing less reflection, or being more regardless of consequences, began, with the most audacious boldness, to advance. His nigh approach, and unshaken step, subdued the spark of bravery, and that dread of ridicule, that had hitherto upheld our adventurer; he turned and fled. But now was the time of danger. The sailor's flight encouraged the bear in his turn to pursue; and being better practised in snow-travelling, and better provided for it, he rapidly gained upon the fugitive. The whale-lance, his only defence, encumbering him in his retreat, he threw it down, and kept on. This fortunately excited the bear's attention; he stopped,—pawed it,—bit it, and then resumed the chase. Again he was at the heels of the panting seaman, who, conscious of the favourable effect of the lance, dropped a mitten: the stratagem succeeded, and, while bruin again stopped to examine it, the fugitive, improving the interval, made considerable progress a-head. Still the bear resumed the pursuit, with the most provoking perseverance, excepting when arrested by another mitten, and finally by a hat, which he tore to shreds between his teeth and his paws, and would no doubt have soon made the incautious adventurer his victim, who was rapidly losing strength and heart, but for the prompt and well-timed assistance of his shipmates, who, observing that the affair had assumed a dangerous aspect, sallied out to his rescue. The little phalanx opened him a passage, and then closed to receive the bold assailant. Though now beyond the reach of his adversary, the dismayed fugitive continued onward, impelled by his fears, and never relaxed his exertions until he fairly reached the shelter of the ship! Bruin once more prudently came to a stand, and for a moment seemed to survey his enemies with all the consideration of an experienced general; when, finding them too numerous for a reasonable hope of success, he very wisely wheeled about, and succeeded in making a safe and honourable retreat.

*

THE RAIN OF THE FORE-PART OF THE DAY, GAVE PLACE, ABOUT NOON, TO hail, which was so sharp that it was scarcely possible to face to windward; and this was succeeded with an intermixture of soft flaky snow, that covered the deck to the depth of several inches. The wind, in the mean time, became more and more fierce, until it blew almost a hurricane. So long as the floe to which we were moored maintained its position, we rode in tolerable safety; but, as the wind increased, it began to "slue" or revolve, until it brought the ship alongside of it. As the fierceness of the gale, and the thickness of the weather, rendered it impossible for human exertion or care to keep a ship in safety under-way, surrounded as we were with ice in innumerable sheets, we determined to retain our hold of the floe as long as practicable; and we were encouraged in this resolution, by observing that, about 4 P.M., the revolution of the ice had ceased, whilst the ship yet rode "head-to-wind." To be prepared for all events, however, we close-reefed the top-sails, and stowed the courses; took out "springs" from the quarters, for casting the ship; had axes in readiness for cutting the hawsers, if necessary; and made every other arrangement for providing against ordinary casualties, which my experience in similar adventures could suggest.

About 6 P.M. the snow became so thick that we could scarcely see a hundred yards distinctly, and the wind was, if possible, more furious. Two small icebergs now appeared setting towards the ship; but as they were not of a magnitude sufficient to endanger us, without auxiliary pressure, we quietly awaited their approach. The first, which was about thirty-six feet above the level of the sea, struck the ship on the starboard quarter, and turned her broadside to the wind; it then slipped clear, after obliging us to lower three of our boats to preserve them, without occasioning us any damage whatever. The second iceberg approached us with more alarming rapidity; but as we had not the power of getting clear of it, we were obliged to receive the shock upon whatever part of the ship it might chance to fall. It came in contact with the rudder, and slightly bruised one of its timbers; then grazing the ship's quarter and broadside, it passed forward to the bows, and being fortunately kept from close contact aloft, by a tongue projecting from its base, it cleared all our boats, and occasioned only a trifling injury to some of the skeeds in its progress. At this juncture, when the ship was so much involved with icebergs as to render casting off impracticable, had the state of the weather permitted it, two floes came in sight from different quarters. One of these appeared to be rapidly closing upon us from the west, and the other from the south, which, with the floe that we were moored to, occupying the eastern quarter, almost completely locked us in. To secure ourselves as far as possible against the crush, which now appeared certain, we fastened, by a hawser, a large heavy piece of ice ahead of the ship, where the floes threatened the first contact; with the view of subjecting the interposed mass to the pressure, and with the hope of being then defended from partaking of it. The last iceberg that passed yet annoying us, we slacked the ship astern until it was quite clear ahead, and had placed itself across the bows, with the deceitful appearance of affording an additional safeguard. As we became more and more exposed to danger from the floe setting up from the southward, as we slacked the ship down, and at the same time retreated from the protection the pieces of ice ahead seemed to promise, —it appeared to me that the nearer the ship was kept to these, so long as they were fairly clear, the greater would be our safety. But an unfortunate revolution among the ice disappointed these expectations, and overcame all our precautions. The first shock of the floes was sustained, as we had expected, by the mass of ice that was expressly placed near the ship for the purpose, and for some time afterwards, all things seemed quiet and safe. Suddenly, however, the pressure was renewed, in consequence, it was presumed, of some new stoppage to the drift of the floes, with tenfold violence. Our barrier was squeezed deeply into the floe, and prodigious blocks of ice were broken off, and reared up by the pressure. While we contemplated these mighty effects with much anxiety, the berg ahead of the ship began a revolving and a retrograde motion, so quick, as to overtake us before we could get the ropes off to slack astern, and suddenly nipped the ship on the larboard beam and bow, against the floe by which we rode. The force was irresistible. It thrust the ship completely up on a broad tongue, or shelf under water, of the floe, until she was fairly grounded, and continued to squeeze her rapidly up the inclined plane formed by the tongue, until the ice came in contact beneath the keel. This was the work of a few moments, and in ten minutes all was again at rest. When the pressure ceased, we found that the ship had risen six or eight feet forward, and about two feet abaft.

The floe on the starboard side was about a mile in diameter, and forty feet in thickness, having a regular wall-side of solid ice, five feet in height above the sea; on the tongue of this the ship was grounded. The iceberg on the larboard side was about twenty feet high, and was in contact with the railing at the bows, and with the gunwale and channel-bends amidships. This berg was connected with a body of floes to the westward, several leagues in breadth. The only clear place was directly astern, where a small interstice and vein of water was produced, by the intervention of the bergs. Any human exertion for our extrication, from such a situation, was now in vain; the ship being firmly cradled upon the tongues of ice, which sustained her weight. Every instant we were apprehensive of her total destruction; but the extraordinary disposition of the ice beneath her, was the means of her preservation. The force exerted upon the ship, to place her in such a situation, must evidently have been very violent. Two or three sharp cracks were heard at the time the ship was lifted, and a piece of plank, which proved to be part of the false keel, was torn off and floated up by the bows; but no serious injury was yet discovered. Our situation, however, was at this time almost as dangerous and painful, immediate hazard of our lives excepted, as possible. Every moment threatened us with shipwreck; while the raging of the storm, —the heavy bewildering fall of sleet and snow, —and the circumstance of every man on board being wet to the skin, rendered the prospect of our having to take refuge on the ice most distressing. Our only hope of safety in such a calamity, was the supposed proximity of the *Fame*. Yet we well knew that she must also be in danger; and, perhaps, in a situation as bad as our own. We could look to no other refuge; since we had reason to apprehend, that the whole of the Greenland fleet, with the exception of a single ship, had left the coast, and proceeded either homeward, or at least to the skirts of the ice. Even in the event of the safety of the *Fame*, as she was not near us, nor had we any conception of her position, we could not have obtained protection from her before a change of weather; and, in the mean time, exposed to such a storm, without the possibility of erecting tents for our shelter, it was to be feared that many of our crew would have sunk under the inclemency of the weather. Impressed with this apprehension, the people not being required to attend to any duty in the immoveable state of the ship, employed themselves in making preparation for the catastrophe that seemed to await us.

We remained in this state of anxiety and apprehension about two hours. On the one hand, we feared the calamity of shipwreck; on the other, in case of her preservation, we looked forward to immense difficulties, before the ship so firmly grounded could be got afloat. While I walked the deck under a variety of con-flicting feelings, produced by the anticipation of probable events, and under the solemnizing influence natural to a situation of extreme peril, I was suddenly aroused by another squeeze of the ice, indicated by the cracking of the ship and the motion of the berg, which seemed to mark the moment of destruction. But the goodness of the ALMIGHTY proved better to us than our fears. This renewed pressure, by a singular and striking providence, was the means of our preser-vation. The nip took the ship about the bows, where it was received on a part rendered prodigiously strong by its arched form, and the thickness of the inte-rior "fortifications." It acted like the propulsion of a round body squeezed between the fingers, driving the ship astern, and projecting her clear of all the ice, fairly afloat, with a velocity equal to that of her first launching!

Fortunately the ropes and anchors held until her stern-way was overcome. As soon as she was brought up, our attention was instantly turned to more dan-gers; and our previous state of anxious inaction instantly gave place to the most persevering and vigorous exertions for our preservation. Hitherto, while the floes were in contact about the ship, there had been a clear vein of water lead-ing directly to leeward, in which it appeared that the ship might ride, under the protection of the icebergs, in safety. But two points of the bounding floes, betwixt which the ship lay, were now observed to be rapidly closing upon us, and threatening us with another squeeze. As the channel running to leeward was so narrow, that there was not room to swing the ship so as to get under-way, our only chance of safety depended upon our being able to drop to leeward with a considerable velocity[3]. Though we had little hope of accomplishing this

3 To *drop* a ship is a nautical phrase, expressive of the operation of removing under the simple action of the wind, by veering out the ropes by which the ship is moored. Thus, in the present example, the wind, blowing directly down the channel betwixt the two floes where the ship was moored, forced her to leeward along the channel, whenever the ropes were slacked.

under such a gale, without some of the ropes or anchors giving way, which would have been almost certain ruin, yet having no other resource, we were obliged to undertake the risk. With all imaginable care and prudence, we began to slack astern, using two hawsers on an end for greater despatch; these carried us past the nearest points, at the moment when they had closed within two or three feet of the breadth of the ship. In five minutes they were in contact, and some hundreds of tons of ice gave way, and squeezed up under the pressure. Before another rope, that had been employed in aid of the hawsers, could be disengaged from its anchor, and replaced near the ship for continuing our movement to leeward, other two points of the floes appeared astern in rapid approximation. Remaining where we were, though but for five minutes, was inevitable shipwreck; and to trust to the strength of a warp of five inches circumference, the only mooring rope we had now at command, afforded but small hope of a better fate; for, in the event of the ship breaking adrift, as there was not breadth between the floes to swing, she must fall astern with such a shock against the ice, as could scarcely fail to be destructive. Possible safety, however, was preferred to certain destruction. We now slacked astern by the warp fastened to the second hawser, which, to our astonishment and delight, sustained the prodigious strain; and although it was not capable of bringing the ship up, yet it so far resisted her velocity, that at the moment when it came to an end, a hawser, that was meanwhile hauled on board, was fastened to another anchor placed for its attachment, whereby the motion astern was suspended. On this occasion, we again escaped the nip by only three or four feet, and the floes came in contact with unabated violence, scarcely a ship's length ahead. But more and more approximating points appearing astern, we dropped the ship the whole length of our last hawser, with the hope of avoiding them; but it only carried us clear of the first. We were then brought to a stand; for the other hawsers and warp, forming a continuous line of 700 yards in length, got entangled, and nipped by the floes, so that we were under the necessity of slipping the end and fastening it to the ice. As we had now no rope left of sufficient strength with which to shift the hawser, our progress would have been suspended, and our previous exertions rendered nugatory, had we not brought into use a small mooring chain that was fortunately at hand. Before the hawser was again fastened, however, the hook of the chain broke, and the ship was entirely adrift. But it providentially happened, that the people who were on the ice having seized upon the end of the hawser, were enabled to cast it over an anchor that an officer was engaged in setting, at the very last moment that could have served for our preservation! The severe strain to which this hawser was subjected, broke one of its strands, and called for the instant renewal of the chain. This was a most narrow escape; but there was another that succeeded which was equally striking. When slacking astern by the hawser, the ship swung alongside the eastern floe into a little bight, and the rudder unfortunately caught behind a point which projected some feet to windward. The floes were so nearly close, that we had not time to heave ahead, had this measure been practicable under such a storm. We were in a state of extreme jeopardy. One of the after-sails was instantly loosed, and hauled over to the starboard quarter; the action of this, happily coinciding with a momentary diminution of the wind, when the tension of the ropes drew the ship ahead, turned her stern clear of the point. We instantly slacked astern and dropped beyond this danger.

It might be tedious to describe all the subsequent exertions made for our deliverance, under the repeated difficulties we encountered. These difficulties will be readily appreciated by persons acquainted with the management of a ship, when they are informed, that our movements, to a considerable distance, were effected by means of a stranded (or partly broken) rope, and a doubtful chain, at a time when the wind blew with such violence, that I could scarcely make myself heard with a speaking trumpet, from the companion to the windlass. It may be sufficient to say, in addition, that b y a most striking and remarkable providence aiding our exertions, suggesting precautions, and timeing our various removals, we continued to drop the ship down the narrow dangerous channel betwixt the floes, until their approximation ceased. Thus was the ship most miraculously preserved, throughout a removal of a mile, under the most dangerous, difficult, and discouraging circumstances, when there was not a single spot in all the distance that we accomplished, in which a ship remaining five or ten minutes after we left it, could have been saved from being crushed. The reason of this was evident. The two floes betwixt which we were involved, though full of little prominences or points, were, in the main, of a circular form. As these were revolving against each other in contrary directions, like the action of a pair of toothed wheels, when one is put in motion by the other, every part of the circumference of each floe became in its turn the point of contact.

These anxious and energetic operations continued until midnight, when we obtained the first respite, on observing that the floes had ceased to revolve. But we were still in jeopardy. A large body of ice having been drifted by the violence of the gale against the floe that we were moored to, urged it so rapidly to leeward for some time that, the southern ice, to which we were now exposed, began to set up with alarming velocity. Nothing dangerous, however, came in the way during the continuance of the gale; and, to our great comfort, about 4 A.M. the weather cleared up, and immediately began to moderate.

By this time our people were so much exhausted by fatigue, that on undertaking the recovery of our ropes, which cost a labour of some hours, several of our able-seamen withdrew from their duty, making a sacrifice of their character and hopes of preferment, and exposing themselves to the loss of their wages, for the sake of the indulgence in a little rest.

WE WILL NOT HAVE OCCASION TO MENTION WHALING AGAIN IN THIS *collection. Except for Scoresby, whalers did little exploring beyond the known whaling grounds. But whalers did know a great deal about conditions in the Arctic and they sometimes lived through adventures as extreme as any the explorers themselves endured. One of the most notable events in northern whaling history occurred in early September 1871 when 39 ships found themselves beset by ice and fierce storms off Icy Cape in northern Alaska. As the ice closed in, crews abandoned their ships and made their way to other ships that were still free of the ice. In the end only seven ships escaped, but they had managed under appalling conditions to take on the crews of all the ships that were abandoned. The fleet did not lose a single man. It was a feat worthy of Ernest Shackleton.*

For all their knowledge and daring, however, the whalers had not penetrated north of Davis Strait. Baffin Bay remained an unknown quantity. Did it have an outlet or was it another dead end, like Repulse Bay? Baffin had found no outlet when he explored it in 1616, but no one thought Baffin's chart was definitive. England came out of the Napoleonic Wars not merely victorious, but the lone master of the world's oceans. At peace now, it had an excess of Royal Navy officers on half pay, itching for something to do, and there was no shortage of Royal Navy ships. What better use for them than to explore those parts of the world that remained unexplored? No one yet knew what lay west of Baffin Bay or north of the mouth of the Coppermine River, where Samuel Hearne had seen open ocean.

Second in command at the British Admiralty—Second Secretary was his official title—was a man named John Barrow. The Lords of the Admiralty were the titular heads of the Admiralty, but the First and Second Secretaries actually ran things, and the First Secretary was more the outside man, dealing with Parliament and with the Admiralty's relationship with the rest of government. Barrow actually administered the Admiralty. He did so for more than forty years, from 1804 until 1845. And his primary interest in life was in exploration. He had traveled early in life, first on an embassy to China during which he learned Chinese, then to South Africa, where he mapped portions of the interior, married, and lived for four years. He was an intelligent man with exceptional bureaucratic skills, well read in the literature of exploration, strongly opinionated. He was certain that the Niger emptied into the Nile. He believed in an open polar sea. And he took it as an obvious matter of fact that there was a Northwest Passage, and that it was navigable.

In 1818 he mounted a two-pronged attack on the passage, sending two ships north toward Spitzbergen to find the open polar sea and two ships to Baffin Bay to find a way west. A year later he would send a third expedition to northern Canada to cross by land from Hudson Bay to the Coppermine River and then map the coastline east of its mouth to see if the sea were open and the passage might be found by that means.

Under the command of Captain David Buchan and Lieutenant John Franklin respectively, the two ships sent to the north found the same conditions that every other expedition that had tried to penetrate the Arctic Ocean north of Spitzbergen had found: impenetrable ice. The two ships barely escaped from it by warping their way out—setting anchors in the ice ahead, then using the winch to drag their way down narrow, rapidly disappearing leads. It took 220 hours of non-stop labor to accomplish their self-rescue and the ships themselves suffered enough damage that they had to lay up in Spitzbergen for repairs before returning to England.

The ships that went into Baffin Bay were only slightly more successful. Under Commander John Ross and Lieutenant William E. Parry, they sailed up the western coast of Greenland with the pack ice of Davis Strait and Baffin Bay lying off to their west some ten miles, still impenetrable. It was June, relatively early in the season, and they worked their way slowly north, past the British whaling fleet, to the top of Baffin Bay, entering waters that had not been sailed since the time of William Baffin himself. Ice and icebergs littered the sea, the conditions were dangerous, and they were still unable by the end of July to find a way across Baffin Bay to Baffin Island.

It was then that they encountered the natives who are the subject of our next excerpt. They noticed them waving at them on August 8 from the Greenland shore, but they were evidently not asking them to approach. When Ross and some of his seamen came on shore they ran away, even though Ross left gifts for them, and it wasn't until the next day that contact was made, and then only by a man named John Sacheuse, himself an Eskimo from southern Greenland that Ross had brought with him to help with translation. These Eskimos spoke a dialect that Sacheuse hardly knew, but that he could, to a degree, understand. They were a band that had separated from the southern Eskimos nearly four centuries before. They retained no memory of their origins. They had lost skills, like the building of kayaks and the use of bows and arrows, that were basic in southern Eskimo life. And they had never before seen other human beings. They believed they were the only people in the world.

The account Ross gives of this encounter is the best section of his book. He gave them the name Arctic Highlanders—the coast of Greenland is mountainous where he found these people—and he spent as many days with them as he could. The Highlanders were enormously curious. Having never seen ships, they thought they were alive. They thought glass was a form of ice. When they saw their faces in mirrors they looked behind the mirrors to see who was standing there. They had no use for English food, spitting it out when they tasted it. They were astonished at the amount of metal on board the ships, and made numerous attempts to steal as much of it as they could.

Ross summarizes their behavior and beliefs in the following excerpt, which we print entire.

JOHN ROSS

A Voyage of Discovery Made Under the Orders of the Admiralty, 1819

THE ORIGIN OF THE ARCTIC HIGHLANDERS, OR INHABITANTS OF PRINCE Regent's Bay, is a question as yet involved in peculiar obscurity. They exist in a corner of the world by far the most secluded which has yet been discovered, and have no knowledge of any thing but what originates, or is found, in their own country; nor have they any tradition how they came to this spot, or from whence they came; having until the moment of our arrival, believed themselves to be the only inhabitants of the universe, and that all the rest of the world was a mass of ice. It is generally believed by the natives of South Greenland, that they are themselves descended from a nation in the north; and the moment they were discovered, Sacheuse exclaimed, "these are *right* Esquimaux, these are *our* fathers!" This supposition is related, as believed by every Esquimaux, that a party of savages having come from the north to the establishments at Woman's Islands, murdered the Esquimaux stationed there; the accounts of which having reached their friends in the south, a party went against them, and destroyed them in return. The similarity of the language proves they are the same people; and it appears most probable, that South Greenland has been peopled from the north, and that the northern parts of Baffin's Bay have been, in the same manner, originally peopled from America. It has been long ascertained, that the land discovered by Davis, on the west side of Davis' Strait was inhabited; and where we landed, on the west side in latitude 70, there were evident marks of its recent occupation. The only parts which appeared to be uninhabitable, were between Whale Sound and Lancaster Sound, a place, no doubt, of very considerable extent; but which, with a sledge on the ice, would be only three days' journey. Their having no knowledge of canoes is easily accounted for, by their total want of wood, and the very short time that canoes could be used in their seas.

The dress of the Arctic highlander consists of three pieces, which are all comprised in the name of *tunnick*. The upper one is made of seal skin, with the hair outside, and is similar to the woman's jacket of the South Greenlander, being open only near the top, so as to equal the size of the wearer's face. At the bottom it is formed like a shirt, but terminating in a tongue before and behind, the hood part being neatly trimmed with fox's skin, and made to fall back on the shoulders, or cover the head, as required. This is lined, in general, with eider-duck, or awk skins; and this lining being close at the bottom, and open near the breast, serves as a pocket. The neck piece of dress, which scarcely reached the knee, is also uncomfortably small in the upper part, so that, in stooping, the skin is exposed. This is made of bear or dog's skin, and fastened up with a string. The boots are made of seal-skin, they reach over the knees, and meet the middle part of the dress. The whole of these are made by the women; the needles used being of ivory, and the thread is of the sinews of the seal, split; the seams are so neat that they can scarcely be distinguished. They informed us, that in the winter, or as the weather got colder, they had a garment of bear-skins, which they put on as a cloak; but this we did not see, nor were able to persuade them to spare any part of their dress.

The Arctic Highlanders are of a dirty copper colour, their stature is about five feet, their bodies corpulent, and their features much resembling the Esquimaux of South Greenland. The following description of Ervick, of whom so much has already been said, and whose portrait is given at full length, and of his nephews, Marshuick and Otooniah, will give a just idea of the whole tribe of these people. This man, who appeared to be about forty years of age, measured five feet one inch in height, his skin being of a dirty copper colour, rather darker than the generality; his face was broad, his forehead narrow and low, with some wrinkles, and the nose small and straight; the cheeks full, round, and ruddy, even through the oil and dirt which covered them; his mouth was large, generally half open, and all shewing that he had lost his fore-teeth, the remainder of which were however, white and regular; his lips were thick, particularly towards the middle; his eyes small, black, oval, and very approximate; the hair was black, coarse, long, and lank, and had certainly never been cut or combed; his beard and mustachios, which were suffered to grow, were scanty, and confined to the upper lip and chin; his body was fleshy, inclining to corpulence; the hands thick and small, fingers short, and the feet very short and thick. Though good humor was fully expressed in his countenance, it also bore that indescribable mixed appearance of ignorance and wildness, that characterizes all uncivilized people. In walking he seemed inactive, and it was with much difficulty he got up the ship's side.

Marshuick appeared to be twenty-three years of age; he was not so dark as his uncle; his features were so pleasing, that he got the name of the "handsome native": he was not so corpulent as the rest, but, in every other respect, his appearance was the same.

Otooniah was about twenty-one years of age; his features were much freckled, and we recognized a likeness between him and a Greenlander we had seen in N.E. Bay; both these, who were brothers, had white regular teeth, and were five feet high. The man, who stole the hammer, was by much the tallest, being five feet six inches and half; his skin was not so dark as Ervick's, the nose was large and aquiline, the forehead very narrow, and lower part of his face broad; the body muscular; the features savage and dishonest; he had less beard than the rest, but was in other respects the same.

The greatest number of natives seen was about eighteen; many attempts were made to discover the numbers of the tribe, but without success, as they could reckon no further than five, and could therefore only say "plenty people," pointing to the north; and it must be recollected, that this was only a party detached from the main body.

Ervick, being the senior of the first party that came on board, was judged to be the most proper person to question on the subject of religion. I directed Sacheuse to ask him, if he had any knowledge of a Supreme Being, but after trying every word used by his own language to express it, he could not make him understand what he meant. It was distinctly ascertained that he did not worship the sun, moon, stars, or any image or living creature. When asked, what the sun or moon was for, he said, to give light. He had no knowledge, or idea, how he came into being, or of a future state; but said, that when he died he would be put into the ground. Having fully ascertained that he had no idea of a beneficent Supreme Being, I proceeded, through Sacheuse, to inquire if he believed in an evil spirit; but he could not be made to understand what it meant. The word "angekok" which means a conjuror, or sorcerer, was then pronounced to him, in the South Greenland Eskimaux language. He said, they had many of them, that it was in their power to raise a storm, or make a calm, and to drive off seals, or bring them; that they learned this art from old Angekoks, when young; that they were afraid of them; but they had generally one in every family. Mejgack gave precisely the same answers, and had the same notions, but he was not so intelligent as Ervick. Finding that Otooniah, the nephew of Ervick, a lad of eighteen years of age, was a young angekok, I got him in the cabin by himself, and, through Sacheuse, asked him how he learned this art. He replied, from an old angekok; that he could raise the wind, and drive off seals and birds. He said that this was done by gestures and words; but the words had no meaning, nor were they said or addressed to any thing but the wind or the sea. He was positive that in this incantation he did not receive assistance from anything, nor could he be made to understand what a good or evil spirit meant. When Ervick was told that there was an omnipotent, omnipresent, and invisible Being, who had created the sea and land, and all therein he shewed much surprise, and eagerly asked where he lived. When told that he was every where, he was much alarmed, and became very impatient to be on deck. When told that there was a future state, and another world, he said that a wise man, who had lived long before his time, had said that they were going to go to the moon, but that it was not now believed, and that none of the others knew any thing of this history; they believed however, that birds, and certainly no proof whatever that this people have any idea of a Supreme Being, or of a spirit, good or bad, the circumstances of their having conjurers, and of their going to the moon after death, are of a nature to prevent any conclusion from being drawn to that effect; especially, as it must be evident, that our knowledge of their language was too imperfect to obtain the whole of their ideas on the subject.

We had not an opportunity of visiting the habitations of the Arctic Highlanders, nor did we see them but at too great a distance to form a judgement either of their construction or comforts, but, from the description given by the natives, they appeared to be situated always near the sea-side, on a spot the least liable to be overwhelmed by snow. These houses are built entirely of stones, the walls being sunk three feet into the earth, and raised to three feet above it; the roof is in the form of an arch, and such holes as would admit air are filled up with mud; they have no windows. The entrance is by a long, narrow, and nearly under-ground passage. The floor is covered with skins, on which they sit or sleep; several families live in one house, and each family has a lamp made of hollowed stone, which is suspended from the roof, and in which they burn the oil, or rather the blubber of the seal and sea-unicorn, using dried moss for a wick; fire is produced from iron and stone. This lamp, which is never extinguished, serves for light and warmth, and, at the same time, for cooking; and we ascertained that they had a method both of boiling and roasting, or scorching their meat, which occupation falls entirely on the women. They eat all kinds of animal food, but the seal and sea-unicorn are preferred, as being more oily and agreeable to their palates. Dogs are also esteemed excellent food, and are bred as live stock, as well as to draw the sledge; but they are only eaten in winter, in times when no other food can be obtained. The men catch the seals, either when they are asleep, or by lying down near the holes in the ice, and making a great noise, which brings them to the surface. When the animal appears they imitate his cry, or grunt, and by this means induce him to come on the ice and approach them; when within reach, they strike him on the nose with a spear made of sea unicorns' horn, and soon despatch him. The sea-unicorn is taken by a harpoon, the barbed part of which is about three inches long, having a line attached to it of about five fathoms in length, the other end of which is fastened to a buoy of a seal's skin made into a bag and inflated. The lade is fixed on the tend of the shaft in such a manner that it may be disengaged from the handle after it is fixed in the animal, and the shaft is then pulled back by a line which is tied to it for the purpose.

The animal immediately plunges, and carries down with him the seal-skin buoy, which fatigues him. As he must come up in some pool to respire, like the black whale, he is followed and despatched with the spears; as this animal frequents the chasms and pools in the ice, he falls an easy prey to the natives,

We could not learn the precise manner in which they kill the bears, but the informed us that they attacked them in the water. The foxes and hares are taken in traps, made of stones, resembling a small grotto and having a narrow entrance which is closed by a stone that falls down when the animals enter to take the bait they left within it. The natives described to us an animal which they called humminick, but said it was too large for them to kill; it has, by their account, a horn on its back, and is very swift, I therefore suppose it must be a reindeer. They have also an animal known to both countries by the name of ancarok, but which I cannot find to be mentioned by writers on Greenland. Sacheuse says, it is not uncommon about North-east Bay and Disco Bay, where its cry is continually heard at night. It is very wild, and can seldom be approached, being very active and fierce; the Esquimaux are afraid of it. He says it resembles a cat, but is three times larger, that it moves by jumping more than by running, and lives in holes and caverns in the rocks; that it eats hares and partridges, which it lies in wait for, and catches by springing on them. The hares, seen by our people, were white. The foxes were generally black, but they were also seen both of a white and of the common colour which they have in southern countries; unfortunately none of them were taken, and therefore they cannot be particularly described. The dogs which are the only animals that have been domesticated by the Arctic Highlanders, are of various colours, but chiefly resembling that given in the plate; they are of the size of a shepherd's dog, they have a head like a wold, and a tail like a fox; their bark resembles the latter, but they have also a howl like the former.

An Arctic Highlander never hunts, or travels any distance, but on his sledge, and he always carries with him his spear and knife; from the rapidity with which they seem to drive, it may be fairly conjectured, they could travel fifty or sixty miles a day, which, indeed, is known to have been done by the natives of South Greenland. The habits of this people appear to be filthy in the extreme; their faces, hands, and bodes, are covered with oil and dirt, and they look as if they never had washed themselves since they were born. Their hair was matted with filth, yet they seemed very tenacious of it, for when a small piece was cut off from the head of one of Meigack's sons, both he and his father were much displeased, and shewed great uneasiness until it was returned, when it was carefully wrapped in a piece of seal-skin, and put by the former into his pocket. We learned that each man took one wife when he was able to maintain a family; if she had children, he took no other, nor was she permitted to have another husband; but, if otherwise, the man may take anotherr wife, and so on a third, until they have children, and the women have the same privilege. Ervick spoke very affectionately of his wife, who he said was a good one, because she had six sons; when they took , or begged any financial thing, as a looking-glass or picture, they all said it was for their wives. They also shew much respect to their mothers; for, one of them said, he would let me have his sledge, and another would have parted with his jacket, but his mother would be displeased. The dress of the women is, from what we could collect, the same as that of the men. We could not make out whether they lived to a great age or not, for the old people had been sent to the mountains, or concealed on our approach, and we never saw them, nor did we see any of the children. I asked both Ervick and Meigack if they would spare one of their sons; to which they answered they would not; nor could either of them be tempted by any presents to consent to part with a child. Indeed, none of them were willing to leave their country; they seemed most happy and contented, their clothing was in good condition, and very suitable to the climate, and by their account, they had plenty of provisions. They all acknowledge Tuloowah as their king, represented him as a strong man, as very good, and very much beloved; the name of his residence was Petowack, which they described to be near a large island. He had a large house built of stone, which they described to be nearly as large as the ship; that there were many houses near it, and that the mass of the natives lived there; that they paid him a portion of all they caught or found, and returned to this place whenever the sun went away, with the fruits of their labours. They could not be made to understand what was meant by war, nor had they any warlike weapons; and I gave strict and positive orders that no firearms, or other warlike weapons, should be shewn them, or given to them on any account, and when they were with us all shooting-parties were called in. They seemed to have no diseases among them, nor could we learn that they died of any complaints peculiar to this or any other country. We saw no deformed persons among them, nor could we find out that there were any; we did not see any of the women or young children, but had we been able to remain I have no doubt but they would have visited us.

Such is the substance of what we collected in our short intercourse with this interesting people, which may appear in some points to be defective; but it must be recollected that the ships were always in motion, principally from the state of the weather, which rendered it impossible for us to send parties on shore after the first day. We still had daily hopes of obtaining a more complete access to them, even to the last moment when we were obliged to leave this part of the coast; and in proceeding northward from our last station, had still the prospect of visiting their king, and filling up the measure of information respecting them. These hopes were ultimately disappointed, as will appear by the events that will be related in the ensuing chapter.

✳

ROSS WAS HOPING TO BRING SOME OF THESE PEOPLE BACK TO LONDON *with him, but he was forced to leave when the pack suddenly opened. He had no choice but to seize the opportunity and sail west. The two ships then crossed the head of Baffin Bay and coasted down the east coast of Baffin Island. They encountered constant trouble with ice and often had to warp the ships through the pack. Late in August, on August 30, they sailed the ships into Lancaster Sound, which William Baffin had named for the Duke of Lancaster. The Sound is 45 miles wide at its mouth and Ross turned west into it. Fog obscured the view west and there was much discussion on board, he says, as to whether they were entering an inlet or a strait, but either way, he continues, he would go on to explore it "completely." Then the fog lifted "for ten minutes" and he was called up on deck where "I distinctly saw the land round the bottom of the bay, forming a chain of mountains connected with those which extended along the north and south sides. This land appeared to be at the distance of eight leagues [24 miles]; and Mr. Lewis, the master, and James Haig, leading man, being sent for, they took its bearings, which were inserted in the log...." Ross named them the Croker Mountains, after the First Secretary of the Admiralty, John Wilson Croker, John Barrow's superior. Then, after some cursory examination of the shoreline, Ross gave orders to return to England.*

Arctic historians have puzzled over this event ever since, because, of course, there are no Croker Mountains, and Lancaster Sound is the entrance to the Northwest Passage ,and had Ross simply sailed on he would have sailed into it. Ferguson thinks one of the Arctic's tricks with atmospheric refraction fooled Ross into thinking he was looking at mountains where there were none. Perhaps. But William Edward Parry, sailing in the Alexander a few miles behind Ross's ship, saw no mountains, nothing indeed that looked like land at all, and he urged Ross to sail on. When the expedition returned to England in November, Parry was summoned to discuss the matter with the First Lord of the Admiralty, Lord Melville. A second expedition to Lancaster Sound was authorized in January 1820. Ross tried to get the command of it for himself. The Admiralty declined. They gave the job to William Edward Parry.

Parry is too discreet to enrich his published journal with any hint of triumph when he describes sailing into Lancaster Sound and straight through the Croker

Mountains. He and his two ships, the Hecla and the Griper, reached the Sound in late July of 1819 and entered it on August 1. As they sailed west officers and crew climbed into the spars and the crow's nest, staring ahead, eager to see whether the mountains existed. In one day they sailed through three degrees of latitude and saw no land ahead. In a few more days Parry had cleared Lancaster Sound and named the western end of it Barrow's Strait, after "my friend John Barrow." He turned south then into what he named Prince Regent Inlet, explored that for 120 miles, then returned to the end of Barrow Strait and turned west again. By September 4th they had reached the 110th meridian and eventually reached the 112th before turning back to seek a harbor to spend the winter. They found one on Melville Island, which Parry had named for the same Lord Melville who had chosen Parry for this voyage.

Among polar explorers Parry is justly famous for showing later explorers how to spend an Arctic winter on a ship frozen into the ice. He had planned for this experience very well, and our next selection describes, in his own words, some of the measures he had taken to keep his men busy and entertained, and to keep them warm.

WILLIAM EDWARD PARRY

Journal of a Voyage for the Discovery of a North-West Passage from the Atlantic to the Pacific...1819-1820.

HAVING NOW REACHED THE STATION, WHERE, IN ALL PROBABILITY, WE were destined to remain for at least eight or nine months, during three of which we were not to see the face of the sun, my attention was immediately, and imperiously, called to various important duties; many of them of a singular nature, such as had, for the first time, devolved on any officer in His Majesty's navy, and might indeed be considered of rare occurrence in the whole history of navigation. The security of the ships, and the preservation of the various stores, were objects of immediate concern. A regular system to be adopted for the maintenance of good order and cleanliness, as most conducive to the health of the crews during the long, dark, and dreary winter, equally demanded my attention.

Not a moment was lost, therefore, in the commencement of our operations. The whole of the masts were dismantled except the lower ones, and the Hecla's main-top-mast, the latter being kept fidded for the purpose of occasionally hoisting up the electrometer-chain, to try the effect of atmospherical electricity. The lower yards were lashed fore and aft amidships, at a sufficient height to support the planks of the housing intended to be erected over the ships, the lower ends of which rested on the gunwale; and the whole of this frame-work was afterwards roofed over with a cloth, composed of wadding-tilt, with which waggons are usually covered; and thus was formed a comfortable shelter from the snow and wind. The boats, spars, running rigging, and sails, were removed on shore, in order to give as much room as possible on our upper deck, to enable the people to take exercise on board, whenever the weather should be too inclement for walking on shore. It was absolutely necessary, also, for the preservation of our sails and ropes, all of which were hard-frozen, that they should be kept in that state till the return of spring; for, as it was now impossible to get them dried, owing to the constantly low temperature of the atmosphere, they would, probably, have soon rotted had they been kept in any part of the ships, where the warmth would occasion them to thaw; they were, therefore, placed with the boats on shore, and a covering of canvass fixed over them. This covering, however, as we afterwards found, might better have been dispensed with; for as we had not the means of constructing a roof sufficiently tight to keep out the fine snow which fell during the winter, it only served, by the eddy wind which it created, to make the drift about it greater; and, I have now no doubt that, with stores in the state in which I have described our sails to be, it would be better simply to lay them on some spars to keep them off the ground, allowing the snow to cover them as it fell. For want of experience in these matters, we also took a great deal of unnecessary trouble in carrying the anchors over the ice to the beach, with an idea of securing the ships to the shore at the breaking up of the ice in the spring; a precaution for which there was not the smallest occasion, and by which the cables suffered unnecessary exposure during the winter.

As soon as the ships were secured and housed over, my undivided attention was in the next place directed to the comfort of the officers and men, and to the preservation of that extraordinary degree of health which we had hitherto enjoyed in both ships. A few brief remarks on this subject by Mr. Edwards (to whose skill and advice, as well as humane and unremitting attention to the few sick, on all occasions, I am much indebted) I need to make no apology for offering, in his own words: "On our arrival in our winter quarters, after a season sufficiently harassing both to officers and men, it was pleasing to reflect on the excellent health they had experienced throughout. On our passage across the Atlantic, indeed, a few ephemeral complaints, arising from wet and cold, appeared among the men, but they were so slight as to be scarcely worthy of notice; and, since our arrival within the Polar circle, a period of between two and three months, not a single medical case had been entered on the sick list. To this favourable account, one exception, however, must be made in the case of Lieutenant Liddon, who had suffered severely from an attack of rheumatism shortly after our leaving England, from which he had not yet recovered. With regard to accidents, we had been no less fortunate; a few injuries from frost, and one from a burn by gunpowder, which had not yet recovered, but which proved only of temporary inconvenience, constituting all the cases of this nature which had hitherto occurred. Not the slightest disposition to scurvy, the disease most to be apprehended under our present circumstances, had yet been evinced in either ship. In fact, the whole of the officers and men, with the few exceptions above mentioned, might be said to exhibit the finest aspect of health; and it was no less gratifying to observe, that their spirits were in perfect unison with their corporeal powers; so that it was impossible not to consider them as effective as at the commencement of the voyage. Under these co-existing circumstances, combined with the powerful preventives with which we were furnished, it was not unreasonable to indulge in a confident hope of finding ourselves at the beginning of the next season with our numbers undiminished, and our energies unimpaired."

In order to prolong this healthy state of the crews, and to promote the comfort of all, such arrangements were made for the warmth and dryness of the berths and bed-places, as circumstances appeared to require; and in this respect some difficulties were to be overcome, which could not, perhaps, have been anticipated. Soon after our arrival in Winter Harbour, when the temperature of the atmosphere had fallen considerably below zero of Fahrenheit, we found that the steam from the coppers, as well as the breath and other vapour generated in the inhabited parts of the ship, began to condense into drops upon the beams and the sides, to such a degree as to keep them constantly wet. In order to remove this serious evil, it was necessary to adopt such means for producing a sufficient warmth, combined with due ventilation, as might carry off the vapour, and thus prevent its settling on any part of the ship. For this purpose a large stone oven, cased with cast iron, in which all our bread was baked during the winter, was placed on the main-hatchway, and the stove-pipe led fore and aft on one side of the lower deck, the smoke being thus carried up the fore-hatchway. On the opposite side of the deck, an apparatus had been attached to the gallery-range, for conveying a current of heated air between decks. This apparatus simply consisted of an iron box or air-vessel about fifteen inches square, through which passed three pipes, of two inches diameter, communicating from below with the external air, and uniting above in a metal box fixed to the side of the gallery-range; to this box a copper stove pipe was attached, and conveyed to the middle part of the lower deck. When a fire was made under the air-vessel, the air became heated in its passage through the three pipes, from which it was conveyed through the stove-pipe to the men's berths. While this apparatus was in good order, a moderate fire produced a current of air of the temperature of 87°, at the distance of seventeen feet from the fire-place; and, with a pipe of wood, or any other imperfect conductor of heat, which would not allow of its escaping by the way, it might undoubtedly be carried to a much greater distance. By these means we were enabled to get rid of the moisture about the berths where the people messed; but when the weather became more severely cold, it still accumulated in the bed-places occasionally to a serious and very alarming degree. Among the means employed to prevent the injurious effects arising from this annoyance, one of the most efficacious perhaps was a screen made of fear-nought fixed to the beams round the gallery, and dropping within eighteen inches of the deck, which served to intercept the steam from the coppers, and prevent it as before from curling along the beams, and condensing upon them into drops. This screen was especially useful at the time of drawing off the beer, which we had lately been in the habit of brewing from essence of malt and hops, and which continued to be served for several weeks as a substitute for part of the usual allowance of spirits. We found the steam arising from this process so annoying during the cold weather, that, valuable as the beer must be considered as an antiscorbutic beverage, it was deemed advisable to discontinue our brewery on that account. While on this subject, I may also add that, when the weather became severely cold, we could not get the beer to ferment, so as to make it palatable.

For the preservation of health, and as a necessary measure of economy, a few alterations were made in the quantity and quality of the provisions issued. I directed the allowance of bread to be permanently reduced to two-thirds, a precaution which, perhaps, it would have been as well to have adopted form the commencement of the voyage. A pound of Donkin's preserved meat, together with one pint of vegetable or concentrated soup per man, was substituted for one pound of salt beef weekly; a proportion of beer and wine was served in lieu of spirits; and a small quantity of sour krout and pickles, with as much vinegar as could be used, was issued at regular intervals. The daily proportion of lime-juice and sugar was mixed together, and, with a proper quantity of water, was drunk by each man in presence of an officer appointed to attend to this duty. This latter precaution may appear to have been unnecessary, to those who are not aware how much sailors resemble children in all those points in which their own health and comfort are concerned. Whenever any game was procured, it was directed to be invariably served in lieu of, and not in addition to, the established allowance of other meat, except in a few extraordinary cases, when such an indulgence was allowed; and in no one instance, either in quantity or quality, was the slightest preference given to the officers.

In the article of fuel, which is of such vital importance in so severe a climate, a system of the most rigid economy was adopted; such a quantity of coal only being expended as was barely sufficient for the preservation of health on board the ships. A search was made for turf or moss immediately after our arrival, and a small quantity of the latter was made use of as fuel; but, without a previous drying, which, from the advanced period of the season, we had no means of giving it, it was found to be too wet to produce any saving of coals. We also looked out most anxiously for a vein of coal on shore, but only a few lumps were picked up during out stay in Winter Harbour.

Great attention was paid to the clothing of the men, who were put into a certain number of divisions, according to the usual custom of the navy, each division being under the command of an officer, who was responsible for the personal cleanliness of the men entrusted to his charge, as well as for their keeping their clothes at all times mended and in good condition. The men were regularly mustered for inspection morning and evening, at which times I always visited every part of the between-decks, accompanied by Lieut. Beechey and Mr. Edwards; and one day in the week was appointed for the examination of the men's shins and gums by the medical gentlemen, in order that any slight appearance of the scurvy might at once be detected, and checked by timely and adequate means.

It was my intention to have caused the bedding of the ships' companies to be brought on deck, for the purpose of airing, at least once a week during the winter; but here, also, a difficulty occurred, which, without previous experience, could not perhaps have been easily anticipated. Whenever a blanket was brought on deck, and suffered to remain there for a short time, it of course acquired the temperature of the atmosphere. When this happened to be rather low, under zero of Fahrenheit for instance, the immediate consequence, on taking the blanket again into the inhabited parts of the ship was, that the vapour settled and condensed upon it, rendering it almost instantly so wet, as to be unfit to sleep on, and requiring, therefore, after all, that it should be dried by artificial heat before it could be returned into the bed-place. We were, therefore, under the necessity of hanging the bedding upon lines between decks, as the only mode of airing it; and what was likely to prove still more prejudicial, we were obliged to have recourse to the same unhealthy measure in drying the washed clothes.

Under circumstances of leisure and inactivity, such as we were now placed in, and with every prospect of its continuance for a very large portion of a year, I was desirous of finding some amusement for the men during this long and tedious interval. I proposed, therefore, to the officers to get up a Play occasionally on board the Hecla, as the readiest means of preserving among our crews that cheerfulness and good-humour which had hitherto subsisted. In this proposal I was readily seconded by the officers of both ships; and Lieutenant Beechey having been duly elected as stage-manager, our first performance was fixed for the 5th of November, to the great delight of the ship's companies. In these amusements I gladly undertook a part myself, considering that an example of cheerfulness, by giving a direct countenance to every thing that could contribute to it, was not the least essential part of my duty, under the peculiar circumstances in which we were placed.

In order still further to promote good-humour among ourselves, as well as to furnish amusing occupation, during the hours of constant darkness, we set foot on a weekly newspaper, which was to be called the North Georgia Gazette and Winter Chronicle, and of which Captain Sabine undertook to be the editor, under the promise that it was to be supported by original contributions from the officers of the two ships: and, though some objection may, perhaps, be raised against a paper of this kind being generally resorted to in ships of war, I was too well acquainted with the discretion, as well as the excellent dispositions of my officers, to apprehend any unpleasant consequences from a measure of this kind; instead of which I can safely say, that the weekly contributions had the happy effect of employing the leisure hours of those who furnished them, and of diverting the mind from the gloomy prospect which would sometimes obtrude itself on the stoutest heart.

Immediately on our arrival in harbour, Captain Sabine had employed himself in selecting a place for the observatory, which was erected in a convenient spot, about seven hundred yards to the westward of the ships. It was also considered advisable immediately to set about building a house near the beach, for the reception of the clocks and instruments. For this purpose we made use of a quantity of fir-plank, which was intended for the construction of spare boats, and which was so cut as not to injure it for that purpose. The ground was so hard frozen that it required great labour to dig holes for the upright posts which formed the support of the sides. The walls of this house being double, with moss placed between the two, a high temperature could, even in the severest weather which we might be doomed to experience, be kept up in it without difficulty by a single stove.

Among the many fortunate circumstances which had attended us during this first season of our navigation, there was none more striking than the opportune time at which the ships were securely placed in harbour; for on the very night of our arrival, the 26th of September, the thermometer fell to -1°; and, on the following day, the sea was observed from the hills to be quite frozen over, as far as the eye could reach; nor was any open water seen after this period. During the first three weeks in October, however, we remarked that the young ice, near the mouth of the harbour, was occasionally squeezed up very much by the larger floes, so that the latter must still have had some space left, in which to acquire motion: but after that time the sea was entirely covered with one uniform surface of solid and motionless ice.

After our arrival in port, we saw several rein-deer, and a few coveys of grouse; but the country is so destitute of every thing like cover of any kind, that our sportsmen were not successful in their hunting excursions, and we procured only three rein-deer, previously to the migration of these and the other animals from the island, which took place before the close of the month of October, leaving only the wolves and foxes to bear us company during the winter. The full-grown deer, which we killed in the autumn, gave us from one hundred and twenty to one hundred and seventy pounds of meat each, and a fawn weighed eighty-four pounds.

On the 1st of October, Captain Sabine's servant having been at some distance from the ships, to examine a fox-trap, was pursued by a large white bear, which followed his footsteps the whole way to the ships, where he was wounded by several balls, but made his escape after all. This bear, which was the only one we saw during our stay in Winter Harbour, was observed to be more purely white than any we had before seen, the colour of these animals being generally that of a dirtyish yellow, when contrasted with the whiteness of the ice and snow.

On the night of the 4th, we had a strong gale from the southward, which gave us a satisfactory proof of the security of the harbour we had chosen, for the main ice was found in the morning to have pressed in very forcibly upon that which was newly formed near the entrance, while within the two points of the harbour, it remained perfectly solid and undisturbed. Some deer being seen near the ships on the 10th, a party was dispatched after them, some of whom having wounded a stag, and being led on by the ardour of pursuit, forgot my order that every person should be on-board before sun-set, and did not return till late, after we had suffered much apprehension on their account. I, therefore, directed that the expense of all rockets and other signals made in such cases, should, in future, be charged against the wages of the offending party. John Pearson, a marine belonging to the *Griper*, who was the last that returned on board, had his hands severely frost-bitten, having imprudently gone away without mittens, and with a musket in his hand. A party of our people most providentially found him, although the night was very dark, just as he had fallen down a steep bank of snow, and was beginning to feel that degree of torpor and drowsiness which, if indulged, inevitably proves fatal. When he was brought on board, his fingers were quite stiff, and bent into the shape of that part of the mukuet which he had been carrying: and the frost had so far destroyed the animation in his fingers on one hand, that it was necessary to amputate three of them a short time after, notwithstanding all the care and attention paid to him by the medical gentlemen. The effect which exposure to severe frost has, in benumbing the mental as well as the corporeal faculties, was very striking in this man, as well as in two of the young gentlemen who returned after dark, and of whom we were anxious to make inquiries respecting Pearson. When I sent for them into my cabin, they looked wild, spoke thick and indistinctly, and it was impossible to draw from them a rational answer to any of our questions. After being on board for a short time, the mental faculties appeared gradually to return with the returning circulation, and it was not till then that a looker-on could easily persuade himself that they had not been drinking too freely. To those who have been much accustomed to cold countries this will be no new remark; but I cannot help thinking (and it is with this view that I speak of it) that many a man may have been punished for intoxication, who was only suffering from the benumbing effects of frost; for I have more than once seen our people in a state so exactly resembling that of the most stupid intoxication, that I should certainly have charged them with that offence, had I not been quite sure that no possible means were afforded them on Melville Island, to procure any thing stronger than snow-water. In order to guard in some measure against the danger of persons losing their way, which was more and more to be apprehended as the days became shorter, and the ground more covered with snow which gives such a dreary sameness to the country, we erected on all the hills within two or three miles of the harbour, finger-posts pointing towards the ships.

I have before remarked that all the water which we made use of while within the polar circle, was procured from snow, either naturally or artificially dissolved. Soon after the ships were laid up for the winter, it was necessary to have recourse entirely to the latter process, which added materially to the expenditure of fuel during the winter months. The snow for this purpose was dug out of the drifts, which had formed upon the ice round the ships, and dissolved in the coppers. We found it necessary always to strain the water thus procured, on account of the sand which the heavy snow-drifts brought from the island, after which it was quite pure and wholesome.

On the evening of the 13th, the Aurora Borealis was seen very faintly, consisting of a stationary white light in the south-west quarter, and near the horizon.

On the 15th, we saw the last covey of ptarmigan which were met with this season. On the same day our people fell in with a herd of fifteen deer to the southward; they were all lying down at first, except one large one, probably a stag, which afterwards seemed to guard the rest in their flight, going frequently round them, and sometimes striking them with his horns to make them go on, which otherwise they did not seem much inclined to do.

On the 16th, it blew a strong gale from the northward, accompanied by such a constant snow-drift, that although the weather was quite clear overhead, the boat-house, at the distance of three or four hundred yards, could scarcely be seen from the ships. On such occasions, no person was permitted on any account to leave the ships. Indeed, when this snow-drift occurred, as it frequently did during the winter, with a hard gale, and the thermometer very low, I believe that no human being could have remained alive after an hour's exposure to it. In order, therefore, to secure a communication between the ships, a distance not exceeding half a cable's length as well as from the ships to the house on shore, a line was kept extended, as a guide from one to the other. About the middle of October the snow began to fall in smaller flakes than during the summer; and soon after this, whenever it fell, it consisted entirely of very minute *spicula*, assuming various forms of crystallization. The meridian altitude of the sun was observed this day by an artificial horizon, which I notice from the circumstance of its being the last time we had an opportunity of observing it for about four months.

On the 17th and 18th, our hunting parties reported that the deer were more numerous than they had been before, which made us conclude, that they were assembling their forces for an immediate departure over the ice to the continent of America, as we only saw one or two on the island after this time. They had been met with, since taking up our quarters, in herds of from eight to twenty, and from forty to fifty were seen in the course of one day. A thermometer placed in the sun at noon, on the 18th, rose only to -9°, the temperature in the shade being -16°.

It had for some time past been a matter of serious consideration with me, whether it would be necessary to cut the ice round the ships, which had by this time become so firmly attached to the bends, that they were completely imbedded in it. There happened to be only two or three persons in the expedition, who had ever been frozen up during a whole winter in any of the cold countries, and I consulted these as to the expediency of doing so. This precaution, it would seem, is considered to be necessary, from the possibility of a ship being hung by the ice attached to her bends, and thus prevented from rising and falling with the tide; in consequence of which, a plank might easily be torn out near the water-line, by the weight of the ship hanging entirely on that particular part. I was relieved from any apprehension on this score, however, by knowing how small the rise and fall of the tides were in this place; and also by having observed that a spring tide caused the whole mass of ice in the harbour to detach itself from the beach, along the whole line of which it split, and was lifted; so that both ships and ice rose and fell in a body with the tide. The only question, therefore, that remained, was, whether the lateral expansion of the ice might not create such a pressure upon the water-line of the ships as to do them some damage. This apprehension was rather increased by Lieutenant Liddon's having reported to me, that his officers had, a night or two before, heard a loud crack about the *Griper's* bends, which gave them the idea of something straining or giving way. This noise, however, which occurred very frequently afterwards, as the cold became more intense, proved to be nothing more than that which is not unusually heard in houses in cold countries, being occasioned by the freezing and expansion of the juices contained in wood not thoroughly seasoned. To put the matter out of all doubt, however, I deemed it prudent to order the ice to be cut round both ships, an operation which occupied the two crews almost the whole of two days, the ice being now twenty-three inches in thickness; and I determined to continue this operation daily, as long as the weather would permit.

The 20th of October was one of the finest days which, as experience has since taught us, ever occur in this climate, the weather being clear, with little or no wind; and though the thermometer remained steadily between -15° and -16° during the day, it was rather pleasant to our feelings than otherwise. Our sportsmen were out from both ships the whole day, and returned, for the first time, without having seen any living animal, though they had walked over a very considerable extent of ground; so that the hope we had indulged of obtaining, occasionally, a fresh meal, was now nearly at an end for the rest of the winter. It was observed from the hills, that the ice in the offing had been thrown into higher hummocks than before; and in the morning we saw a number of little vertical streams of vapour rising from the sea, near the mouth of the harbour, which was probably that phenomenon vulgarly called the "barber," in North America, and which is occasioned, I believe, by the vapour arising from the water being condensed into a visible form by the coldness of the atmosphere. It is probable, therefore, from the two circumstances now mentioned, that a motion had taken place among the floes in the offing, producing first the pressure by which the hummocks were thrown up, and then a partial separation leaving, for a time, a small space of unfrozen surface.

Between six and eight P.M., we observed the Aurora Borealis, forming a broad arch of irregular white light, extending from N.N.W. to S.S.E., the centre of the arch being 10° to the eastward of the zenith. It was most bright near the southern horizon; and frequent, but not vivid, coruscations were seen shooting from its upper side, towards the zenith. The magnetic needle was not sensibly affected by this phenomenon.

Between two and three P.M. on the 21st, the weather being still remarkably clear and fine, and the sun near the horizon, a parhelion strongly prismatic was seen on each side of it, at the distance of 23°, resembling the legs of a rainbow resting upon the land.

On the 26th, the sun afforded us sufficient light for writing and reading in my cabin, the stern-windows exactly facing the south, from half past nine till half past two; for the rest of the four-and-twenty hours we lived, of course, by candle-light. Nothing could exceed the beauty of the sky to the south-east and south-west at sun-rise and sun-set about this period: near the horizon there was generally a rich bluish purple, and a bright arch of deep red above, the one mingling imperceptibly with the other. The weather about this time was remarkably mild, the mercury in the thermometer having stood at or above zero for more than forty-eight hours. By a register of the temperature of the atmosphere, which was kept by Captain Sabine at the observatory, it was found that the thermometer, invariably, stood at least from 2° to 5°, and even on one or two occasions as much as 7° higher on the outside of the ships, than it did on shore, owing probably to a warm atmosphere, created round the former by the constant fires kept up on board.

On the 29th the weather was calm and clear, and we remarked, for the first time, that the smoke from the funnels scarcely rose at all, but skimmed nearly horizontally along the housing, the thermometer having got down to -24°[1], and the mercury in the barometer standing at 29.70 inches. It now became rather a painful experiment to touch any metallic substance in the open air with the naked hand; the feeling produced by it exactly resembling that occasioned by the opposite extreme of intense heat, and taking off the skin from the part affected. We found it necessary, therefore, to use great caution in handling our sextants and other instruments, particularly the eye-pieces of the telescopes, which, if suffered to touch the face, occasioned an intense burning pain; but this was easily remedied by covering them over with soft leather. Another effect,

[1] By a Meteorological Journal in my possession, kept at York Fort, Hudson's Bay, in the year 1795, it appears that this phenomenon did not occur til the thermometer indicated a temperature of about -36°. The height of the barometer is not mentioned.

with regard to the use of instruments, began to appear about this time. Whenever any instrument, which had been some time exposed to the atmosphere, so as to be cooled down to the same temperature, was suddenly brought below into the cabins, the vapour was instantly condensed all around it, so as to give the instrument the appearance of smoking, and the glasses were covered almost instantaneously with a thin coating of ice, the removal of which required great caution to prevent the risk of injuring them until it had gradually thawed, as they acquired the temperature of the cabin. When a candle was placed in a certain direction form the instrument, with respect to the observer, a number of very minute *spicula* of snow were also seen sparkling around the instrument, at the distance of two or three inches from it, occasioned, as we supposed, by the cold atmosphere produced by the low temperature of the instrument almost instantaneously congealing into that form the vapour which floated in its immediate neighbourhood.

The month of November commenced with mild weather, which continued for the first ten days. It is generally supposed, by those who have not experienced the effects produced upon the feelings by the various alterations in the temperature of the atmosphere, when the thermometer is low, that a change of 10° or 15° makes no sensible difference in the sensation of cold; but this is by no means the case, for it was a remark continually made among us, that our bodies appeared to adapt themselves readily to the climate, that the scale of our feelings, if I may so express it, was soon reduced to a lower standard than ordinary; so that, after living for some days in a temperature of -15° or -20°; it felt quite mild and comfortable when the thermometer rose to zero, and *visa versa*.

The 4th of November being the last day that the sun would, independently of the effects of refraction, be seen above our horizon till the eighth of February, an interval of ninety-six days, it was a matter of considerable regret to us that the weather about this time was not sufficiently clear to allow us to see and make observations on the disappearance of that luminary, in order that something might be attempted towards determining the amount of the atmospherical refraction at a low temperature. But, though we were not permitted to take a last farewell, for at least three months, of that cheering orb, "of this great world, both eye and soul," we nevertheless felt that this day constituted an important and memorable epoch in our voyage. We had, some time before, set about the preparations for our winter's amusements; and the theatre being ready, we opened on the 5th of November, with the representation of *Miss in her Teens*, which afforded to the men such a fund of amusement as fully to justify the expectations we had formed of the utility of theatrical entertainments under our present circumstances, and to determine me to follow them up at stated periods. I found, indeed, that even the occupation of fitting up the theatre, and taking it to pieces again, which employed a number of men for a day or two before and after each performance, was a matter of no little importance, when the immediate duties of the ship appeared by no means sufficient for that purpose; for I dreaded the want of employment as one of the worst evils that was likely to befall us.

On the 6th we tried the temperature of the sea at the bottom, the depth being five fathoms, and found it to be 30°, whilst that of the surface was 28°, and of the air -16°. On the 9th, the temperature of the bottom was as high as 31°, the surface being still at 28°. The specific gravity of the surface water was 1.0264, at the temperature of 52°, and that of the water brought from the bottom 1.0265 at 50°. On the same evening, the weather being fine and clear, the Aurora Borealis was seen for nearly two hours, forming a long, low, irregular arch of light, extending from north to south in the western quarter of the heavens, its altitude in the centre being 3° or 4°. The electrometer-chain was hoisted up to the mast-head, and its lower end brought down to the ice, so as to keep it perfectly clear of all the masts and rigging, which method was used throughout the winter; but no sensible effect was produced on the gold-leaf. It was tried a second time, after the sky became full of white fleecy clouds, but with as little success.

On the forenoon of the 11th, the thermometer having again fallen to -26°, the smoke, as it escaped from the funnels, scarcely rose at all above the housing. Mr. Ross, having gone to the mast-head at noon, reported that he saw the sun. There was no time for measuring the altitude, but Lieutenant Beechey, who went up to observe it, considered that about twenty-four minutes of its disk appeared above the horizon, according to which the amount of refraction would appear to be 2° 09' 05". The temperature of the atmosphere at this time was -27°, and the mercury in the barometer stood at 30.07 inches. The thermometer having fallen to -31° on the following day, we expected to have seen the sun again, and looked out from the mast-head for that purpose, but it did not re-appear. At six P.M. the Aurora Borealis was seen in a broken irregular arch, about 6° high in the centre, extending from N.W.b.N. to

S.b.W., from whence a few coruscations were now and then faintly emitted towards the zenith. From eight P.M. till midnight on the 13th, it was again seen in a similar manner from S.W. to S.E., the brightest part being in the centre, or due south. On the 15th, Lieutenant Beechey informed me that he had seen, in the N.N.W. and S.E. quarters, some light transparent clouds, from which columns of light were thrown upwards, resembling the Aurora Borealis; those to the S.E. being opposed to a very light sky, had a light-brown appearance. This phenomenon was again observed on the 16th, consisting of a bright stationary light from S.S.W. to S.b.E. and reaching from the horizon to the height of about 6° above it.

About the time of the sun's leaving us, the wolves began to approach the ships more boldly, howling most piteously on the beach near us, sometimes for hours together, and, on one or two occasions, coming alongside the ships, when every thing was quiet at night; but we seldom saw more than one or two together, and, therefore, could form no idea of their number. The animals were always very shy of coming near our people, and, though evidently suffering much from hunger, never attempted to attack any of them. The white foxes used also to visit the ships at night, and one of these (*Canis Lagopus*) was caught in a trap, set under the *Griper's* bows. The uneasiness displayed by this beautiful little animal during the time of his confinement, whenever he heard the howling of a wolf near the ships, impressed us with an opinion, that the latter is in the habit of hunting the fox as his prey.

The rapidity with which the ice formed round the ships had now become so great, as to employ our people for several hours each day in cutting it; and for the last three days our utmost labour, during the time of twilight, could scarcely keep it clear. As it was evident, therefore, that, as the frost increased, we could not possibly effect this, and as the men almost always got their feet wet in sawing the ice, from which the most injurious effects upon their health were likely to result, I gave orders to leave off cutting it any more during the severity of the winter. The average formation of ice round the ships, during the time we continued to remove it, was usually from three to five inches in twenty-four hours; and once it froze eight inches in twenty-six hours, the mean temperature of the atmosphere being -12°. At noon to-day we saw, for the first time at this hour, a star of the first magnitude (*Capella*), and at half an hour past noon, those of the second magnitude in Ursa Major were visible; which circumstance will, perhaps,

give the best idea of the weakness of the sun's light at this period. At three P.M.
a remarkable variety of the Aurora Borealis was seen by several of the officers.
Having about this time been confined for a few days to my cabin by indisposition, I am indebted to Lieutenant Beechey for the following description of it:
"Clouds of a light-brown colour were seen, diverging from a point near the
horizon bearing S.W.b.S., and shooting pencils of rays upwards at an angle of about
45° with the horizon. These rays, however, were not stationary as to their position, but were occasionally extended and contracted. From behind these, as it
appeared to us, flashes of white light were repeatedly seen, which sometimes
streamed across to the opposite horizon, some passing through the zenith, others at a considerable distance on each side of it. This phenomenon continued to
display itself brilliantly for half an hour, and then became gradually fainter till
it disappeared, about four o'clock. The sun, at the time of the first appearance of
this meteor, was on nearly the same bearing, and about 5° below the horizon."

The temperature of the atmosphere having, about this time, become considerably lower than before, the cracking of the timbers was very frequent and
loud for a time; but generally ceased altogether in an hour or two after this fall
had taken place in the thermometer, and did not occur again at the same temperature during the winter. The wind blowing fresh from the northward, with
a heavy snow-drift, made the ship very cold below; so that the breath and other
vapour accumulated during the night in the bed-places and upon the beams,
and then immediately froze; hence it often occupied all hands for two or three
hours during the day to scrape the ice away, in order to prevent the bedding from
becoming wet by the increase of temperature occasioned by the fires. It was therefore found necessary to keep some of the fires in between decks at night, when
the thermometer was below -15° or -20° in the open air, especially when the wind
was high. To assist in keeping the lower decks warm, as well as to retard, in some
slight degree, the formation of ice immediately in contact with the ships'
bends, we banked the snow up against their sides, as high as the main-chains;
and canvass screens were nailed round all the hatchways on the lower deck.

✳

PARRY'S ACCOUNT FAILS TO DO JUSTICE TO THE BRILLIANCE OF HIS
planning. The paper the ships published, the North Georgia Gazette *and* Winter

Chronicle, was truly a stroke of genius, even if the writing within it tended toward silly jokes, bad puns, even worse poems, and other you-had-to-be-there sorts of humor. But it kept men busy and amused who otherwise had little to do. The theatricals took place on the upper deck and often in bitter cold, but they, too, were fun—and unprecedented.

Problems did arise, to be sure. The cold was intense and it was death to be caught in it. Men who stayed out hunting too long suffered frostbite. Fighting a fire that started in a hut outside the ship where they were storing scientific instruments, one man lost seven fingers to the cold. One case of scurvy appeared, which Parry solved by using mustard grown on warm pipes inside the cabins. And when spring came a more serious problem arose: the ice surrounding the ships did not melt. They had sailed into a harbor, but could they sail out? Ice was clearing out of the deeper waters beyond, but not in their harbor. Not until the last of July was Parry able to take his ships out of their winter quarters and into the sound. He tried then to complete his task and find the rest of the Northwest Passage, but ice to the west defeated him. In mid-September, 1820, he turned for home.

The Admiralty, of course, was ecstatic. Parry had broken through the Croker Mountains, successfully wintered over in the Arctic (only one man was lost; he died of disease), and sighted straits and inlets, any one of which might be the Northwest Passage or the route into it. John Wilson Croker, showing not the least displeasure that the mountains named after him had proven fictitious, saw to it that Parry was promoted to Commander. He sold his journal to a publisher for a thousand guineas, a small fortune then. Parry's success also gave the coup de grace to the reputation of John Ross. When he went back to the Arctic, it was under private sponsorship, not in command of an Admiralty ship.

The Arctic was creating other English heroes, in the meantime, on the shore of the Arctic Ocean in northern Canada. While Ross, and then Parry, were sailing into Baffin Bay and Lancaster Sound, the 1819 expedition on the ground was moving west and north from Hudson Bay to map the coastline east of the mouth of the Coppermine River, where Samuel Hearne had discovered in 1771 that the polar ocean at that point was free of ice. The expedition was under the command of a career naval officer named John Franklin. His instructions were that, having reached the mouth of the Coppermine, he was to move east—or west; the instructions were vague, and much was left for him to decide on the spot—by canoe, map the coastline as far as he could, and possibly meet up with Parry coming through the Passage from the east. He was to use Indian guides, or else guides hired from the Hudson's Bay Company and/or its rival, the North West Company, to supplement the several Navy men he was taking with him. So began one of the most remarkable careers in Arctic history.

Actually Franklin's career as an explorer had begun somewhat earlier, but not in so notable a fashion. Franklin had commanded the second ship in David Buchan's abortive attempt to penetrate the pack and sail to the North Pole two years before. Franklin had been serving in the Navy since the age of fourteen and had fought in the Battle of Trafalgar. He had fought the Americans at the Battle of New Orleans. But this was a much more rigorous assignment, and more challenging. Indeed, Franklin was an odd choice. He was 33 years old, overweight, not at all fit, and most of all he had spent his entire career to date on board ships. He had no experience of land travel, particularly wilderness land travel. One of the Hudson's Bay Company men noted that he could not travel more than eight miles a day and that he was insistent that he have his tea every afternoon at four.

He took four countrymen with him: Dr. John Richardson, a surgeon in the Royal Marines; a midshipman named Robert Hood, who painted some wonderful watercolors on the trip before he died; another named George Back who would later lead his own expedition across the Canadian tundra; and an ordinary seaman named John Hepburn. They reached York Factory in Hudson Bay in August, 1819, and moved west some 500 miles in a small boat through the complex waterways of upper Canada in increasingly cold weather to Cumberland House, a Hudson's Bay Company depot on the Saskatchewan River, where further travel by boat became impossible as the rivers and lakes froze up. In January Franklin left Cumberland House with Hepburn and Back on snowshoes for Fort Chipewyan, 857 miles away, to hire voyageurs and arrange for food supplies for the summer journey ahead.

There were no food supplies to spare at Fort Chipewyan. He could not find voyageurs who wanted to make such a long journey into unknown territory. Not until July, when the rest of the party appeared, was he able to round up sixteen men willing to make the trip. He also managed to gather some meager food supplies, and to arrange with the chief of the Coppermine Indians, a man named Akaitcho, to hunt food for him along the way. And then they set out—for their next winter camp, near the Coppermine itself, where they built two buildings before winter came, one large log cabin for the five Navy men, a smaller one for the voyageurs. The Indians were left to their own devices for shelter. They called this place Fort Enterprise. They spent an interesting winter there. Back and Hood nearly fought a duel over an Indian girl named Greenstockings, and Hood fathered a child by her. The two fur companies were so deeply locked into their rivalry that they refused, until Back browbeat them into it, to supply Franklin's party with food or anything else; both believed Franklin had taken the other's side. The Indians turned out not to know the country at all. The voyageurs grew restless at Franklin's leadership.

Nevertheless the expedition finally set out toward the Coppermine in early June, 1821, two years after Franklin had left England. He had with him his own four Navy men, an interpreter named Wentzel, the Indians, and fifteen voyageurs. When they reached the Arctic Ocean in July, the Indians turned around and went home. So did Wentzel. That left Franklin, a party of nineteen, and three bark canoes, in which they set sail—to the east. They moved east along the coast until August 18, which found them on what became known as the Kent Peninsula, at a point he named Point Turnagain—more than 500 miles from the mouth of the Coppermine. The snow geese were already flying south. The deer had begun to move toward their winter feeding grounds farther south. Winter weather was closing in earlier than usual. The seas were stormy.

Franklin had to abandon the idea of moving back to the Coppermine in the canoes. They would have to trek overland up the Hood River, named after Robert Hood, and hope to cross overland from the Hood to the Coppermine. Food was getting low. They ran out of pemmican on September 4. On September 7 they ran out of soup. Franklin had gone too far.

Disaster rapidly followed disaster. The three ocean-going canoes were broken up and rebuilt into two smaller canoes but the voyageurs dropped one of them as they walked across the landscape. The voyageurs were carrying 90 pounds of gear per man, and they required eight to nine pounds of food per day, which is normal for men bearing huge loads, but the only food was an occasional deer. They probably dropped the canoe on purpose, but it would prove to be a mistake. They needed the canoes. A man fell into the water and nearly froze to death. Game was disappearing quickly, and they took to eating lichen, which they dubbed tripes de roche. It was close to inedible, and it gave them severe diarrhea. The voyageurs, carrying all the load, were ravenous. They took to eating rotting scraps of deerskin they found at old wolf kills. We join them on September 22, 1821.

JOHN FRANKLIN

Narrative of a Journey to the Shores of the Polar Sea

September 22

Our progress next day was extremely slow, from the difficulty of managing the canoe in passing over the hills, as the breeze was fresh. Peltier who had it in charge, having received several severe falls, became impatient, and insisted on leaving his burden, as it had already been much injured by the accidents of this day; and no arguments we could use were sufficient to prevail on him to continue carrying it. Vaillant was, therefore, directed to take it, and we proceeded forward. Having found that he got on very well, and was walking even faster than Mr. Hood could follow, in his present debilitated state, I pushed forward to stop the rest of the party, who had got out of sight during the delay which the discussion respecting the canoe had occasioned. I accidentally passed the body of the men, and followed the tracks of two persons who had separated from the rest, until two P.M., when not seeing any person, I retraced my steps and on my way met Dr. Richardson, who had also missed the party whilst he was employed gathering *tripe de roche,* and we went back together in search of them. We found they had halted among some willows, where they had picked up some pieces of skin, and a few bones of deer that had been devoured by the wolves last spring. They had rendered the bones friable by burning, and eaten them as well as the skin; and several of them had added their old shoes to the repast. Peltier and Vaillant were with them, having left the canoe, which, they said, was so completely broken by another fall, as to be rendered incapable of repair, and entirely useless. The anguish this intelligence occasioned may be conceived, but it is beyond my power to describe it. Impressed, however, with the necessity of taking it forward, even in the state these men represented it to be, we urgently desired them to fetch it; but they declined going, and the strength of the officers was inadequate to the task. To their infatuated obstinacy on this occasion, a great portion of the melancholy circumstances which attended our subsequent progress may, perhaps, be attributed. The men now seemed to have lost all hope of being preserved; and all the arguments we could use failed in stimulating them to the least exertion. After consuming the remains of the bones and horns of the deer we resumed our march, and in the evening, reached a contracted part of the lake, which. perceiving it to be shallow, we forded, and encamped on the opposite side. Heavy rain began soon afterwards, and continued all night. On the following morning the rain had so wasted the snow, that the tracks of Mr. Back and his companions, who had gone before with the hunters, were traced with difficulty; and the frequent showers during the day almost obliterated them. The men became furious at the apprehension of being deserted by the hunters, and some of the strongest throwing down their bundles, prepared to set out after them, intending to leave the more weak to follow as they could. The entreaties and threats of the officers, however, prevented their executing this mad scheme; but not before Solomon Belanger was despatched with orders for Mr. Back to halt until we should join him. Soon afterwards a thick fog came on, but we continued our march and overtook Mr. Back, who had been detained in consequence of his companions having followed some recent tracks of deer. After halting an hour, during which we refreshed ourselves with eating our old shoes, and a few scraps of leather, we set forward in the hope of ascertaining whether an adjoining piece of water was the Copper-Mine River or not, but were soon compelled to return and encamp, for fear of a separation of the party, as we could not see each other at ten yards' distance. The fog diminishing towards evening, Augustus was sent to examine the water, but having lost his way he did not reach the tents before midnight, when he brought the information of its being a lake. We supped upon *tripe de roche*, and enjoyed a comfortable fire, having found some pines, seven or eight feet high, in a valley near the encampment.

The bounty of Providence was most seasonably manifested to us next morning, in our killing five small deer out of a herd, which came in sight as

we were on the point of starting. This unexpected supply re-animated the drooping spirits of our men, and filled every heart with gratitude.

The voyageurs instantly petitioned for a day's rest which we were most
reluctant to grant, being aware of the importance of every moment at this crit-
ical period of our journey. But they so earnestly and strongly pleaded their
recent sufferings, and their conviction that the quiet enjoyment of two substantial
meals, after eight days' famine, would enable them to proceed next day more vigorously, that we could not resist their entreaties. The flesh, the skins, and even
the contents of the stomachs of the deer were equally distributed among the party
by Mr. Hood, who had volunteered, on the departure of Mr. Wentzel, to perform
the duty of issuing the provision. This invidious task he had all along performed with great impartiality, but seldom without producing some grumbling
amongst the Canadians; and, on the present occasion, the hunters were displeased
that the heads and some other parts, had not been added to their portions. It is
proper to remark, that Mr. Hood always took the smallest portion for his own
mess, but this weighed little with these men, as long as their own appetites
remained unsatisfied. We all suffered much inconvenience from eating animal
food after our long abstinence, but particularly those men who indulged themselves beyond moderation. The Canadians, with their usual thoughtlessness, had
consumed above a third of their portions of meat that evening.

We set out early on the 26th, and after walking about three miles along the
lake, came to the river which we at once recognised, from its size, to be the
Copper-Mine. It flowed to the northward, and after winding about five miles,
terminated in Point Lake. Its current was swift, and there were two rapids in
this part of its course, which in a canoe we could have crossed with ease and
safety. These rapids, as well as every other part of the river, were carefully
examined in search of a ford; but finding none, the expedients occurred, of
attempting to cross on a raft made of the willows which were growing there,
or in a vessel framed with willows, and covered with the canvas of the tents;
but both these schemes were abandoned, through the obstinacy of the interpreters and the most experienced voyageurs, who declared that they would
prove inadequate to the conveyance of the party, and that much time would
be lost in the attempt. The men, in fact, did not believe that this was the
Copper-Mine River, and so little confidence had they in our reckoning, and
so much had they bewildered themselves on the march that some of them

asserted it was Hood's River, and others that it was the Bethe-tessy. (A river which rises from a lake to the northward of Rum Lake, and holds a course to the sea parallel with that of the Copper-Mine.) In short, their despondency had returned, and they all despaired of seeing Fort Enterprise again. However, the steady assurances of the officers that we were actually on the banks of the Copper-Mine River, and that the distance to Fort Enterprise did not exceed forty miles, made some impression upon them, which was increased upon our finding some bear-berry plants (*arbutus uva ursi*), which are reported by the Indians not to grow to the eastward of that river. They then deplored their folly and impatience in breaking the canoe, being all of opinion, that had it not been so completely demolished on the 23rd, it might have been repaired sufficiently to take the party over. We again closely interrogated Peltier and Vaillant as to its state, with the intention of sending for it; but they persisted in the declaration that it was in a totally unserviceable condition. St. Germain being again called upon to endeavour to construct a canoe frame with willows, stated that he was unable to make one sufficiently large. It became necessary, therefore, to search for pines of sufficient size to form a raft; and being aware that such trees grow on the borders of Point Lake, we considered it best to trace its shores in search of them; we, therefore, resumed our march, carefully looking, but in vain, for a fordable part, and encamped at the east end of Point Lake.

As there was little danger of our losing the path of our hunters whilst we coasted the shores of this lake, I determined on again sending Mr. Back forward, with the interpreters to hunt. I had in view, in this arrangement, the further object of enabling Mr. Back to get across the lake with two of these men, to convey the earliest possible account of our situation to the Indians. Accordingly I instructed him to halt at the first pines he should come to, and then prepare a raft; and if his hunters had killed animals, so that the party could be supported whilst we were making our raft, he was to cross immediately with St. Germain and Beauparlant, and send the Indians to us as quickly as possible with supplies of meat.

We had this evening the pain of discovering that two of our men had stolen part of the officers' provision, which had been allotted to us with strict impartiality. This conduct was the more reprehensible, as it was plain that we were suffering, even in a greater degree than themselves, from the effects of famine, owing to our being of a less robust habit, and less accustomed to privations. We had no means of punishing this crime, but by the threat that they should forfeit their wages, which had now ceased to operate.

Mr. Back and his companions set out at six in the morning, and we started at seven. As the snow had entirely disappeared, and there were no means of distinguishing the footsteps of stragglers, I gave strict orders, previously to setting out, for all the party to keep together: and especially I desired the two Esquimaux not to leave us, they having often strayed in search of the remains of animals. Our people, however, through despondency, had become careless and disobedient, and had ceased to dread punishment, or hope for reward. Much time was lost in halting and firing guns to collect them, but the labour of walking was so much lightened by the disappearance of the snow, that we advanced seven or eight miles along the lake before noon, exclusive of the loss of distance in rounding its numerous bays. At length we came to an arm, running away to the north-east, and apparently connected with the lake which we had coasted on the 22nd, 23rd, and 24th, of the month.

The idea of again rounding such an extensive piece of water and of travelling over so barren a country was dreadful, and we feared that other arms, equally large, might obstruct our path, and that the strength of the party would entirely fail, long before we could reach the only part where we were certain of finding wood, distant in a direct line twenty-five miles. While we halted to consider of this subject, and to collect the party, the carcass of a deer was discovered in the cleft of a rock into which it had fallen in the spring. It was putrid, but little less acceptable to us on that account, in our present circumstances; and a fire being kindled, a large portion was devoured on the spot, affording us an unexpected breakfast, for in order to husband our small remaining portion of meat, we had agreed to make only one scanty meal a day. The men, cheered by this unlooked-for supply, became sanguine in the hope of being able to cross the stream on a raft of willows, although they had before declared such a project impracticable, and they unanimously entreated us to return back to the rapid, a request which accorded with our own opinion, and was therefore acceded to. Crédit and Junuis, however, were missing, and it was also necessary to send notice of our intention to Mr. Back and his party. Augustus being promised a reward, undertook the task, and we agreed to wait for him at the rapid. It was supposed he could not fail meeting with the two stragglers on his way to or from Mr. Back, as it was likely they would keep on the borders of the lake. He accordingly set out after Mr. Back, whilst we returned about a mile towards the rapid, and encamped in a deep valley amongst some large willows. We supped on the remains of the putrid deer, and the men having gone to the spot where it was found. scraped together the contents of its intestines which were scattered on the rock, and added them to their meal. We also enjoyed the luxury today of eating a large quantity of excellent blueberries and cranberries (*vaccinium uliginosum* and *v. vitis idaea*) which were laid bare by the melting of the snow, but nothing could allay our inordinate appetites.

In the night we heard the report of Crédits gun in answer to our signal muskets, and he rejoined us in the morning, but we got no intelligence of Junius. We set out about an hour after daybreak, and encamped at two P.M. between the rapids, where the river was about one hundred and thirty yards wide, being its narrowest part.

Eight deer were seen by Michel and Crédit, who loitered behind the rest of the party, but they could not approach them. A great many shots were fired by those in the rear at partridges, but they missed, or at least did not choose to add what they killed to the common stock. We subsequently learned that the hunters often secreted the partridges they shot, and ate them unknown to the officers. Some *tripe de roche* was collected, which we boiled for supper, with the moiety of the remainder of our deer's meat. The men commenced cutting the willows for the construction of the raft. As an incitement to exertion, I promised a reward of three hundred livres to the first person who should convey a line across the river, by which the raft could be managed in transporting the party.

September 29.—Strong south-east winds with fog in the morning, more moderate in the evening. Temperature of the rapid 38°. The men began at an early hour to bind the willows in fagots for the construction of the raft, and it was finished by seven; but as the willows were green, it proved to be very little buoyant, and was unable to support more than one man at a time. Even on this, however, we hoped the whole party might be transported, by hauling it from one side to the other, provided a line could be carried to the other bank. Several attempts were made by Belanger and Benoit, the strongest men of the party, to convey the raft across the stream, but they failed for want of oars. A pole constructed by tying the tent poles together, was too short to reach the bottom at a short distance from the shore; and a paddle which had been carried from the sea-coast by Dr. Richardson, did not possess sufficient power to move the raft in opposition to a strong breeze, which blew from the other side. All the men suffered extremely from the coldness of the water, in which they were necessarily immersed up to the waists, in their endeavours to aid Belanger and Benoit; and having witnessed repeated failures, they began to consider the scheme as hopeless. At this time Dr. Richardson, prompted by a desire of relieving his suffering companions, proposed to swim across the stream with a line, and to haul the raft over. He launched into the stream with the line round his middle, but when he had got a short distance from the bank, his arms became benumbed with cold, and he lost the power of moving them; still he persevered, and, turning on his back, had nearly gained the opposite bank when his legs also became powerless, and to our infinite alarm we beheld him sink. We instantly hauled upon the line and he came again to the surface, and was gradually drawn ashore in an almost lifeless state. Being rolled up in blankets, he was placed before a good fire of willows, and fortunately was just able to speak sufficiently to give some slight directions respecting the manner of treating him. He recovered strength gradually, and through the blessing of God was enabled in the course of a few hours to converse, and by the evening was sufficiently recovered to remove into the tent. We then regretted to learn that the skin of his whole left side was deprived of feeling, in consequence of exposure to too great heat. He did not perfectly recover the sensation of that side until the following summer. I cannot describe what everyone felt at beholding the skeleton which the Doctor's debilitated frame exhibited. When he stripped, the Canadians simultaneously exclaimed, "Ah! que nous sommes maigres!" I shall best explain his state and that of the party, by the following extraction from his journal: "It may be worthy of remark that I should have had little hesitation in any former period of my life, at plunging into water even below 38° Fahrenheit; but at this time I was reduced almost to skin and bone, and, like the rest of the party, suffered from degrees of cold that would have been disregarded in health and vigour. During the whole of our march we experienced that no quantity of clothing could keep us warm whilst we fasted, but on those occasions on which we were enabled to go to bed with full stomachs, we passed the night in a warm and comfortable manner."

In following the detail of our friend's narrow escape, I have omitted to mention, that when he was about to step into the water, he put his foot on a dagger, which cut him to the bone; but this misfortune could not stop him from attempting the execution of his generous undertaking.

In the evening Augustus came in. He had walked a day and a half beyond the place from whence we turned back, but had neither seen Junius nor Mr. Back. Of the former he had seen no traces, but he had followed the tracks of Mr. Back's party for a considerable distance, until the hardness of the ground rendered them imperceptible. Junius was well equipped with ammunition, blankets, knives, a kettle, and other necessaries; and it was the opinion of Augustus that when he found he could not rejoin the party, he would endeavour to gain the woods on the west end of Point Lake, and follow the river until he fell in with the Eskimaux, who frequent its mouth. The Indians too with whom we have since conversed upon this subject, are confident that he would be able to subsist himself during the winter. Crédit, on his hunting excursion today, found a cap, which our people recognised to belong to one of the hunters who had left us in the spring. This circumstance produced the conviction of our being on the banks of the Copper-Mine River, which all the assertions of the officers had hitherto failed in effecting with some of the party; and it had the happy consequence of reviving their spirits considerably. We consumed the last of our deer's meat this evening at supper.

Next morning the men went out in search of dry willows, and collected eight large fagots, with which they formed a more buoyant raft than the former, but the wind being still adverse and strong, they delayed attempting to cross until a more favourable opportunity. Pleased, however, with the appearance of this raft, they collected some *tripe de roche*, and made a cheerful supper. Dr. Richardson was gaining strength, but his leg was much swelled and very painful. An observation for latitude placed the encampment in 65° 00' 00" N., the longitude being 112° 20' 00" W., deduced from the last observation.

On the morning of the 1st of October, the wind was strong, and the weather as unfavourable as before for crossing on the raft. We were rejoiced to see Mr. Back and his party in the afternoon. They had traced the lake about fifteen miles farther than we did, and found it undoubtedly connected, as we had supposed, with the lake we fell in with on the 22nd of September; and dreading, as we had done, the idea of coasting its barren shores, they returned to make an attempt at crossing here. St. Germain now proposed to make a canoe of the fragments of painted canvas in which we wrapped our bedding. This scheme appearing practicable, a party was sent to our encampment of the 24th and 25th last, to collect pitch amongst the small pines that grew there, to pay over the seams of the canoe.

In the afternoon we had a heavy fall of snow, which continued all night. A small quantity of *tripe de roche* was gathered; and Crédit, who had been hunting, brought in the antlers and back bone of a deer which had been killed in the summer. The wolves and birds of prey had picked them clean, but there still remained a quantity of the spinal marrow which they had not been able to extract. This, although putrid, was esteemed a valuable prize, and the spine being divided into portions, was distributed equally. After eating the marrow, which was so acrid as to excoriate the lips, we rendered the bones friable by burning, and ate them also.

October 4.–The canoe being finished, it was brought to the encampment, and the whole party being assembled in anxious expectation on the beach, St. Germain embarked, and amidst our prayers for his success, succeeded in reaching the opposite shore. The canoe was then drawn back again, and another person transported, and in this manner by drawing it backwards and forwards, we were all conveyed over without any serious accident. By these frequent traverses the canoe was materially injured; and latterly it filled each time with water before reaching the shore, so that all our garments and bedding were wet, and there was not a sufficiency of willows upon the side on which we now were, to make a fire to dry them.

That no time might be lost in procuring relief, I immediately despatched Mr. Back with St. Germain, Solomon Belanger, and Beauparlant, to search for the Indians, directing him to go to Fort Enterprise, where we expected they would be, or where, at least, a note from Mr. Wentzel would be found to direct us in our search for them. If St. Germain should kill any animals on his way, a portion of the meat was to be put up securely for us, and conspicuous marks placed over it.

It is impossible to imagine a more gratifying change than was produced in our voyageurs after we were all safely landed on the southern banks of the river. Their spirits immediately revived, each of them shook the officers cordially by the hand, and declared they now considered the worst of their difficulties over, as they did not doubt of reaching Fort Enterprise in a few days, even in their feeble condition. We had, indeed, every reason to be grateful, and our joy would have been complete had it not been mingled with sincere regret at the separation of our poor Esquimaux, the faithful Junius.

The want of *tripe de roche* caused us to go supperless to bed. Showers of snow fell frequently during the night. The breeze was light next morning, the weather cold and clear. We were all on foot by daybreak, but from the frozen state of our tents and bed-clothes, it was long before the bundles could be made, and as usual, the men lingered over a small fire they had kindled, so that it was eight o'clock before we started. Our advance, from the depth of the snow, was slow, and about noon, coming to a spot where there was some *tripe de roche*, we stopped to collect it and breakfasted. Mr. Hood, who was now very feeble, and Dr. Richardson, who attached himself to him, walked together at a gentle pace in the rear of the party. I kept with the foremost men, to cause them to halt occasionally, until the stragglers came up. Resuming our march after breakfast, we followed the track of Mr. Back's party, and encamped early, as all of us were much fatigued, particularly Crédit, who having today carried the men's tent, it being his turn so to do, was so exhausted, that when he reached the encampment he was unable to stand. The *tripe de roche* disagreed with this man and with Vaillant, in consequence of which, they were the first whose strength totally failed. We had a small quantity of this weed in the evening, and the rest of our supper was made up of scraps of roasted leather. The distance walked today was six miles. As Crédit was very weak in the morning, his load was reduced to little more than his personal luggage, consisting of his blanket, shoes, and gun. Previous to setting out, the whole party ate the remains of their old shoes, and whatever scraps of leather they had, to strengthen their stomachs for the fatigue of the day's journey. We left the encampment at nine, and pursued our route over a range of black hills. The wind having increased to a strong gale in the course of the morning, became piercingly cold, and the drift rendered it difficult for those in the rear to follow the track over the heights; whilst in the valleys, where it was sufficiently marked, from the depth of the snow, the labour of walking was proportionably great. Those in advance made, as usual, frequent halts, yet being unable from the severity of the weather to remain long still they were obliged to move on before the rear could come up, and the party, of course, straggled very much.

About noon Samandré coming up, informed us that Crédit and Vaillant could advance no farther. Some willows being discovered in a valley near us,

I proposed to halt the party there, whilst Dr. Richardson went back to visit them. I hoped too, that when the sufferers received the information of a fire being kindled at so short a distance they would be cheered, and use their utmost efforts to reach it, but this proved a vain hope. The Doctor found Vaillant about a mile and a half in the rear, much exhausted with cold and fatigue. Having encouraged him to advance to the fire, after repeated solicitations he made the attempt, but fell down amongst the deep snow at every step. Leaving him in this situation, the Doctor went about half a mile farther back, to the spot where Crédit was said to have halted, and the track being nearly obliterated by the snow drift, it became unsafe for him to go farther. Returning he passed Vaillant, who having moved only a few yards in his absence, had fallen down, was unable to rise, and could scarcely answer his questions. Being unable to afford him any effectual assistance, he hastened on to inform us of his situation. When J.B. Belanger had heard the melancholy account, he went immediately to aid Vaillant, and bring up his burden. Respecting Crédit, we were informed by Samandré that he had stopped a short distance behind Vaillant, but that his intention was to return to the encampment of the preceding evening.

When Belanger came back with Vaillant's load, he informed us that he had found him lying on his back, benumbed with cold, and incapable of being roused. The stoutest men of the party were now earnestly entreated to bring him to the fire, but they declared themselves unequal to the task; and, on the contrary, urged me to allow them to throw down their loads, and proceed to Fort Enterprise with the utmost speed. A compliance with their desire would have caused the loss of the whole party, for the men were totally ignorant of the course to be pursued, and none of the officers, who could have directed the march, were sufficiently strong to keep up at the pace they would then walk; besides, even supposing them to have found their way, the strongest men would certainly have deserted the weak. Something, however, was absolutely necessary to be done to relieve them as much as possible from their burdens, and the officers consulted on the subject. Mr. Hood and Dr. Richardson proposed to remain behind, with a single attendant, at the first place where sufficient wood and *tripe de roche* should be found for ten days' consumption; and that I should proceed as expeditiously as possible with the men to the house, and thence send them immediate relief. They strongly urged that this arrangement would contribute to the safety of the rest of the party, by relieving them from the burden of a tent, and several other articles; and that they might afford aid to Crédit, if he should unexpectedly come up. I was distressed beyond description at the thought of leaving them in such a dangerous situation, and for a long time combated their proposal; but they strenuously urged, that this step afforded the only chance of safety for the party, and I reluctantly acceded to it. The ammunition, of which we had a small barrel, was also to be left with them, and it was hoped that this deposit would be a strong inducement for the Indians to venture across the barren grounds to their aid. We communicated this resolution to the men, who were cheered at the slightest prospect of alleviation to their present miseries, and promised with great appearance of earnestness to return to those officers, upon the first supply of food.

The party then moved on; Vaillant's blanket and other necessaries were left in the track, at the request of the Canadians, without any hope, however, of his being able to reach them. After marching till dusk without seeing a favourable place for encamping, night compelled us to take shelter under the lee of a hill, amongst some willows, with which, after many attempts, we at length made a fire. It was not sufficient, however, to warm the whole party, much less to thaw our shoes; and the weather not permitting the gathering of *tripe de roche*, we had nothing to cook. The painful retrospection of the melancholy events of the day banished sleep, and we shuddered as we contemplated the dreadful effects of this bitterly cold night on our two companions, if still living. Some faint hopes we entertained of Crédits surviving the storm, as he was provided with a good blanket, and had leather to eat.

The weather was mild next morning. We left the encampment at nine, and a little before noon came to a pretty extensive thicket of small willows, near which there appeared a supply of *tripe de roche* on the face of the rocks. At this place Dr. Richardson and Mr. Hood determined to remain, with John Hepburn, who volunteered to stop with them. The tent was securely pitched, a few willows collected, and the ammunition and all other articles were deposited, except each man's clothing, one tent, a sufficiency of ammunition for the journey, and the officers' journals. I had only one blanket, which was carried for me, and two pair of shoes. The offer was now made for any of the men, who felt themselves to weak to proceed, to remain with the officers, but none of them accepted it. Michel alone felt some inclination to do so. After we had united in thanksgiving and prayers to Almighty God, I separated from my companions, deeply afflicted that a train of melancholy circumstances should have demanded of me the severe trial of parting, in such a condition, from friends who had become endeared to me by their constant kindness and co-operation, and a participation of numerous sufferings. This trial I could not have been induced to undergo, but for the reasons they had so strongly urged the day before, to which my own judgment assented, and for the sanguine hope I felt of either finding a supply of provision at Fort Enterprise, or meeting the Indians in the immediate vicinity of that place, according to my arrangements with Mr. Wentzel and Akaitcho. Previously to our starting, Peltier and Benoit repeated their promises, to return to them with provision, if any should be found at the house, or to guide the Indians to them, if any were met.

Greatly as Mr. Hood was exhausted, and indeed, incapable as he must have proved, of encountering the fatigue of our very next day's journey, so that I felt his resolution to be prudent, I was sensible that his determination to remain, was chiefly prompted by the disinterested and generous wish to remove impediments to the progress of the rest. Dr. Richardson and Hepburn, who were both in a state of strength to keep pace with the men, besides this motive which they shared with him, were influenced in their resolution to remain, the former by the desire which had distinguished his character, throughout the Expedition, of devoting himself to the succour of the weak, and the latter by the zealous attachment he had ever shown towards his officers.

We set out without waiting to take any of the *tripe de roche*, and walking at a tolerable pace, in an hour arrived at a fine group of pines, about a mile and a quarter from the tent. We sincerely regretted not having seen these before we separated from our companions, as they would have been better supplied with fuel here, and there appeared to be more *tripe de roche* than where we had left them.

Descending afterwards into a more level country, we found the snow very deep, and the labour of wading through it so fatigued the whole party, that we were compelled to encamp, after a march of four miles and a half. Belanger and Michel were left far behind, and when they arrived at the encampment appeared quite exhausted. The former, bursting into tears, declared his inability to proceed, and begged me to let him go back next morning to the tent, and shortly afterwards Michel made the same request. I was in hopes they might recover a little strength by the night's rest, and therefore deferred giving any permission *until* morning The sudden failure in the strength of these men cast a gloom over the rest, which I tried in vain to remove, by repeated assurances that the distance to Fort Enterprise was short, and that we should, in all probability, reach it in four days. Not being able to find any *tripe de roch*, we drank an infusion of the Labrador tea plant (*ledum palustre*), and ate a few morsels of burnt leather for supper. We were unable to raise the tent, and found its weight too great to carry it on; we, therefore, cut it up, and took a part of the canvas for a cover. The night was bitterly cold, and though we lay as close to each other as possible, having no shelter, we could not keep ourselves sufficiently warm to sleep. A strong gale came on after midnight, which increased the severity of the weather. In the morning Belanger and Michel renewed their request to be permitted to go back to the tent, assuring me they were still weaker than on the preceding evening, and less capable of going forward; and they urged that the stopping at a place where there was a supply of *tripe de roche* was their only chance of preserving life; under these circumstances, I could not do otherwise than yield to their desire. I wrote a note to Dr. Richardson and Mr. Hood, informing them of the pines we had passed, and recommending their removing thither. Having found that Michel was carrying a considerable quantity of ammunition, I desired him to divide it among my party, leaving him only ten balls and a little shot, to kill any animals he might meet on his way to the tent. This man was very particular in his inquiries respecting the direction of the house, and the course we meant to pursue; he also said, that if he should be able, he would go and search for Vaillant and Crédit; and he requested my permission to take Vaillant's blanket, if he should find it, to which I agreed, and mentioned it in my notes to the officers.

Scarcely were these arrangements finished, before Perrault and Fontano were seized with a fit of dizziness, and betrayed other symptoms of extreme debility. Some tea was quickly prepared for them, and after drinking it, and eating a few morsels of burnt leather, they recovered, and expressed their desire to go forward; but the other men, alarmed at what they had just witnessed, became doubtful of their own strength, and, giving way to absolute dejection, declared their inability to move. I now earnestly pressed upon them the necessity of continuing our journey, as the only means of saving their own lives, as well as those of our friends at the tent; and, after much entreaty, got them to set out at ten A.M.: Belanger and Michel were left at the encampment, and proposed to start shortly afterwards. By the time we had gone about two hundred yards, Perrault became again dizzy, and desired us to halt, which we did, until he, recovering, offered to march on. Ten minutes more had hardly elapsed before he again desired us to stop, and, bursting into tears, declared he was totally exhausted, and unable to accompany us farther. As the encampment was not more than a quarter of a mile distant, we recommended that he should return to it, and rejoin Belanger and Michel, whom we knew to be still there, from perceiving the smoke of a fresh fire; and because they had not made any preparation for starting when we quitted them. He readily acquiesced in the proposition, and having taken a friendly leave of each of us, and enjoined us to make all the haste we could in sending relief, he turned back, keeping his gun and ammunition. We watched him until he was nearly at the fire, and then proceeded.

AT THIS POINT IN THE STORY WE TURN TO JOHN RICHARDSON, WHO *tells us in his official report to the authorities in England what happened when Franklin left him on the trail.*

JOHN RICHARDSON

Arctic Ordeal: The Journal of John Richardson

DR. JOHN RICHARDSON'S REPORT TO THE GOVERNMENT

AFTER CAPTAIN FRANKLIN HAD BIDDEN US FAREWELL WE REMAINED seated by the fireside as long as the willows, the men had cut for us before they departed, lasted. We had no *tripe de roche* that day, but drank an infusion of the country tea-plant, which was grateful for its warmth, although it afforded no sustenance. We then retired to bed, where we remained all the next day [October 8], as the weather was stormy, and the snow-drift so heavy, as to destroy every prospect of success in our endeavours to light a fire with the green and frozen willows, which were our only fuel. Through the extreme kindness and forethought of a lady, the party, previous to leaving London, had been furnished with a small collection of religious books, of which we still retained two or three of the most portable, and they proved of incalculable benefit to us. We read portions of them to each other as we lay in bed, in addition to the morning and evening service, and found that they inspired us on each perusal with so strong a sense of the omnipresence of a beneficent God, that our situation, even in these wilds, appeared no longer destitute; and we conversed, not only with calmness, but with cheerfulness, detailing with unrestrained confidence the past events of our lives, and dwelling with hope on our future prospects. Had my poor friend been speared to revisit his native land, I should look back to this period with unalloyed delight.

On the morning of the 29th [October 9th], the weather, although still cold, was clear, and I went out in quest of the *tripe de roche*, leaving Hepburn to cut willows for a fire, and Mr. Hood in bed. I had no success, as yesterday's snow drift was so frozen on the surface of the rocks that I could not collect any of the weed; but, on my return to the tent, I found that Michel, the Iroquois, had come with a note from Mr. Franklin, which stated, that this man, and Jean Baptiste Belanger being unable to proceed, were about to return to us, and that a mile beyond our present encampment there was a clump of pine trees, to which he recommended us to remove the tent. Michel informed us that he quitted Mr. Franklin's party yesterday morning, but, that having missed his way, he had passed the night on the snow a mile or two to the northward of us. Belanger, he said, being impatient, had left the fire about two hours earlier, and, as he had not arrived, he supposed he had gone astray. It will be seen in the sequel, that we had more than sufficient reason to doubt the truth of this story.

Michel now produced a hare and a partrdige which he had killed in the morning. This unexpected supply of provision was received by us with a deep sense of gratitude to the Almighty for his goodness, and we looked upon Michel as the instrument he had chosen to preserve all our lives. He complained of cold, and Mr. Hood offered to share his buffalo robe with him at night; I gave him one of two shirts which I wore, whilst Hepburn, in the warmth of his heart, exclaimed, "How I shall love this man if I find that he does not tell lies like the others." Our meals being finished, we arranged that the greatest part of the things should be carried to the pines the next day; and, after reading the evening service, retired to bed full of hope.

October 10th

Early in the morning Hepburn, Michel, and myself, carried the ammunition, and most of the other heavy articles to the pines. Michel was our guide, and it did not occur to us at the time that his conducting us perfectly straight was incompatible with his story of having gone astray on his way to us. He now informed us that he had, on his way to the tent, left on the hill above the pines a gun and forty-eight balls, which Perrault had given to him when with the rest of Mr. Franklin's party, he took leave of him. It will be seen, on a reference to Mr. Franklin's journal, that Perrault carried his gun and ammunition with him when they parted from Michel and Belanger. After we had made a fire, and drank a little of the country tea, Hepburn and I returned to the tent, where we arrived in the evening, much exhausted with our journey. Michel preferred sleeping where he was, and requested us to leave him the hatchet, which we did, after he had promised to come early in the morning to assist us in carrying the tent and bedding. Mr. Hood remained in bed all day. Seeing nothing of Belanger to-day, we gave him up for lost.

October 11th
After waiting until late in the morning for Michel, who did not come, Hepburn and I loaded ourselves with the bedding, and, accompanied by Mr. Hood, set out for the pines. Mr. Hood was much affected with dimness of sight, giddiness, and other symptoms of extreme debility, which caused us to move very slow, and to make frequent halts. On arriving at the pines, we were much alarmed to find that Michel was absent. We feared that he had lost his way in coming to us in the morning, although it was not easy to conjecture how that could have happened, as our footsteps of yesterday were very distinct. Hepburn went back for the tent, and returned with it after dusk, completely worn out with the fatigue of the day. Michel too arrived at the same time, and relieved our anxiety on his account. He reported that he had been in chase of some deer which passed near his sleeping-place in the morning, and although he did not come up with them, yet that he found a wolf which had been killed by the stroke of a deer's horn, and had brought a part of it. We implicitly believed this story then, but afterwards became convinced from circumstances, the detail of which may be spared, that it must have been a portion of the body of [J.B.] Belanger or Perrault. A question of moment here presents itself; namely, whether he actually murdered these men, or either of them, or whether he found the bodies on the snow. Captain Franklin, who is the best able to judge of this matter, from knowing their situation when he parted from them, suggested the former idea, and that both Belanger and Perrault had been sacrificed. When Perrault turned back, Captain Franklin watched him until he reached a small group of willows, which was immediately adjoining to the fire, and concealed it from view, and at this time the smoke of fresh fuel was distinctly visible. Captain Franklin conjectures, that Michel having already destroyed Belanger, completed his crime by Perrault's death, in order to screen himself from detection. Although this opinion is founded only on circumstances,

and is unsupported by direct evidence, it has been judged proper to mention it, especially as the subsequent conduct of the man shewed that he was capable of committing such a deed. The circumstances are very strong. It is not easy to assign any other adequate motive for his concealing from us that Perrault had turned back, and his request overnight that we should leave him the hatchet; and his cumbering himself with it when he went out in the morning, unlike a hunter who makes use only of his knife when he kills a deer, seem to indicate that he took it for the purpose of cutting up something that he knew to be frozen. These opinions, however, are the result of subsequent consideration. We passed this night in the open air.

October 12th
On the following morning the tent was pitched, and Michel went out early, refused my offer to accompany him, and remained out the whole day. He would not sleep in the tent at night, but chose to lie at the fire-side.

October 13th
On the 13th there was a heavy gale of wind, and we passed the day by the fire.

October 14th
About two, P.M., the gale abating, Michel set out as he said to hunt, but returned unexpectedly in a very short time. This conduct surprised us, and his contradictory and evasory answers to our questions excited some suspicions, but they did not turn towards the truth.

October 15th
In the course of this day Michel expressed much regret that he had stayed behind Mr. Franklin's party, and declared that he would set out for the house at once if he knew the way. We endeavoured to soothe him, and to raise his hopes of the Indians speedily coming to our relief, but without success. He refused to assist us in cutting wood, but about noon, after much solicitation, he set out to hunt. Hepburn gathered a kettle of *tripe de roche*, but froze his fingers. Both Hepburn and I fatigued ourselves much to-day in pursuing a flock of partridges from one part to another of the group of willows, in which the hut was situated, but we were too weak to be able to approach

them with sufficient caution. In the evening Michel returned, having met with no success.

October 16th

Michel refused either to hunt or cut wood, spoke in a very surly manner, and threatened to leave us. Under these circumstances, Mr. Hood and I deemed it better to promise if he would hunt diligently for four days, that then we would give Hepburn a letter for Mr. Franklin, a compass, inform him what course to pursue, and let them proceed together to the fort. The non-arrival of the Indians to our relief, now led us to fear that some accident had happened to Mr. Franklin, and we placed no confidence in the exertions of the Canadians that accompanied him, but we had the fullest confidence in Hepburn's returning the moment he could obtain assistance.

October 17th

On the 17th I went to conduct Michel to where Vaillant's blanket was left, and after walking about three miles, pointed out the hills to him at a distance, and returned to the hut, having gathered a bagful of *tripe de roche* on the way. It was easier to gather this weed on a march than at the tent, for the exercise of walking produced a glow of heat, which enabled us to withstand for a time the cold to which we were exposed in scraping the frozen surface of the rocks. On the contrary, when we left the fire, to collect it in the neighbourhood of the hut, we became chilled at once, and were obliged to return very quickly.

Michel proposed to remain out all night, and to hunt next day on his way back.

October 18th

Michel returned in the afternoon of the 18th, having found the blanket, together with a bag containing two pistols, and some other things which had been left beside it. We had some *tripe de roche* in the evening, but Mr. Hood, from the constant griping it produced, was unable to eat more than one or two spoonfuls. He was now so weak as to be scarcely able to sit up at the fire-side, and complained that the least breeze of wind seemed to blow through his frame. He also suffered much from cold during the night. We lay close to each other, but the heat of the body was no longer sufficient to thaw the frozen rime formed by our breaths on the blankets that covered him.

At this period we avoided as much as possible conversing upon the hopelessness of our situation, and generally endeavoured to lead the conversation towards our future prospects in life. The fact is, that with the decay of our strength, our minds decayed, and we were no longer able to bear the contemplation of the horrors that surrounded us. Each of us, if I may be allowed to judge from my own case, excused himself from so doing by a desire of not shocking the feelings of the others, for we were sensible of one another's weakness of intellect though blind to our own. Yet we were calm and resigned to our fate, not a murmur escaped us, and we were punctual and fervent in our addresses to the Supreme Being.

October 19th
Michel refused to hunt, or even to assist in carrying a log of wood to the fire, which was too heavy for Hepburn's strength and mine. Mr. Hood endeavoured to point out to him the necessity and duty of exertion, and the cruelty of his quitting us without leaving something for our support; but the discourse far from producing any beneficial effect, seemed only to excite his anger, and amongst other expressions, he made use of the following remarkable one: "It is no use hunting, there are no animals, you had better kill and eat me." At length, however, he went out, but returned very soon, with a report that he had seen three deer, which he was unable to follow from having wet his foot in a small stream of water thinly covered with ice, and being consequently obliged to come to the fire. The day was rather mild and Hepburn and I gathered a large kettleful of *tripe de roche;* Michel slept in the tent this night.

Sunday, October 20th
In the morning we again urged Michel to go a hunting that he might if possible leave us some provision, to-morrow being the day appointed for his quitting us; but he shewed great unwillingness to go out, and lingered about the fire, under the pretence of cleaning his gun. After we had read the morning service I went about noon to gather some *tripe de roche,* leaving Mr. Hood sitting before the tent at the fire-side, arguing with Michel; Hepburn was employed cutting down a tree at a short distance from the tent, being desirous of accumulating a quantity of fire wood before he left us. A short time after I went out I heard the report of a gun, and about ten minutes afterward Hepburn

called to me in a voice of great alarm, to come directly. When I arrived, I found poor Hood lying lifeless at the fire-side, a ball having apparently entered his forehead. I was at first horrorstruck with the idea, that in a fit of despondency he had hurried himself into the presence of his Almighty Judge, by an act of his own hand; but the conduct of Michel soon gave rise to other thoughts, and excited suspicions which were confirmed, when upon examining the body, I discovered the shot had entered the back part of the head, and passed out at the forehead, and that the muzzle of the gun had been applied so close as to set fire to the night-cap behind. The gun, which was of the longest kind supplied to the Indians, could not have been placed in a position to inflict such a wound, except by a second person. Upon inquiring of Michel how it happened, he replied, that Mr. Hood had sent him into the tent for the short gun, and that during his absence the long gun had gone off, he did not know whether by accident or not. He held the short gun in his hand at the time he was speaking to me. Hepburn afterwards informed me that previous to the report of the gun Mr. Hood and Michel were speaking to each other in an elevated angry tone; that Mr. Hood being seated at the fire-side, was hid from him by intervening willows, but that on hearing the report he looked up, and saw Michel rising up from before the tent-door, or just behind where Mr. Hood was seated, and then going into the tent. Thinking that the gun had been discharged for the purpose of cleaning it, he did not go to the fire at first; and when Michel called to him that Mr. Hood was dead, a considerable time had elapsed. Although I dared not openly to evince any suspicion that I thought Michel guilty of the deed, yet he repeatedly protested that he was incapable of committing such an act, kept constantly on his guard, and carefully avoided leaving Hepburn and me together. He was evidently afraid of permitting us to converse in private, and whenever Hepburn spoke, he inquired if he accused him of the murder. It is to be remarked, that he understood English very imperfectly, yet sufficiently to render it unsafe for us to speak on the subject in his presence. We removed the body into a clump of willows behind the tent, and, returning to the fire, read the funeral service in addition to the evening prayers. The loss of a young officer, of such distinguished and varied talents and application, may be felt and duly appreciated by the eminent characters under whose command he had served; but the calmness with which he contemplated the probable termination of a life of uncommon promise; and the patience and fortitude with which he sustained, I may venture to say, unparalleled bodily sufferings, can only be known to the companions of his distresses. Owing to the effect that the *tripe de roche* invariably had, when he ventured to taste it, he undoubtedly suffered more than any of the survivors of the party. *Bickersteth's Scripture Help* was lying open beside the body, as if it had fallen from his hand, and it is probable that he was reading it at the instant of his death. We passed the night in the tent together without rest, every one being on his guard.

October 21st
Having determined on going to the Fort, we began to patch and prepare our clothes for the journey. We singed the hair off a part of the buffalo robe that belonged to Mr. Hood, and boiled and ate it. Michel tried to persuade me to go to the woods on the Copper-Mine River, and hunt for deer instead of going to the Fort. In the afternoon a flock of partridges coming near the tent, he killed several which he shared with us.

October 22nd
Thick snowy weather and a head wind prevented us from starting the following day.

October 23rd
The morning of the 23rd we set out, carrying with us the remainder of the singed robe. Hepburn and Michel had each a gun, and I carried a small pistol, which Hepburn had loaded for me. In the course of the march Michel alarmed us so much by his gestures and conduct, was constantly muttering to himself, expressed an unwillingness to go to the Fort, and tried to persuade me to go to the southward to the woods, where he said he could maintain himself all the winter by killing deer. In consequence of this behaviour, and the expression of his countenance, I requested him to leave us and to go to the southward by himself. The proposal increased his ill-nature, he threw out some obscure hints of freeing himself from all restraint on the morrow; and I overheard him muttering threats against Hepburn, whom he openly accused of having told stories against him. He also, for the first time, assumed such a tone of superiority in addressing me, as evinced that he considered us to be completely in his power, and he gave vent to several expressions of hatred towards the white

people, or as he termed us in the idiom of the voyageurs, the French, some of whom, he said, had killed and eaten his uncle and two of his relations. In short, taking every circumstance of his conduct into consideration, I came to the conclusion, that he would attempt to destroy us on the first opportunity that offered, and that he had to be hitherto abstained from doing so from his ignorance of the way to the Fort, but that he would never suffer us to go thither in company with him. In the course of the day he had several times remarked that we were pursuing the same course that Mr. Franklin was doing when he left him, and that by keeping towards the setting sun he could find his way himself. Hepburn and I were not in a condition to resist even an open attack, nor could we by any device escape from him. Our united strength was far inferior to his, and, beside his gun, he was armed with two pistols, and Indian bayonet, and a knife. In the afternoon, coming to a rock on which there was some *tripe de roch,* he halted, and said he would gather it whilst we went on, and that he would soon overtake us. Hepburn and I were now left together for the first time since Mr. Hood's death, and he acquainted me with several material circumstances, which he had observed of Michel's behaviour, and which confirmed me in the opinion that there was no safety for us except in his death, and he offered to be the instrument of it. I determined, however, as I was thoroughly convinced of the necessity of such a dreadful act, to take the whole responsibility upon myself; and immediately upon Michel's coming up, I put an end to his life by shooting him through the head with a pistol. Had my own life alone been threatened, I would not have purchased it by such a measure; but I considered myself as intrusted also with the protection of Hepburn's, a man, who, by his humane attentions and devotedness, had so endeared himself to me, that I felt more anxiety for his safety than for my own. Michel had gathered no *tripe de roche,* and it was evident to us that he had halted for the purpose of putting his gun in order, with the intention of attacking us, perhaps, whilst we were in the act of encamping.

I have dwelt in the preceding part of the narrative upon many circumstances of Michel's conduct, not for the purpose of aggravating his crime, but to put the reader in possession of the reasons that influenced me in depriving a fellow-creature of life. Up to the period of his return to the tent, his conduct had been good and respectful to the officers, and in a conversation between Captain Franklin, Mr. Hood, and myself, at Obstruction Rapid, it had been proposed to give him a reward upon our arrival at a post. His principles, however, unsupported by a belief in the divine truths of Christianity, were unable to withstand the pressure of severe distress. Hs countrymen, the Iroquois, are generally Christians, but he was totally uninstructed and ignorant of the duties inculcated by Christianity; and from his long residence in the Indian country, seems to have imbibed, or retained, the rules of conduct which the southern Indians prescribe to themselves.

October 24th & 25th
On the two following days we had mild but thick snowy weather, and as the view was too limited to enable us to preserve a straight course, we remained encamped amongst a few willows and dwarf pines, about five miles from the tent. We found a species of *cornicularia,* a kind of lichen, that was good to eat when moistened and toasted over the fire; and we had a good many pieces of singed buffalo hide remaining.

October 26th
The weather being clear and extremely cold, we resumed our march, which was very painful from the depth of the snow, particularly on the margins of the small lakes that lay in our route. We frequently sunk under the load of our blankets, and were obliged to assist each other in getting up. After walking about three miles and a half, however, we were cheered by the sight of a large herd of reindeer, and Hepburn went in pursuit of them; but his hand being unsteady through weakness he missed. He was so exhausted by this fruitless attempt that we were obliged to encamp upon the spot, although it was a very unfavourable one.

October 27th
We had fine and clear, but cold, weather. We set out early, and, in crossing a hill, found a considerable quantity of *tripe de roche*. About noon we fell upon Little Marten Lake, having walked about two miles. The sight of a place that we knew inspired us with fresh vigour, and there being comparatively little snow on the ice, we advanced at a pace to which we had lately been unaccustomed. In the afternoon we crossed a recent track of a wolverene, which, from a parallel mark in the snow, appeared to have been dragging something. Hepburn traced it, and

upon the borders of the lake found the spine of a deer, that it had dropped. It was clean picked, and, at least, one season old; but we extracted the spinal marrow from it, which, even in its frozen state, was so acrid as to excoriate the lips. We encamped within sight of the Dog-rib Rock, and from the coldness of the night and the want of fuel, rested very ill.

October 28th

We rose at day-break, but from the want of the small fire, that we usually made in the mornings to warm our fingers, a very long time was spent in making up our bundles. This task fell to Hepburn's share, as I suffered so much from the cold as to be unable to take my hands out of my mittens. We kept a straight course for the Dog-rib Rock, but, owing to the depth of the snow in the valleys we had to cross, did not reach it until late in the afternoon. We would have encamped, but did not like to pass a second night without fire; and though scarcely able to drag our limbs after us, we pushed on to a clump of pines, about a mile to the southward of the rock, and arrived at them in the dusk of the evening. During the last few hundred yards of our march, our track lay over some large stones, amongst which I fell down upwards of twenty times, and became at length so exhausted that I was unable to stand. If Hepburn had not exerted himself far beyond his strength, and speedily made the encampment and kindled a fire, I must have perished on the spot. This night we had plenty of dry wood.

October 29th

We had clear and fine weather. We set out at sunrise, and hurried on in our anxiety to reach the house, but our progress was much impeded by the great depth of the snow in the valleys. Although every spot of ground over which we travelled to-day had been repeatedly trodden by us, yet we got bewildered in a small lake. We took it for Marten Lake which was three times its size, and fancied that we saw the rapid and the grounds about the fort, although they were still far distant. Our disappointment when this illusion was dispelled, by our reaching the end of the lake, so operated on our feeble minds as to exhaust our strength, and we decided upon encamping; but upon ascending a small eminence to look for a clump of wood, we caught a glimpse of the Big-Stone, a well known rock upon the summit of a hill opposite to the Fort, and determined upon proceeding. In the evening we saw several large herds of rein-deer, but Hepburn who used to be considered a good marksman, was now unable to hold the gun straight, and although he got near them all his efforts proved fruitless. In passing through a small clump of pines we saw a flock of partridges, and he succeeded in killing one after firing several shots. We came in sight of the fort at dusk.

IN THE END NINE OF THE TWENTY MEN WHO STARTED ON THE EXPEDITION *survived. Eleven were dead, four of them, including Hood, having been killed, two apparently having been eaten by the crazed voyageur Michel. The remainder died of starvation. Franklin had mapped a small portion of coastline. He had led his men beyond the point of no return, and that return was an unmitigated disaster for them all.*

Yet he returned to England a hero. The Admiralty elevated him to the rank of captain. London lionized him. He had eaten his boots to survive, and that seemed to be enough to make him, not a fool, not incompetent, but a figure of romance. It is an amazing story, most of all for this very fact—that Franklin's failures of judgment led to such grand rewards.

While John Franklin was struggling to survive in the Barren Lands of northern Canada, William Parry was back in the Arctic looking for the Northwest Passage in the unlikely vicinity, once again, of Hudson Bay. It should have been obvious by now that neither Hudson Bay nor Foxe Basin above it had an exit to the west. Foxe in the seventeenth century and Middleton in the eighteenth had explored these areas thoroughly enough to demonstrate that there was no way out. But John Barrow was not persuaded. Barrow had his own conceptions of geography and he held to them stubbornly and no matter what. Off Parry went, therefore, and with him went George F. Lyon, another naval officer who had already achieved a measure of fame by surviving a trip into sub-Saharan Africa in search of the Niger River, another of John Barrow's pet projects. So Parry spent the late summer of 1821 searching Repulse Bay—once again—fruitlessly, and the summer of 1822 in Foxe Basin.

This time, however, they did find a passage: Fury and Hecla Strait, named after their ships. But it is a narrow passage, so narrow that the ice in it seldom, if ever, melts (now, with global warming, that situation may have changed). It was as good as finding nothing. Parry resolved to spend a second winter in the Arctic to make sure the next summer that the strait stayed frozen, but he was pessimistic about the result, and he was right to be so. His last glimpse of Fury and Hecla Strait found it frozen solid.

The voyage is notable nevertheless for the degree of intimacy with which the men on board the two ships became acquainted with the Eskimos of Foxe Basin, who had little previous contact with white men, even the men of the Hudson's Bay Company. Frozen in, with the Eskimos often camped right beside them, it was a golden opportunity to do some early anthropological work, and George F. Lyon in particular took advantage of it. Lyon already, in Africa, had had a great deal of contact with other ways of life and had eaten things no ordinary Englishman would dream of touching. Lyon in the Arctic even submitted to a tattoo on his arm, done by an Eskimo tattoo artist. Our next excerpt comes from Lyon's journal of the voyage and describes some of the native life he observed. It is a richer portrait than even John Ross's portrait of the "Arctic Highlanders" in Greenland.

GEORGE F. LYON

The Private Journal of Captain George F. Lyon of the

H   Hecla, *1824*

THE PECULIAR SHAPE OF THE CANOES MAY BE CONCEIVED FROM THE
above account; but the dimensions of one may serve as a description of all the
rest. It may be that some differ in length, but in width or form they are the same.
The head and stern, if they may be so called, are equally sharp, and the whole
body of the vessel has been very justly compared in shape with a weaver's shut-
tle. The ribs, of which there are sixty or seventy, are made of ground willow, small
bones, whalebone, or if it can be procured, of good grained wood. The whole
contrivance does not weigh above 50 or 60 lbs., so that a man easily carries his
kayak on his head, which, by the form of the rim, he cando without the assistance of his hands.

An Eskimaux prides himself in the neat appearance of his boat, and has a
warm skin placed in its bottom to sit on. His posture is with the legs pointed
forward, and he cannot change his position unless with the assistance of
another person: in all cases where a weight is to be lifted, and alteration of
stowage, or any movement to be made, it is customary for two kayaks to lie
together; and the paddle of each being placed across the other, they form a steady
double boat. These Eskimaux have not the art of turning their boat over, and
recovering themselves by a skillful management of the paddle, under water, like
the Greenlanders. An inflated seal's bladder forms, invariably, part of the
equipage of a canoe, and the weapons are confined in their places by small lines
of whalebone, stretched tightly across the upper covering, so as to receive the

points or handles of the spears beneath them. Flesh is frequently stowed within the stem or stern, as are also birds and eggs; but a seal, although round, and easily made to roll, is so neatly balanced on the upper part of the boat as seldom to require a lashing. When the Eskimaux are not paddling, their balance must be nicely preserved, and a trembling motion is always observable in the boat.

The most difficult position for managing a kayak, is when going before the wind, and with a little swell running. Any inattention would instantly, by exposing the broadside, overturn this frail vessel. The dexterity with which they are turned, the velocity of their way, and the extreme elegance of form of the kayaks, renders an Eskimaux an object of the highest interest when sitting independently, and urging his course towards his prey.

The next object of importance to the boat is the sledge, which finds occupations during at least three-fourths of the year. A man who possesses both this and a canoe is considered a person of property. To give a particular description of the sledge would be impossible, as there are no two actually alike; and the materials of which they are composed are as various as their form. The best are made of the jaw-bones of the whale, sawed to about two inches in thickness, and in depth from six inches to a foot. These are the runners, and are shod with a thin plank of the same material: the side pieces are connected by means of bones, pieces of wood, or deers' horns, lashed across with a few inches space between each, and they yield to any great strain which the sledge may receive. The general breadth of the upper part of the sledge is about twenty inches, but the runners lean inwards, and therefore at bottom it is rather greater. The length of bone sledges is from four feet to fourteen. Their weight is necessarily great; and one of moderate size, that is to say, about ten or twelve feet, was found to be 217 lbs. The skin of the walrus is very commonly used during the coldest part of the winter, as being hard frozen, and resembling an inch board, with ten times the strength, for runners. Another ingenious contrivance is, by casing moss and earth in seal's skin, so that by pouring a little water, a round hard bolster is easily formed. Across all these kinds of runners there is the same arrangement of bones, sticks, &c. on the upper part; and the surface which passes over the snow is coated with ice, by mixing snow with fresh water, which assists greatly in lightening the load for the dogs, as it slides forwards with ease. We sometimes saw a person who had but one or two dogs, driving in a little tray made of a rough piece of walrus hide, or a flat slab of ice, hollowed like a bowl. Boys frequently amuse themselves by yoking several dogs to a small piece of seal's skin, and sitting on it, holding by the traces. Their plan is then to set off at full speed; and he who bears the greatest number of bumps before he relinquishes his hold, is considered a very fine fellow.

There are various kinds of spears, but their difference is chiefly in consequence of the substances of which they are composed, and not in their general form. A want of proper materials has been the means of restricting the northern tribes to few varieties; but I shall describe those we procured in Hudson's Strait collectively with others obtained at Igloolik. The principal spears are four in number, and are as follows:

Ka-te-leek, which is a large and strong-handled spear, with an ivory point for despatching any wounded animal in the water. It is never thrown, but has a place appropriated for it on the kayak, and is seldom seen amongst the northern tribes.

Akliak, or oonak. A lighter kind than the former; also ivory headed. It has a bladder fastened to it, and has a loose head with a line attached; this being darted into an animal, is instantly liberated from the handle which give the impetus. Some few of these weapons were constructed of the solid ivory of the unicorn's horn, about four feet in length, and remarkably well rounded and polished. These were seen at Igloolik only; ivory being more easily attainable than wood, or bone of the whale's ribs, which is also used.

Ip-poo-too-yoo, is another kind of hand-spear, varying but little from the one last described. It has, however, no appendages.

Noogh-wit. This is one of two kinds, but both are used for striking birds, young animals, or fish. The first has a double fork at the extremity, and there are three other barbed ones at about half its length, diverging in different directions, so that if the end pair should miss, some of the centre ones might strike. The second kind has only three barbed forks at the head. All the points are of ivory, and the natural curve of the walrus tusk favours and facilitates their construction.

The whole of the above weapons as described by Crantz under the same names, as being used by the Greenlanders. There is, however, an instrument of which I believe he gives no account, as probably it does not exist there. It is a kind of nippers called kak-ke-way, which are used in taking salmon, and even smaller fish. When sealing on the ice, spare khiat-kos and liners are taken, and the panna and oonak are the only weapons. The others are merely carried on the kayak. A large inflated seal's skin or bladder is used, with a khiat-ko attached to it, in wearying a whale, unicorn, or walrus, and is called awataak.

Amongst the minor instruments of the ice-hunting are a long bone feeler for plumbing any cracks through which seals are suspected of breathing, and also for trying the safety of the road. Another contrivance is occasionally used with the same effect as the float of a fishing line. Its purpose is to warn the hunter who is watching a seal hole, when the animal rises to the surface, so that he may strike without seeing, or being seen by his prey. This is a most delicate little rod of bone or ivory, of about a foot in length, and the thickness of a fine knitting-needle. At the lower end is a small knob like a pin's head, and the upper extremity has a fine piece of sinew tied to it, so as to fasten it loosely to the side of the hole. The animal on rising does not perceive so small an object hanging in the water, and pushes it up with his nose, when the watchful Eskimaux observing his little beacon in motion, strikes down, and secures his prize.

Small ivory pegs or pins are used to stop the holes made by the spears in the animal's body; thus the blood, a great luxury to the natives, is saved.

The same want of wood which renders it necessary to find substitutes in the construction of spears, also occasions the great variety of bows. The horn of the musk ox, thinned horns of deer, or other bony substances, are as frequently used or met with, as wood in the manufacture of these weapons, in which elasticity is a very secondary consideration. Three or four pieces of horn or wood are frequently joined together in one bow, —the strength lying alone in a vast collection of small plaited sinews; these, to the number of perhaps a hundred, run down the back of the bow, and being quite tight, and having the spring of catgut, cause the weapon, when unstrung, to turn the wrong way: when bent, their united strength and elasticity are amazing. The bowstring is of fifteen or twenty plaits, each loose from the other, but twisted round when in use, so that a few additional turns will at any time alter its length. The general length of the bows is about three feet and a half.

The arrows are short, light, and formed according to no general rule as to length or thickness. A good one has half the shaft of bone, and a head of hard slate, or a small piece of iron; others have sharply pointed bone heads: none are barbed. Two feathers are used for the end, and are tied opposite each other with the flat sides parallel. A neatly formed case contains the bow and a few arrows: seal's skin is preferred for this purpose, as more effectually resisting the wet than any other. A little bag, which is attached to the side, contains a stone for sharpening, and some spare arrowheads carefully wrapped up in a piece of skin.

The bow is held in a horizontal position, and though capable of great force, is rarely used at a greater distance than from twelve to twenty yards.

The peculiar term by which the search for sea-animals is distinguished, is ma-ook-pok; but the severity of the climate prevented our people from seeing any regular chase; and as we could only judge from report, and from the expressive pantomimic description of the natives, I cannot pretend to offer any connected account on this subject.

Where the ice is of sufficient strength to bear a particular form, the breathing-places of seals bear great resemblance to mole-hills, and have a small crack in the upper part. By this kind of mound the hunter stands, and listens until he hears the animal breathing, which assures him that the place is tenanted, and his operations commence accordingly. On striking, the first care is to catch the line behind one leg, so as to act as a strong check; and for farther security, a hitch is also taken round the ring finger, which sometimes is terribly lacerated, and even torn off by the struggles of a large animal. The spear being at liberty, is now used to stab the seal until it dies, and the hole being enlarged, it is drawn out on the ice. The carcass speedily freezes, and is then fit to be drawn home to the huts. The walrus is occasionally taken in the same manner; but it is only when he has no open water to range in, that he is found under young ice. The general manner of striking him is when he rises amongst loose, heavy pieces of ice, which are moving under the influence of wind or tide. If two or three men are together, the operation is comparatively easy; but we have many accounts of unfortunate persons who have been drawn under the ice and drowned, owing to insecure footing, or an entangled line. The animals caught amongst the young or moving ice, and in those places where particularly favourable or the contrary, are three: the walrus, *trichicus rosmarus* of Linnaeus, or ay-wek of the Eskimaux. Small seal, *p. vitellina* of Linnaeus, or net-yek of the Eskimaux.

One method of killing these animals in the summer is ingenious. When the hunters, in their canoes, perceive a large herd sleeping on the floating ice, as is their custom, they paddle to some other piece near them, which is small enough to be moved. On this they lift their canoes, and then bore several holes, through which they fasten their tough lines, and when every thing is ready, they silently paddle the hummock towards their prey, each man sitting by his own line and spear. In this manner they reach the ice on which the walruses are lying snoring; and if they please, each man may strike an animal, though, in general, two persons attack the same beast. The wounded and startled walrus rolls instantly to the water, but the shatko, or harpoon, being well fixed, he cannot escape from the hummock on which the Eskimaux have fastened the line. When the animal becomes a little weary, the hunter launches his canoe, and lying out of his reach spears him to death.

The ooghioo rises occasionally in holes at no great distance from the edge of the field, but the netyek is found many miles from any open water. The latter, therefore, is the principal and only certain support during the greater portion of the severe winter, and it makes a perfectly circular hole, by which it rises to breathe, even through ice many feet in thickness. This opening it keeps continually cleared, of a sufficient size for the admission of its body, allowing the top alone to freeze partially over. It is thus easily discovered by the Eskimaux, an inhabited hole being always distinguished by its perfect form. The process in taking seals in these situations is rather different from the way of killing them in the young ice; and I have seen what I believe is a general custom, practised in two instances. A small wall of slabs of snow being raised near the hole, the hunter sits within it, having previously enlarged the seal-hole, when the animal raises its head and shoulders out of the water, without fear. This he repeats once or twice with increased confidence, and being in no haste to dive again, the hunter rises suddenly, and throws his spear into him. A second way is by covering the seal hole over with snow, and then putting the end of the spear through it, to make an opening about as large as the neck of a bottle. The spear is then withdrawn. The hunter meanwhile having a wall to shelter him from the wind, sits quietly on a snow bench near the hole, and having his weapons ready, listens attentively until he hears the seal breathing beneath the snow. He then rises without noise, and with all his force strikes through the light snow, generally with success. This is the plan during the severe and dark part of the winter; and a poor fellow will sometimes sit ten or twelve hours in this manner, at a temperature of 30 or 40 degrees below zero, without even hearing a seal.

It would be needless for me to attempt any description of the Polar bear. An

Eskimaux, with three or four dogs, will instantly attack one of these animals without thinking of any thing but the capture of a delicate meal, and a good skin for clothing. The dogs no sooner see the unwieldy bear, than giving tongue, they chase and keep him at bay until their master comes up, who throws the khiatko into him, if he finds a piece of ice around which he can secure the line, or otherwise darts the spear alone behind the shoulder. He then trusts entirely to his own activity and the spirit of his dogs, and leaping from side to side, avoids the furious springs of the wounded animal. If the spear drops from the wound, it is again thrown, and with better effect; but if it holds, the dogs attack the animal's legs, and the man rushes on with his panna, and despatches his enemy.

The females which have their young cubs with them, are far more to be dreaded than the males, though not much more than half their size. An Eskimaux will, however, attack the mother first, and afterwards kill the two cubs, even when nearly as large as their dam.

Dogs. These useful creatures being indispensable attendants on the Eskimaux, drawing home whatever captures are made, as well as frequently carrying their masters to the chase, I know of no more proper place to introduce them, than as a part of the hunting establishment. Having myself possessed, during our second winter, a team of eleven very fine animals, I was enabled to become better acquainted with their good qualities than could possibly have been the case by the casual visits of Eskimaux to the ships.

The form of the Eskimaux dog is very similar to that of our shepherd's dogs in England, but he is more muscular and broad chested, owing to the constant and severe work to which he is brought up. His ears are pointed, and the aspect of the head is somewhat savage. In size a fine dog is about the height of the Newfoundland breed, but broad like a mastiff in every part, except the nose. The hair of the coat is in summer, as well as in winter, very long, but during the cold season, a soft downy under covering is found, which does not appear in warm weather. Young dogs are put into harness as soon as they can walk, and being tied up, soon acquire a habit of pulling, in their attempts to recover their liberty, or to roam in quest of their mothers. When about two months old, they are put into the sledge with the grown dogs, and sometimes eight or ten little ones are under the charge of some steady old animal, where with frequent, and sometimes cruel beatings, they soon receive a competent education. Every dog is distinguished by a particular name, and the angry repetition of it has an effect as instantaneous as an application of the whip, which instrument is of an immense length, having a lash of from eighteen to twenty-four feet, while the handle is of one foot only. With this, by throwing it on one side or the other of the leader, and repeating certain words, the animals are guided or stopped. Wah-aya,- aya, whooa, to the right. A-wha, a-wha, a-whut, to the left. A-look, turn, and wooa, stop. When the sledge is stopped, they are all taught to lie down, by throwing the whip gently over their backs, and they will remain in this position even for hours, until their master returns to them.

Such of the natives as have not a sufficient number of dogs to draw a sledge are followed to Maookpok by all which belong to them. A walrus is frequently drawn along by three or four of them, and seals are sometimes carried home in the same manner, though I have, in some instances, seen a dog bring home the greater part of a seal in panniers placed across his back. This mode of conveyance is often used in the summer, and the dogs also carry skins or furniture overland to the sledges, when their masters are going on any expedition.

It might be supposed that in so cold a climate these animals had peculiar periods of gestation, like the wild creatures; but on the contrary, they bear young at every season of the year, and seldom exceed five at a litter. In December, with the thermometer 40° below zero, the females were, in several instances, in heat. Cold has very little effect on these animals, for although the dogs at the huts slept within the snow passages, mine at the ships had no shelter, but lay alongside, with the thermometer at 42° and 44°, and with as little concern as if the weather had been mild.

I found, by several experiments, that three of my dogs could draw me on a sledge, weighing 100 lbs., at the rate of one mile in six minutes; and as a proof of the strength of a well-grown dog, my leader drew 196 lbs. singly, and to the same distance in eight minutes.[1] Whoever has had the patience to read this account, will laugh at my introducing my team so frequently in a professed account of

---

[1] At another time, seven of my dogs ran a mile in four minutes thirty seconds, drawing a heavy sledge full of men. I stopped to time them; but had I ridden they would have gone equally fast: in fact, I afterwards found that ten dogs took five minutes to go over the same space. Afterwards, in carrying stores to the Fury, one mile distant, nine dogs drew 1611 lbs. in the space of nine minutes! My sledge was on wooden runners, neither shod nor iced; had they been the latter, at least 40 lbs. might have been added for every dog.

Eskimaux dogs generally; but I can only offer, as my excuse, the merits of my poor animals, with which I have often, with one or two persons besides myself, on the sledge, returned home from the *Fury*, a distance of near a mile, in pitchy darkness, and amidst clouds of snow drift, entirely under the care of those trusty servants, who, with their noses down to the snow, have galloped on board entirely directed by their sense of smelling. Had they erred, or been at al restive, no human means could have brought us on board until the return of clear weather.

I shall first enumerate such creatures as are procured by the bow, and amongst these shall include birds of different species.

Of the form of the rein-deer it is unnecessary for me to attempt a particular description. He visits the polar regions at the latter end of May or the early part of June, and remains until late in September. On his first arrival he is thin, and his flesh is tasteless, but the short summer is sufficient to fatten him to two or three inches on the haunches. When feeding on level ground, an Eskimaux makes no attempt to approach him, but should a few rocks be near, the wary hunter feels secure of his prey. Behind one of these he cautiously creeps, and having laid himself very close, with his bow and arrow before him, imitates the bellows of the deer when calling to each other. Sometimes, for more complete deception, the hunter wears his deer-skin coat and hood so drawn over his head, as to resemble, in a great measure, the unsuspecting animals he is enticing. Though the bellow proves a considerable attraction, yet if a man has great patience, he may do without it, and may be equally certain that his prey will ultimately come to examine him; the rein-deeer being an inquisitive animal, and at the same time so silly, that if he sees any suspicious object which is not actually chasing him, he will gradually, and after many caperings and forming repeated circles, approach nearer and nearer to it. The Eskimaux rarely shoot until the creature is within twelve paces, and I have frequently been told of their being killed at a much shorter distance. It is to be observed, that the hunters never appear openly, but employ stratagem for their purpose; thus by patience and ingenuity rendering their rudely formed bows, and still worse arrows, as effective as the rifles of Europeans. When two men hunt in company, they sometimes purposely show themselves to the deer, and when his attention is fully engaged, walk slowly away from him, one before the other. The deer follows, and when the hunters arrive near a stone, the foremost drops behind it and prepares his bow, while his companion continues walking steadily forward. This latter the deer still follows unsuspectingly, and thus passes near the concealed man, who takes a deliberate aim and kills the animal. When the deer assemble in herds, there are particular passes which they invariably take, and on being driven to them are killed with arrows by the men, while the women, with shouts, drive them to the water. Here they swim with the ease and activity of waterdogs; the people in kayaks chasing and easily spearing them: the carcasses float, and the hunter then presses forward and kills as many as he finds in his track. No springes, or traps, are used in the capture of these animals, as is practised to the southward, in consequence of the total absence of standing wood. Musk-oxen are killed in the same manner as deer; and with both it is requisite, on account of their quick scent, to make advances against the wind, or, to use a sea phrase, to have them in the "wind's eye." Hares are also killed with arrows, and being quiet animals, are easily caught sitting, by those who know their haunts. Grouse being in large coveys, present an extensive mark for the hunter; and as they are stupid, and not easily persuaded to fly, will see the arrow fall amongst them with the greatest unconcern. The shooter walks to pick it up, and they remove a few paces only before him, so that he has repeated shots. Swans, geese, ducks, and other birds, if lying in the hunter's path, are killed by the same weapon; but they are so much more easily obtained by other means, that he never moves out for the express purpose of shooting them. Opinions vary considerably respecting the skill which the Eskimaux display in archery; but I am of that party which condemns them as very indifferent marksmen.

Ducks and divers of all descriptions, which frequent lakes, are caught by whalebone nooses, which being fastened in great numbers to a long line, and stretched between stones, placed at intervals across shallow lakes, easily catch the birds while diving for their prey, or more frequently, from being alarmed by women and children stationed for the purpose. The noose hangs below the water, but no sooner closes on a bird than the captive rises to the surface, where, when seen, some one wades in and secures him. Swans are caught by springes set in their nest, or near it, and the whalebone has sufficient strength to hold the bird by the foot until it can be taken out. The moulting season is the great bird harvest, as a few persons, wading in the shallow lakes, can soon tire out and catch the birds by hand. Marmottes and ermines, but more especially the former, are caught by women, who suspend a noose over their hole, and catch them with great ease. Marmotte skins are frequently procured, in one summer, by a single female, to make herself a pair of breeches, in which she takes great pride; and some even equip a child or two besides themselves.

I now come to the traps used to catch wolves and foxes, and which are of two kinds in winter. The first is made of strong slabs of ice, long and narrow, so that a fox can with difficulty turn himself in it, but a wolf must actually remain in the position in which he is taken. The door is a heavy portcullis of ice, sliding in two well secured grooves of the same substance, and is kept up by a line, which, passing over the top of the trap, is carried through a hole at the farthest extremity: to the end of the line is fastened a small hoop of whalebone, and to this any kind of flesh bait is attached. From the slab which terminates the trap, a projection of ice, or a peg of wood or bone, points inwards near the bottom, and under this the hoop is lightly hooked: the slightest pull at the bait liberates it, and the door falls in an instant. Foxes are sometimes taken out by hand, but a wolf is speared as he lies confined. The second kind of trap is like a small lime-kiln in form, having a hole near the top, within which the bait is placed, and the foxes, for these animals alone are thus taken, are obliged to advance to it over a piece of whalebone, which, bending beneath their weight, lets them into prison, and then resumes its former position: thus a great number of them are sometimes caught in a night. In the summer they are but rarely taken, and it is then by means of a trap of stones, formed like the ice-trap, with a falling door.

There is less art practised in procuring fish than any other article of Eskimaux food. One kind only is caught in salt water; this is the sillock, a small dark fish, left in pools at certain spots, by the falling of the tide, when it is easily taken by the children.

In fresh water, at the spawning season, salmon are caught in great numbers at the little rushes of water which fall from particular lakes or rivulets into the sea. The Eskimaux wade up to the middle in the water, and with the kak-ke-way, or little nippers, continue striking down until a fish is taken; they then throw their captive on shore, and continue striking for others. One man can load a sledge with them in a day, but the season does not last long, and many hands render the prey timid. The salmon we saw were small sweet-flavoured fish, weighing about 6 or 7 lbs. The other very simple process of taking salmon trout in lakes, is by having a small ivory fish attached to a string, continually bobbed in the water until some curious trout comes to gaze at it, when he is immediately struck by the kakkeway. The fishers are generally boys, and the season is at the close of the year, when the newly formed ice will safely bear their weight.

I have seen a rude kind of fish-hook, but whether it is used for taking fish with bait, or by jigging for them, I know not, although, from the description of the natives, I suspect the latter.

The propensity to ramble is one of the remarkable characteristics of the Eskimaux, who, in this particular, resemble the Arabs of the desert, prefering the most desolate and inhospitable countries to those which are clothed with food and vegetation. It is true that the sea animals are found in abundance in the icy ocean, yet there are some stations which have also rein-deer, musk oxen, and birds, in addition to these, but which are rarely visited, though in nearly the same parallel of latitude. There are no regularly established settlements along an immense extent of coast, at which the Eskimaux can be said to have a fixed habitation; but there are three or four which are considered as general mustering places, and are, from year to year, changing their population. Thus for instance, Igloolik, in consequence of our known intention of visiting it, proved the most attractive wintering quarter, and at least half the dwellers along the coast hurried to assemble there. This last place, Repulse Bay, Akoolee (by all accounts three days west of it, and on the sea coast), and Noowook, or Wager River, are the principal rendezvous along the N.E. shores of America: and at some one of these there is annually a gathering of the small hunting parties, who have roamed about during the summer, and who winter in a body. There are few people who have not seen each of the above-named places; and the importance assumed by a great Eskimaux traveller, is fully equal to that displayed by Europeans who have seen the world. Nothing indeed affords more gratification to a man newly arrived, than to ask him of the places he has recently quitted, unless it be to inquire also of his success in hunting or fishing, or the abundance of food he has enjoyed during the summer. In travelling, the Eskimaux are entirely guided by well-known points or objects on the shore; and therefore, though they know the cardinal points of the compass, and are also acquainted with particular stars, they have, as far as I can learn, but little occasion to depend on the clearness of the heavens, or the presence of the sun. The setting in of winter, when the ground is well covered with snow, and the land ice firmly formed, is one of the principal times of moving, as the sledges can then travel conveniently, and food is obtained from day to day, in consequence of their vicinity to open water.

At night snow huts are speedily constructed, warm skins are spread, and the lamps are lighted for cooking and heating the dwellings. In the morning the travellers pursue their route. Of the rate at which certain space may be travelled over, it is impossible to have an idea, as all accounts vary; for this reason, if a great prize of flesh is taken, it is customary to remain and feed until it is devoured; if repeated success attends the hunters, many of these feasting stoppages occur; but if, on the other hand, their captures are few, they have nothing to impede their progress. The second time of journeying is in the early summer, before the land ice has parted from the shores; along this the sledges proceed easily, as it is then free from snow. At night tents are pitched on the shore, from which also the winter clothing has began to disappear, and in consequence, deer are found travelling northwards.

Here, as in autumn, success, or the contrary, determines the period of travelling. A third way of passing from place to place, in summer, is by moving along amongst the hills, killing deer, catching fish and small animals. At the close of this short season of happiness, the settlement nearest at hand is selected for the winter quarters. If small rivers or lakes lie across the track, the men ferry over their wives and children on their kayaks, which generally are carried with them in frames, one person being taken across at a time: if grown up, they lie on their belly, and balance with hands and legs on the hind covering of the boat; but if children, they are seated in the lap of the man who paddles. Any weighty goods, for example, a bone sledge, &c. are frequently left in store on the banks; and as every streamlet, lake, bay, point, or island, has a name, and even certain piles of stones have also appellations, it is easy, in some ensuing year, to find the things which are buried, or even to describe their situation to others. It is remarkable, that in enumerating the various sleeps, or days' journeys along the shore, every one has a particular name, in the same manner as the Alams, or piles of stones on the African desert, and which are also placed by travellers to mark the usual resting-places or wells.

The Eskimaux, even those who have roamed to a short distance only, are acquainted traditionally with their own country; and I have seen charts of a line of coast drawn by persons who never were on it, with nearly the same remarks, and exactly the same names, as those traced by experienced travellers.

The whole space of country traversed by the tribe with whom we were acquainted extends from Noowook to Igloolik, and is about ninety miles north of this latter; a distance of but few miles in a direct line, but comprehending an immense number of deep inlets, bays, and islands. There are again distant tribes, with whom communication is occasionally held, and who are situated eight or ten days to the north-eastward. This distant tribe, from all accounts, differs, and indeed is distinct from our people, yet intermarriages have taken place amongst them, and there are annually some travellers to and from them; but this occurs before the sea begins to break up, as it is over salt water ice that four days' journey must be performed. There are, besides, some smaller establishments on various northern islands, and in bays, of which, as I have not obtained satisfactory intelligence, I shall make no other mention than that they are strangers. One nation, however, is nearer at hand, respecting whom none of our informants seem well acquainted; those are the inhabitants of Southampton Island, which, though in sight from Repulse Bay and Noowook, appears never to be visited. Our people gave to it, and to its natives, the name of Khiad-ler-mi-o; and it is observable, that they hold these near, but unknown neighbours, in the most sovereign contempt, considering them as savages, and as vastly inferior to themselves.

Captain Parry agrees with me in opinion, that the term I have employed is used by our polished acquaintances in the same manner, and to the same extent, as the appellation of barbari, which the Greeks, and after them the Romans, so liberally bestowed on all other nations but their own. The savages we saw in Hudson's Strait, and the land they occupy, appear to be quite unknown, and for a very clear reason. No oomiaks have been seen, or are used by our tribe, and no direct communication therefore we can ever have taken place by families, and perhaps so rarely by single kayaks, as not to be remembered.

The Eskimaux do not, like many other wild people, imagine that there is no world besides that which they occupy; but have some faint ideas of what the unseen countries are, and take great pleasure in hearing of them. They have many traditionary stories of Kabloona and Indians; of the latter of whom, under the name It-kagh-lie, they speak with fear and abhorrence: but the former, unlike the kabloonas of the early Greenlanders, are not looked upon as differing in species from themselves, but as a good people, who have plenty of wood and iron. This character, of course, may be traced from the time of the establish-

ment of our factories in Hudson's Bay, which have a constant communication
with the Noowook people through the intervening tribes, who however do not
constitute a part of the northern family, or, as far as I can learn, form any settlements north of Chesterfield Inlet, and rarely even so high as that place.

The limits of our certain information are these: Noowook to the southward,
Igloolik to the northward, and the land between them bounded on either side
by sea. Thus, at Akkolee, three days to the westward of Repulse Bay, according
to all accounts, the main ocean is arrived at. It stretches to the westward as far
as can be seen from the settlement; but a farther knowledge does not seem to
have been obtained, as it is the opinion of the Eskimaux that no animals for
food are to be found along its banks. From Akkoolee the sea is traced to the
northward as far as the strait which we examined in September 1822, and which
is named by the natives Khee-mig, or the closed, being, as we found it, constantly
choked with ice. None have passed this by water, yet it opens to the westward
in the main ocean. The islands to the north of this strait are large, but it is known
that a sea, perhaps a frozen one, is beyond them. Of the eastern coast I need
make no mention, as we have examined it all from Repulse Bay; but I cannot
conclude without bestowing deserved praise on several of our native hydro-
graphers, for the wonderful correctness of their charts of the coast.

I verily believe that there does not exist a more honest set of people than
the tribe with whom we had so long an acquaintance. Amongst themselves they
never even touch each other's property without permission, and on board the
ships their scruples were the same. I have mentioned a few trifling appropri-
ations, for thefts I can hardly call them, which were made without our consent;
but it is only justice to allow that our unreserved distribution of iron, and the
quantity of empty tin vessels thrown away on the dirt heap alongside, were of
themselves sufficient inducement for some few of the natives to take such articles away, even from the decks.

We should also consider the amazing temptations constantly thrown in the
way of poor ignorant savages, possessed neither of wood nor iron, and esteeming these two substances as much as we do gold or jewels. Our acquaintances,
on the whole, amounted to about 200 people, yet only three out of that number were considered as determined thieves, and they performed their work so
clumsily as to be instantly detected. To weigh with these, very numerous
instances of honesty might be mentioned; and when things have been really

dropped on the ice, or otherwise lost, the Eskimaux, on picking them up, have invariably brought them to be owned on board. Notwithstanding this, however, they have one very glaring and yet natural fault, which is Envy. This passion exists amongst them to the highest degree. The possession of any desirable article by another, is sufficient to draw down on him a bad name from the man who covets it; and the women are much addicted to blackening the character of any sister who enjoys a more than usual quantity of beads, tin pots, &c. This vice leads naturally to its very near relation,

Every one begs; but their demands are invariably introduced with a piteous story of the favour conferred on some other, and an assertion of their own right to be equally well treated. Yet, when presents are given, they are never content, and the passion appears to increase with the favours received.

Gratitude is not only rare, but absolutely unknown amongst them, either by action, word, or look, beyond the first outcry of satisfaction. Nursing their sick, burying the dead, clothing and feeding the whole tribe, furnishing the men with weapons, and the women and children with ornaments, are insufficient to awaken a grateful feeling, and the very people who relieved their distresses when starving, are laughed at in time of plenty, for the quantity and quality of the food which was bestowed in charity.

The envious disposition of these people naturally leads them into falsehood; but their lies consist only in vilifying each other's character, with false accusations of theft or ill behaviour. When asking questions of an individual, it is but rarely that he will either advance or persist in an untruth. They are very tenacious of being termed "thief," or "liar." I am sorry to be so ungallant as to agree with Crantz, that lying, envy, and quarrelling, are almost exclusively confined to the ladies; and to this list begging may safely be added.

Of hospitality, we had a most convincing proof in the treatment we received when strangers, wet and cold, we found shelter for a night in their tents, July 16th, 1822. On that occasion, both sexes gave up their clothes and bedding for our use, warming us, hauling our boat over the ice, and assisting us in every way, and in the kindest manner. The women in particular, though insufferably dirty, and covered with train [*whale*] oil, showed the greatest tenderness and solicitude for our comfort, though subsequently they were too apt to remind us, whenever they wanted any thing, of the shelter they had once afforded us. An Eskimaux is equally hospitable as an Arab, and whatever food he possesses is free to all who enter.

He never eats with closed doors, but by his manner convinces his visitors they are welcome. I have slept seven or eight times, without another European, in different huts; and invariably have met with the same attention; my property was respected by my hosts, even though begged by others; the best seat was assigned, and a portion of food offered me, while I was even thanked for accepting and eating it. As a proof that all this proceeded from motives of pure hospitality, if I the next day entered the hut, and asked even a bit of moss, I was required to pay for it, besides which every thing in my possession was begged of me.

Though the Eskimaux do not possess much of the milk o f human kindness, yet their even temper is in the highest degree praiseworthy. In pain, cold, starvation, disappointment, or under rough treatment, their good humor is rarely ruffled. Few have ever shown symptoms of sulkiness, and even then for a short time only. Those who for an instant feel anger at neglect, or at being punished for some offence, are, in a few moments, as lively and as well disposed to the persons who affronted them as if nothing had occurred. No serious quarrels or blows happen amongst themselves, and the occasional little instances of spite which I have mentioned are the only disagreement they have.

Revenge, the detestable passion of almost all savages, is I believe here unknown, and I could learn of no instances of any one man having ever killed another, or of a son imbibing from his father any dislike towards particular persons. At the distant northern settlements, however, of which we know nothing but by report, murders are said to be frequently committed.

Courage, and that too in an eminent degree, must be allowed to a people who dare to face the terrific Polar bear, and even to kill it in single combat, with only the assistance of their dogs. There is an independent fearless expression in the countenance and person of an Eskimaux, which is highly striking. The firm walk, erect head, and unbending eye, all denote a man who feels confident of himself. An insensibility of danger is acquired also in venturing amongst young or loose ice, which by a change of wind or unseen ruption, might carry them to certain starvation and death at sea. This very indifference has, however, been the means of many men having fallen through the ice, and some few women also, who have never risen again, and whose families have told the story of their fate.

It is a very general custom for parents to betroth their children in infancy, and this compact being understood, the parties, whenever they are inclined, and able to keep house, may begin living as man and wife. Thus it is that so many very young couples are seen, and that our arrival was the means of some marriages being made in consequence of the youthful bridegrooms being enriched by our presents of household and hunting furniture. The husband, though young, is still a manly person, and a good hunter; but the wife, in two or three instances, could not be above twelve or thirteen years of age, and to all appearance a mere child. Where previous engagements are not made, the men select wives amongst their relatives or connexions, paying but little regard to beauty of face; and as to person, that is equally out of the question. Young men naturally prefer youthful females; but the middle-aged will connect themselves with old widows, as being more skilled in household duties, and better able to take care of their mutual comforts. I cannot pretend to guess at what are the requisite qualifications of a woman in the eye of an Eskimaux, independent of her skill in housewifery. There is decidedly no ceremony by which married people are connected, and I am quite unable to distinguish in what a wife differs from a concubine, for there are some women in that situation, as both, for the time, receive the same title. I never, however, observed a woman living in this manner in the same family with an acknowledged wife. Bigamy is common, but I could hear of no instances of men, having more than two wives; the greater portion, indeed, of those we knew had but one. Divorced women are frequent, but they soon, by marriage, or otherwise, form other connexions. Widows who have friends and good health, fare equally well with those females who have husbands; but illness, or want of friends, seals their fate, and if they are unable by prostitution to support themselves, they are left to starve with their children. Cousins are allowed to marry, but a man will not wed two sisters. A son or daughter-in-law does not consider father or mother-in-law in the light of relations. The most extraordinary connexion is that by adoption, for there are few families which have not one or two adopted sons, their proper progeny being in like manner adopted by others. A wealthy man will, in this manner, take fine stout youths under his protection, and is thereby insured of being supported in his old age, and having good assistance, while yet himself a hunter. This curious connexion binds the parties as firmly together as the ties of blood; and an adopted son, if senior to one by nature, is the heir to all the family riches. This exchange of children is frequently made between families already related or connected, and I am aware of but one instance of a girl being Tegoo-wa-gha, while her natural parents were alive.

The women are treated well; are rarely, if ever, beaten; are never compelled to work, and are always allowed an equal authority in household affairs with the men. Though a phlegmatic people, the Eskimaux may be said to treat them with fondness; and young couples are frequently seen rubbing noses, their favourite mark of affection, with an air of tenderness. Yet even those men and women who seem most fond of each other, have no scruples on the score of mutual infidelity, and the husband is willingly a pander to his own shame. A woman details her intrigues to her husband with the most perfect unconcern, and will also answer to any charge of the kind made before a numerous assemblage of people. Husbands prostitute wives, brothers sisters, and parents daughters, without showing the least signs of shame. It is considered extremely friendly for two men to exchange wives for a day or two, and the request is sometimes made by the women themselves. These extraordinary civilities, although known, are never talked of, and are contrived as secretly as possible.

Even the very early age of a female is not considered, either by herself or her wretched companions, who are all equally willing to assist in bringing her forward. In this deplorable state of morals and common decency, it is extraordinary that in general conversation not an immodest word or gesture can be detected; when men and women are mixed together, and in dancing or singing parties, the females have a seat apart, the conduct of both sexes being extremely decorous.

When parties are out fishing, such young men as are at home make no scruple of intriguing with others' wives, yet if the injured husband hears of it, it gives him little or no uneasiness. Divorced women and widows, and even young and well-looking girls, are equally liberal of their persons. There is one very remarkable fact attached to this general depravity, which is that we never heard of any quarrels arising respecting women, and this may be attributed to the men being totally unacquainted with such a passion as love, or its frequent attendant, jealousy. Two wives, however, will sometimes have a quarrel about the preference of their husband, and a pull by the hair, or a scratched face, has been known to have passed between the disputants. It is a generally allowed opinion that the farther North man is settled, the more dwindled in his form, his intellect, and his passions; and in these last, the Eskimaux are certainly different from any race of beings I ever saw or heard of. With all their indifference to morality, these people, but particularly the women, have a great dread of exposing any part of their persons, and in this respect are really very bashful. Blushes are by no means unknown, and may be easily excited, even in the men. I have already, in my journal, mentioned an instance of the loose behaviour of the women when the men are absent, and believe that at these female assemblages their conduct, when not liable to interruption, is frantic and licentious in the extreme.

Although no Eskimaux can have the least certainty of being the father of his wife's children, yet if she brings progeny, he is very indifferent as to their legitimacy, and considers them as undoubtedly his own. Nothing can be more delightful than the fondness which parents show to their little ones during infancy. The mothers carry them naked on their backs, until they are stout and able walkers, and their whole time and attention are occupied in nursing and feeding them. The fathers make little toys, play with, and are constantly giving them whatever assistance lies in their power. A child is never corrected or scolded, but has its own way in every thing. Their tempers are, however, excellent; their spirits good, and they are affectionate towards their parents. As they grow up, however, they become independent, but still consider it their duty to obey and assist their father and mother. Amongst themselves the little ones never quarrel or fight, and they even play at the roughest games without losing their temper. Little boys frequently attach themselves to each other, and are inseparable companions ever after. The amusements of each sex consist in imitations of their future occupations, and while the boys are making bows, spears, &c. the little girls are gravely affecting to superintend the care of a hut and lamp. Parties sometimes join forces and build small snow places, in which they put rude models of the furniture of real dwellings.

Old and helpless persons lead a quiet undisturbed life, while their own or adopted children live; but should their natural supporters die, no one would move a foot to save them from being frozen or starved to death. The protection afforded to the poor old wretches is of a negative sort, for they are fed merely because food is brought for all the inmates of the hut, but no one of their nearest relatives would in a time of scarcity forego a mouthful for their accommodation. In moving them about, they are handled as roughly as if they were in full vigour; and if they are performing a journey, and sinking from fatigue, the stoutest, even of their own descendants, will not resign to them a seat on the sledge. The old people, on their side, think nothing of this neglect: having themselves practised it to their parents, they do not expect attention in their own helpless state.

To the sick who have relations living under the same roof, little or no attention is paid; sympathy or pity being equally unknown. A wife attends on her sick husband, because she knows that his death would leave her destitute; but if any other person would take the trouble off her hands, she would never even ask to see or at all inquire after him. A man will leave his dying wife without caring who attends her during his absence; a woman will walk to the ships in high spirits while her husband is lying neglected and at death's door in a solitary hut. A brother will not be able to inform you if his sick sister be better or worse, and in her turn a sister will laugh at the sufferings of her brother. A sick woman is frequently built or blocked up in a snow-hut, and not a soul goes near to look in and ascertain whether she be alive or dead. I shall have occasion to speak more at length of this brutal insensibility in my regular journal, and shall therefore now turn to their care of the dead. The relatives alone attend to the corpse, on which a few slabs of snow are placed, and if the dogs choose to devour the body, they do so undisturbed, for not a soul would take the trouble again to cover it. The survivors speak of these horrors with far less concern than they would of a dog's stealing a small piece of meat.

Parry would go on to make two more trips to the Arctic, the *first in the Hecla and the Fury in 1824 to explore Prince Regent Inlet and points south, the second yet another try at reaching the North Pole. The first was yet another disaster. It was a bad year for ice in the Canadian Arctic. Parry spent the winter in the Inlet and then in July headed south, only to have an iceberg nip the Fury against the shore and damage it so severely it could not be repaired. The stores were left on the beach, and the Fury as well, while the Hecla, the crews of both ships aboard, sailed for London, the whole voyage a total failure. George F. Lyon, on a separate voyage to Repulse Bay, had already been forced to turn back by heavy pack ice in northern Hudson Bay after almost losing his ship in some of the bad weather that characterized that season.*

Three years later, in 1827, Parry sailed for the Pole. No one entertained any hopes this time that he could sail through the pack into an open sea. The idea now was to reach the Pole over the ice, on sledges, dragging boats overland with the sledges using teams of reindeer. Perhaps this was where the world got the notion that reindeer drew Santa Claus's sleigh. Parry's plan was at least equally as silly. One man who objected to it was William Scoresby, the whaler. Scoresby knew that the only way to travel efficiently, long distance, over ice was the Eskimo way—with light sledges drawn by dog teams. But the navy ignored Scoresby once more.. When the boats proved too heavy for reindeer to pull, Parry reverted to man-hauling them over the ice, each man pulling 260 pounds. The pressure ridges were a nightmare, the ice was full of leads, the temperature fluctuated between below freezing and the 60s, and they discovered what all Arctic travelers discover, that while they were struggling to move north the pack was moving south beneath their feet. They reached 82 degrees north before they gave up. Seldom was an Arctic expedition so ill-conceived. Parry never went to the Arctic again.

But John Ross did. For ten years Ross had hung out to dry, the nonexistent Croker Mountains, rising out of the fog across Lancaster Sound, still fresh in the British Navy's memory. They were never going to give him another chance to rescue his reputation, and they never did. What he got instead was a private sponsor—Felix Booth, the founder of the company that still makes Booth's Gin. Booth got nothing for placing his trust in John Ross but his name on the land. The Boothia Peninsula and the Gulf of Boothia, which lies at the end of Prince Regent Inlet, are named for him. He may have wanted nothing more. The real prize would have been the honor of having sponsored the voyage that finally discovered the Northwest Passage, had Ross done so.

Ross set sail in 1829 in a steamship called the Victory. The very act of going did much to restore his reputation. Dozens of navy officers applied to go with him, even though this was not a navy expedition. Among the men he did take with him was his nephew, James Ross, who would discover the North Magnetic Pole on this voyage and, a decade later, command the expedition to Antarctica on which he discovered the Ross Sea. The Victory left port on May 23 for Lancaster Sound.

The steam engine gave him trouble from the start, and in Greenland he switched to sail. He entered Prince Regent Inlet on August 10 and turned south, stopping at Fury Beach to pick up some of the supplies Parry had left there four years earlier. They were in excellent condition. He sailed farther south, past Parry's farthest south, naming the landscape after Felix Booth and his family, as well as his own family. He looked every day for the exit from Prince Regent Inlet to the west, and the Northwest Passage. He passed it by, without seeing it—Bellot Strait, named for the Frenchman who did find it later on—a narrow, dangerous passage between Somerset Island and Boothia Peninsula, which he did not yet know was a peninsula. Then winter froze him in.

It was not a wholly unproductive winter. James Ross, John Ross's nephew, did enough sledge exploring with Eskimo guides on Eskimo sledges to discover that the Boothia Peninsula was indeed a peninsula, and that there was water to the west of it—but not open water. He discovered King William Island, although he did not know it was an island, and explored portions of it. The entire crew became accustomed to the presence of Eskimos, who camped beside the ship, and the Eskimos helped them acquire fresh meat. There was no scurvy that winter.

But the following summer the Arctic took over. They had sailed into the Gulf of Boothia in a warm summer with little ice. Getting out was another story. Ross could not get out. He was able to cut a channel for the ship less than a quarter of a mile from their winter quarters, and then they had to cut another channel into the next harbor—two hours' walk from the first. They had moved perhaps a mile from one winter's quarters to the next. The men had little to do. Ross lacked Parry's gift for keeping his men entertained and interested. He was more the old tough, stern navy type. The crew grew increasingly unhappy. It was during the following spring that James Ross discovered the North Magnetic Pole, claiming it, for what that's worth, for England, but he returned to the ship to find that nothing had changed. The ice did not melt that summer, either. They had plenty of provisions, thanks to all they had taken from Fury Beach, but they faced a third winter with nothing to do, no way to escape. Scurvy crept up on the crew, the Eskimos having moved on to other hunting grounds and fresh meat being thin on the ground.

We take our next excerpt from an account of Ross's expedition written by a free-lance writer of no particular repute named Robert Huish. He was using material, perhaps a diary, furnished him by one of Ross's crew, a man named William Light, the ship's steward. Light clearly hated Ross, and the book shows it, but it also shows what an Arctic expedition felt like below decks, as it were, when it went wrong and things got tough. Everything depends on the commander in tough times, and Ross was not likeable enough to inspire either confidence or loyalty among his crew. The excerpt describes a moment when the crew thought they might escape from the ice at last, but when, according to Light's interpretation, he lost courage. Ross himself describes the moment as one of those when he delivered them all from certain death. Here it is.

ROBERT HUISH

The Last Voyage of Capt. Sir John Ross to the Arctic Regions for the Discovery of a Northwest Passage 1829-30-31-32 and 33

ON THE 17TH OF SEPTEMBER THE ICE OPENED IN A MOST EXTRAORDINARY manner, with the wind from the north-north-west and the Aurora shining most brilliantly. A boat was despatched to examine the ice, and, from the report, that was received on its return, at 2 o'clock P.M., the *Victory* was once more under sail, and she stretched along the land until 4 P.M , when, having made nearly four miles, a boat was sent a-head with a whale line, and the ship was made fast to a berg, with the intention of remaining in that position until the following morning.

A considerable degree of censure was attached to Capt Ross, by the whole of the crew, for the most injudicious act of fastening the ship to a berg, under the circumstances, in which they were then placed, nor does it appear, that the censure so passed, was not in every respect well founded. This was, however, not the only error of judgement, of which Capt. Ross was accused, in the management of the ship, through the difficult and intricate navigation, which he had to encounter, and which required not only the most consummate skill, but a most extraordinary degree of presence of mind, which are seldom found confined in the same person.

There were some on board the *Victory*, who had sailed on former expeditions to the Polar seas, and who had witnessed the tact and ability, with which certain circumstances were taken advantage of, and seized, as it were, by the forelock, showing at once the determined spirit of the commander, and his noble daring, in dashing through the difficulties by which he was beset.

We will not lay timidity to the charge of Capt. Ross; but there is a great difference between that animal courage, which displays itself amidst the carnage of the quarter-deck of a man of war, and that old and invincible fortitude, which is the touchstone of the man, in the hour of dangers and difficulties. The man who, in the heat of an engagement, will show, that he has a lion heart within him, will frequently show himself the effeminate, or, more properly speaking, he will appear as daunted and unnerved, when his physical energies are to be called into action, for the purpose of avoiding or surmounting an impending evil. This appears, in some respects, to have been the character of Capt. Ross, for, in many of the trying situations, in which he was placed, either from pusillanimity or indiscretion, he acted in direct variance with the judgement of those, who, although, they might have been his inferior in rank, were perhaps his superior in nautical skill, and in that boldness and promptitude of action, which are the most striking features of the great and noble character in the immediate hour of danger.

The *gravamen* of the accusation against Capt. Ross, in the present instance, consisted in the unnecessary act of his fastening the *Victory* to the iceberg, when circumstances so combined, as to have enabled him to dash through the passage, and thereby brought the vessel into an open sea, instead of exposing her to be momentarily so severely nipped by the ice, as perhaps to render her unfit altogether to prosecute the voyage.

At the time of the *Victory* leaving Felix Harbour, the wind was south, and the ice running north; the wind then veered round to the west north-west, and the ice still running to the north; it then changed to the south-west, but the ice still running in the same direction. Now, if the *Victory* had been pushed through, instead of being fastened to a berg, the north-easternmost point, as well as all the islands, that lay off it, would have been cleared: this was the current opinion amongst the crew, and one of the mates in particular openly avowed his sentiments on the subject, viz. that if he had had charge of the vessel, he would have shoved her out into the ice, because it was then running to the north, and the inlet became broader, the further they advanced. It was well known to all the crew, that Capt. Ross always entertained a strong objection to carry the vessel amongst the ice; but, that had she been under the command of Capt. Parry, a very different fate would have befallen the Victory, than when under the command of Capt. Ross. We have the authority of several of the crew, for stating that a greater degree of danger was experienced with Capt. Parry in one hour, than was incurred on board the Victory, from the period of her reaching the ice, to the moment of her abandonment: and further, that if a strong desire had not been manifested to return to England, a greater advance to the northward might have been obtained, which, however, was relinquished, wither from timidty or an indisposition to endure any longer the perils of the voyage.

During the 18th and 19th, the wind shifted to almost all the two-and-thirty points of the compass, driving the ice in every direction. But the Victory had got into such an unfavourable situation, that very little hope remained, of emancipating her from it: no other prospect therefore presented itself, than passing another winter within four miles of the former harbour, with the dread of a scarcity of provisions staring them in the face, and, perhaps, their ultimate fate, being the abandonment of the ship, with the chance of being frozen to death in their endeavor to reach the seas frequented by the whalers, which, at all events, could not be done for nearly nine months to come.

On the 20th, the wind got round to the south-west, blowing strong: but it was too late for the Victory to take any advantage of it, as she was completely frozen in, and the young ice pouring in upon her, in all directions. The labor of the crew was here sever indeed, in cutting away the young ice, to keep the ship clear: but it was a most disheartening task, for they had no sooner cleared her in one quarter, than she was blocked up in another, and faint, indeed was now the hope of ever moving the vessel from the perilous situation in which she lay.

On the morning of the 21st, the wind blew from the eastward, but the ice deviated not from its usual direction; toward midday however, it veered suddenly round to the northward, and on account of this sudden change, the ice came rushing in, driving every thing before it. At that time, the Victory was fast to two large bergs: but the pressure of the ice was so great, that it sent the bergs and the ship right on shore, so that at low water she was lying aground, on some very heavy pieces of ice, the ice itself being aground also. As the tide rose, she floated, but with every ebb she rested on the ice, endangering her bottom, and rendering her situation one of the greatest peril. All hands were now employed in clearing away the ice from under her bottom;

the consequence of which was, that when the tide ebbed, she careened nearly on her broadside.

It now amounted almost to a certainty, that they were in their winter harbour, the whole blame of which was attributed to Capt. Ross; and it occasioned some bitter bickerings between that officer and his nephew, who was, from the commencement, decidedly adverse to the course of proceedings, which were adopted, and to which their present disastrous situation was alone to be ascribed. It must indeed have been most galling to the feelings of the crew, to be cooped up in an inlet, when about, two miles further outside of the land ice, there were an abundance of clear water, and the signs of it, to a considerable distance. The very elements however, seemed to conspire against them; for the prevalence of the northerly winds drove the ice into the inlet, and the frost was so severe, that the young ice began to assume a thickness, through which it was difficult to effect a passage.

On the 21st, the wind was variable, but blowing very hard; the ice cleared away a ltttle, but left the ship a-ground on ground ice. At 5 p.m., the wind veered round to the north-ward, and drove the ice into the inlet, carrying every thing before it, and forced the ship two or three feet closer in shore. The ice was now closely packed, and, at low water, the ship careened four streaks.

In the 27th, the rudder was unshipped; the wind still blowing hard from the north-east, and about two miles off, a vast expanse of clear water, with a very dark watery sky; but the ship was so blocked up, that it was then reduced to a certainty, that their progress for that season, was at an end, Commader Ross left the ship, to take a view of the position, in which the *Victory* lay, and to seek for a place, where she might harbour for the winter. He ascended a hill, and to the northward saw a clear sea, in which the *Victory* ought to have been, if she had kept on her course, on the day that she left Felix Harbour, instead of being fastened to the bergs, from which act, the whole of their disasters were to be ascribed. Commander Ross marked out a place for a harbour, but, on examining it more minutely, it was found to be too shallow.

From the 29th September to the 3rd October, the crew were laboriously employed in getting the ship into her winter harbour, and in five days they got her no further than 35 feet. The crew were principally engaged in cutting a canal for the ship to winter in, or rather the canal was cut for the purpose of getting the ship into deeper water, for where she then lay, the heavy ice was clear of her bottom; but, at low water, she would fall on her broadside, if she were not shored up every tide, which was one of the severest labors, which the crew had to undergo, during the whole of the voyage: in fact, it may be affirmed, that the privations, which they underwent at this period, and the constant and unremitting labor, to which they were exposed, may be denominated as the most trying part of the voyage. In the first place, each man had to keep his watch every night, with the thermometer as low as 15 below zero. As soon as morning broke, all hands were turned out to saw the ice, for the purpose of making the canal; and every piece, that was cut, had to be got on the ice, for there was not depth of water sufficient to suck it under it. The whole of this ice, that was cut, was not less than four feet in thickness, and every piece had to be boused up in the other side, by the capstern. By admeasurement, the crew cut 855 feet of ice, before they got into their winter harbour: the men often working like horses, during the whole of the day, and then to turn out two or three times in the night, accordingly as the tide served, to shore the vessel up, to prevent her careening on her broadside. Some of the men would fall in the canal, head over ears; and before they could get to the ship, their clothes would be frozen, the jacket to the waistcoat, and the former so hard, that it would almost stand upright. But, on those occasions, Capt. Ross never followed the example of Capt. Parry: nor did he cheer his men, by saying, "Come my lads, bear a-hand, out again, and tell my steward to give you a good glass of grog." But the first thing, that was heard from Capt. Ross, was his well-known grunt of displeasure, and then the exclamation, "It serves you right—come make haste, and shift yourselves." And even when a man got wet in the *Victory*, there was no warm air stove, to thaw or dry his clothes, for the ship had nothing but a small stove of Slater's Patent: but, to keep up as large a fire as possible, the stove would not consume more than two pecks a day; and the whole consumption of fuel on board the *Victory*, in the dead of winter, was no more than three pecks and a half or four pecks a day: whereas, in the *Hecla* and the *Fury*, the consumption was, five pecks to the warm air stove, five to the galley, 1 ¼ to the cabin, 1 ¼ to the gun-room, ½ of a peck to the midshipmen's berth, and a peck to the sick bay: making in all 14 per day; the temperature of the men's berths on the lower deck, was never below 60; whereas the temperature of the *Victory's* lower deck was seldom higher than 36, except on baking days, which was once a week, when the lower deck was as high as 54, which may be considered as the maximum: whereas, in the cabin, the thermometer was as high as 70, the average being 65.

It was not however, only the shoring up of the vessel, that deprived the men of their rest; but if at any time it was high water during the night, they were called up to heave the ship astern, as far as they had cut the canal during the day, and then when the ship was close up, they were not allowed to return to their berths, but they were obliged to wait, exposed to the severity of the frost, until the tide ebbed, that the vessel might be propped up, to prevent her falling on her broadside, as they had no more than four or five feet of water, the whole length of the canal. By the end of October, the *Victory* may be considered to be in her winter harbour, her forehead 10 feet, 4 inches, aft 10 feet 6 inches, and a few feet further there was no more than 9 feet 6 inches.

From the 1st November to the 10th, the principal duty of the crew was unrigging the vessel, and preparing her for her wintering; the wind blowing strong, sometimes accompanied with snow, from the northward and the westward. The ship was banked up as during the preceding winter, and a snow deck was raised as a protection against the violence of the weather. Snow walls were also built about the ship, and an observatory was commenced on the highest hill in the immediate vicinity of the harbour. The powder was got out of the ship, for fear of fire, and the boats housed up, and covered with snow, to keep them from renting. A spar was placed on a high hill as a flag-staff, for the purpose of guiding the Esquimaux to the ship, whose visits, during the preceding winter, had been highly acceptable, as they were the purevyors of different kinds of food, and of materials, from which the winter clothing was to be made. In fine weather a flag was hoisted on the spar; but it was necessary to keep a constant watch upon it, as it was an object, which the Esquimaux women had a great desire to obtain possession of, as an ornament round their necks.

On the 30th October, the sun took his departure for three months: and trebly steeled as the heart may be, and competent to bear up with fortitude against the accidents and casualties of life, there was something most trying to the feelings, in the thought, that the great luminary, which dispenses light and cheerfulness upon the earth, was to be a stranger to them for three months, and they removed from all the comforts, which could render life desirable.

As it was considered necessary to re-establish the intercourse with the natives, for various reasons, but particularly on account of the regular supply of food, which they were in the habit of bringing for the dogs, Capt. Ross took the earliest opportunity of visiting the old harbour, where he drew upon the boilers, which were left on the ice, some figures, and a large hand, as a guide to the natives to their new station: when, however, the trifling distance is considered, which the second harbour was from the first, it was not likely that a roving people like the Esquimaux, would not discover the vessel; for although she might not be exactly visible from Felix Harbour, the sound of her guns, which were now and then fired for experimental purposes, would have been a sure indication to them, that the *Kabloonas* were still in their vicinity. It must, however, be remarked, that the Esquimaux had no very urgent motives for visiting the ship; they had already, in their commercial dealings with Capt. Ross, denuded themselves of almost their whole stock of clothing; and until the seals began to be plentiful, they had scarcely any other article, which they could barter away with the Europeans, for their fish-hooks, needles, files, and old pieces of iron.

On the 1st December, the crew were put into five watches, the principal reason of which was, to keep all the men in a regular state of exercise. Two of the watches were continually walking in the day-time; two were at work; and one was down below, for the purpose of keeping the lower deck dry, and in good order. The working party about the ship, were employed in building a snow wall four feet high, which reached from stem to stern, and which served the purpose of a screen to the men, in their various operations about the ship.

The officers now began their usual occupation of the chase, and seldom a day elapsed, that some animal or game was not brought to the ship. A very rare animal, a black fox, was killed on the 3rd of December; and the following day a white one and a hare. During the whole month of December, not a Sunday elapsed, that a roasted hare did not smoke on the table in the cabin; and in truth it may be said that the gun was the best purveyor of food for the cabin, which was known, during the whole of the time, that the vessel was blocked up.

✶

ROSS AND HIS MEN ESCAPED IN THE END BY ABANDONING THE VICTORY, *dragging small boats, and, when that failed, what supplies they could carry, to Fury Beach, commandeering the remaining small boats left there by Parry so many years before, and sailing out of Prince Regent Inlet to hail a passing whaler—just in time.*

It's a great story, like so many Arctic stories, but while Ross had survived, he had also failed. The Northwest Passage had yet to be discovered.

Naturally, he returned a hero.

Not for long, though. Controversy surrounded John Ross. John Barrow hated him and attacked him in print. The Huish book did the same. Ross attacked back, starting arguments with the man who had made the useless steam engine he had finally simply discarded, with fellow naval officer Francis Beaufort, even with his own nephew. History has generally not been kind to Ross. Yet he did manage to get his men out of an appalling situation, and most of them returned alive. In the Arctic that is a genuine accomplishment. Ray Edinger's recent book, Fury Beach, ably defends him. And he had shown that Prince Regent Inlet was not the way west. As for Felix Booth, he must have been pleased. Not only did his name grace a piece of the world's real estate, he had been awarded a baronetcy. He was now Sir Felix Booth.

As for the Northwest Passage, when asked by a committee of parliament whether it would be worthwhile to continue to search for it, John Ross said, "I think it would be utterly useless."

But the search went on. John Franklin, despite the disasters of his first overland trip, had already gone to and come back from northern Canada a second time, taking a small expedition down the Mackenzie River to the coast of the Arctic Ocean. His assignment was to map the coastline to the west of the Mackenzie, into Russian Alaska, while a second party, his old friend John Richardson leading the way, mapped the coast to the east. Franklin had clearly learned something from the first trip. This one was relatively free of trouble. It began, to be sure, on a tragic note. Franklin left England as his wife was dying of tuberculosis. His schedule did not allow him to stay home and wait it out. The whole enterprise depended on his leaving early. One can only imagine his feelings as he walked away. She died six days after he sailed.

This aside, the expedition was a success, opening up most of the coastline of northern Canada. Only a small portion remained unmapped, the portion east of Point Turnagain, which Franklin had reached on his first expedition to the area. It was a considerable achievement and it earned both Franklin and Richardson their own knighthoods. Six years later another expedition had the chance to fill in some of that blank space when another veteran of Franklin's first overland trek, George Back, led a small expedition to the northeast out of Great Slave Lake in northern Canada and discovered the Great Fish River, which empties into the Chantry Inlet, an arm of the Arctic Ocean south of King William Island and west of the Boothia Peninsula. Back could have gone on and explored to the east, crossing the Boothia Peninsula to find out more about the area, and the only other officer with him, a surgeon named Richard King, urged him to do so. But Back, running out of provisions, turned, well, back. The purpose of his trip had been to find John Ross, then trying to work his way out of the ice of Prince Regent Inlet. He had heard even before he left for the Great Fish River that Ross was safely home. He was free to explore if he wanted to. But he gave up and went home. He had found the Great Fish River, and that was enough. His reward, which came after a calamitous expedition to Repulse Bay in 1836, from which he was to set out by land to cross the bottom of the Boothia Peninsula into unknown territory, was also a knighthood. The Great Fish River is now known as the Back River.

And now the Admiralty, and John Barrow, paused. He was still interested in the Northwest Passage, but he had ambitions in other parts of the world as well, and in 1838 he sent James Clark Ross, John Ross's nephew, south to Antarctica on a voyage that lasted three years. The younger Ross had discovered the North Magnetic Pole; his mission now was to discover the South. He did not, but he left his own name on the Ross Sea (to his credit, he did not bestow this name; it was named after him subsequent to his return) and the names of just about every Englishman of any prominence on the mountains which border it, and he discovered a seal, the Ross Seal, and a sea gull as well: Ross's gull. Over the two years 1837-39, the Hudson's Bay Company sent two of its factors, George Simpson and Peter Dease, back to the coast of northern Canada. Simpson made it all the way to Point Barrow, and then east all the way to Chantrey Inlet, discovering on the way that King William Island was separated on its south side from the mainland by a narrow strait, now named Simpson Strait. It happens to be an important link in the Northwest Passage. The water channel north of King William Island is more or less perpetually blocked by ice. What he did not recognize was that King William Island is an island. He thought it was connected farther north to the Boothia Peninsula. He also thought that Boothia Peninsula was an island, with a strait somewhere just beyond his explorations that detached it from the mainland. If he had gone just a little farther he would have rectified those errors, and he might have achieved far more fame than he did.

This was a fur company exploration, however, not an Admiralty. John Barrow was getting old. He would retire in 1845, having spent more than 40 years directing traffic into the unknown parts of the Arctic and Africa. He wanted only one more prize, the Northwest Passage, and he waited until 1845 to set it up. He would send the Erebus and the Terror, James Ross's Antarctic ships, into the Canadian archipelago and this time they would do it. They would bull their way through the ice and complete the map. That was now the only goal. No one believed any longer that the Northwest Passage might be a viable route to the Pacific. National honor was at stake, nothing more.

By right James Ross should have led it. He had become, after Parry, England's reigning polar hero after his successful completion of the Antarctic voyage, and he had a great deal of experience in the Arctic as well, thanks to his uncle. But Ross had just married, and he had promised his wife's family that he would stay home. It was now understood that a voyage like this might take two or three years. And another man wanted the job.

Wanted it desperately. John Franklin had spent the last few years in Van Diemen's Land (i.e., Tasmania) serving as the colony's governor. He had not done well. He had, in fact, been fired from the job for his inability to understand and master the political intrigue that characterized Tasmanian colonial politics. Franklin was a navy man, good on board a ship, inept at administering a bureaucracy, even worse at dealing with the craft and guile of the political animal. He had remarried after he returned from his second exploration in northern Canada, a woman named Jane Griffin, and she was exceedingly strong-willed and ambitious. She had no compunctions about interfering in the political game herself, shocking all of Tasmania in the process. She was formidable. Now that the couple was back in England, she was not about to lead a quiet provincial life on her husband's half-pay as a retired British naval officer. She wanted this final, crowning achievement for him. Franklin wanted it for himself, partly to satisfy his wife's ambitions, and partly, perhaps,—we will never know—to get out of her presence for a while. After Ross turned the job down, the Admiralty reluctantly gave it to Franklin. They thought that at 60 he was just too old. No no, he hurried to correct them. He was only 59.

John Franklin's final mission to the Arctic is the hinge on which all subsequent Arctic history turns, yet we know almost nothing about it, for he never came back. He took two ships and 129 men with him. The ships disappeared. Not one man survived. They were last seen by a whaler in Lancaster Sound, in the summer of 1845, sailing west. Then—nothing. We know what happened to them in general, but no journals, no letters, only a few notes left in stone cairns by the survivors, some skeletons, a small boat, and a fair amount of detritus and debris, have ever been found. People are still trying to find the ships themselves on the bottom in the areas where they were thought to have gone down. The fate of the Franklin expedition remains one of the great unsolved mysteries of the Arctic.

But the search for Franklin opened the Arctic up. From 1848 on, when the Admiralty finally began to become alarmed, expedition after expedition came at the Arctic from every available direction in hopes of rescuing the presumed survivors or, failing that, finding out what happened to them. When the Admiralty gave up Lady Jane Franklin stepped in and prodded and shamed the government into trying again, and again. She got the Americans involved in Arctic exploration. She used the press, she found private financing, she financed expeditions herself. Before Franklin, one or two expeditions might set out for the Arctic in a year, or in two years, or three. In the ten years after Franklin disappeared, no fewer than 40 expeditions set out in search of him.

When it was over the final link in the Northwest Passage had been found, the maze of islands, straits, inlets and channels that was the Canadian archipelago had been mapped, and the mantle of Arctic exploration had been transferred from the British to the Americans. But still no one knew why 130 men had died when they had provisions for four years or more on board and Parry's supplies still stacked at Fury Beach and Eskimos living all through the archipelago who might have helped them.

It would be impossible in a book of this size to use excerpts from all of the expeditions that went after Franklin. We will do what we can. We begin with an excerpt from the journal of Robert Carter, a junior officer on one of the two ships manned by the U. S. Navy and financed by Henry Grinnell, an American shipbuilder of considerable wealth who was developing an interest in Arctic exploration. The search for Franklin was well underway by the time the U. S. Navy got involved in 1850. A number of expeditions had gone out, and come back with nothing to report. But interest around the world remained high. It would continue to remain high. The search for Franklin was one of the major events of the nineteenth century.

A number of other expeditions besides what became known as the first Grinnell Expedition left for Baffin Bay in the summer of 1850, and Lancaster Sound was crowded with rescue ships when Carter's ship arrived. Leading the Grinnell Expedition was Lt. DeHaven on board the Advance. DeHaven was considered an expert on polar sailing; he had been with Wilkes on the U. S. Exploring Expedition that coasted Antarctica for some 1500 miles in the early 1840s. Robert Carter, an FFV, a member of the First Families of Virginia, was first officer (i.e., second in command) on board the Rescue. His account of the expedition has a freshness to it that stands in contrast to the often more formal accounts of Arctic experience written by the leaders of expeditions. Carter was young, hated the cold, hated his ship, did not want to spend the winter in the Arctic, and never intended to publish his comments, which are, as a result, honest and unsparing. And fun to read. This excerpt covers the period when the decision was made that they would have to overwinter in Barrow Strait at the western end of Lancaster Sound, much against Carter's most fervent wishes.

ROBERT R. CARTER

Private Journal of a Cruise in the Brig RESCUE
in Search of Sir John Franklin

Saturday August 31st 1850

Quite a gale making the moderate temperature very unpleasant to the feelings; much colder to the feeling than any weather we have yet had. The tide was very high and the field to which we are fast drifting Northward and closing in with the land so that both the vessels had to shift their berths, we several times. The ice is so hard that digging for an anchor is a labour of 10 or 15 minutes.

I see now what the arctic writers mean by hummocky ice and how disagreeable travelling over it must be, tenfold worse than new ploughed ground and quite as bad as loose lava.

Three bears swam near the ship at breakfast time and Griffin & myself manned a boat and pulled to the attack. About half way bearward we found that our weapons consisted of my shot gun (one barrel with buck and one with bird shot) and his musket with a doubtful charge however as no time could be sparsed we went on. His musket snapped the first time but upon being recapped brought one and reloaded by an accidental charge in Brooks pocket brought another and my load of buckshot by coming within ten yards laid out the third. Pretty fair—three bears with three loads. The one I shot is the first male we have got but is small being young all were shot in the head, mine least dammaged, those muskets make such awful holes. The chance of getting out of this pool to the Southward are getting slim, the ice being jammed up against

Cape Spencer for a mile and that too with a high tide leaving the chance of finding a harbour horribly small.

Commo made my heart jump for joy by saying that if we get out and find no opening to Southwestward that he will endeavour to return home this winter.

Sunday September 1st 1850
Gale continues till night and the drifting snow renders the open air unpleasant. Passage Southward still closing. Drifted two miles Nd. All in all rather bad. But all for the best as everything yet has turned out. Suppose the commo hadnt got ashore and stayed so long at Cape Riley that we ran back, we would most probably have been jammed with Ommanneys vessels. By the way all our suspicions of him and Capt Kater [Cator] were as unjust and unfounded as galley yarns generally are.

More say [talk] about home. Commo dined here, says that he expects to winter either 300 miles west of this or at home, but is very disheartened at the present prospect- the first time I have heard him at all despond[ent].

The only thing that we can gain by wintering in the Sound is the advantage of Spring foot parties, for which while we're entirely unprepared (not having even a tent, and so few men) the English are fully equipped, have a strong force and less ground than will occupy half their time. And by refering to former winters up here, no vessel has ever been freed from her winter quarters as early as we got here in this season, so backward that not a Whaler got through Baffins Bay.

Monday September 2nd 1850
Capt Griffin & Brooks went hare hunting without seeing any near enough to shoot. Griffin dined with Penny whom he likes still more. Dr. Kane returned from the English ships (where he has been for three days during the gale) giving glowing accounts of their comforts, he actually had sheets to sleep in every night. He staid on board Austins ship says that they have regular Man o war discipline, had prayers morning and evening at quarters, and are inspected regularly and make as much ado, reporting &c. about a small piece of drift ice as we do about being nipped and thrown on our beam ends. All the officers and men receive double pay and the officers certain of promotion after this cruise. Aint dat hi? Commo Austin came back with the doc and dined aboard the commo is the jolliest old Englishman ever seen. Talks to our commo

about the expeditions to be sent in cohoot in the spring saying that he will fit us out. They are trying to get old Ross home to carry news of the squadron.

One of the baloons for distributing news over the Arctic world was sent up from Beechey Island during the gale. About a thousand bits of paper marked with (Date, Ship, position, future intentions, and naming depots of provisions) put up in packages of ten or more are fast to the baloon and so arranged that by the burning of a slow match a bundle is bursted and scattered at regular intervals during its flight. Three of the papers were found by a party from the *Advance* about five miles from Beechey Island which were probably some of the first bundle showing that it had worked well thus far. Saw numbers of Narwhal and some were shot but not struck in the right place. It being almost impossible to harpoon this fish- it is oftener caught by shooting it in the spine. The tusks which are several feet long are the finest ivory. During the disagreeable weather of the last few days we have had our hatch doors closed and now we find everything damp with condensed vapour. The *Advance*s say that even in their lockers the clothes are all damp. Sheets wouldn't suit that.

The English officers on hearing our Commo say that his force was 33 men asked in surprize "thirty three all in your vessel"? and perhaps their surprize increased a little when told that the thirty three included officers, men, cooks, and stewards of both vessels. Still we have beaten them with their steam, experience, faster vessels, and strong force.

Tuesday September 3rd 1850
The floe to which we have been fast during the gale commenced drifting South with the ebb tide so at 10:30 we cast of[f] and commenced beating against the tide loosing a little every tack until about 6 P.M. when at slack water we found ourselves very little to Southward of the mornings position we stood to the Westward in a long lead towards Cape Hothany about six miles. At midnight the lead closing with the continuance of the flood we had to tie up. The tides here run about 12 hours each way so that this lead ought to be open tomorrow afternoon with the ebb unless a southerly wind comes when we shall probably be jammed. Dr. Kane shot a seal and got him falsifying the assertions of all the knowing ones that they will sink when killed in the water. He says that the Englishmen have shot several and got them. Going this way don't look homeward and our cakes look doughy.

Wednesday September 4th 1850

This is a beautiful morning but rather cool. Dressing on deck Ther 27° the water in the tumbler would freeze after each pouring on the toothbrush put the sun was so welcome that I didn't want to shame him by going below, especially as we have not come to that yet, and a beautiful mess we would have if we did dress below. At 3 the ice opened so that we had a lead as far as we could see to Westward of which taking advantage we make about six miles toward Cape Hothany and by Midnight are fast again. The pack to Southward of us drifting by to Westward at a lick o two knots carrying with it loose pieces several feet higher than our rail making our position any thing but comfortable and letting us see that the marvelous accounts of Ross and Back may have a little truth mixed with the poetry.

A most enormous bear was shot from the *Advance* just before we made fast here measuring 8 ft 8 in—two inches larger than any on record; a male very old and swam near the ship without fear. We were in hopes that they did not see him as the lead was narrow and the vessels going three knots when suddenly they stood right for him, the port bow bristling with fire arms, however, only two were fired, the first killing and the second missing but they were fired so nearly at the same instant that Lovell and Dr Kane don't know which of them did it. Poor Lovell- he put one ball in the head of the first one they killed but one of the men did the same and he is most ambitious to kill a polar bruin. Saw the *Assistance* and *Intrepid* off Cape Hothany under sail but our chance seems rather slim to get there or any where else just now. Therm at 20° and bay ice forming fast. Saw lots of stars to-night the first of the season. Compasses are humplugs. Az gives only 111° var today.

Thursday September 5th 1850

The *Advance*'s bear is immense and can only be compared with small elephants being too large for 'orses and hoxen. Made a start at one P.M. and at quarter fore six made fast to the land ice about 300 yds from the North Cape of Barlows inlet in eleven feet water the *Advance* being beached just ahead of us but she did it so softly that they had to measure to discover it, and at low water too. The tide commenced to flow and by eight we have lots of ice around us. I took a cruise around the inlet which is a beautiful and land locked harbour extending three miles from the mouth and spacious, as a horse shoe but I don't know the depths as it was frozen or rather filled with ice of years standing. We are not near the middle of the enterance which accounts for our shoal water. We found a dead seal with a fine silk handkerchief tied round it, and opened a cairn erected only yesterday with a paper in the same bombastic style of Capt Ommanney's other document not mention[in]g which way he is going nor where provisions are left &c. but that no traces have been found on Cornwallis Island of which perhaps he has examined one one hundredth and that $\frac{1}{100}$ poorly if no better than Beechey Island which they thoroughly examined without finding Franklins winter quarters with a conspicuous cairn pointing them out. Perhaps this isnt the place to express such uncharitable sentiments but it does look so ridiculous for that party to be rushing ahead so as to be first at every place then leaving it unexamined to say that no traces are found there (Cornwallis Island is a young continent). Commo Austins barque and steamer crossed the sound to-day and the steamer is towing her in among the loose ice toward us. Once of their boats has just returned having come in to see whether all that flashing and firing was for warning to them. And having learned that it was Dr. Kane trying to get his rifle off took another drink and returned. That's the rifle as shot the bear after snapping only once thinks Dr. Kane but Lovell thinks his Polly longlips done it. We saw three bear this afternoon as we sailed rapidly along the edge of the field and some of the men fired at one but only alarmed him; one was feeding on the carcass of a bear left skinned by the Englishmen so I daresay bruin can eat his fellow bruins without compunctions. This looks less like home than ever and as Capt Ommanney doubled Cape Hothany this afternoon I suppose we may tomorrow. Hoping which, I'll take the meteorogicals and call my relief.

Friday September 6th 1850
No possibility of advancing or returning all day being closely surrounded by ice which drifts South and North with the tides at a great rate. The English commo also sticks pretty fast and I daresay regrets not squeezing in here last night as he is in a fine position for drifting out of the Sound a la James Ross. Murdaugh sounded across the enterance of this inlet and found six and seven fathoms in the channell which runs nearer the Southern cape agreeing with the rule "In entering bays, harbours, &c in Limestone regions avoid the side which terminates in a cliff." Cleaned my bear skin as much as possible which

wasn't much though requiring some labour. The bay ice formed so thick during the night that parties have been skating all day. But today it is mild again. The Englishmen came ashore near us but don't come aboard.

Saturday September 7th 1850
Ice still closer until 6 P.M. when a North wind getting a little fresh we perceive the whole pack to drift slowly Southward taking Commo Austin with it. We being inside of a point on which are a number of grounded bergs maintain our position having the power to force our way further in the harbour if desirable. About this time a large fragment of the floe to which we were fast broke off and both vessels drift rapidly across the mouth of the harbour toward a berg grounded to leeward of us. The *Advance* goes clear but the poor little *Rescue* was caught again. Providentailly in the vortex of an angle and was popped out like a melon seed with no dammage the ice very considerably unshipping the rudder just as we most desired it to be done[,] however as the ice could not stop to run it up to the davits that had to be done, and seeing some men humbugging at it to sling it and keep dry feet, I jumped into the water and slung it myself somewhat to their amusement perhaps but at all events better than losing the rudder. Hauled the vessels a short distance farther in and made fast to the lee bergs being protected from this wind by those grounded on the point (above mentioned) but still not in a secure place as quite large pieces drift against us with the tide. Austin is drifting yet and closely beset. Begin to talk about having to winter in this desolate spot where even the bears wont come. I had almost rather winter at home. Read in Parry to-day that he put all his compasses below except the Azimuth which was also a poor dependence and am quite satisfied to learn that I am not the first master to make funny variations by azimuths taken near the same position. The variation I got on the 29th ulto agrees within 2° of Parrys nearest to that position.

Sunday September 8th 1850
Another day of confinement by the ice one of the few remaining and precious days of open season. Expecting a gale all day the Barometer having risen higher than it has ever done before. Austin still beset has drifted about six miles South of us. Old Penny seems to be as cautious as a fox he keeps astern of us all and profits by our experience. He appeared last evening five miles to Northward of this port in a stream of open water next the land ice and

holding on to it so as not to share what seems to be Austins misfortune. The bay ice formed thick enough for all the men who can raise skates to be breaking the sabbath all day, and firmly cementing the loose fragments that drifted around us with the last flood tide so that two hours of the afternoon were employed in breaking it around them so that the ebb cleared us again. I spent a very quiet sabbath reading, but this is no place to pass a satisfactory one and more particularly in this weather where one is suffering from cold except while in bed or during active exercise. I sent a bundle of tracts which I selected from our supply into the forecastle but I am afraid they will hardly be noticed. Every one in the expedition appears so utterly indifferent to the one thing needful in spite of the constant evidence that Providence alone can protect us and in this cruise by special interposition.

Monday September 9th 1850
Got underway at 4 A.M. and stood for Cape Hothany doubling it and commenced beating to the Westward. Austin towed by his steam tender got out of the ice and went to windward fast. Penny caught and passed us, so that by night we are again last because of our dull vessels. Penny boarded us as he passed and got some 300 pounds of bears meat for his dogs of which he has thirty eight. We gave him of an old bear as we think the young one fine eating. Saw Griffith Island twenty miles ahead. The young ice is so troublesome now that we apprehend having to hunt for winter quarters soon, lest our dull vessels should be caught in it and drifted S.E. Home stock so high a few days ago is not worth shucks now and Melville Island stock is up and as such seems the design of Providence. I shall e'en content myself with the prospect of a winter in one of these brigs which the remembrance of last winter renders doubly gloomy. Penny says he sailed some distance up Wellington Channel and thinks Griffin mistaken about its being a bay.

Tuesday September 10, 1850
Until 4 P.M. beating to the Westward when we got a fair wind stopping the snow and cheering us up. At 6:30 we doubled the Southern extremity of Griffith Island and saw Austins four vessels and Pennys brigs fast to a field of ice three miles West of the Island and extending North and South as far as we can see. Came to among them (man o war style). Capt Ommanney had been here only 24 hours

having examined a good deal more of Cornwallis Island without finding traces of Sir John. Austin & Penny had been here only twelve hours and all say that there is no going farther. The *Intrepid* has examined in shore and between Griffith Island & Cornwallis finding a harbour on the latter which they have named Assistance Harbour and where Commo Austin thinks of wintering as the season is shutting up so early and on dit [it is said] that Ommanney is to survey Wellington Channel. So what do now Messrs Yankees but go home if ye can as your instructions direct ye, saying to the effect that if you cant get far enough West to go to [blank] in the spring you will return and examine Jones & Smith Sounds and finding them closed not let the young ice catch you but return to New York. A great deal of the snow that fell into the water was formed into round balls about the size to throw so that the mermaids have millions of them all ready for their sport. One of the English middies spent the evening with us and entertained us much being quite funny. But he tells us that in addition to the double pay and certain promotion, that Govt furnishes them with clothes, and better ones than they could have purchased themselves. The list he gave us of one years allowance being about equal to my whole supply plus two pairs of boots such as we never even saw before. Old Penny is right in saying that those fellows don't deserve any credit, steamboats and all taken into consideration.

Wednesday September 11th 1850

A very dirty day. One incessant snow storm to half of which I have been exposed and find it like everything else nothing when you are used to it. Worked three hours of the morning to wind the ship and warp her a cables length to a good lee. The *Assistance*'s tender cruised about all the forenoon to find an opening to the Westward without success. Penny made sail and stood to S. Westward into some loose ice and the tender reports him fast in it a few miles south of us. Too thick to see half a mile.

I met a most interesting gentlemen on board the *Advance* of the uncommon name of Brown, an English Lieut who was with Sir Jas Ross last cruise in these regions and he gave us among other interesting information an exact account of the equipment and conduction of the Spring parties, of which however I can tell better after we have tried one. Commo Austin sent a letter to our Commo advising him of his plans. The *Assistance* is to winter near here and survey Wellington Chan and examine as far as possible the Northern shore of Barrow Strait while he endeavours to get farther West in his vessels. Home stock is again in the Market and I think that if there is no going West in a few days we will try still harder to get East and home. Doc wishes for a fair wind to go home and hear Jenny Lind; of course in much finer poetry that the above. The Aurora Borealis wants to know what bug abounds these regions which accompanied Noah on his cruise. I suppose it must be the Ark-tick.

Thursday September 12th 1850
I have seen days of suffering, hard winds, and some cold work but, this was one in which those unpleasant things, combined with danger, made quite an event in the life of every one of us.

At midnight last night I turned in leaving all calm and secure but in half an hour I felt her bump against the ice, heard the wind roar, and the captain turn out so of course I lay expecting to be called every minute. However not till 1:30 did they make my tally, when I was up quickly and found that our nice lee by a change of wind had become a lee shore against which she was thumping heavily. Captain on the ice planting anchors & wanted me to drop the brig round the point, but changing his mind he came aboard and commenced veering. When just at the point all four anchors broke adrift and we were blown off leaving two men and one of our boats on the ice (near the *Advance*). Making sail we commenced beating up, under considerable anxiety lest not being able to make any weather we should drift on the ice two miles to leeward of us where human efforts wouldn't have been worth shucks to save the brig and little more to save our lives. But after two or three tacks we found that we gained a little and thought that we would stand off and on until the gale abated when we could make fast to the ice again. So at 4 I turned in having been two & a half hours at the helm, but under such excitement that I scarcely felt the cold, although the Capt had the helm relieved every half hour afterwards, the therm being 18° and snowing fast. At 6 I was again called to relieve the capt who had not slept all night either, having been aboard the Commo until Midt so I worked her up among washing ice until 12 when finding that we had gained enough to run under the lee of Griffith Island and anchor I called him and made the proposition which he determined to attempt seeing the exhausted state of the men (who were now reduced to six, three being sick and two absent). So we ran her to within stones cast of the ice grounded on the beach and let go an anchor in 9 fms water but it wouldn't hold, and we dragged off in a giffey; drifting into a piece of washing ice and smashed the rudder so as to render it almost useless. However made sail and beat up again to within biscuit throw of the shore and let go in 4 fms water which held for a while so that she swung round alongside the land ice and a man jumped ashore to plant an ice anchor but before he could do it the arm of our best bower broke short off and we began to drift off so rapidly that with difficulty the man was dragged aboard leaving the ice anchor. The men were now nearly exhausted but we made sail again hove up the broken anchor and worked up a third time, shortening sail and running alongside of a grounded berg we put ropes over some of its projecting points and were thankful to see them hold until we could get out ice anchors and secure her for the night. By this time all hands were completely worn out so that few were capable of any exertion even to save their lives.

It must be remembered that we had all been doing heavy and annoying work all day. The weather very cold and snowy, while underway constantly looking out for ice which the blinding snow and spray made it difficult to avoid. Our clothes were saturated with the spray in half an hour after starting, but they froze immediately and so were perhaps warmer. But the annoyance was the stiffness of the ropes which were iced and twice their usual size. The head guys, shrouds, and bobstays made a kind of net work which, being dipped as the vessel pitched, soon formed a solid mass of ice out to the bowsprit cap and the sea breaking over the bow rail soon had a solid mass from the knight heads to the windlass and being coated with ice outside she looked like an iceberg under sail. The small boat which we got from the *Advance* having been smashed against the ice and filling with water made us steer wild, so I cut her adrift with one blow of a hatchet and said good bye as she dove and rose bottom up astern. Only two men had their fingers frost bitten and both might have escaped it by more care, for although cautioned about taking off their mits they wouldn't believe that a minutes exposure could do the business. One was the old Boatswains mate whom I had ordered to put on his mits about six times during the day. Giving the Doctor and Brooks the first & mid watches (they having been in bed all day,) the captain and mate with all hands got some needful repose.

Friday September 13th 1850

Were very glad to see the *Advance* and Commo Austins squadron standing down for the Island at 11 o'clock. But not so glad as they said they were because they didn't expect to see us again supposing of course that we had been caught in the ice to leeward and the Commo having determined to try and go home they feared that having to hunt for us would knock that in the head. They made signal to us to get underway and followed and upon hearing of our crippled condition took us in tow and we are going to Eastward finely. At 8 we were off Cape Hothany and stood across the channel until 10 A.M. when we fetched up in the young ice. The *Advances* saw Penny and a schooner anchored close under the land about half way between Capes Martyr & Hothany. We left Commo Austin going into the harbour which the Assistance found for winter quarters. Home stock was up high but the young ice has caused a great fall.

Saturday September 14th 1850

We are afraid that we're caught for the winter. There was open water for several hours as far as we could see to the Eastward but we couldn't get into it until shortly before it was closed that we sailed only two miles and are again fast in the new ice with a six knot SW wind and the temperature so low that there is little hope of a break up. Commo Austin didn't write by us but asked our Commo to write to the Admiralty which is strange none of his officers seem to have known of our homeward intentions and we suppose that their commander didn't wish them to.

Sunday September 15th 1850

It is sometimes hard to say "Thy will be done." And this my 25th birth day is one of those times. Yes one day of open water would have put us whence we have every reason to suppose returning home certain or at all events in some harbour. But here we are fast, tight as wax in the middle of the mouth of Wellington Strait with a six knot fair wind. There has been no opening to-day and the field has drifted a little to NE so as to bring us with the capes of the strait and near the middle of it. The ice is so thick (4 inc[hes]) that while there was hope of getting on all hands were cutting sawing and breaking upon it, but it is so soft and tenacious that it doesn't crack; a stick makes a hole through it like mud, and closing after the sun, in five minutes it becomes hard as before. The ways of Providence are inscrutable and it is doubtless all for the best, but one can scarcely help thinking it hard to be kept up here away from all that is dear to us away from even the companionship of the English vessels for nine or ten long months at least and away from a safe harbour.

"What! winter in the pack" said old Penny, "Perfect madness!" and then enumerated the many disadvantages and dangers which we now unavoidably must suffer and experience. The danger to be apprehended most is the breaking up of the ice in Spring which being so far off I leave for a future Jeremiatic reflection. But the present inconvenience is that we cant prepare our vessels for winter until six weeks after John Bull in his harbour has been comfortably housed for we dare not put our stores on the ice out here until the lateness of the season makes it improbable that a gale would give them to the mermaids and in fact Parry says that he saw the ice outside the harbour agitated in the gales during all winter. So here we must remain without fire until winter is well begun. Our apartments are now so cold and damp that the Docs call them unwholesome and those of the men are worse. Could ships and men have a more gloomy prospect? But it may all be for good even in a worldly sense an early break up in the spring might liberate us early enough to be the farthest West next season or if we have an awful time Government may give us extra pay eclat &c. Again! May it not be a just punishment? Ours were the only vessels of the nine up here, in which there was no public worship of God, no mention made of his name nor his goodness in having enabled us to do as much as the English with all their advantages. So perhaps we are brought out from among them lest they be consumed with us. But since with God, miracles are small things I yet hope that he may convince some of us that he has done all for us heretofore by liberating us after all hope has vanished. For it seems that even the worst of us could be better employed almost any where else.

Monday September 16th 1850

Another day of fast in this horrid young ice. There was a small opening at 6 o'clock P.M. and we were carried into it about half a mile North in which direction we are daily being carried at a rate very annoying to those who still hope for a liberation this season, very gratifying to those who wish to remain and survey the channel and very perceptible to those who like myself are indifferent which way we go since it is so plainly the hand of Providence guiding us. The young ice has got so strong now that it plays with our vessels like toys swinging and thumping us about constantly so as to keep us constantly at work repairing its dammages. To day after almost finishing our rudder it [the ice] swung the *Advance* into us nearly crushing out white whale boat and then commenced squeezing us so as to make every timber creak and the poor little brig quake and quiver constantly; leaving it at this rascally sport which having lasted an hour seems still to afford it amusement, I will bid it good night.

Tuesday September 17th 1850
Drifting Northward with the pack about five miles NE of Cape Bowden today at noon. The ice kept up the squeezing and grinding all night and is much broken. The heavy pack ice coming North seems to have done this and if there is any hope left of getting out this season the loosening of the ice will cherish it until another freeze blasts it entirely. This South wind contrary to anything ever known in these regions seems to have no end. The South wind is rare at this season and generally of short duration.

Wednesday September 18th 1850
Drifting Northward still, came to a floe of heavy ice and being hard up for water got some fresh ice from it. All hands have given up hopes and the commo doesn't want to go home. Talking of going on land journeys this fall which I call a double extract of the essence of humbug and want to see it tried by some of those who propose sending the party.

Thursday September 19th 1850
The wind has been kind enough to change so that the Northerly drift seems checked. It is quite a gale from North but too thick and snowy to see far. The home is done for and the object now is to get in near the land and find a harbour which a few pools stretching toward the West coast seem to render practicable. So all hands were set to work to see how the cutting into the nearest pool (a large one to Westward of us) would go but I judge that it was thought rather difficult as we were ordered to knock off after two hours work, having made no impression, for although the ice is only a few inches thick it is so piled up and overlapped that all around us six feet of thickness is common. I am in hopes that we may be drifted entirely out of Lancaster Sound before we are lib-

erated as I cant perceive the good of wintering any where near here, it being certain that if the lost party have gone no farther West than our spring parties could reach they would have returned years ago in the same manner that we would go, and besides we know that from the low temperature, and South wind driving the ice on the North shore of Barrow strait that Austin, Penny, & Ross cant be far off and that they intend examining this channel. However our carpenter is making a sledge and a tent is under construction aboard the *Advance* for the proposed party to go to Assistance Harbour as soon as we are considered fast for the winter.

Friday September 20th 1850
So be it! No home this winter and that given up I am content, although wintering in the pack to initiated ones has connected with it ideas of suffering, danger, the almost impossibility of return next fall, and the improbability of taking the vessels back at all and lastly the almost certainty that some of our number will find a long home here. Who can say, "it wont be me"?

A fresh South wind commencing at noon and increasing to a gale by midnight send us at a great rate up the channel, and my hopes of being drifted out of the sound with those of the commo of getting into a harbour are driven before it at too rapid a pace to return any more. Some few leads and pools were seen near us but we are still fixed as stone and our cement seems to harden dayly. Better as tis perhaps because having been piled around us in a soft state it did us no injury and now serves to guard us from the shocks and squeezes of the heavy masses drifting about us. I was quite anxious and unhappy while there was a hope of going home but now that has vanished I am as indifferent and trusting that it is for some good end and thankful to say earnestly "They will be done."

Saturday September 21st 1850
The fresh Southerly wind made a rupture in the ice about the *Advance* leaving her adrift in a pool so she makes an ice anchor of the *Rescue* and moors by us head and stern. Drifted much to the Northward. Got an imperfect for lat. The sun on the mer being so low as to be scarcely seen in the art hor and entirely useless for longitude. Commo wants us to get alts of stars but thanks to be none have been seen yet through the mist, to give Jack Frost a bite at my fingers holding a sextant for the amusement of commodores and captains of the American Arctic fleet.

Transferred Wm Benson to the *Advance*, he having been sick with the scurvy for a long time and am in hopes that the little fleet surgeon understands its cure as I see he has gone very actively to work on this patient making him scrub and exercise. *The Crows Nest* (Lovell & Griffin editors) came out to-night. I haven't read the first number but understand that it is a dirty pill which didn't go down.

Sunday September 22nd 1850
Strange indeed does it seem to me that Enlightened Americans should openly profane the Sabbath. All hands have been employed to-day cutting the ice between us and the pool in which the *Advance* is. By 4 P.M. a canal was cut to within twenty feet of our stern when they discovered that we are entirely imbedded in the crushed and lapped cakes of bay ice which for twenty or thirty feet around us is from 8 to 15 feet thick and of course impossible to get out unless there was room to float off layer after layer of it so the sabbath has been a lost day in every respect. As I have the forenoon watch I had the afternoon below and so o[n]ly lost four hours of the Sabbath in that scrape. Read the Sabbath Manual by J. Edwards and am afraid it behooves me to leave a service where such work may be required. Indeed my conscience spites me, for not having considered this matter before, though I had never any idea that I would ever be places where the Sabbath was purposely made the day of work as it is with us. Last Sunday the Commo mentioned here that to employ his men he has set them to breaking out the hold. Most of the preceding week tho had been idle. The S. Manual, together with several other religious books furnished by some Society in New York I got out of a waste paper locker on board the *Advance* where are many others being torn up perfectly new. A large bundle of tracts having been exhausted in the same cause. This is perhaps speaking against my superiors & brother officers, but as this is a private journal and only intended for the perusal of my friends at home with whom these officers will probably never come in contact, I deem it no harm and if on our return this should be demanded by the commander of the expedition, I am willing that this days record be the first to meet his eye. This cutting ice with a cold wind and half the time wet to the knees is unpleasant and if the cold feet I have had all day is an earnest of our future winter work I am afraid that some of us will suffer from the effects of this cruise. The Northerly drift has been less

to-day and at Midt we have a fine NE Wind. The ice is again piling up around us and our canal is a mound several feet high. I walked to the *Advance* on ice of to-days formation. The channel seems to widen up here the Western coast taking a Northwesterly direction. Got a good 2° for lat.

Monday September 23, 1850
The ice has been in a state of great excitement all day overlaying and piling itself around the vessels in a manner to give us apprehension for their safety and show-ing us that with perfect ease it could overwhelm us. I am afraid that it is only waiting for the season to become more inclement to leave those of use who can rush out, sans every thing on the ice. This business of wintering in the pact com-mences with difficulties, I only hope we may be able to tell how it ends. About a foot of snow has fallen to-day and looks just like home snow falling fast, silently, and in large flakes, so different from the fine driving snow coming into every crevice that we have hitherto had that I went up and enjoyed the scene often being delighted with one reminding me of home as it did. Griffin accuses all hands of desponding at the prospect which gloomy as it can be rendered more so by constantly expecting the worst. Dr. Kane says "all this extra annoyance just to be called fools for our pains while the Englishmen amply provided, meet only the common evils of the undertaking to be honoured and promoted." Verily we would be fools to repeat the visit under like circumstances.

Tuesday September 24th 1850
More squeezing and piling. The little *Rescue* was forced twelve feet ahead through her bed of hummocks and mounds of this ice are raised in every direc-tion some of them ten feet high. Quite cool to-day but pleasant below with doors shut except for the constant dripping which has no cure and keeps numerous vessels employed at its regular depots and little puddles where its deposits are not known till thus discovered.

Wednesday September 25th 1850
Quite a pleasant day out. Taking active exercise after breakfast was oppressed with heat. This seems so strange, but with no wind and a low temperature, we are comfortable sitting in the open air whereas with a rise of 20° and a mod-erate breeze it is difficult to keep warm at all and with a fresh one impossible

even with violent exercise. Our tent (of felt cloth) was finished and pitched to-
day and being found to be too large is to be turned into a depot tent. The floe
in which we are so firmly imbedded broke adrift and is a very small one
appearing to-day in the middle of a large pool and showing its ability to drift
wherever open water will permit it carrying us along captives. I wish it would
go down the bank s of Newfoundland on a fishing excursion and get stuck there.

Thursday September 26th 1850
Very pleasant day. Commenced a snow or rather an ice house for exercise cutting and carrying the blocks of ice being hard work. Murdaugh & Lovell soon
joined me and I daresay we shall have a tower of Babel after a few mornings
work using ice for brick and water for cement.

Dr. Kane shot another seal and was as much pleased with himself as after
his first one.

Broke out our stove to prepare the pipes (which to save room were ordered
to be put up in sheets all punched and cut) and find that we have none at all,
the box containing only the parts of the stove and any quantity of shavings.
Wouldn't we have been comfortable this winter by ourselves? The *Advance* has
been making her pipes for several days and has nearly enough when lo! the
rivets have given out. Verily some of our countrymen are knaves. Knowing how
we were hurried off and that none of us would suspect rascality where all
seemed to wish to aid, our stove man had a fine opportunity to display his kind.
Saw a black fox quite near the vessels but under too much way to give hope
of a chase. Our floe has drifted to the Northern side of the water mentioned
yesterday and is also leaving the land.

Finding every thing in my bunk damp and some articles touching the beams
saturated, I kept a solar lamp burning inside the bunk all day and determined
not to draw the curtains at night any more.

Friday September 27th 1850
Rather sombre day and being pretty cool withall not so pleasant. Exercise at the
snow hut. Lovell made a swing from *Advance*'s fore yard. Some skating but the
ice was too rough and one man looking for smoother got into the drink and being
some distance from the strong ice came near joining the mermaids. All hands
rushed toward the spot but no one thought to carry a line or board until at the

place, giving the man ample time to drown if he had lost his strength or presence of mind as some do when floundering about in this cold water.

✳

CARTER, INTERESTINGLY ENOUGH, HAD SEEN, A WEEK OR TWO EARLIER, *the earliest evidence of Franklin anyone had yet found. One of the English ships had come upon the site of his first winter camp, occupied in 1845-46. The ground was littered with debris—scraps of paper, a pair of gloves held down by a rock, a huge pile of empty meat cans, a clay pipe. And three graves. What they did not find was a cairn with a note inside detailing their projected route for the next season. It was standard operating procedure in the Arctic to leave notes in stone cairns giving just that information. They found cairns, but no notes. They did, however, find the tracks of sledges leading north up the frozen Wellington Channel. That seemed to be a clue to where Franklin might have gone, or tried to go, the following summer. Based on this slender clue, subsequent expeditions looked north, up Wellington Channel, which as it happens was precisely the wrong way to turn. No one actually knew what Franklin's route had been.*

Although Lady Jane Franklin kept hope alive and persuaded others to do the same, it was already too late in 1850 to hold out much hope that Franklin or any of his men might be alive. The Franklin expedition had left in 1845. The first attempts to send out rescuers did not leave until 1848, when Sir James Ross led two ships into winter harbor on Somerset Island. Ross's sledge parties actually went the next spring along the route Franklin had taken, down Peel Sound to the west of Somerset Island, but ice held them where they were for most of the summer, and they cut for home. A party led by Sir John Richardson, Franklin's old friend, traversed the northern coast of Canada, thinking they might find that Franklin had found the Northwest Passage and was stuck somewhere near the Coppermine River. No such luck.

In fact the last of the Franklin survivors died in the spring of 1848. But by 1850, with nothing and no one having been found, the search only became more intense. Ships sailed through the Bering Strait and across the top of Alaska to look for something there. Still other ships approached from the east, through Lancaster Sound. The rescue expeditions had to winter over in the ice themselves. That had been Robert Carter's big worry, and it was indeed something to worry about—they got caught in the ice in Barrow Strait, unable to reach harbor, and spent a miserable winter in which food froze so hard that it took a mallet and cold chisel to carve pieces of butter and barrels of fruit had to be opened and broken up with an ax. Scurvy stalked them, too.

But men continued to join the search. French and German explorers, as well as American, volunteered. Nothing. Just those three graves, and the pile of meat tins, a pair of gloves, some scraps of paper. Money was at stake. The Admiralty had offered 20,000 pounds to anyone who could help save the lives of Franklin and/or his men, and half that sum for news of what had happened to them. Lady Jane continued to organize and badger and hold out hope, indeed to insist upon it. She became an international figure, persistent, indomitable, someone whose movements and activities were the subject of regular press reports. She raised money for still further expeditions. She traveled to the United States and met with the President of the United States.

John Rae found the first real evidence of what had happened to Franklin and his men. Rae is one of those great figures who has never been given his due, mostly because he was not a member of the establishment, particularly the Admiralty establishment with its old Arctic hands, now gathered into something known as the Arctic Council. A Hudson's Bay Company man, a medical doctor, and a natural scientist who published studies of plants and animals as well as anthropological and glaciological studies, Rae was one of the first white men to understand fully how to live comfortably in the Arctic in all kinds of conditions—like the Eskimos. He traveled light as they did, mastered dogs and dog sleds as they did, carried little in the way of provisions but lived off the land as they did, took no tents but built much warmer igloos out of snow instead, wore furs rather than wool (something the Admiralty had still, stubbornly, not learned to do), and ate what the Eskimos ate: fresh meat, uncooked if necessary, blubber, and fish. The Admiralty particularly scorned fish.

Equipped in this fashion, Rae made epic treks across northern Canada with no trouble at all. He served as a guide to Sir John Richardson in his 1849 search for Franklin. In the summer of 1851 he made another journey along the shores of the Arctic Ocean, covering ground near where Franklin's two ships had met their end. He found two pieces of wood that had obviously come off ships, but which ships there was no way of telling. Then, in 1854, when most of the other searches for Franklin were winding down, when the Admiralty had officially given up on the project, when it was obvious to everyone except Lady Jane that the entire company, officers and men, 130 English souls, had perished, John Rae, on an excursion up the Boothia Peninsula to finish off the chart of the coastline east of the Great Fish River, not yet named the Back, found out what had happened. To the survivors, that is. He tells us in a letter he wrote to the Secretary of the

Hudson's Bay Company in London. Rae, it's worth noting, reported almost all his accomplishments in letters to his superiors. He was not looking for fame. Here is his letter, up to and including his report on what the Eskimos told him about the fate of Franklin's last survivors.

JOHN RAE

Correspondence with the Hudson's Bay Company

on Arctic Exploration, 1844–1855

Yorkfactory Hudson's Bay *1st September 1854*
Archibald Barclay Esquire
Secretary
Hudson's Bay House
London

SIR,

I have the honor to report for the information of the Governor, Deputy Governor and Committee, that I arrived here yesterday with my party all in good health, but from causes which will be explained in their proper place, without having effected the object of the Expedition. At the same time information has been obtained, and articles purchased from the Natives which prove, beyond a doubt, that a portion, if not all, of the then survivors of the long lost and unfortunate party under Sir John Franklin, had met with a fate as melancholy and dreadful as it is possible to imagine.

By a Letter dated Chesterfield Inlet, 9th August 1853, you are in possession of my proceedings up to that time. Late on the evening of that day we parted company with our small consort, she steering down to the southward, whilst we took the opposite direction towards Repulse Bay.

Light and variable winds sadly retarded our advance northward, but by anchoring during the flood, and sailing or rowing with the tide, we gained some ground daily; On the 11th, we met with upwards of three hundred Walrus, lying on a rock a few miles off shore. They were not at all shy, and several were mortally wounded, but one only, (an immensely large fellow) was shot dead by myself. The greater part of the fat was cut off and taken on board, which supplied us abundantly with Oil for our Lamps all Winter.

On the forenoon of the 14th having a fair wind, we rounded Cape Horn [Hope], and ran up Repulse Bay, but as the weather was very foggy, completely hiding every object, at the distance of a quarter of a mile; we made the Land about seven miles east of my old winter quarters: next day, midst heavy rain, we ran down to North Pole River, moored the boat, and pitched the tents.

The weather being still dark and gloomy the surrounding Country presented a most dreary aspect. Thick masses of ice clung to the shore, whilst immense drifts of snow filled each ravine, and lined every steep bank that had a southerly exposure. No Esquimaux were to be seen, nor any recent traces of them: appearances could not be less promising for wintering safely, yet I determined to remain until the 1st September, by which date, some opinion could be formed as to the practicability of procuring sufficient food and fuel for our support during the winter, all the provisions on hand at that time being equal to only three months consumption.

The weather fortunately improved, and not a moment was lost. Nets were set: Hunters were sent out to procure Venison; and the majority of the party was constantly employed collecting fuel. By the end of August a supply of the latter essential article, (Andromeda Tetragona,) for fourteen weeks was laid up, thirteen deer and one musk bull had been shot, and one hundred and thirty six salmon caught. Some of the favorite haunts of the Esquimaux had been visited, but no indications were seen, to lead us to suppose, that they had been lately in the neighbourhood.

The absence of the Natives caused me some anxiety, not that I expected any aid from them, but because I could attribute their having abandoned so favourable a locality, to no other cause than a scarcity of food, arising from the deer having taken another route in their migrations to and from the north.

On the 1st September, I explained our position to the Men; the quantity of provisions we had, and the prospects, which were far from flattering, of getting more. They all most readily volunteered to remain, and our preparations for a nine months winter were continued with unabated energy. The weather, generally speaking, was favorable, and our exertions were so successful, that by the end of the month, we had a quantity of provisions and fuel collected, adequate to our wants up to the period of the spring migrations of the deer.

One hundred and nine deer, one musk ox, (including those killed in August,) fifty three brace of Ptarmigan, and one Seal had been shot; and the nets produced fifty four Salmon: Of the larger Animals above enumerated, forty nine deer and the musk ox were shot by myself, twenty one deer by Mistegan the deer hunter, fourteen by another of the Men, nine by William Ouligbuck, and sixteen by the remaining four Men.

The cold weather set in very early and with great severity. On the 20th, all the smaller and some of the larger Lakes were covered with ice four to six inches thick. This was far from advantageous for deer shooting, as these animals were enabled to cross the Country in all directions, instead of following their accustomed passes.

October was very stormy and cold. About the 15th the migrations of the deer terminated, and twenty five more were added to our Stock. Forty two Salmon and twenty Trout were caught with nets and hooks set in lakes under the ice, On the 28th, the snow was packed hard enough for building, and we were glad to exchange the cold and dismal tents (in which the temperature had latterly been 36° or 37° below the freezing point,) for the more comfortable shelter of snowhouses, which were built on the S.S.E. side of Beacon Hill, by which they were well protected from the prevailing N.W. Gales. The houses were nearly half a mile south of my winter quarters of 1846/7.

The weather in November was comparatively fine but cold, the highest, lowest and mean temperature uncorrected for error of thermometer being respectively 38° and 18.3° below Zero. Some deer were occasionally seen, but only four were shot, some wolves, several foxes and one wolverine were killed and from the nets 59 Salmon, and 22 Trout were obtained.

Our most productive Fishery was in a Lake about three miles distant, bearing East, (magnetic) from Beacon Hill or the mouth of the North Pole River.

The whole of December a very few days excepted was one continued gale with snow and drift. When practicable the men were occupied scraping under snow for fuel, by which means our stock of that very essential article was kept up. The mean temperature of the month was 23° below zero. The produce of our nets and guns was extremely small, amounting to one partridge, one wolf, and twenty seven fish.

1854 On the first of January the temperature rose to the very unusual height of 18°above zero, the wind at the time being S E with snow. Our nets after being set in different lakes without success, were finally taken up on the 12th, only five small fish having been caught. The thermometer was tested by freezing mercury and found to be in error the temperature indicated by it being 4°5 too high.

The cold during February was steady and severe, but there were fewer storms than usual. Deer were more numerous and generally were travelling northward. One or two were wounded but none killed. On two occasions, (1st and 27th) that beautiful but rare appearance of the Clouds near the Sun, with three fringes of pink and green following the outline of the Cloud, was seen, and I may add that the same splendid phenomenon was frequently observed during the Spring, and was generally followed by a day of two of fine weather.

During the latter part of the Month, preparations were being made for our Spring journies. A Carpenters work shop was built of snow, and our sledges were taken to pieces, reduced to as light a weight as possible, and then re-united more securely than before. The mean temperature of February, corrected for error of thermometer was 39°below zero. The highest and lowest being −20° and −53°.

On the 1st of March a female deer in fine Condition was shot, and on the 9th and 10th two more were killed. Three men were absent some days during this month in search of Esquimaux from whom we wished to obtain dogs. They went as far as the head of Ross Bay but found no traces of these people.

On the 14th I started with three men hauling sledges with provisions, to be placed in "cache" for the long spring Journey. Owing to the stormy state of the weather, we got no farther than Cape Lady Pelly, on the most northerly point of which our stores were placed under a heap of large stones secure from any Animal except Man or the bear. We returned on the 24th, the distance walked together being 170 miles.

On the 31st of March leaving three men in charge of the boat and stores, I set out with the other four including the Interpreter, with the view of tracing the west coast of Boothia from the Castor and Pollux River to Bellot Strait. The weight of our provisions &c. with those deposited on the way amounted to 865 lbs, an ample supply for 65 days.

The route followed for part of the Journey being exactly the same as that of Spring 1847, it is unnecessary to describe it. During the first two days, although we did not travel more than fifteen miles per day, the men found the work extremely hard, and as I perceived that one of them (a fine active young fellow but a light weight,) would be unable to keep pace with the others, he was sent back and replaced by Mistegan, a very able man and an experienced sledge hauler. More than a day was lost in making this exchange, but there was still abundance of time to complete our work if not opposed by more than common obstacles.

On the 6th April, we arrived at our provision "caches" and found it all safe. Having placed the additional stores on the sledges, which made those of the men weigh more than 160 lbs each, and my own about 110 lbs, we travelled seven miles further, then built a snow house on the ice two miles from shore. We had passed among much rough ice, but hitherto the drift banks of snow, by lying in the same direction in which we were travelling, made the walking tolerably good. As we advanced to the northward however, these crossed our track, (shewing that the prevailing winter gales had been from the westward,) and together with stormy weather, impeded us so much that we did not reach Colville Bay until the 10th. The position of our snowhouse was in Latitude 68°13' 5" N, Longde. by Chronometer 88°14" W., the variation of the Compass being 26° 20" W. From this place it was my intention to strike across Land as straight as possible for the Castor and Pollux River.

The 11th day was so stormy that we could not move, and the next day after placing "en cache" two days provisions, we had walked only six miles, in a westerly direction, when a gale of wind compelled us to get under shelter. The weather improved in the Evening, and having the benefit of the full moon, we started again at a few minutes to 8 P.M. Our course at first was the same as it had been in the morning, but the snow soon became so soft and deep, that I turned more to the northward in search of firmer footing. The walking was excessively fatiguing, and would have been so even to persons travelling unencumbered, as we sank at every step nearly ankle deep in snow. Eight and a half miles were accomplished in six and a half hours, at the end of which, as we required some rest, a small snow house was built, and we had some tea and frozen pemican.

After resting three hours, we resumed our march, and by making long detours, found the snow occasionally hard enough to support our weight. At 30 minutes to noon on the 13th, our days journey terminated in Latde. 68°23' 30" N, Longde. 89°3' 53" W, variation of Compass 83°30' W. At a mile and a half from our bivouac, we had crossed the arm of a lake of considerable extent, but the Country around was so flat, and so completely covered with snow, that its limits could not be easily defined and our snowhut was on the borders of another lake apparently somewhat smaller.

A snow storm of great violence raged during the whole of the 14th, which did not prevent us from making an attempt to get forward; after persevering two and a half hours, and gaining a mile and a half distance, we were again forced to take shelter.

The 15th was very beautiful with a temperature of only 8°below zero. The heavy fall of snow had made the walking and sledge hauling worse than before. It was impossible to keep a straight course, and we had to turn much out of our way, so as to select the hardest drift banks. After advancing several miles, we fortunately reached a large Lake containing a number of Islands, on one of which I noticed an old Esquimaux tent site. The fresh footmarks of a partridge (Tetrao Rupestris) were also seen, being the only signs of living thing, (a few tracks of foxes excepted,) that we had observed since commencing the traverse of this dreary waste of snow clad country. To the lake above mentioned, and to those seen previously, the name of Barrow was given, as a mark of respect to John Barrow Esquire, of the Admiralty, whose zeal in promoting and liberality in supporting many of the Expeditions to the Arctic Sea are too well known to require any comment; further, than that he presented a very valuable Halketts Boat for the Service of my party, which unfortunately by some irregularity in the Railway baggage trains between London and Liverpool did not reach the latter place in time for the Steamer although sent from London some days before. Our snow hut was built on the edge of a small lake in Late. 68°31' 38 N, Longde. 89°11. 55 W, Variation of Compass 83°30 W.

The difficulties of walking were somewhat diminished on the 16th, by a fresh breeze of wind which drifted the snow off the higher ground, and we were enabled to make a fair day's Journey. Early on the 17th we reached the shore of Pelly Bay, but had barely got a view of its rugged ice covering, before a dense fog came on: we had to *steer* by compass for a large rocky Island, some miles to the westward, and we stopped on an islet near to its east shore until the fog cleared away. This luckily happened some time before noon, and afforded an opportunity of obtaining observations, the results of which were Latde. 68°44' 53" N, Longde. by chron 89°34' 47 W, and variation 84° 20 W. Even on the ice we found the snow soft and deep, a most unusual circumstance. The many detentions I had met with caused me now, instead of making for the Castor and Pollux River, to attempt a direct course towards the magnetic Pole, should the land west of the bay be smooth enough for travelling over. The large island west of us was so rugged and steep, that there was no crossing it with sledges we therefore travelled along its shore to the northward, and stopped for the night, within a few miles of its northern extremity. The track of an Esquimaux sledge drawn by dogs was observed to day, but was of old date.

The morning of the 18th was very foggy, but after rounding the north point of the Island, it became clear and we travelled due west or very nearly so, until within three miles of the west shore of the bay, which presented an appearance so rocky and mountainous, that it was evident we could not traverse it, without loss of time. As the Country towards the head of the bay looked more level I turned to the southward, and after a most circuitous walk of more than sixteen miles, we built our snow house on the ice, five miles from shore. Many old traces of Esquimaux were seen on the ice to day.

On the 19th we continued travelling southward, and our day's journey (about equal to that of yesterday) terminated near the head of the bay.

20th April. The fresh footmarks of Esquimaux, with a sledge having been seen yesterday on the ice within a short distance of our resting place, the interpreter and one man were sent to look for them, the other two being employed in hunting and collecting fuel, whilst I obtained excellent Observations, the results of which were Latde. 68°28' 29" N Longde. by Chronr. 90°18' 32" W, Variation of Compass 98°30 W. The latter is apparently erroneous, probably caused by much local attraction.

After an absence of eleven hours the Men sent in search of Esquimaux returned in company with seventeen natives, (five of whom were Women,) and several of them had been at Repulse Bay when I was there in 1847. Most of the others had never before seen "Whites", and were extremely forward and troublesome, they would give us no information on which any reliance could be placed, and none of them would consent to accompany us for a day or two, although I promised to reward them liberally. Apparently there was a great objection to our travelling across the Country in a westerly direction. Finding that it was their object to puzzle the Interpreter and mislead us, I declined purchasing more than a small piece of Seal from them, and sent them away, not however, without some difficulty, as they lingered about with the hope of stealing something, and notwithstanding our vigilance, succeeded in abstracting from one of the sledges a few pounds of Biscuit and Grease.

The morning of the 21st was extremely fine, and at 3 A.M. we started across land towards a very conspicuous hill, bearing west of us. On a rocky eminence some miles inland, we made a "cache" of the Seals flesh we had purchased. Whilst doing this our Interpreter made an attempt to join his Countrymen, fortunately his absence was observed before he had gone back very far, and he was overtaken after a sharp race of four or five miles. He was in a great fright when we came up to him, and was crying like a child, but expressed his readiness to return, and pleaded sickness as an excuse for his conduct. I believe he was really unwell, probably from having eaten too much boiled Seals flesh, with which he had been regaled in the snowhuts of the Natives.

Having taken some of the lading off Ouligbuck's sledge, we had barely resumed our Journey when we were met by a very intelligent Esquimaux, driving a dog's sledge laden with musk ox beef. This man at once consented to accompany us two days Journey, and in a few minutes had deposited his load on the snow, and was ready to join us. Having explained my object to him, he said that the road by which he had come was the best for us, and having lightened the men's sledges we travelled with more facility. We were now joined by another of the Natives who had been absent Seal hunting yesterday, but being anxious to see us, had visited our snow house early this morning, and then followed up on our track. This man was very communicative, and on putting to him the usual questions as to his having seen "white men" before, or any ships or boats—he replied in the negative; but said, that a party of "Kabloonans", had died of starvation, a long distance to the west of where we then were, and beyond a large River;—He stated that, he did not know the exact place; that he had never been there; and that he could not accompany us so far.

The substance of the information then and subsequently obtained from various sources, was to the following effect:

In the Spring, four winters past, (1850) whilst some Esquimaux families were killing Seals near the north shore of a large Island named in Arrowsmith's Charts, King William's Land, about forty white men were seen travelling in company southward over the ice, and dragging a boat and sledges with them. They were passing along the west shore of the above named Island. None of the party could speak the Esquimaux language so well as to be understood, but by signs the Natives were led to believe that the Ship or Ships had been crushed by ice, and that they were then going to where they expected to find deer to shoot. From the appearance of the Men (all of whom with the exception of one Officer, were hauling on the drag ropes of the sledge and were looking thin)—they were then supposed to be getting short of provisions, and they purchased a small Seal or piece of Seal from the natives. The Officer was described as being a tall, stout, middle aged man: When their days journey terminated, they pitched Tents to rest in.

At a later date the same Season but previous to the disruption of the ice, the corpses of some thirty persons and some Graves were discovered on the Continent, and five dead bodies on an Island near it, about a long day's journey to the north west of the mouth of a large stream, which can be no other than Backs Great Fish River, (named by the Esquimaux Ool-koo-i-hi-ca-lik,) as its description, and that of the low shore in the neighborhood of Point Ogle and Montreal Island agree exactly with that of Sir George Back. Some of the bodies were in a tent or tents; others were under the boat which had been turned over to form a shelter, and some lay scattered about in different directions. Of those seen on the Island, it was supposed that one was that of an Officer, (chief) as he had a telescope strapped over his shoulders, and his double barrelled gun lay underneath him.

From the mutilated state of many of the bodies and the contents of the kettles, it is evident that our wretched Countrymen had been driven to the last dread alternative, as a means of sustaining life. A few of the unfortunate Men must have survived until the arrival of the wild fowl, (say until the end of May,) as shots were heard, and fresh bones and feathers of geese were noticed near the scene of the sad event.

There appears to have been an abundant store of ammunition, as the Gunpowder was emptied by the Natives in a heap on the ground out of the kegs or cases containing it and a quantity of shot and ball was found below high water mark, having probably been left on the ice close to the beach before the spring thaw commenced. There must have been a number of telescopes, guns, (several of them double barrelled,) watches, compasses &c. all of which seem to have been broken up, as I saw pieces of these different articles with the Natives, and I purchased as many as possible, together with some silver spoons and forks, an order of merit in the form of a Star, and a small silver plate engraved Sir John Franklin K.O.H.

Inclosed is a list of the principal articles bought, with a note of the initials and a rough pen and ink sketch of the crests on the forks and spoons. The articles themselves I shall have the honor of handing over to you, on my arrival in London.

None of the Esquimaux with whom I had communication saw the "white men" either when living or after death, nor had they ever been at the place where the Corpses were found, but had their information from Natives who had been there, and who had seen the party when travelling over the ice. From what I could learn, there is no reason to suspect that any violence had been offered to the sufferers by the Natives.

As the dogs in the sledge were fatigued before they joined us, our days journey was a short one. Our snow house was built in Latde. 68°29' N & Londe. 90 42. 42. W on the bed of a river having high mud banks, and which falls into the west side of Pelly Bay about Latde. 68°47' N, and Longde. 90°25' W.

On the 22nd, we travelled along the north bank of the River, (which I named after Capt. Beecher of the Admiralty) in a westerly direction for seven or eight miles (until abreast of the lofty and peculiarly shaped hill already alluded to, and which I named Ellice Mountain,) when we turned more to the northward. We soon arrived at a long narrow lake on which we encamped a few miles from its east end, our days march being little more than thirteen miles. Our Esquimaux auxiliaries were now anxious to return, being in dread or professing to be so, that the wolves or wolverines would find their "cache" of meat and destroy it. Having paid them liberally for their aid and information, and having bade them a most friendly farewell, they set out for home, as we were preparing to go to bed.

Next morning provisions for six days were secured under a heap of ponderous stones, and we resumed our march along the Lake. Thick weather, snow storms and heavy walking sadly retarded our advance. The Esquimaux had recommended me, after reaching the end of the chain of lakes, (which ran in a N' Westerly direction for nearly twenty miles, and then turned sharply to the southward,) to follow the windings of a brook that flowed from them. This I attempted to do, until finding that we would be led thereby far to the South, we struck across land to the west among a series of hills and valleys. Tracks of deer now became numerous, and a few traces of musk cattle were observed.

At 2 A.M. on the 26th we fell upon a River with banks of mud and gravel 20 to 40 feet high, and about a quarter of a mile in width. After a most laborious walk of more than 18 miles, we found an old snow hut, which after a few repairs was made habitable, and we were snugly housed at 6h.40m. A.M. Our position was in Latde. 68°25'27"N, Longde. 92°53' 14" W.

One of my men who from carelessness some weeks before, had severely frozen two of his toes, was now scarcely able to walk; and as by Esquimaux report, we could not be very far from the Sea, I prepared to start in the evening with two men and four days provisions for the Castor and Pollux River, leaving the lame man and another to follow at their leisure a few miles on our track, to some rocks that lay in our route, where they were more likely to find both fuel and game, than on the bare flat ground where we then were.

The morning of the 26th was very fine as we commenced tracing the course of the River seaward, sometimes following its course, at other times travelling on its left or right bank to cut off points. At 4 A.M. on the 27th, we reached the mouth of the river, which by subsequent observation I found to be situate in Lat 68°32 N, Longde. 93. 20 W. It was rather difficult to discover when we had reached the Sea, until a mass of rough ice settled the question beyond a doubt. After leaving the river we walked rapidly due west for six miles, then built our usual snug habitation on the ice, three miles from shore, and had some partridges ,(Tetrao mutas,) for supper, at the unseasonable hour of 8 A.M. We had seen great numbers of these birds during the night. Our latitude was 68° 32 1 N, Longde. 93°33' 48" West, being 3' 38" N and about 40' East of Simpsons position of the mouth of the Castor and Pollux River.

The weather was overcast with snow, when we resumed our journey at 8h. 30m.P.M. on the 27th; we directed our course directly for the shore, which we reached after a sharp walk of one and a half hours, in doing which we crossed a long stony island of some miles in extent. As by this time it was snowing heavily, I made my men travel on the ice, the walking being better there, whilst I followed the winding of the shore, closely examining every object along the beach.

After passing several heaps of stones, which had evidently formed Esquimaux "Caches", I came to a collection larger than any I had yet seen, and clearly not intended for the protection of property of any kind. The stones generally speaking were small, and had been built in the form of a pillar, but the top had fallen down, as the Esquimaux had previously given me to understand was the case.

Calling my men to land, I sent one to trace what looked like the bed of a small river immediately west of us, whilst I and the other man cleared away the pile of stones in search of a document. Although no document was found there could be no doubt in my own mind, and in that of my companion, that its construction was not that of the natives: My belief that we had arrived at the Castor and Pollux River was confirmed, when the person who had been sent to trace the apparent stream bed, returned with the information that it was clearly a River.

THAT, IN ITS LACONIC UNDERSTATED WAY, IS IT. THIRTY OR FORTY MEN *had made it to the area of the Great Fish River, and they had all died. Ironically, it was in the area of the Great Fish River that Richard King, another doctor, who had been with George Back on his discovery of it, had urged the Admiralty to look for Franklin survivors. The Admiralty had ignored him. King had a way of alienating people even as he gave them good, indeed excellent advice. Like a Cassandra, nobody would listen to him. Had they taken his advice, the Admiralty might have found a few of these men alive. But probably not. They were seen straggling down the shorelines in the spring of 1848. None of the rescue expeditions really got going until 1849.*

The big news was not that the truth had been learned—no one expected any survivors at this point, perhaps not even Lady Franklin—but that these men had evidently eaten their dead. That was a thought the English could not bear. One of the most interesting aspects of this event, in fact, is the way the English reacted to this news. Rae, who came to England to pick up the 10,000£ reward for finding out what had happened to the expedition, became a pariah. The press condemned him for even suggesting such a thing. Other explanations were offered. Eskimos had no doubt attacked them and mutilated the bodies. One officer's skeleton had been found lying on top of his gun. Surely that meant that someone had attacked him from behind. Treacherous natives, no doubt. When Rae, who knew the Eskimos as well as anyone alive, defended them, he was further condemned. Charles Dickens became involved, writing in Household Words, the magazine he owned and edited, that while Rae had had no choice but to report what he had heard, surely it was the natives who had killed the survivors and then, trying to conceal the crime, had made up this story. In collaboration with the novelist Wilkie Collins, Dickens soon after wrote a play, The Frozen Deep, upholding the honor of Franklin and his men. Dr. Rae did collect his reward, but virtually alone among the English Arctic explorers he received no knighthood, no medals, no respect.

Dr. Rae's findings were not enough to satisfy Lady Franklin. She continued to urge that expeditions be sent to fill out the story. Various veterans of other Arctic expeditions did the same, petitioning the government to do something more when the Crimean War ended in 1856. At the last it was Lady Franklin herself who organized it, buying a small ship, hardly more than a yacht, named the Fox, and sending it, under Arctic veteran Leopold McClintock, to the Canadian archipelago in 1857. She financed the expedition partly through contributions from the public.

The Fox spent two winters in the Arctic before it was able to send out sledge parties, in the spring of 1859, fourteen years after Franklin left England, to search the area where the last survivors had been reported. The excerpt that follows tells us what McClintock found.

LEOPOLD MCCLINTOCK

The Voyage of the FOX in the Arctic Seas:
A Narrative of the Discovery of the Fate of Sir John
Franklin and His Companions

7TH MAY.—TO AVOID SNOW-BLINDNESS, WE COMMENCED NIGHTMARCH-ING. Crossing over from Matty Island towards the King William Island shore, we continued our march southward until midnight, when we had the good fortune to arrive at an inhabited snow-village. We found here ten or twelve huts and thirty or forty natives of King William's Island; I do not think any of them had ever seen white people alive before, but they evidently knew us to be friends. We halted at a little distance, and pitched our tent, the better to secure small articles from being stolen whilst we bartered with them.

I purchased from them six pieces of silver plate, bearing the crests or initials of Franklin, Crozier, Fairholme, and McDonald; they also sold us bows and arrows of English woods, uniform and other buttons, and offered us a heavy sledge made of two short stout pieces of curved wood, which no mere boat could have furnished them with, but this of course we could not take away; the silver spoons and forks were readily sold for four needles each.

They were most obliging and peaceably disposed, but could not resist the temptation to steal, and were importunate to barter every thing they possessed; there was not a trace of fear, every countenance was lighted up with joy; even the children were not shy, nor backward either, in crowding about us, and poking in everywhere. One man got hold of our saw, and tried to retain it, holding it behind his back, and presenting his knife in exchange; we might have had some trouble in getting it from him, had not one of my men mistaken his object in presenting the knife towards me, and run out of the tent with a gun in his hand; the saw was instantly returned, and these poor people seemed to think they never could do enough to convince us of their friendliness; they repeatedly tapped me gent on the breast, repeating the words "Kammik toome" (We are friends).

Having obtained all the relics they possessed, I purchased some seal's flesh, blubber, frozen venison, dried and frozen salmon, and sold some of my puppies. They told us it was five days' journey to the wreck, —one day up the inlet still in sight, and four days overland; this would carry them to the western coast of King William's Land; they added that but little now remained of the wreck which was accessible, their countrymen having carried almost every thing away. In answer to an inquiry, they said she was without masts; the question gave rise to some laughter amongst them, and they spoke to each other about *fire*, from which Petersen thought they had burnt the masts through close to the deck in order to get them down.

There had been *many books* they said, but all have long ago been destroyed by the weather; the ship was forced on shore in the fall of the year by the ice. She had not been visited during the past winter, and an old woman and a boy were shown to us who were the last to visit the wreck; they said they had been at it during the winter of 1857-8.

Petersen questioned the woman closely, and she seemed anxious to give all the information in her power. She said many of the white men dropped by the way as they went to the Great River; that some were buried and some were not; they did not themselves witness this, but discovered their bodies during the winter following.

We could not arrive at any approximation to the numbers of the white men nor of the years elapsed since they were lost.

This was all the information we could obtain, and it was with great difficulty so much could be gleaned, the dialect being strange to Petersen, and the natives far more inclined to ask questions than to answer them. They assured us we should find natives upon the south shore of King William's Island only three days' journey from here, and also at Montreal Island; moreover they said we might find some at the wreck. For these reasons I did not prolong my stay with them beyond a couple of hours. They seemed to have but little intercourse with other communities, not having heard of our visit to the Boothians two months before; one man even asked Petersen if he had seen his brother, who lived in Boothia, not having heard of him since last summer.

It was quite a relief to get away from these good-humored, noisy thieves, and rather difficult too, as some of them accompanied us for miles. They had abundance of food, were well clothed, and are a finer race than those who inhabit North Greenland, or Pond's Inlet: the men had their hair cropped short, with the exception of one long, straggling lock hanging down on each side of the face; like the Boothians, the women had lines tattooed upon their cheeks and chins.

We now proceeded round a bay which I named Latrobe in honor of the late Governor of Victoria, and of his brother, the head of the Moravian Church in London, both esteemed friends of Franklin.

Finding the "Mathison Island" of Rae to be a flat-topped hill, we crossed over low land to the west of it, and upon the morning of the 10th May reached a single snow hut off Point Booth. I was quite astonished at the number of poles and various articles of wood lying about it, also at the huge pile of walrus' and reindeer's flesh, seal's blubber, and skins of various sorts. We had abundance of leisure to examine these exterior articles before the inmates would venture out; they were evidently much alarmed by our sudden appearance.

A remarkably fine old dog was tied at the entrance—the line being made fast within the long passage—and although he wagged his tail, and received us as old acquaintances, we did not like to attempt an entrance. At length an old man and an old woman appeared; they trembled with fear, and could not, or would not, say any thing except "Kammik toomee:" we tried every means of allaying their fears, but their wits seemed paralyzed and we could get no information. We asked where they got the wood? They purchased it from their countrymen. Did they know the Great River? Yes, but it was a long way off. Were there natives there now? Yes. They even denied all knowledge of white people having died upon their shores. A fine young man came out of the hut, but we could learn nothing of him; they said they had nothing to barter, except what we saw, although we tempted them by displaying our store of knives and needles.

The wind was strong and fair, and the morning intensely cold, and as I could not hope to overcome the fears of these poor people without encamping, and staying perhaps a day with them, I determined to push on, and presented the old lady with a needle as a parting gift.

The principal articles which caught my attention here were eight or ten fir poles, varying in length from 5 to 10 feet, and up to 2 ½ inches in diameter (these were converted into spear handles and tent poles), a kayak paddle constructed out of the blade of two ash oars, and two large snow shovels 4 feet long, made of thin plank, painted white or pale yellow; these might have been the bottom boardsof a boat. There were many smaller articles of wood.

Half a mile further on we found seven or eight deserted snow huts. Bad weather had now fairly set in, accompanied by a most unseasonable degree of cold. On the morning of the 12th May we crossed Point Ogle, and encamped upon the ice in the Great Fish River the same evening; the cold and the darkness of our more southern latitude, having obliged us to return to day-travelling. All the 13th we were imprisoned in our tent by a most furious gale, nor was it until late on the morning of the 14th that we could proceed; that evening we encamped 2 miles from some small islands which lie off the north end of Montreal Island.

On the morning of the 15th we made only a short march of 6 miles, as one of the men suffered severely from snow-blindness, and I was anxious to recommence night travelling; encamped in a little bay upon the N.E. side of Montreal Island. The same evening we again set out, although it was blowing very strongly, and "snowing for a wager," as the men expressed it, but it was only necessary for us to keep close along the shore of the island: we discovered, however, a narrow and crooked channel which led us through to the west side of the island, and, one of the men appearing seriously ill, we encamped about midnight.

Whilst encamped this day, explorations were made about the N.E. quarter of the island; islets and rocks were seen to abound in all directions; eventually it proved to be a separate island upon which we had encamped. The only traces or relics of Europeans found were the following articles, discovered by Petersen, beside a native mark (one large stone set upright on the top of another), at the east side of the Main—or Montreal—island:–a piece of preserved meat tin, two pieces of iron hoop, some scraps of copper, and an iron-hoop bolt. These probably are part of the plunder obtained from the boat, and were left here until a more favorable opportunity should offer, or perhaps necessity should compel the depositor to return for them.

All the 16th we were unable to move, not only because Hampton was ill, but the weather was extremely bad, and snow thickly falling with temperature at zero; certainly strange weather for the middle of May! We have not had a single clear day since the first of the month.

On the 17th the weather, though dull, was clear, so Petersen, Thompson, and I, set off with the dog-sledge to complete the examination of Montreal Island, leaving the other three men with the tent: we hoped also to find natives, but had not seen any recent traces of them since passing Point Booth. Petersen drove the dog-sledge south, as far up the east side as to meet our previously explored portion of it, whilst Thompson and I walked along on the land, the one close down to the beach, and the other higher up, examining the more conspicuous parts: in this order we traversed the remaining portion of the island.

Although the snow served to conceal from us any traces which might exist in hollows or sheltered situations, yet it rendered all objects intended to serves as marks proportionably conspicuous; and we may remember that it was in its winter garb that the retreating crews saw Montreal Island, precisely as we ourselves saw it. The island was almost covered with native marks, usually of one stone standing upright upon another, sometimes consisting of three stones, but very rarely of a greater number.

No trace of a cairn could be found.

In examining, with pickaxe and shovel, a collection of stones which appeared to be arranged artificially, we found a quantity of seal's blubber buried beneath; this old Esquimaux cache was near the S.E. point of the island. The interiors of the island and the principal islets adjacent were also examined without success, nor was there the slightest evidence of natives having been here during the winter: it is not to be wondered at that we returned in the evening to our tent somewhat dispirited. The total absence of natives was a bitter disappointment; circles of stones, indicating the sites of their tenting places in summer, were common enough.

Montreal Island is of primary rock, chiefly grey gneiss, traversed with whitish vertical bands in a N. and S. direction (by them I often directed my route when crossing the island). It is of considerable elevation, and extremely rugged. The low beaches and grassy hollows were covered with a foot or two of hard snow, whilst all the level, the elevated, or exposed parts were swept perfectly bare; had a cairn, or even a grave existed (raised as it must be, the earth being frozen hard as rock), we must at once have seen it. If any were constructed they must have been levelled by the natives; every doubtful appearance was examined with the pickaxe.

A remark made by my men struck me as being shrewd; they judged from the washed appearance of the rock upon the east side of Montreal Island that it must be often exposed to a considerable sea, such as would effectually remove everything not placed far above its reach; when looking over the smooth and frozen expanse one is apt to forget this.

Since our first landing upon King William's Island we have not met with any heavy ice; all along its eastern and southern shore, together with the estuary of this great river, is one vast unbroken sheet formed in the early part of last winter where *no ice previously existed;* this I fancy (from the accounts of Back and Anderson) is unusual, and may have caused the Esquimaux to vary their seal-hunting localities. Mr. Petersen suggested that they might have retired into the various inlets after the seals; and therefore I determined to cross over into Barrow's Inlet as soon as we had examined the Point Ogle Peninsula.

Upon Montreal Island I shot a hare and a brace of willow-grouse. Up to this date we had shot during our journey only one bear and a couple of ptarmigan. The first recent traces of reindeer were met with here.

On the 18th May we crossed over to the mainland near Point Duncan, but Hampton again complaining, I was obliged to encamp. When away from my party, and exploring along the shore towards Elliot Bay, I saw a heard of eight reindeer and succeeded in shooting one of them. In the evening Petersen saw another. Some willow-grouse also were seen. Here we found much more vegetation than upon King William's Island, or any other Arctic land I have yet seen.

On the evening of the 19th we commenced our return journey, but for the three following weeks our route led us over new ground. Hampton being unable to drag, I made over my puppy-team to him, and was thus left free to explore and fully examine every doubtful object along our route. I shall not easily forget the trial my patience underwent during the six weeks that I drove that dog-sledge. The leader of my team, named "Omar Pascha," was very willing, but very lame; little "Rose" was coquettish, and fonder of being caressed than whipped; from some cause or other she ceased growing when only a few months old; she was therefore far too small for heavy work; "Darky" and "Missy" were mere pups; and last of all came the two wretched starvelings, reared in the winter, "Foxey" and "Dolly." Each dog had its own harness, formed of strips of canvas, and was attached to the sledge by a single trace 12 feet long. None of them had ever been yoked before, and the amount of cunning and perversity they displayed to avoid both the whip and the work, was quite astonishing. They bit through their traces, and hid away under the sledge, or leaped over one another's backs, so as to get into the middle of the team out of the way of my whip, until the traces became plaited up, and the dogs were almost knotted together; the consequence was I had to halt every few minutes, pull off my mits, and, at the risk of frozen fingers, disentangle the lines. I persevered, however, and, without breaking any of their bones, succeeded in getting a surprising amount of work out of them. Hobson drove his own dog-sledge likewise, and as long as we were together we helped each other out of difficulties, and they were frequently occurring, for, apart from those I have above mentioned, directly a dog-sledge is stopped by hummocks, or sticks fast in deep snow, the dogs, instead of exerting themselves, lie down, looking perfectly delighted at the circumstance, and the driver has to extricate the sledge with a hearty one, two, three haul! and apply a little gentle persuasion to set his canine team in motion again.

Having searched the east shore of this land for 7 or 8 miles further north, we crossed over into Barrow's Inlet, and spent a day in its examination, but not a trace of natives were met with.

Regaining the shore of Dease and Simpson's Strait, some miles to the west of Point Richardson, we crossed over to King William's Island upon the morning of the 24th, striking in upon it a short distance west of the Peffer River. The south coast was closely examined as we marched along towards Cape Herschel. Upon a conspicuous point, to the westward of Point Gladman, a cairn nearly five feet high was seen, which, although it did not appear to be a recent construction, was taken down, stone by stone, and carefully examined, the ground beneath being broken up with the pickaxe, but nothing was covered.

The ground about it was much exposed to the winds, and consequently devoid of snow, so that no trace could have escaped us. Simpson does not mention having landed here, or anywhere upon the island except at Cape Herschel, yet it seemed to me strange that natives should construct such a mark here, since a huge boulder, which would equally serve their purpose, stood upon the same elevation, and within a couple of hundred yards. We had previously examined a similar but smaller cairn, a few miles to the eastward.

We were now upon the shore along which the retreating crews must have marched. My sledges of course travelled upon the sea-ice close along the shore; and, although the depth of snow which covered the beach deprived us of almost every hope, yet we kept a very sharp look-out for traces, nor were we unsuccessful. Shortly after midnight of the 24th May, when slowly walking along a gravel ridge near the beach, which the winds kept partially bare of snow, I came upon a human skeleton, partly exposed, with here and there a few fragments of clothing appearing through the snow. The skeleton—now perfectly bleached—was lying upon its face, the limbs and smaller bones either dissevered or gnawed away by small animals.

A most careful examination of the spot was of course made, the snow removed, and every scrap of clothing gathered up. A pocket-book afforded strong grounds of hope that some information might be subsequently obtained respecting the unfortunate owner and the calamitous march of the lost crews, but at the time it was frozen hard. The substance of that which we gleaned upon the spot may thus be summed up:

This victim was a young man, slightly built, and perhaps above the common height; the dress appeared to be that of a steward or officer's servant, the loose bow-knot in which his neck-handkerchief was tied not being used by seamen or officers. In every particular the dress confirmed our conjectures as to his rank or office in the late expedition, —the blue jacket with slashed sleeves and braided edging, and the pilot-cloth great-coat with plain covered buttons. We found, also, a clothes-brush near, and a horn pocket-comb. This poor man seems to have selected the bare ridge top, as affording the least tiresome walking, and to have fallen upon his face in the position in which we found him.

It was a melancholy truth that the old woman spoke when she said, "they fell down and died as they walked along."

I do not think the Esquimaux had discovered this skeleton, or they would have carried off the brush and comb; superstition prevents them from disturbing their own dead, but would not keep them from appropriating the property of the white man, if in any way useful to them. Dr. Rae obtained a piece of flannel, marked "F.D.V., 1845," from the Esquimaux of Boothia or Repulse Bay: it had doubtless been a part of poor Des Voeux's garments.

At the time of our interview with the natives of King William's Island, Petersen was inclined to think that the retreat of the crews took place in the fall of the year, some of the men in boats, and others walking along the shore; and as only five bodies are said to have been found upon Montreal Island with the boat, this fact favored his opinion, because so small a number could not have dragged her there over the ice, although they could very easily have taken her there by water. Subsequently this opinion proved erroneous. I mention it because it shows how vague our information was—indeed all Esquimaux accounts are naturally so—and how entirely we were dependent upon our own exertions for bringing to light the mystery of their fate.

The information obtained by Dr. Rae was mainly derived second-hand from the Fish River Esquimaux, and should not be confounded with that received by us from the King William's Island Esquimaux. These people told us they did not find the bodies of the white men (that is, they did not know any had died upon the march) until the following winter. This probably true, as it is only in winter and early spring they can travel overland to the west shore, or that they make a practice of wandering along the shore in search of seals and bears.

The remains of those who died in the Fish River may very probably have been discovered in the summer shortly after their decease.

Along the south coast of King William's Land, as upon the mainland, I was sadly disappointed in my expectation of meeting natives. We found only six or eight deserted snow huts, showing that they had recently been here, and consequently there was less chance of meeting with them on our further progress, as the season had now arrived when they seek the rivers and the favorite haunts and passes of the reindeer in their northern migration.

Hobson was, however, upon the western coast, and I hoped to find a note left for me at Cape Herschel, containing some piece of good news. After minutely examining the intervening coast-line, it was with strong and reasonable hope I ascended the slope which is crowned by Simpson's conspicuous cairn. This summit of Cape Herschel is perhaps 150 feet high, and about a quarter of a mile within the low stony point which projects from it, and on which there was no considerable ice pressure and a few hummocks heaped up, the first we had seen for three weeks. Close round this point, or by cutting across it as we did, the retreating party *must* have passed; and the opportunity afforded by the cairn of depositing in a known position—and that, too, where their own discoveries terminated—some record of their own proceedings, or, it might be, a portion of their scientific journals, would scarcely have been disregarded.

Simpson makes no mention of having left a record in this cairn, nor would Franklin's people have taken any trouble to find it if he had left one; but what now remained of this once "pondrous cairn" was only four feet high; the south side had been pulled down and the central stones removed, as if by persons seeking for something deposited beneath. After removing the snow with which it was filled, and a few loose stones, the men laid bare a large slab of limestone; with difficulty this was removed, then a second, and also a third slab, when they came to the ground. For some time we persevered with a pickaxe, in breaking up the frozen earth, but nothing whatever was found, nor any trace of European visitors in its vicinity. There were many old caches and low stone walls, such as natives would use to lurk behind for the purpose of shooting reindeer; and we noticed some recent tracks of those animals which had crossed direct hither from the mainland.

Chapter XV

As the Esquimaux of this land, as well as those of Boothia and Pond's Inlet, have long since given up the practice of building stone dwellings—passing their winters in snow huts, and summers in tents—no other traces of them than those described reamin; so that when or in what numbers they may have been here one cannot form any opinion, the same caches and hiding-places serving for generations.

I cannot divest myself of the belief that *some record was left here* by the retreating crews, and perhaps some most valuable documents which their slow progress and fast failing strength would have assured them could not be carried much further. If any such were left they have been discovered by the natives, and carried off, or thrown away as worthless. Doubtless the natives, when they ascertained that famine and fatigue had caused many of the white men to "fall down and die" upon their fearful march, and heard, as they might have done, of its fatal termination upon the mainland, lost no time in following up their traces, examining every spot where they halted, every mark they put up, or stone displaced.

It is easy to tell whether a cairn has been put up or touched within a moderate period of years; if very old, the outer stones have a weathered appearance, lichens will have grown upon the sheltered portions and moss in the crevices; but if recently disturbed, even if a single stone is turned upside down, these appearances are altered. If a cairn has been recently built it will be evident, because the stones picked up from the neighborhood would be bleached on top by the exposure of centuries, whilst underneath they would be colored by the soil in which they were imbedded.

To the eye of the native hunter these marks of a recent cairn are at once apparent: and unless Simpson's cairn (built in 1839) had been disturbed by Crozier, I do not think the Esquimaux would have been at the trouble of pulling it down to plunder the cache; but having commenced to do so, would not have left any of it standing, *unless they found what they sought.*

I noticed with great care the appearance of the stones, and came to the conclusion that the cairn itself was of old date, and had been erected many years ago, and that it was reduced to the state in which we found it by people having broken down one side of it; the displaced stones, from being turned over, looking far more fresh than those in that portion of the cairn which had been left standing. It was with a feeling of deep regret and much disappointment that I left this spot without finding some certain record of those martyrs to their country's fame. Perhaps in all the wide world there will be few spots more hallowed in the recollection of English seamen than this cairn on Cape Herschel.

A few miles beyond Cape Herschel the land becomes very low; many islets and shingle-ridges lie far off the coast; and as we advanced we met with hummocks of unusually heavy ice, showing plainly that we were now travelling upon a far more exposed part of the coast-line. We were approaching a spot where a revelation of intense interest was awaiting me.

About 12 miles from Cape Herschel I found a small cairn built by Hobson's party, and containing a note for me. He had reached this extreme point, six days previously, without having seen anything of the wreck, or of natives, but he had found a record—the record so ardently sought for, of the Franklin Expedition—at Point Victory, on the N.W. coast of King William's Land.

That record is indeed a sad and touching relic of our lost friends, and, to simplify its contents, I will point out separately the double story it so briefly tells. In the first place, the record paper was one of the printed forms usually supplied to discovery ships for the purpose of being enclosed in bottles and thrown overboard at sea, in order to ascertain the set of the currents, blanks being left for the date and position; any person finding one of these records is requested to forward it to the Secretary of the Admiralty, with a note of time and place; and this request is printed upon it in six different languages. Upon it was written apparently by Lieutenant Gore, as follows:

"28 of May, 1847 {H.M. ships 'Erebus' and 'Terror' wintered in the ice in lat. 70° 05'N.; long. 98° 23' W.

Having wintered in 1846-7 at Beechey Island, in lat. 74° 43'28" N.; long. 91° 39' 15" W., after having ascended Wellington Channel to lat. 77°, and returned by the west side of Cornwallis Island.

"Sir John Franklin commanding the expedition.

"All well.

"Party consisting of 2 officers and 6 men left the ships on Monday, 24th May, 1847.

"Gm. Gore, Lieut.

"Chas. F. Des Voeus, Mate."

There is an error in the above document, namely, that the 'Erebus' and 'Terror' wintered at Beechey Island in 1846-7, -the correct dates should have been 1845-6—a glance at the date at the top and bottom of the record proves this, but in all other respects the tale is told in as few words as possible of their wonderful success up to that date, May, 1847.

We find that, after the last intelligence of Sir John Franklin was received by us (bearing date of July, 1845), from the whalers in Melville Bay, that his Expedition passed on to Lancaster Sound, and entered Wellington Channel, of which the southern entrance had been discovered by Sir Edward Parry in 1819. The 'Erebus' and 'Terror' sailed up that strait for one hundred and fifty miles, and reached in the autumn of 1845 the same latitude as was attained eight years subsequently by H.M.S. 'Assistance' and 'Pioneer.' Whether Franklin intended to pursue this northern course, and was only stopped by ice in that latitude of 77° north, or purposely relinquished a route which seemed to lead away from the known seas off the coast of America, must be a matter of opinion; but this the document assures of, that Sir John Franklin's Expedition, having accomplished this examination, returned southward from latitude 77° north, which is at the head of Wellington Channel, and re-entered Barrow's Strait by a new channel between Bathurst and Cornwallis Islands.

Seldom has such an amount of success been accorded to an Arctic navigator in a single season, and when the 'Erebus' and 'Terror' were secured at Beechey Island for the coming winter of 1845-6, the results of their first year's labor must have been most cheering. These results were the exploration of Wellington and Queen's Channel, and the addition to our charts of the extensive lands on either hand. In 1846 they proceeded to the southwest, and eventually reached within twelve miles of the north extreme of King William's Land, when their progress was arrested by the approaching winter of 1846-7. That winter appears to have passed without any serious loss of life; and when in the spring Lieutenant Gore leaves with a party for some especial purpose, and very probably to connect the unknown coast-line of King William's Land between Point Victory and Cape Herschel, those on board the 'Erebus' and 'Terror' were "all well," and the gallant Franklin still commanded.

But, alas! round the margin of the paper upon which Lieutenant Gore in 1847 wrote those words of hope and promise, another hand had subsequently written the following words:—

"April 25, 1848.—H.M. ships 'Terror' and 'Erebus' were deserted on the 22d April, 5 leagues N.N.W. of this, having been beset since 12th September, 1846. The officers and crews, consisting of 105 souls, under the command of Captain F.R.M. Crozier, landed here in lat. 69° 37'42" N., long. 98° 41' W. Sir John Franklin died on the 11th June, 1847; and the total loss by deaths in the expedition has been to this date 9 officers and 15 men.

(Signed)	(Signed)
"F.R.M. Crozier,	"James Fitzjames,
"Captain and Senior Officer.	"Captain H.M.S. Erebus
"and start (on) to-morrow, 26th, for	
Back's Fish River."	

The marginal information was evidently written by Captain Fitzjames, excepting only the note stating when and where they were going, which was added by Captain Crozier.

There is some additional marginal information relative to the transfer of the document to its present position (viz., the site of Sir James Ross's pillar) from a spot four miles to the northward, near Point Victory, where it had been originally deposited by the *late* Commander Gore. This little word *late* shows us that he too, within the twelve-month, had passed away.

In the short space of twelve months how mournful had become the history of Franklin's expedition; how changed from cheerful "All well" of Graham Gore! The spring of 1847 found them within 90 miles of the known sea off the coast of America; and to men who had already in two seasons sailed over 500 miles of previously unexplored waters, how confident must they have felt that the forthcoming navigable season of 1847 would see their ships pass over so short an intervening space! It was ruled otherwise. Within a month after Lieutenant Gore placed the record on Point Victory, the much-loved leader of the expedition, Sir John Franklin, was dead; and the following spring found Captain Crozier, upon whom the command had devolved at King William's Land, endeavoring to save his starving men, 105 souls in all, from a terrible death, by retreating to the Hudson Bay territories up the Back or Great Fish River.

A sad tale was never told in fewer words. There is something deeply touching in their extreme simplicity, and they show in the strongest manner that both the leaders of this retreating party were actuated by the loftiest sense of duty, and met with calmness and decision the fearful alternative of a last bold struggle for life, rather than perish without effort on board their ships; for we well know that the 'Erebus' and 'Terror' were only provisioned up to July, 1848.

Another discrepancy exists in the second part of the record written by Fitzjames. The original number composing the expedition was 138 souls, and the record states the total loss by death to have been 9 officers and 15 men, consequently that 114 officers and men remained; but it also states that 105 only landed under Captain Crozier's command, so that 9 individuals are unaccounted for.

Lieutenant Hobson's note told me that he found quantities of clothing and articles of all kinds lying about the cairn, as if these men, aware that they were retreating for their lives, had there abandoned every thing which they considered superfluous.

Hobson had experienced extremely bad weather—constant gales and fogs—and thought he might have passed the wreck without seeing her; he hoped to be more successful upon his return journey.

Encouraged by this important news, we exerted our utmost vigilance in order that no trace should escape us.

Our provisions were running very short, therefore the three remaining puppies were of necessity shot, and their sledges used for fuel. We were also enabled to lengthen our journeys, as we had very smooth ice to travel over, the off-lying islets keeping the rough pack from pressing in upon the shore.

Upon the 29th of May we reached the western extreme of King William's Island, in lat. 69° 08' N., and long. 100° 08W. I named it after Captain Crozier of the 'Terror', the gallant leader of that "Forlorn Hope" of which we now just obtained tidings. The coast we marched along was extremely low—a mere series of ridges of limestone shingle, almost destitute of fossils. The only tracks of animals seen were those of a bear and a few foxes—the only living creatures a few willow grouse. Traces even of the wandering Esquimaux became much less frequent after leaving Cape Herschel. Here were found only a few circles of stones, the sites of tenting-places, but so moss-grown as to be of great age. The prospect to seaward was not less forbidding—a rugged surface of crushed-up pack, including much heavy ice. In these shallow ice-covered seas, seals are but seldom found: and it is highly probable that all animal life in them is as scarce as upon the land.

From Cape Crozier the coast-line was found to turn sharply away to the eastward; and early in the morning of the 30th May we encamped alongside a large boat—another melancholy relic which Hobson had found and examined a few days before, as his note left here informed me: but he had failed to discover record, journal, pocket-book, or memorandum of any description.

A vast quantity of tattered clothing was lying in her, and this we first examined. Not a single article bore the name of its former owner. The boat was cleared out and carefully swept that nothing might escape us. The snow was then removed from about her, but nothing whatever was found.

This boat measured 28 feet long, and 7 feet 3 inches wide; she was built with a view to lightness and light draught of water, and evidently equipped with the utmost care for the ascent of the Great Fish River; she had neither oars nor rudder, paddles supplying their place, and as a large remnant of light canvas, commonly known as No. 8, was found, and also a small block for reeving a sheet through, I suppose she had been provided with a sail. A sloping canvas roof or rain-awning had also formed part of her equipment. She was fitted with a weather-cloth 9 inches high, battened down all round the gunwale, and supported by 24 iron stanchions so placed as to serve likewise for rowing thowells. There were 50 fathoms of deep-sea sounding-line near her, as well as an ice grapnel. She appeared to have been originally "carvel" built; but for the purpose of reducing weight, very thin fir planks had been substituted for her seven upper strakes, and put on "clincher" fashion.

The weight of the boat alone was about 700 or 800 lbs. only, but she was mounted upon a sledge of unusual weight and strength. It was constructed of two oak planks 23 feet 4 inches in length, 8 inches in width, and with an average thickness of 2 1/2 inches. These planks formed the sides or runners of the sledge; they were connected by five cross bars of oak, each 5 feet long, and 4 inches by 3 1/2 inches thick, and bolted down to the runners; the underneath parts of the latter were shod with iron. Upon the crossbars five saddles or supporting chocks for the boat were lashed, and the drag-ropes by which the crew moved this massive sledge, and the weights upon it, consisted of 2 3/4 inch whale line.

I have calculated the weight of this sledge to be 650 lbs.; it could not have been less, and may have been considerably more. The total weight of boat and sledge may be taken at 1,400 lbs., which amounts to a heavy load for seven strong healthy men.

The only markings about the boat were those upon her stem, by which we learned that she was built by contract, was received into Woolwich Dockyard in April, 184-, and was numbered 61. There may have been a fourth figure to the right hand, as the stem had been reduced in order to lighten the boat. The ground the sledge rested upon was the usual limestone shingle, perfectly flat, and probably overflowed at times every summer, as the stones were imbedded in ice.

The boat was partially out of her cradle upon the sledge, and lying in such a position as to lead me to suppose it the effect of a violent northwest gale. She was barely, if at all, above the reach of occasional tides.

One hundred yards from her, upon the land side, lay the stump of a fir-tree 12 feet long, and 16 inches in diameter at 3 feet above the roots. Although the ice had used it roughly during its drift to this shore, and rubbed off every vestige of bark, yet the wood was perfectly sound. It may have been and probably has been lying there for twenty or thirty years, and during such a period would suffer less decay in this region of frost than in one-sixth of the time at home. Within two yards of it I noticed a few scanty tufts of grass.

But all these were after observations; there was that in the boat which transfixed us with awe. It was portions of two human skeletons. One was that of a slight young person; the other of a large, strongly-made, middle-aged man. The former was found in the bow of the boat, but in too much disturbed a state to enable Hobson to judge whether the sufferer had died there; large and powerful animals, probably wolves, had destroyed much of this skeleton, which may have been that of an officer. Near it we found the fragment of a pair of worked slippers, of which I give the pattern, as they may possibly be identified. The liens were white, with a black margin; the spaces white, red and yellow. They had originally been 11 inches long, lined with calf-skin with the hair left on, and the edges bound with red silk ribbon. Besides these slippers there were a pair of small strong shooting half-boots. The other skeleton was in a somewhat more perfect state, and was enveloped with clothes and furs; it lay across the boat, under the after-thwart. Close beside it were found five watches; and there were two double-barrelled guns—one barrel in each loaded and cocked— standing muzzle upward against the boat's side. It may be imagined with what deep interest these sad relics were scrutinised, and how anxiously every fragment of clothing was turned over in search of pockets and pocket-books, journals, or even names. Five or six small books were found, all of them scriptural or devotional works, except the 'Vicar of Wakefield.' One little book, 'Christian Melodies', bore an inscription upon the titlepage from the donor to G.G. (Graham Gore?) A small Bible contained numerous marginal notes, and whole passages underlined. Besides these books, the covers of a New Testament and Prayerbook were found.

Amongst an amazing quantity of clothing there were seven or eight pairs of boots of various kinds—cloth winter boots, sea boots, heavy ankle boots, and strong shoes. I noted that there were silk handkerchiefs—black, white, and figured—towels, soap, sponge, tooth-brush, and hair-combs; mackintosh gun-cover, marked outside with paint A 12, and lined with black cloth. Besides these articles we found twine, nails, saws, files, bristles, wax-ends, sailmakers' palms, powder, bullets, shot, cartridges, wads, leather cartridge-case, knives—clasp and dinner ones—needle and thread cases, slow-match, several bayonet-sabbards cut down into knife-sheaths, two rolls of sheet-lead, and, in short, a quantity of articles of one description and another truly astonishing in variety, and such as, for the most part, modern sledge-travelers in these regions would consider a mere accumulation of dead weight, but slightly useful, and very likely to break down the strength of the sledge-crews.

The only provisions we could find were tea and chocolate; of the former very little remained, but there were nearly 40 pounds of the latter. These articles alone could never support life in such a climate, and we found neither biscuit nor meat of any kind. A portion of tobacco and an empty pemmican-tin, capable of containing 22 pounds of weight, were discovered. The tin was marked with an E; it had probably belonged to the

'Erebus.' None of the fuel originally brought from the ships remained in or about the boat, but there was no lack of it, for a drift-tree was lying on the beach close at hand, and had the party been in need of fuel they would have used the paddles and bottom-boards of the boat.

In the after part of the boat wediscovered eleven large spoons, eleven forks, and four teaspoons, all of silver; of these twenty-six pieces of plate, eight bore Sir John Franklin's crest, the remainder had the crests or initials of nine different officers, with the exception of a single fork which was not marked; of these nine officers, five belonged to the 'Erebus,'—Gore, Le Vesconte, Fairholme, Couch, and Goodsir. Three others belonged to the 'Terror,'—Crozier, (a teaspoon only,) Hornby, and Thomas. I do not know to whom the three articles with an owl engraved on them belonged, nor who ws the owner of the unmarked fork, but of the owners of those we can identify, the majority belonged to the 'Erebus.' One of the watches bore the crest of Mr. Couch, of the 'Erebus,' and as the pemmican tin also came from that ship, I am inclined to think the boat did also; the authorities at Woolwich could tell (by her number) to which ship she was supplied; and as one of the pocket chronometers found in the boat was marked "Parkinson and Frodsham 980," and the other "Arnold 2020," it could also be ascertained to which ship they had been issued.

Sir John Franklin's plate perhaps was issued to the men for their use, as the only means of saving it; and it seems probable that the officers generally did the same, as not a single iron spoon, such as sailors always use, has been found. Of the many men, probably twenty or thirty, who were attached to this boat, it seemed most strange that the remains of only two individuals were found, nor were there any graves upon the neighboring flat land; indeed, bearing in mind the season at which these poor fellows left their ships, it should be remembered that the soil was then frozen hard, and the labor of *cutting* a grave very great indeed.

I was astonished to find that the sledge was directed to the N.E., exactly for the next point of land for which we ourselves were travelling!

The position of this abandoned boat is about 50 miles—as a sledge would travel— from Point Victory, and therefore 65 miles from the position of the ships; also it is 70 miles from the skeleton of the steward, and 150 miles from Montreal Island; it is moreover in the depth of a wide bay, where, by crossing over 10 or 12 miles of very low land, a great saving of distance would be effected, the route by the cost-line being about 40 miles.

A little reflection led me to satisfy my own mind at least, that the boat was returning to the ships: and in no other way can I account for two men having been left in her, than by supposing the party were unable to drag the boat further, and that these two men, not being able to keep pace with their shipmates, were therefore left by them supplied with such provisions as could be spared, to last until the return of the others from the ship with a fresh stock.

Whether it was the intention of the retroceding party to await the result of another season in the ships, or to follow the track of the main body to the Great Fish River, is now a matter of conjecture. It seems highly probable that they had purposed revisiting the boat, not only on account of the two men left in charge of it, but also to obtain the chocolate, the five watches, and many other articles which would otherwise scarcely have been left in her.

The same reasons which may be assigned for the return of this detachment from the main body, will also serve to account for their not having come back to their boat. In both instances they appear to have greatly overrated their strength, and the distance they could travel in a given time.

Taking this view of the case, we can understand why their provisions would not last them for anything like the distance they required to travel; and why they would be obliged to send back to the ships for more, first taking them from the detached party all provisions they could possibly spare. Whether all or any of the remainder of this detached party ever reached their ships is uncertain; all we know is, that they did not revisit the boat, and which accounts for the absence of more skeletons in its neighborhood, and the Esquimaux report that there was no one alive in the ship when she drifted on shore, and that but one human body was found by them on board of her.

After leaving the boat we followed an irregular coastline to the N. and N.W., up to a very prominent cape, which is probably the extreme of land seen from Point Victory by Sir James Ross, and named by him Point Franklin, which name, as a cape, it still retains.

I need hardly say that throughout the whole of my journey along the shores of King William's Land I caused a most vigilant look-out to be kept to seaward for any appearance of the stranded ship spoken of by the natives: our search was however fruitless in that respect.

Chapter XVI

On the morning of 2nd June we reached Point Victory. Here Hobson's note left for me in the cairn informed me that he had not found the slightest trace of a wreck anywhere upon the coast, or of natives to the north of Cape Crozier.

Although somewhat short of provisions, I determined to remain a day here in order to examine an opening at the Bottom of Back Bay, called so after Sir George Back, by his friend Sir James Ross, and which had not been explored. This proved to be an inlet nearly 13 miles deep, with an average width of 1 1/2 or 2 miles; I drove round it upon the dog sledge, but found no trace of human beings; it was filled with heavy old ice, and was therefore unfavorable for the resort of seals, and consequently of natives also.

The direction of the inlet is to the E.S.E.; we found the land on either side rose as we advanced up it, and attained a considerable elevation, except immediately across its head, where alone it was very low; I have conferred upon it the name of Collinson, after one who will ever be distinguished in connection with the Franklin search, and who kindly relieved Lady Franklin of much trouble by taking upon himself the financial business of this expedition.

An extensive bay, westward of Cape Hershel, I have named after Captain Washington, the hydrographer, a steadfast supporter of this final search.

All the intermediate coast-line, along which the retreating crews performed their fearful march, is sacred to their names alone.

Hobson's note informed me of his having found a second record, deposited also by Lieutenant Gore in May, 1847, upon the south side of Back Bay, but it afforded no additional information.

It is strange that both these papers state the ships to have wintered in 1846-7 at Beechey Island! So obvious a mistake would hardly have been made had any importance been attached to these documents. They were soldered up in thin tin cylinders, having been filled up on board prior to the departure of the travellers; consequently the day upon which they were *deposited* was not filled in; but already the papers were much damaged by rust, —a very few more years would have rendered them wholly illegible. When the record left at Point Victory was opened to add thereto the supplemental information which gives it its chief value, Captain Fitzjames, as may be concluded by the color of the ink, filled in the date—28th— in May, when the record was originally deposited. The cylinder containing the record had not been soldered up again; I suppose they had not the means of doing so; it was found on the ground amongst a few loose stones which had evidently fallen along with it from the top of the cairn. Hobson removed every stone of this cairn down to the ground and rebuilt it.

Brief as these records are, we must needs be contented with them; they are perfect models of official brevity. No log-book could be more provokingly laconic. Yet, that *any record at all* should be deposited after the abandonment of the ships, does not seem to have been intended; and we should feel the more thankful to Captains Crozier and Fitzjames, to whom we are indebted for the invaluable supplement; and our gratitude ought to be all the greater when we remember that the ink had to be thawed, and that writing in a tent during an April day in the Arctic regions is by no means an easy task.

Besides placing a copy of the record taken away by Hobson from the cairn, we both put records of our own in it; and I also buried one under a large stone ten feet true north from it, stating the explorations and discoveries we have made.

A great quantity and variety of things lay strewed about the cairn, such as even in their three days' march from the ships the retreating crews found it impossible to carry further. Amongst these were four heavy sets of boat's cooking stoves, pickaxes, shovels, iron-hoops, old canvas, a large single block, about four feet of a copper lightning conductor, long pieces of hollow brass curtain rods, a small case of selected medicines containing about twenty-four phials, the contents in a wonderful state of preservation; a dip circle by Robinson, with two needles, bar magnets, and light horizontal needle all complete, the whole weighing only nine pounds; and even a small sextant engraved with the name of "Frederick Hornby" lying beside the cairn without its case. The colored eye-shades of the sextant had been taken out, otherwise it was perfect; the movable screws and such parts as come in contact with the observer's hand were neatly covered with thin leather to prevent frostbite in severe weather.

The clothing left by the retreating crews of the 'Erebus' and 'Terror' formed a huge heap four feet high; every article was searched, but the pockets were empty, and not one of all these articles were marked, —indeed sailors' warm clothing seldom is. Two canteens, the property of marines, were found, one marked "88 C°. Wm. Hedges," and the other "89 C°. Wm. Hether." A small panniken made out of a two-pound preserved-meat tin had scratched on it "W. Mark."

When continuing my homeward march, and, as nearly as I could judge, 2 1/2 or 2 3/4 miles to the north of Point Victory, I saw a few stones placed in line, as if across the head of a tenting place to afford some shelter; here it was I think that Lieutenant Gore deposited the record in May, 1847, which was found in 1848 by Lieutenant Irving, and finally deposited at Point Victory. Some scraps of tin vessels were lying about, but whether they had been left by Sir James Ross' party in May, 1830, or by the Franklin Expedition in 1847 or 1848, is uncertain.

Here ended my own search for traces of the lost ones. Hobson found two other cairns, and many relics, between this position and Cape Felix. From each place where any trace was discovered the most interesting of the relics were taken away, so that the collection we have made is very considerable.

Of these northern cairns I will write a description when I have received Hobson's account of his journey; but here it is as well to state his opinion, as well as my own, that no part of the coast between Cape Felix and Cape Crozier has been visited by Esquimaux since the fatal march of the lost crews in April, 1848; none of the cairns or numerous articles strewed about—which would be invaluable to the natives—or even the drift-wood we noticed, had been touched by them. From this very significant fact it seems quite certain that they had not been discovered by the Esquimaux, whose knowledge of the "white men falling down and dying as they walked along" must be limited to the shoreline southward and eastward of Cape Crozier, and where, of course, no traces were permitted to remain for us to find. It is not probable that such fearful mortality would have overtaken them so early in their march as within 80 miles by sledge-route from the abandoned ships—such being their distance from Cape Crozier; nor is it probable that we could have passed the wreck had she existed there, as there are no off-lying islands to prevent a ship drifting in upon the beach; whilst to the southward they are very numerous; so much so that a drifting ship could hardly run the gauntlet between them so as to reach the shore.

The coast from Point Victory northward is considerably higher than that upon which we have been so many days; the sea also is not so shallow, and the ice comes close in; to seaward all was heavy close pack, consisting of all descriptions of ice, but for the most part old and heavy.

From Walls' Bay I crossed overland to the eastern shore, and reached my depot near the entrance of Port Parry on the 5th June, after an absence of thirty-four days. Hence I purposed travelling alongshore to Cape Sabine, in order to avoid the rough ice which we encountered when crossing direct from Cape Victoria in April, and also hoping to obtain a few more observations for the magnetic inclination.

✳

IT WOULD BE THE BOAT THAT WOULD MOST BAFFLE ARCTIC HISTORIANS— *the boat, that is, and what was in it. The boat itself weighed between 700 and 800 pounds, and the sledge that hauled it was another 650 pounds. Add it up, as McClintock did, and it comes to 1,400 pounds to be pulled over the rough Arctic ice by seven men—for that was the number of tow ropes they found attached to it. That in itself was work enough, the kind of labor that demanded eight or nine pounds of meat per man per day to sustain. Now add to that what was in it: dead weight. Fancy silverware from the officers' mess, tools of all kinds, scientific instruments, two rolls of sheet lead—these men were dragging a couple of hundred pounds, in other words, of largely useless stuff. It must have been impossible. They could have made only a few miles a day. Why did they keep all those things? Where was the food that should have been on the boat?*

More facts would trickle out over the years. The American explorer Charles Francis Hall found more skeletons in the 1860s and traded for more relics with the Eskimos. He also collected Eskimo stories of what had happened to Franklin's men. Eskimo oral tradition, with respect to Franklin and to many other events, has been shown to be quite accurate, if hazy on dates and periods of time. Hall also found further evidence of cannibalism—bones cut with a saw, for example, and holes in skulls. Eskimo lore has Crozier, Franklin's second in command, surviving for some years living with the Eskimos. Lt. Frederick Schwatka of the U. S. Navy returned to King William Island in the late 1870s and revisited the area of McClintock's finds, discovering more skeletons and more relics. He also gathered more oral testimony. Natives had found, he was told, corroborating the reports Hall had heard, bones sawed in half, evidence of cannibalism. They had found a tin box full of human bones. Eskimos had also found a tin box full of books. The Eskimos had thrown the books away and kept the box. Schwatka was convinced that the books contained the journals of Franklin and other members of the party. Eskimo children used the books as playthings for a while, but in the end they were all destroyed.

The Franklin story just goes on and on. In 1923 the Norwegian anthropologist Knud Rasmussen picked up still more oral tradition from the tribe he was studying. Eskimos had gone on a great ship just to the west of King William Island. It had been deserted.

They found dead bodies inside. Trying to let in some light, they foolishly broke a hole in the boat at the waterline, and the boat soon sank. Dr. Owen Beattie, a Canadian forensic anthropologist, exhumed the bodies found on Beechey Island in 1851, found very high levels of lead in the hair samples, and concluded that the Franklin expedition may have suffered from lead poisoning from the tin cans in which the expedition's meat was stored. Preserving food in tins was a new technology at the time, and the tins were sealed by soldering them with lead. But lead poisoning is not a sufficient explanation for the disaster. At the time the London water supply was carried in lead pipes. Lead paint covered the interior and exterior walls of England.

We shall never know for sure why the 130 members of this expedition died. The general conclusion reached by many historians is that they died of any number of causes: scurvy, starvation, exhaustion, disease, all the killers that accompanied Arctic exploration in the nineteenth century. Vilhjalmur Stefansson believes that they died, in the final analysis, of culture—that they were unable to learn from or to live like Eskimos, and could not have survived under the best of circumstances without doing so.

But if a certain amount of mystery still surrounds the fate of the Franklin expedition, the search for it did solve another mystery—the location of the Northwest Passage. By the time the search was over the map of the Canadian Arctic was more or less complete. Indeed Robert McClure, leading one of the searching expeditions, found the last link in the Passage early on, in October, 1850—and was then stuck in the ice with all his men for four winters. Men had swarmed over the ice looking for Franklin without finding him, but they had mapped the Arctic. Whether it was worth the cost, in time, money, and lives, is impossible to say. Between 1903 and 1906 Roald Amundsen actually sailed the Northwest Passage in his little converted herring schooner, the Gjoa. Like most of Amundsen's expeditions, it was an uneventful trip. He discovered that the waters south of Victoria Island, in the narrow straits through which the Passage makes its way, are so shallow that only a small ship like his own could comfortably make the trip. The Northwest Passage existed, in short, but even if the ice did not make it impracticable, it would never have been useful for commerce. If big ships could not pass through it, there could be no big profits.

*

PART THREE

To the Top
of the World

*

To the Top of the World

AFTER THE DEATH OF FRANKLIN AND HIS 129 MEN, THE BRITISH *understandably lost interest in Arctic exploration. The costs of searching for him had been huge, other men had died in the search, and the Northwest Passage itself was not worth the paper the map of it was printed on. Emotionally the British seemed drained by the whole affair. It would be a generation before they returned to the north, and then they would return only once, in a fruitless attempt to get to the North Pole.*

But explorers from other countries did begin to take an interest in the Arctic, most notably explorers from the United States. These were individual explorers. The United States Government had no interest in Arctic exploration. Along with most of the rest of the country, the Government was still focused on exploring and settling the unknown regions of the West. During the 1860s the nation would turn its attention to the Civil War. But United States involvement in the search for Franklin had excited the passions of a few men for the Arctic, and two in particular—Elisha Kent Kane and Charles Francis Hall—would become American Arctic heroes.

They were both fascinating men. Kane was a Navy surgeon of slight stature and a damaged heart who was an unlikely candidate for Arctic exploration, or any other kind, thanks to his habitually poor health. Robert Carter, in the journal from which we drew the preceding excerpt, called him "little doc." He was a member of the first U. S. Grinnell expedition of 1850 that sent the Advance and the Rescue to Lancaster Sound to search for Franklin, and Carter came to know him reasonably well when they were all trapped in the pack during that winter.

Despite his stature and his health, Kane had already had an unusually active and adventurous life. The first child of a prominent Philadelphia family, he spent his youth traveling. In the Philippines he descended on a vine into an active volcano. In 1847, during the war with Mexico, he was in Mexico, serving with a detachment of Mexican irregulars and bandits working for the Americans, and fought a hand-to-hand battle with Mexican troops in which he was wounded twice with a lance but fought off his attackers and then, working as a doctor, saved the life of a man he himself had almost killed. Shortly afterwards Kane sickened with typhus. He spent twelve days in a coma. The Mexican officer whose life he had saved thought of him as a hero, and he was indeed heroic, brave enough, indeed reckless enough, to take on anything.

He volunteered for the first Grinnell expedition three years later and he found in the Arctic the fulfillment of his dreams: a theater of action in which he felt well physically for almost the first time in his life; and a place in which courage was a character trait often in demand. He loved the Arctic, its miracles of refraction—ships, icebergs hanging upside down in the sky—and its wildlife, its strange terrifying beauty. He shot a polar bear and skinned it. He treated scurvy on the two ships as they drifted, stuck in the ice, down Lancaster Sound and into Baffin Bay during the winter. And he kept a journal. Capt. De Haven, leader of the expedition, was no writer and left the task to Kane. When the ships returned Kane wrote a book about their experiences, The U. S. Grinnell Expedition in Search of Sir John Franklin: A Personal Narrative. Published in 1854, it was gripping and compelling, all that the drier official British polar narratives tended not to be. It sold 65,000 copies in just a few months.

Kane was in demand even before the book came out. He lectured to huge audiences for large fees. His name became a household word. He was primed to return to the Arctic and go even farther in search of Franklin. Kane was one of those who thought Franklin had gone north, up Wellington Channel into the supposedly open polar sea. The first Grinnell expedition had sailed up Wellington Channel, only to be stopped by ice. Kane wanted to sail up Baffin Bay to the top into Smith Sound and enter the open polar sea via that route. No one knew yet that Franklin had gone south from Beechey Island, down Peel Sound. Kane first proposed this expedition in 1852. The public was enthusiastic. The authorities were sympathetic. Henry Grinnell offered him the use of the Advance. In May, 1853, Kane set sail for the Arctic once again, purportedly in search of Franklin but really in search of the Arctic experience he had come to love.

It was not to be a happy experience. Kane was a naval surgeon but he did not have a proper Navy crew, only a motley collection of volunteer U. S. Navy sailors and riff-raff he had scrambled to recruit at the last moment. The Advance was a small ship and Kane went without a sister ship. He had eighteen men on board including himself. In Greenland he would add two more, an Eskimo named Hans Hendrik who ultimately went on four polar expeditions, and a Dane, Carl Petersen, a sledge driver who spoke the local language. Another member of the crew was one John Blake, a tough from the Baltimore docks who used assumed names. Yet another was William Godfrey, a water-front tough whom one of the officers would describe as "a most audacious villain."

Kane had never before commanded a ship, nor did he have the natural gift of command. Trouble boiled up even before they got to Greenland when Blake and Godfrey objected to an order that had been given them. Kane punished them by confining them in a tiny space between decks for a couple of days. It had no effect. A few days later Godfrey acted up again. Kane should have put him aboard a whaler going south at once, but he failed to get rid of him. He would regret it.

The men, meanwhile, already regretted Kane. He was proving to be not just inex-perienced as a leader, but bad—dogmatic, inconsistent, snobbish, and sure that he knew all there was to know about ice. He knew very little about ice and plunged north through the pack and the bergs with the recklessness that had led him into battle in Mexico. He made it through Baffin Bay in August and headed into Smith Sound. He ultimately reached the larger body of water beyond that would henceforth bear his name: Kane Basin. He decided to winter there in a harbor he named after his family's estate in Philadelphia. But he had not brought enough coal to keep the ship warm. He was plan-ning to make an assault on the open polar sea in the spring, but most of his dogs died that winter, no one knew why. On March 19—much too early in the season—he sent one of his officers and seven men north to establish a supply depot for the move. Because the dogs had died the men had to haul the sledge themselves in temperatures 40 degrees below zero. They got about 30 miles from the ship before they collapsed. Three men were sent back to get help. Our excerpt begins where they stumbled on board the ship, more dead than alive.

ELISHA KENT KANE

Arctic Explorations: The Second Grinnell Expedition in Search of Sir John Franklin, 1853, 54, 55

MARCH 27, MONDAY, WE HAVE BEEN FOR SOME DAYS IN ALL THE FLURRY OF preparation for our exploration trip: buffalo hides, leather, and tailoring utensils everywhere. Every particle of fur comes in play for mitts and muffs and wrappers. Poor Floria is turned into a pair of socks, and looks almost as pretty as when she was heading the team.

Everything looked promising, and we were only waiting for intelligence that our advance party had deposited its provisions in safety to begin our transit of the bay. Except a few sledge lashings and some trifling accoutrements to finish, all was ready.

We were at work cheerfully, sewing away at the skins of some moccasins by the blaze of our lamps, when, toward midnight, we heard the noise of steps above, and the next minute Sontag, Ohlsen, and Petersen came down into the cabin. Their manner startled me even more than their unexpected appearance on board. They were swollen and haggard, and hardly able to speak.

Their story was a fearful one. They had left their companions in the ice, risking their own lives to bring us the news: Brooks, Baker, Wilson, and Pierre were all lying frozen and disabled. Where? They could not tell: somewhere in among the hummocks to the north and east; it was drifting heavily round them when they parted. Irish Tom had stayed by to feed and care for the others; but the chances were sorely against them. It was in vain to question them further. They had evidently traveled a great distance, for they were sinking with fatigue and hunger, and could hardly be rallied enough to tell us the direction in which they had come.

My first impulse was to move on the instant with an unencumbered party: a rescue, to be effective or even hopeful, could not be too prompt. What pressed on my mind most was, where the sufferers were to be looked for among the drifts. Ohlsen seemed to have his faculties rather more at command than his associates, and I thought that he might assist us as a guide; but he was sinking with exhaustion, and if he went with us we must carry him.

There was not a moment to be lost. While some were still busy with the newcomers and getting ready a hasty meal, others were rigging out the "Little Willie" with a buffalo cover, a small tent, and a package of pemmican; and, as soon as we could hurry through our arrangements, Ohlsen was strapped on in a fur bag, his legs wrapped in dog skins and eiderdown, and we were off upon the ice. Our party consisted of nine men and myself. We carried only the clothes on our backs. The thermometer stood at minus forty-six degrees, seventy-eight degrees below the freezing point.

A well-known peculiar tower of ice, called by the men the "Pinnacle Berg," served as our first landmark; other icebergs of colossal size, which stretched in long beaded lines across the bay, helped to guide us afterward; and it was not until we had traveled for sixteen hours that we began to lose our way.

We knew that our lost companions must be somewhere in the area before us, within a radius of forty miles. Mr. Ohlsen, who had been for fifty hours without rest, fell asleep as soon as we began to move, and awoke now with unequivocal signs of mental disturbance. It became evident that he had lost the bearing of the icebergs, which in form and color endlessly repeated themselves; and the uniformity of the vast field of snow utterly forbade the hope of local landmarks.

Pushing ahead of the party, and clambering over some rugged ice-piles, I came to a long level floe, which I thought might probably have attracted the eyes of weary men in circumstances like our own. I gave orders to abandon the sledge, and disperse in search of foot marks. We raised our tent, placed our pemmican in cache, except a small allowance for each man to carry on his person; and poor Ohlsen, now just able to keep his legs, was liberated from his bag. The thermometer had fallen by this time to $-49.3°$, and the wind was setting in sharply from the northwest. It was out of the question to halt: it required brisk exercise to keep us from freezing. I could not even melt ice for water; and, at these temperatures, any resort to snow for the purpose of allaying thirst was followed by bloody lips and tongue: it burnt like caustic.

It was indispensable then that we should move on, looking out for traces as we went. Yet when the men were ordered to spread themselves, so as to multiply the chances, though they all obeyed heartily, some painful impress of solitary danger, or perhaps it may have been the varying configuration of the ice-field, kept them closing up continually into a single group. The strange manner in which some of us were affected I now attribute as much to shattered nerves as to the direct influence of the cold. Men like McGary and Bonsall, who had stood out our severest marches, were seized with trembling fists and short breath; and, in spite of all my efforts to keep up an example of sound bearing, I fainted twice on the snow.

We had been nearly eighteen hours without water or food, when a new hope cheered us. I think it was Hans, our Esquimaux hunter, who thought he saw a broad sledge track. The drift had nearly effaced it, and we were some of us doubtful at first whether it was not one of those accidental rifts the gales make in the surface snow. But, as we traced it on the deep snow among the hummocks, we were led to footsteps; and, following these with religious care, we at last came in sight of a small American flag fluttering from a hummock, and lower down a little Masonic banner hanging from a tent pole hardly above the drift. It was the camp of our disabled comrades: we reached it after an unbroken march of twenty-one hours.

The little tent was nearly covered. I was not among the first to come up; but, when I reached the tent curtain, the men were standing in silent file on each side of it. With more kindness and delicacy of feeling than is often supposed to belong to sailors, but which is almost characteristic, they intimated their wish that I should go in alone. As I crawled in, and, coming upon the darkness, heard before me the burst of welcome gladness that came forth from the four poor fellows stretched on their back, and then for the first time the cheer outside, my weakness and gratitude together almost overcame me. "They had expected me: they were sure I would come!"

We were now fifteen souls; the thermometer seventy-five degrees below the freezing point; and our sole accommodation a tent barely able to contain eight persons: more than half our party were obliged to keep from freezing by walking outside while the others slept. We could not halt long. Each of us took a turn of two hours' sleep; and we prepared for our homeward march.

We took with us nothing but the tents, furs to protect the rescued party, and food for a journey of fifty hours. Everything else was abandoned. Two large buffalo bags, each made of four skins, were doubled up to form a sort of sack, lined on each side by fur, and closed at the bottom but opened at the top. This was laid on the sledge; the tent, smoothly folded serving as a floor. The sick, with their limbs sewed up carefully in reindeer skins, were placed upon the bed of buffalo robes, in a half-reclining posture; other skins and blanket bags were thrown above them; and the whole litter was lashed together so as to allow but a single opening opposite the mouth for breathing capacity.

This necessary work cost us a great deal of time and effort; but it was essential to the lives of the sufferers. It took us no less than four hours to strip and refresh them, and then to embale them in the manner I have described. Few of us escaped without frostbitten fingers: the thermometer was at 55.6° below zero, and a slight wind added to the severity of the cold.

It was completed at last, however; all hands stood round; and, after repeating a short prayer, we set out on our retreat. It was fortunate indeed that we were not experienced in sledging over the ice. A great part of our track lay among a succession of hummocks; some of them extending long lines, fifteen and twenty feet high, and so uniformly steep that we had to turn them by a considerable deviation from our direct course; others that we forced our way through, far above our heads in height, lying in parallel ridges, with the space between too narrow for the sledge to be lowered into it safely, and yet not wide enough for the runners to cross without the aid of ropes to stay them. These spaces too were generally choked with light snow, hiding the openings between the ice-fragments. They were fearful traps to disengage a limb from, for every man knew that a fracture or a sprain even would cost him his life. Besides all this, the sledge was top-heavy with its load: the maimed men could not bear to be lashed down tight enough to secure them against falling off. Notwithstanding our caution in rejecting every superfluous burden, the weight, including bags and tent, was a total of eleven hundred pounds.

And yet our march for the first six hours was very cheering. We made by vigorous pulls and lifts nearly a mile an hour, and reached the new floes before we were absolutely weary. Our sledge sustained the trial admirably.

Ohlsen, restored by hope, walked steadily at the leading belt of the sledge lines; and I began to feel certain of reaching our halfway station of the day before, where we had left our tent. But we were still nine miles from it, when, almost without premonition, we all became aware of an alarming failure of our energies.

I was of course familiar with the benumbed and almost lethargic sensation of extreme cold; and once, when exposed for some hours in the midwinter of Baffin's Bay, I had experienced symptoms I compared to the diffused paralysis of the electro-galvanic shock. But I had treated the sleepy comfort of freezing as something like the embellishment of romance. I had evidence now to the contrary.

Bonsall and Morton, two of our stoutest men, came to me, begging permission to sleep: "They were not cold: the wind did not enter them now: a little sleep was all they wanted." Presently Hans was found nearly stiff under a drift; and Thomas, bolt upright, had his eyes closed, and could hardly articulate. At last, John Black threw himself on the snow, and refused to rise. They did not complain of feeling cold; but it was in vain that I wrestled, boxed, ran, argued, jeered or reprimanded. An immediate halt could not be avoided.

We pitched our tent with much difficulty. Our hands were too powerless to strike a fire: we were obliged to do without water or food. Even the spirits (whisky) had frozen at the men's feet under all the coverings. We put Bonsall, Ohlsen, Thomas, and Hans, with the other sick men, well inside the tent, and crowded in as many others as we could. Then, leaving the party in charge of Mr. McGary, with orders to come on after four hours' rest, I pushed ahead with William Godfrey, who volunteered to be my companion. My aim was to reach the halfway tent, and thaw some ice and pemmican before the others arrived.

The floe was of level ice, and the walking excellent. I cannot tell how long it took us to make the nine miles; for we were in a strange sort of stupor, and had little apprehension of time. It was probably about four hours. We kept ourselves awake by imposing on each other a continued articulation of words; they must have been incoherent enough. I recall these hours as amongst the most wretched I have every gone through: we were neither of us in our right senses and retained a very confused recollection of what preceded our arrival at the tent. We both of us, however, remember a bear, who walked leisurely before us and tore up as he went a jumper that Mr. McGary had improvidently thrown off the day before. He tore it into shreds and rolled it into a ball, but never offered to interfere with our progress. I remember this and, with it, a confused sentiment that our tent and buffalo robes might probably share the same fate. Godfrey, with whom the memory of this day's work may atone for many faults of a later time, had a better eye than myself; and, looking some miles ahead, he could see that our tent was undergoing the same unceremonious treatment. I thought I saw it too, but we were so drunken with cold that we strode on steadily and, for aught I know, without quickening our pace.

Probably our approach saved the contents of the tent; for when we reached it the tent was uninjured, though the bear had overturned it, tossing the buffalo robes and pemmican into the snow; we missed only a couple of blanket bags. What we recollect, however, and perhaps all we recollect, is that we had a great difficulty raising the tent. We crawled into our reindeer sleeping bags, without speaking, and for the next three hours slept on in a dreamy but intense slumber. When I awoke, my long beard was a mass of ice, frozen fast to the buffalo skins: Godfrey had to cut me out with his jackknife. Four days after our escape, I found my woolen comfortable with a goodly share of my beard still adhering to it.

We were able to melt water and get some soup cooked before the rest of our party arrived: it took them but five hours to walk the nine miles. They were doing well, and, considering the circumstances, in wonderful spirits. The day was almost providentially windless, with a clear sun. All enjoyed the refreshment we had got ready. The crippled were repacked in their robes, and we sped quite briskly toward the hummock ridges that lay between us and the Pinnacle Berg, clearly visible against the bright sky.

It required desperate efforts to work our way over it—literally desperate, for our strength failed us anew, and we began to lose our self control. We could not abstain any longer from eating snow: our mouths had swelled, and some of us became speechless. Happily the day was warmed by a clear sunshine, and the thermometer rose to minus four degrees in the shade: otherwise we must have frozen.

Our halts multiplied, and we fell half sleeping on the snow. I could not prevent it. Strange to say, it refreshed us. I ventured upon the experiment myself, making Riley wake me at the end of three minutes; and I felt so much benefited by it that I timed the men in the same way. They sat on the runners of the sledge, fell asleep instantly, and were forced to wakefulness when their three minutes were out.

By eight o'clock in the evening we emerged from the floes. The sight of the Pinnacly Berg revived us. Brandy, an invaluable resource in emergency, had already been served out in tablespoonful doses. We now took a longer rest, and a last but stouter dram, and reached the brig at 1:00 P.M., we believe without a halt.

I say we believe; and here perhaps is the most decided proof of our sufferings: we were quite delirious and had ceased to entertain a sane apprehension of the circumstances about us. We moved on like men in a dream. Our foot marks seen afterwards showed that we had steered a beeline for the brig. It must have been by a sort of instinct, for it left no impress on the memory. Bonsall was sent staggering ahead, and reached the brig, God knows how, for he had fallen repeatedly at the track lines; but he delivered with punctilious accuracy the messages I had sent by him to Dr. Hayes. I thought myself the soundest of all; I went through all the formuli of sanity, and can recall the muttering of delirium of my comrades when we got back into the cabin of our brig. Yet I have been told since of some speeches and some order too of mine, which I should have remembered for their absurdity if my mind had retained its balance.

Petersen and Whipple came out to meet us about two miles from the brig. They brought my dog team, with the restoratives I had sent for by Bonsall. I do not remember their coming. Dr. Hayes entered with judicious energy upon the treatment our condition called for, administering morphine freely, after the usual frictions. He reported that none of our brain symptoms was serious, referring them properly to the class of those indications of exhausted power that yield to generous diet and rest. Mr. Ohlsen suffered some time from strabismus[1] and blindness: two others underwent amputation of parts of the foot[2], without an unpleasant consequence; and two died in spite of all our efforts. This rescue party had been out for seventy-two hours. We had halted in all eight hours, half of our number sleeping at a time. We traveled between eighty and ninety miles, most of the way dragging a heavy sledge. The mean temperature of the whole time, including the warmest hours of three days, was at minus 41.2°. We had no water except at our two halts, and were at no time able to intermit vigorous exercise without actually freezing.

[1] Means squinting

[2] Amputation was necessary if frozen limbs became gangrenous.

April 4, Tuesday. Four days have passed, and I am again at my record of failures, sound but aching still in every joint. The rescued men are not out of danger, but their gratitude is very touching. Pray God that they may live!

✳

TWO MEN DIED, UNABLE TO RECOVER FROM THIS EXPERIENCE, AND *another lost his toes to frostbite. Things did not improve over the summer. The ship could not break free of the ice, and Kane's attempts to send out sledge teams came to nothing. Scurvy was now a serious problem, and he had no fresh food except for the seals Hans Hendrik, the Eskimo, shot. On one of the sledge trips William Godfrey, the New York wharf thug, had tried to shoot his companion, who was able to take the gun away from him before he could fire it. Kane had only one success. His last sledge party, a two-man operation that included Hans Hendrik, had discovered a channel out of Kane Basin to the north. Kane called it Kennedy Channel and it does, indeed, lead out of the Basin to the Arctic Ocean. It was clogged with ice. But beyond the channel Morton, the sailor, thought he saw open water. It was a mirage, but Kane was sure he had found the open polar sea people had been talking about for so many centuries.*

August of 1854, a year after their arrival, found the Advance still ice-bound and Kane desperate. He tried to reach Lancaster Sound and rescue in a small boat, but had to turn back when the ice proved impenetrable. They settled in for a second winter, and, as one of his own chapter headings put it, "desolation descends." They depended heavily on Hans Hendrik for food. They were at each other's throats. The next excerpt is Kane's description of what happened when Godfrey persuaded some of the crew that they would do better by leaving the ship and finding and living with Eskimos farther south.

✳

FEBRUARY 22, THURSDAY. Washington's birthday: all our colors flying in the new sunlight. A day of good omen, even to the sojourners among the ice. Hans comes in with great news. He has had a shot at our bennesoak, a long shot; but it reached him. The animal made off at a slow run, but we are sure of him now. This same deer has been hanging round the lake at the fiord through all the dim returning twilight; and so many stories were told of his appearance and movements that he had almost grown into a myth. Tomorrow we shall desire his better acquaintance.

February 23, Friday. "Hans was out early this morning on the trail of the wounded deer. Rhina, the least barbarous of our sledge dogs, assisted him. He was back by noon, with the joyful news, 'The tukkuk dead only two miles up big fiord!' The cry found its way through the hatch, and came back in a broken huzza from the sick men.

"We are so badly off for strong arms that our reindeer threatened to be as great an embarrassment to us as the auction-drawn elephant was to his lucky master. We had hard work with our dogs carrying him to the brig, and still harder, worn down as we were, in getting him over the ship's side. But we succeeded, and were tumbling him down the hold, when we found ourselves in a dilemma like the Vicar of Wakefield[3] with his family picture. It was impossible to drag the prize into our little moss-lined dormitory; the *tossut* was not half big enough to let him pass: and it was equally impossible to skin him anywhere else without freezing our fingers in the operation. It was a happy escape from the embarrassments of our hungry little council to determine that the animal might be carved before skinning as well as he could be afterward; and in a very few minutes we proved our united wisdom by a feast on his quartered remains.

"It was a glorious meal, such as the compensations of Providence reserve for starving men alone. We ate, forgetful of the past, and almost heedless of the morrow; cleared away the offal wearily; and now, at 10:00 P.M., all hands have turned in to sleep, leaving to their commanding officer the solitary honor of an eight hours' vigil."

February 24, Saturday. "A bitter disappointment met us at our evening meal. The flesh of our deer was nearly uneatable from putrefaction; the liver and intestines, from which I had expected so much, utterly so. The rapidity of such a change, in a temperature so low as minus thirty-five degrees, seems curious; but the Greenlanders say that extreme cold is rather a promoter than otherwise of the putrefactive process. All the graminivorous[4] animals have the same tendency, as is well known to the butchers. Our buffalo hunters, when they clean a carcass, do it at once; they have told me that the musk ox is sometimes tainted after five minutes' exposure. The Esquimaux, with whom there is no fastidious sensibility of palate, are in the practice at Yotlik and Horses' Head,

[3] Oliver Goldsmith's semtimental novel, *The Vicar of Wakefield.*

[4] *Gramninivorous:* grass-eating.

in latitude 73° 40' even in the severest weather, of withdrawing the viscera imme-diately after death and filling the cavity with stones."

February 25, Sunday. "Today, blessed the Great Author of Light! I have once more looked upon the sun. I was standing on deck, thinking over our prospects, when a familiar berg, which had been hid in shadow, flashed out in sun birth. I knew this berg well: it stood between Charlotte Wood Fiord and Little Willie's Monument. One year ago I traveled toward it from Fern Rock to catch the sunshine. Then I had to climb the hills beyond, to get the luxury of basking in its brightness; but now, though the sun is but a single degree above the horizon, it is so much elevated by refraction that the sheen stretched across the trough of the fiord like a flaming tongue. I could not resist the influ-ence. It was a Sunday act of worship: I started off at an even run, and caught him as he rolled slowly along the horizon, and before he sank. I was the first of my party to rejoice and meditate in sunshine. It is the third sun I have seen rise for a moment above the long night of an Arctic winter."

February 28, Wednesday. February closes: thank God for the lapse of its twenty-eight days! Should the thirty-one of the coming March not drag us fur-ther downward, we may hope for a successful close to this dreary drama. By the tenth of April we should have seal; and when they come, if we remain to welcome them, we can call ourselves saved.

MY JOURNAL FOR THE BEGINNING OF MARCH IS LITTLE ELSE THAN A chronicle of sufferings. Our little party was quite broken down. Every man on board was tainted with scurvy, and it was not common to find more than the three who could assist in caring for the rest. The greater number were in their bunks, absolutely unable to stir.

The circumstances were well fitted to bring out the character of individu-als. Some were very grateful for every little act of kindness from their more for-tunate messmates; some querulous; others desponding; others again wanted only strength to become mutinous. Brooks, my first officer, as stalwart a man-o'-war's man as ever faced an enemy, burst into tears when he first saw himself in the glass. On Sunday, the fourth, our last remnant of fresh meat had been doled out. Our invalids began to sink rapidly. The wounds of our amputated men opened afresh. The region about our harbor ceased to furnish its scanty contingent of game. One of our huntsmen, Petersen, never very reliable in anything, declared himself unfit for further duty. Hans was unsuccessful: he made several wide circuits, and saw deer twice; but they were beyond range.

I tried the hunt for a long morning myself, without meeting a single thing of life, and was convinced, by the appearance of things on my return to the brig, that I should peril the morale, and with it the only hope, of my command by repeating the experiment.

I labored, of course, with all the ingenuity for a well-taxed mind to keep up the spirits of my comrades. I cooked for them all imaginable compounds of our unvaried diet list, and brewed up flaxseed and lime juice and quinine and willow stems into an abomination which was dignified as beer, and which some were persuaded for the time to believe such. But it was becoming more and more certain every hour that, unless we could renew our supplies of fresh meat, the days of the party were numbered.

I spare myself, as well as the readers of this hastily compiled volume, when I pass summarily over the details of our condition at this time.

I look back at it with recollections like those of a nightmare. Yet I was borne up wonderfully. I never doubted for an instant that the same Providence that had guarded us through the long darkness of winter was still watching over us for good, and that it was yet in reserve for us—for some; I dared not hope for all—to bear back the tidings of our rescue to a Christian land. But how I did not see.

On the sixth of the month I made the desperate venture of sending off my only trusted and effective huntsman on a sledge journey to find the Esquimaux of Etah.

In clearing out Riley's bunk, we found that a rat had built its nest in my insect box, destroying all our specimens. This is a grave loss; for, besides that they were light of carriage and might have accompanied us in the retreat which now seems inevitable, they comprised our entire collection, and, though few in numbers, were rich for this stinted region. I had many spiders and bees. He is welcome to the whole of them, however, if I only catch him the fatter for the ration."

March 10, Saturday. "Hans has not yet returned so that he must have reached the settlement. His orders were, if no meat be obtained of the Esquimaux, to borrow their dogs and try for bears along the open water. In this resource I have confidence. The days are magnificent.

I had hardly written the above, when 'Bim, bim, bim!' sounded from the deck, mixed with the chorus of our returning dogs. The next minute Hans and myself were shaking hands.

"He had much to tell us; to men in our condition Hans was as a man from cities. We of the wilderness flocked around him to hear the news. Sugar teats of raw meat are passed around. 'Speak loud, Hans, that they may hear in the bunks.'

"The 'wind-loved' Anoatok he had reached on the first night after leaving the brig: no Esquimaux there of course; and he slept not warmly at a temperature of fifty-three degrees below zero. On the evening of the next day he reached Etah Bay and was hailed with joyous welcome. But a new phase of Esquimaux life had come upon its indolent, happy, blubber-fed denizens. Instead of plump, greasy children and round-cheeked matrons, Hans saw around him lean figures of misery: the men looked hard and bony, and the children shrivelled in the hoods that cradled them at their mothers' backs. Famine had been among them; and the skin of a young sea unicorn, lately caught, was all that remained to them of food. It was the old story of improvidence and its miserable train. They had even eaten their reserve of blubber, and were seated in darkness and cold, waiting gloomily for the sun. Even their dogs, their main reliance for the hunt and for an escape to some more favored camping ground, had fallen a sacrifice to hunger. Only four remained out of thirty: the rest had been eaten.

"Hans behaved well, and carried out my orders in their full spirit. He proposed to aid them in the walrus hunt.

"I have not time to detail Hans's adventurous hunt, equally important to the scurvied sick of Rensselaer and the starving residents of Etah Bay. Metek (the eider-duck) speared a medium-sized walrus, and Hans gave him no less than five Marston balls before he gave up his struggles. The beast was carried back in triumph, and all hands fed as if they could never know famine again. It was a regular feast, and the kablunah interest was exalted to the skies.

"I had directed Hans to endeavor to engage Myouk, if he could, to assist him in hunting. A most timely thought: for the morning's work made them receive the invitation as a great favor. Hans got his share of the meat, and returned to the brig accompanied by the boy, who is now under my care on board. This imp—for he is full of the devil—has always had a relishing fancy for the kicks and cuffs with which I recall the forks and teaspoons when they get astray; and, to tell the truth, he always takes care to earn them. He is very happy, but so

wasted by hunger that the work of fattening him will be a costly one. Poor little fellow! born to toil and necessity and peril; stern hunter as he already is, the
lines of his face are still quite soft and childlike. I think we understand one
another better than our incongruities would imply."

MARCH 15, THURSDAY. "Today we have finished burning our last Manilla
hawser for fuel, the temperature remaining at the extraordinary mean of
minus 52 degrees. Our next resort must be to the tebling of the brig: Petersen-
what remains of him, for the man's energies are gone—is now at work cutting
it off. It is a hard trial for me. I have spared neither exertion, thought, nor suffering to save the seaworthiness of our little vessel, but all to no end: she can
never bear us to the sea. Want of provisions alone, if nothing else, will drive
us from her; for this solid case of nine-foot ice cannot possibly give way until
the late changes of fall, nor then unless a hot summer and a retarded winter
afterward allow the winds to break up its iron casing."

March 16, Friday. "We have just a scant two day's meat for the sick. Hans
is doing his best; but there is nothing to be found on the hills: and I fear that
a long hunting journey to the south is our only resource."

March 17, Saturday. "I have been getting Hans ready for the settlement, with
a five-sinnet line of Maury's sounding twine. The natives to the south have lost
nearly all their *allunaks* or walrus lines by the accidents of December or
January, and will be unable to replace them till the return of the seal. A good
or even serviceable allunak requires a whole ussuk to cut it from. It is almost
the only article whose manufacture seems to be conducted by the Esquimaux
with any care and nicety of process. Our sounding line will be a valuable contribution to them, and may, like some more ostentatious charities, include the
liberal givers among those whom it principally blesses."

March 18, Sunday. "I have a couple of men on board whose former history
I would give something to know—bad fellows—both of them, but daring, energetic, and strong. They gave me trouble before we reached the coast of
Greenland; and they keep me constantly on the watch at this moment, for it
is clear to me that they have some secret object in view, involving probably a
desertion or escape to the Esquimaux settlements. They are both feigning
sickness this morning; and, from what I have overheard, it is with the view of

getting thoroughly rested before a start. Hans's departure with the sledge and dogs would give them a fine chance, if they could only waylay him, of securing all our facilities for travel; and I should not be surprised if they tried to compel him to go along with them. They cannot succeed in this except by force.

"I am acting very guardedly with them. I cannot punish till I have the evidence of an overt act. Nor can I trust the matter to other hands. It would not do to depress my sick party by disclosing a scheme which, if it could be carried out fully, might be fatal to the whole of us. All this adds to my other duties those of a detective policeman. I do not find them agreeable."

March 19, Monday. "Hans got off at eleven. I have been all right in my suspicions about John and Bill. They were anxious to get together this morning, and I was equally resolved to prevent any communication between them. I did this so ingeniously that they did not suspect my motive, by devising some outside duty for one or the other of them and keeping his comrade in the plot at work under my own eye. Their impatience and cunning little resorts to procure the chance of a word in private were quite amusing. It might be very far otherwise if they could manage to rob us of our dogs and gain the Netlik settlements.

"I hope the danger is over now. I shall keep the whole thing to myself for even the frustration of a mutinous purpose had best be concealed from the party."

March 20, Tuesday. "This morning I received information from Stephenson that Bill had declared his intention of leaving the brig today at some time. John, being now really lame, could not accompany him. This Stephenson overheard in whispers during the night and in faithful execution of his duty, conveyed it to me.

"I kept the news to myself; but there was no time to be lost. William, therefore, was awakened at 6:00 A.M. after my own night watch—and ordered to cook breakfast. Meantime I watched him. At first he appeared troubled and had several stealthily whispered interviews with John: finally his manner became more easy, and he cooked and served our breakfast meal. I now felt convinced that he would meet John outside as soon as he could leave the room, and that one or both would then desert. I therefore threw on my furs and armed myself, made Bonsall and Morton acquainted with my plans, and then, crawling out of our dark passage, concealed myself near its entrance. I had hardly waited half an hour—pretty cold work too—when John crawled out, limping and grunting. Once fairly out, he looked furtively round, and then, with a sigh of satisfaction, mounted our rickety steps entirely cured of his lameness.

Within ten minutes after he had gained the deck the door opened again, and William made his appearance, booted for travel and clad in buffalo. As he emerged into the hold, I confronted him. He was ordered at once to the cabin; and Morton was despatched on deck to compel the presence of the third party, while Mr. Bonsall took his station at the door, allowing no one to pass out.

"In a very few minutes John crawled back again, as lame and exhausted as when he was last below, yet growing lamer rapidly, as recovering from the glare of the light, he saw the tableau. I then explained the state of things to the little company and detailed step by step to the principles in the scene every one of their plans.

"Bill was the first to confess. I had prepared myself for the emergency, and punished him on the spot. As he rose with some difficulty, I detailed from the logbook the offenses he had committed and adduced the proofs.

"The short-handed condition of the brig made me unable to confine him; therefore I deemed it best to remove his handcuffs, to accept his protestations of reform and put him again to work. He accepted my lenity with abundant thanks, went to duty, and in less than an hour deserted. I was hunting at the time, but the watch reported his having first been discovered on the ice-foot and out of presenting distance. His intention undoubtedly is to reach Etah Bay, and, robbing Hans of sledge and dogs, proceed south to Netik.

"Should he succeed, the result will be a heavy loss to us. The dogs are indispensable in the hunt and in transporting us to Anoatok. The step however is not likely to be successful. At all events, he is off, and I regret that duty prevents my rejoicing at his departure. John remains with us, closely watched, but apparently sincere in his protestations of absolute reform."

MARCH 21, WEDNESDAY. "The day had been beautifully clear, and so mild that our midday thermometers gave but seven degrees above zero. This bears badly upon the desertion of Godfrey, for the probabilities are that he will find Hans's buffalo robe at the hut, and thus sleep and be refreshed. In that case, he can easily reach the Esquimaux of Etah Bay, and may easily seize upon the sledge dogs, rifle, and trading articles. The consequences of such an act would be very disastrous; nearly all my hopes of lifting the sick, and therefore of escaping in boats to the south, rest upon these dogs."

March 22, Thursday. "Petersen's ptarmigan are all gone, (five of them) and of the rabbit, but two rations of eight ounces each remain. We three, Bonsall, Petersen, and myself, have made up our minds to walk up Mary River Ravine until we reach the deer plains, and there separate and close in upon them. Today is therefore a busy one, for we must prepare beforehand the entire daily requirements of the sick: the ice for melting water must be cut in blocks and laid near the stove; the wood, of which it requires one entire day to tear enough out for two days, must be chopped and piled within arm reach; the bread must be cooked and provisions arranged before we can leave our comrades. When we three leave the brig, there will not be a single able man on board. McGary is able to leave his bed and stump about a little; but this is all. Need the dear home folks, who may some day read this, wonder that I am a little careworn, and that I leave the brig with reluctance? Of we three God-supported men, each has his own heavy load of scurvy."

March 23, Friday. "We started this morning, overworked and limping, rather as men ending a journey than beginning one. After four hours of forced walking, we reached the reindeer feeding grounds, but were too late: the animals had left at least two hours before our arrival. We scouted it over the protruding syenites, and found a couple of ptarmigan and three hares: these we secured.

"My people had done well during my absence, and welcomed me back impressively."

March 24, Saturday. "Our yesterday's ptarmigan gave the most sick a raw ration, and today we killed a second pair, which will serve them for tomorrow. To my great joy, they seem on that limited allowance to hold their ground.

"Bonsall and Petersen are now woodmen, preparing our daily fuel. My own pleasant duty consists in chopping from an iceberg six half-bushel bagfuls of frozen water, carrying it to the brig and passing it through the scuttle into our den; in emptying by three several jobs some twelve to fifteen bucketfuls from the slop barrel; in administering both as nurse and physician to fourteen sick men; in helping to pick eiderdown from its soil as material for boat bedding; in writing this wretched daily record, eating my meals, sleeping my broken sleeps, and feeling that the days pass without congenial occupation.

"Hans has not returned. I give him two days more before I fall in with the opinion which some seem to entertain, that Godfrey has waylaid or seized upon his sledge. This wretched man has been the very bane of the cruise. My conscience tells me that almost any measure against him would be justified, but aversion to extreme measures binds my hands."

XXII
THE DESERTER RETURNS

MARCH 25, SUNDAY. "A hard-working, busy Sunday it has been—a cheerless, scurvy-breeding day; and now by the midnight, which is as it were the evening of its continued light, I read the thermometers unaided except by the crimson fires of the northern horizon. It is, moreover, cold again, minus thirty-seven degrees.

"Refraction with all its magic is back upon us; the 'Delectable Mountains' appear again; and, as the sun has now worked his way to the margin of the north-western horizon, we can see the blaze stealing out from the black portals of these uplifted hills, as if there was truly beyond it a celestial gate."

March 31, Saturday. 'This month, badly as its daily record reads, is upon review a cheering one. We have managed to get enough game to revive the worst of our scurvy patients, and have kept in regular movement the domestic wheel of shipboard. Our troubles have been greater than at any time before; perhaps I ought to say they are greatest as the month closes: but, whatever of misery Bonsall and Petersen and myself may have endured, it seems nearly certain now that at least four men will soon be able to relieve us. Brooks, McGary, Riley, and Thomas have seen the crisis of their malady, and, if secured from relapse, will recover rapidly. Ohlsen also is better, but slow to regain his powers. But the rest of the crew are still down.

"The game season besides is drawing nearer; and, once able to shoot seal upon the ice, I have little fears for the recovery of the larger portion of our party. Perhaps I am too sanguine; for it is clear that those of us who have till now sustained the others are beginning to sink. Bonsall can barely walk in the morning, and his legs become stiffer daily; Petersen gives way at the ankles; and I suffer much from the eruption, a tormenting and anomalous symptom, which affects eight of our sick. It has many of the characteristics of exanthemata;[1] but is

---

[1] *Exanthmata:* an eruption of the skin

singularly persistent, varied in its phases, and possibly in its result dangerous.

"The moral value of this toilsome month to myself has been the lesson of sympathy it has taught me with the laboring man. The fatigue and disgust and secret trials of the overworked brain are bad enough, but not to me more severe than those which follow the sick and jaded body to a sleepless bed. I have realized the sweat of the brow, and can feel how painful his earnings must be to whom the grasshopper has become a burden."

April 2, Monday. "At eleven o'clock this morning, Mr. Bonsall reported a man about a mile from the brig, apparently lurking on the ice-foot. I thought it was Hans, and we both went forward to meet him. As we drew closer we discovered our sledge and dog team near where he stood; but the man turned and ran to the south.

"I pursued him, leaving Mr. Bonsall, who carried a Sharpe rifle, behind; and the man, whom I now recognized to be Godfrey, seeing me advance alone stopped and met me. He told me that he had been to the south as far as Northumberland Island; that Hans was lying sick at Etah, a consequence of exposure; that he himself had made up his mind to go back and spend the rest of his life with Kalutunah and the Esquimaux; and that neither persuasion nor force should divert him from his purpose.

"Upon my presenting a pistol, I succeeded in forcing him back to the gangway of the brig; but he refused to go farther; and, being loath to injure him, I left him under the guardianship of Mr. Bonsall's weapon while I went on board for irons; for both Bonsall and myself were barely able to walk, and utterly incapable of controlling him by manual force, and Petersen was out hunting: the rest, thirteen in all, are down with scurvy. I had just reached the deck when he turned to run. Mr. Bonsall's pistol failed at the cap. I jumped at once to the gun stand; but my first rifle, affected by the cold, went off in the act of cocking, and a second, aimed in haste at long but practicable distance, missed the fugitive. He made good his escape before we could lay hold of another weapon.

"I am now more anxious than ever about Hans. The past conduct of Godfrey on board, and his mutinous desertion, make me aware that he is capable of daring wrong as well as deception. Hans has been gone more than a fortnight: he has been used to making the same journey in less than a week. His sledge and dogs came back in the possession of the very man whom I suspected of an intention to waylay him; and this man, after being driven by menaces to the ship's side, perils his life rather than place himself in my power on board of her.

"Yet he came back to our neighborhood voluntarily, with sledge and dogs and walrus meat! Can it have been that John, his former partner in the plot, was on the lookout for him, and had engaged his aid to consummate their joint desertion?

"One thing is plain. This man at large and his comrade still on board, the safety of the whole company exacts the sternest observance of discipline. I have called all hands, and announced it as a standing order of the ship, and one to be observed inflexibly, that desertion, or the attempt to desert, shall be met at once by the sternest penalty. I have no alternative. By the body of my crew, sick, dependant, unable to move, and with everything to lose by the withdrawal of any portion of our efficient force, this announcement was received as a guarantee of their personal safety. But it was called for by other grave considerations. There is at this time on the part of all, men as well as officers, a warm feeling toward myself, and a strict, staunch fidelity to the expedition. But, for moral reasons which would control me, even if my impulses were different, I am constrained for the time to mingle among them without reserve, to act as a servant to their wants, to encourage colloquial equality and good humor; and, looking only a little way ahead to the juncture when a perfectly regulated subordination will become essential, I know that my present stand will be of value.

"This sledge load of Godfrey's meat, coming as it does, may well be called a Godsend: one may forgive the man in consideration of the good which it has done us all. We have had a regular feed all round, and exult to think we need no catering for the morrow. It has cheered our downhearted sick men wonderfully. Our brew of beer, too—the 'Arctic Linseed Mucilage Adaptation'—turns out excellent. Our grunts and growls are really beginning to have a good-natured twang. Our faces lessen as our shadows promise to increase. I think I see a change which points to the happier future.

"Our sick, however, are still nonoperatives, and our one room is like the convalescent ward of a hospital, with Bonsall and myself for the only nurses."

April 3, Tuesday. "Today I detained Petersen from his hunt, and took a holiday rest myself—that is to say, went to bed and-sweated—tomorrow I promise as much for Bonsall."

April 6, Friday. "Our little family is growing more and more uneasy about Hans. William reported him sick at Etah; but we had no faith in this story, and looked on his absence as merely the result of fatigue from exposure. But there seems ground for serious apprehension now. My own fear is that William may have conveyed to him some false message, or some threat of reproof, using my name, and in this way deterred him from returning. Hans is very faithful; but he is entirely unaware of William's desertion, and he is besides both credulous and sensitive. I am attached to Hans: he has always been a sort of henchman, a bodyguard, the companion of my walks. He is a devout Moravian and when the party withdrew from the brig last fall he refused to accompany them on grounds of religious obligation. The boy has fixed, honorable principles. Petersen thinks that he ought to be sent for, but he has not thought out the question who is to be sent. Bonsall is too lame to travel; Petersen himself is infinitely the best fitted, but he shirks the duty, and today he takes to his bed. I alone am left.

"Clearly duty to this poor boy calls me to seek him, and clearly duty to these dependent men calls upon me to stay. Long and uncomfortably have I pondered over these opposing calls, but at last have come to a determination. Hans was faithful to me: the danger to him is imminent; the danger to those left behind only contingent upon my failure to return. With earnest trust in that same supervising Agency which has so often before in graver straits interfered to protect and carry me through, I have resolved to go after Hans.

"The orders are given. In three hours I will be equipped and ready to take advantage of the first practicable moment for the start. It makes me write gravely; for I am far from well, very far from strong, and am obliged to drive our reduced team twice seventy miles. The latter half of the journey I shall have to do entirely on foot, and our lowest night temperatures are under minus forty degrees."

✲

THEY ESCAPED NEXT SUMMER, IN SMALL BOATS, MAKING A PERILOUS *trip south to the Eskimo settlement at Upernavik. There Kane learned that the entire expedition had been for nothing. Franklin had gone south, as John Rae had discovered, and all the Franklin crew had died. One more of Kane's crew had died on the trip south, too.*

But for all his faults and for all the turmoil on board the Advance, *he had discovered Kane Basin and, more to the point, Kennedy Channel, which would become, from then on, the route most favored by those seeking the North Pole. He had mapped areas that* were previously unknown. And when he returned to the U. S. he was, once again, accorded hero status. His second book, the one from which the excerpts above were taken, was even more of a success than the first. The book glosses over the cause of many of the interpersonal difficulties that plagued the expedition from the first, namely Kane himself, and William Godfrey, who returned to the ship and was rescued with the others, felt compelled to write his own account of the trip to counter Kane's charges. But it remains a great compelling read, and the original is beautifully illustrated. Kane was already famous, but this was a crowning touch.

Kane's second expedition effectively ruined his health. He was very sick when he sailed for England in the fall of 1856, to help Lady Franklin in yet another appeal for funds to mount yet another search for her husband. He died in Cuba, where he had gone in hopes of recovering, early in 1857. He had just passed his 37th birthday. Such was his fame that his funeral cortege took a month to sail up the Mississippi and then the Ohio to Cincinnati, the rivers lined with people the whole way. His body was taken by train from Cincinnati to Pennsylvania. In Xenia the train was forced to inch along through the mourners who lined the tracks. He lay in state in city after city, and thousands of people paid their respects. In Philadelphia he lay in state for three days while the crowds filed past. It was the biggest funeral America had ever seen, topped only by Abraham Lincoln's eight years later.

There was no cortege when Charles Francis Hall died. The whole nation did not mourn. He did not lie in state in his home city of Cincinnati. Hall was almost certainly murdered. One or more of his crew killed him—the killer remains unknown—and he was buried unceremoniously on the shores of Thank God Harbor, far up the Robeson Channel, which succeeds the Kennedy Channel and is even farther north than Elisha Kent Kane had gone, in 1871. We know he was murdered because in 1969 Chauncy Loomis, who was working on a book about Hall and the Polaris expedition he was leading, traveled to Thank God Harbor, exhumed the body, which was remarkably well preserved, thanks to the cold, and took hair samples. They contained killer amounts of arsenic. Someone had apparently put it in his food. He certainly thought so, at any rate. Unable to speak, sitting up in his bunk trying to write something down, all he could get out was "murder" before he died.

Hall was another explorer who did well until he was in command, and then did badly. In that sense it was fitting that Elisha Kent Kane should be Hall's inspiration.

Hall was a printer in Cincinnati and the owner of a small newspaper when Arctic fever came upon him in 1859. He sold his business, left a wife and two children behind, and went to New York to organize his own expedition to the Arctic. God had called him, he said, to search for Sir John Franklin. Everyone knew that Franklin and his men were long dead, but Hall persuaded himself that there might be a few survivors on King William Island, living with Eskimos. Eskimos fascinated Hall as much as the Arctic itself did. In New York he met Isaac Hayes, a young doctor who had sailed with Kane on his second expedition and was planning his own to that fabulous open polar sea. He got in touch with Henry Grinnell, who encouraged him, he listened to the tales of the Arctic whalers, and he tried to raise money. He raised less than a thousand dollars. With it he hitchhiked to the Arctic on a whaling ship in the summer of 1860 and they left him off on Baffin Island to live with the Eskimos. And here Hall found himself, living with a small group of natives, two of whom, Joe and Hannah—"Joe" Ebierbing and his wife, Tookoolito—had spent two years in London and spoke English.

Joe and Hannah would become Hall's companions from then until his death eleven years later—they went with him on the Polaris expedition— and Hall would spend, over the next decade, a total of five years living with Eskimo peoples as an Eskimo, in igloos and the summer tents made of animal skins, traveling with them, eating with them, sharing their dangers and their pleasures: going native, in short, to the extent that it was possible for him to do. He was a natural loner, naïve about the Eskimos but accepting of their ways, and he fit in nicely, at least for a while. The result was a book called Life with the Esquimaux that is often a delight to read, and quite informative about Eskimo life. Our excerpt is taken from an early chapter of the book, in which Hall accompanies a group of natives on a hunting trip in the winter of 1861.

CHARLES FRANCIS HALL

Life Among the Esquimaux

HAVING A GREAT DESIRE TO TRY AND DO SOMETHING IN THE WAY OF exploring, and particularly to accustom myself to actual life among the Innuits, I at length determined to venture on an excursion by sledge and dogs to Cornelius Grinnell Bay, whither Ugarng had already gone. Accordingly, after due preparation, myself and party were ready on the 10th of January, 1861, and away we went.

The following account of the first day's journey is from my journal, as written every evening in an igloo-snow hut:

"Thursday, January 10th, 1861. Thermometer 30° below zero, or 62° below freezing point! My company consists of self, Ebierbing, Tookoolito, and Koodloo, the cousin of the deceased Nukertou. By 4 A.M. I was up, and, with lantern in hand, went and called Ebierbing and his wife. They arose, and at once proceeded to gather up whatever things they would require during our stay. I then returned to the ship and packed up my own material. The outfit for this trip consisted, in provisions, of 1 ½lb. preserved boiled mutton in cans, 3 lbs. raw salt pork, 15 cakes (4 lbs.) sea-bread, ½lb. pepper, 2 lbs. ground burnt coffee, 1 quart molasses, 1 quart corn-meal, and 3 lbs. Cincinnati cracklings for soup. Then, for bedding, 1 double wool blanket, 1 sleeping-bag, 1 cloak and 1 shawl for bed-covering. For clothing, besides my native dress upon me, I took 1 extra under-shirt, 1 woolen shirt, 2 pairs extra stockings, 1 pair extra pants, 2 towels, and 2 pairs mittens. My books were Bowditch's Navigator, Burrit's Geography *and Atlas of the Heavens*, Gillespie's *Land Surveying, Nautical Almanac for 1861*, a *Bible*, and 'Daily Food.' My instruments were, 1 telescope, 1 self-registering thermometer, 1 pocket sextant, 2 magnetic compasses, and 1 marine glass. I had also a rifle and ammunition, oil for lamp, and a hand-saw, besides paper, ink, pens, memorandum and journal book.

"At 10 A.M. we were in readiness— Ebierbing with the loaded sledge and team of dogs (five of his and five of my Greenlanders)— alongside the *George Henry*. Tookoolito was gayly dressed in new tuktoo shirt, tuktoo pants, jacket, etc. Bidding adieu to our friends on board, we then started, Tookoolito leading the way –tracking for the dogs— for about one mile to the shore, in a northeasterly direction. Thence our course was that which Ugarng had evidently taken the day before. Over hill and mountain, through vale and valley, away we went.Sometimes, when on a descent, our speed was rapid. Now and then we all got on the sledge for a ride. My spirits were high, for this was my first sledge-traveling trip. Ebierbing managed the dogs admirably. Indeed, I should consider him a capital dog-driver. I think I never perspired so profusely as I have this day. Some of the events during our journey have been most amusing. Once we were descending a steep incline, all of the company holding on to the sledge, so as to prevent its too great speed downward, when, one of my feet breaking through the treacherous snow-crust, headlong I went, and, like a hoop, trundled to the bottom of the hill. Tookoolito hastened to my relief, and, seeing a frostbite on my face, she instantly applied her warm hand, the Innuit way, till all was right again. Another steep incline caused the sledge to descend so rapidly that at length it went over three or four of the dogs, who were unable to keep ahead of it, though running at great speed.

"By 3 P.M. we neared the frozen waters of the ocean, after passing over some very abrupt and rocky ground. On the margin of the sea the cliffs were almost perpendicular, and it was necessary to *lower* the sledge down to the ice below. Accordingly, the dogs were detached, and while Tookoolito, whip in hand, held on by their traces, which were from twenty to thirty feet long, we lowered the sledge. The tide, however, was out, and it caused some difficulty in getting on the main ice. At length all was safely accomplished, and once more we started on our way, Tookoolito again leading. Then we proceeded for about five miles, when we came to an igloo out on the ice, which had evidently been erected and occupied the night before by Ugarng and his party. Here we should have stopped; but, as the igloo was too small for us, we went on another mile, and then, finding good material for building a snow house, we encamped at 5 P.M."

Ebierbing and Koodloo at once commenced sawing out snowblocks, while I carried them to a suitable spot for erecting the igloo, which took us one hour to make. And a right good one it was, as I soon found. The door sealed up, and the cheerful lamp in full blaze, with a hot supper preparing, made me feel remarkably comfortable, though in a house of snow, built so speedily upon the frozen surface of the treacherous ocean. I will here give this matter more in detail.

Soon the igloo was completed, Tookoolito entered and commenced placing the stone lamp in its proper position. It was then trimmed, and soon a kettle of snow was over it making water for coffee and soup. She then proceeded to place several pieces of board we had brought with us on the snow platform where our beds were to be made. Upon these pieces was spread the canvas containing some of that small dry shrub I have alluded to. Over this went the tuktoo skins, and thus our sleeping accommodations were complete.

I should mention that every article on the sledge is passed in through an opening at the back of the igloo, for the purpose of convenience. When all is thus within, then this opening is closed, and a proper entrance made on the side opposite the beds. The dogs are left outside.

The drying of whatever has been worn during the day, or whatever has become wet with perspiration, falls to the lot of the "igloo-wife." She places the things on the *in-ne-tin* (a net over the fire-lamp), and through the night attends to the turning of them, as occasion requires. Her other duties in the repairing of such clothing as may be needed. Nothing is allowed to go one day without repair. Every thing, where *care* is required, even to pipes and tobacco, is placed in the igloo wife's hands— in this case, Tookoolito's. These matters I particularly noticed on the occasion of *my first night* spent in an arctic igloo.

Presently our evening meal was ready. It consisted of Cincinnati crackling soup, a small piece of raw salt pork for each of us, half a biscuit and coffee. Tookoolito proved herself an excellent cook; and I soon felt convinced that no party should think of traveling in these regions without an Innuit man and his wife, for the latter, above every thing, is the "all in all," or at least the "better half."

After supper, myself and the two male Esquimaux had each a pipe, and then turned in, my position being between the hot-blooded Innuits Ebierbing and Koodloo.

I slept as well as I would ever wish, and on the following morning, about nine o'clcok, after breakfast and repacking the sledge, we again started. Our proper course was due north, but, owing to hummocky ice, we could not follow it. In truth, sometimes we were obliged to make a retrograde movement to get out of "a fix" that we were occasionally in among icebergs and hummocks. Owing to this, we made but five miles direct toward our destination during the day.

It had been expected that we could reach Cornelius Grinnell Bay in one day from the vessel, but too many obstacles existed to allow it, and thus a second night came upon us while still upon the frozen sea. A storm was also gathering, and its darkness, with the howling wind, which had changed from off the land to right upon it, was foreboding. We were likewise much wearied with the day's labors, and it was some time after we stopped before a suitable place was found and our second igloo erected. At length, though long after dark, we were comfortably located, enjoying a hot supper beneath the snowy dome, the foundation of which rested on the frozen bosom of the mighty deep. But not too soon were we under shelter. The storm had burst in all its fury, and we could hear the wind roaring outside as we warmed ourselves within.

All night long the gale continued, and the next morning— the third of our journey— it was found impossible to go on. It was blowing a strong gale, and continued so all day, with snow in impenetrable thickness. We were therefore obliged to keep inside our shelter, wrapped in furs.

While thus detained, I took the opportunity to have my hair cut by Tookoolito. It had grown to a great length, even to my shoulders, and I now found it very inconvenient. My beard, whiskers, and mustache were also shorn nearly close to my face. In musquito time they were serviceable, but now they had become quite an evil, owing to the masses of ice that clung to them. Indeed, on the previous night I had to lose a portion of my whiskers. They had become so ice-locked that I could not well get my reindeer jacket off over my head, therefore I used my knife, and *cut* longer attachments to them.

I may here mention that, after this, when we vacated the snowhouse, our dogs rushed in to devour whatever they could find, *digestible* or *not digestible*, and my locks were a portion of what they seized. In went my discarded hair to fill up their empty stomachs! A few days later, I saw the very same hirsute material, just as clipped from my head, lining a step leading to another igloo, having passed through the labyrinthian way from a dog's mouth onward.

About 4 P.M. Ebierbing ventured outside to see how matters looked, but he soon returned with the astounding news that *the ice was breaking, and water had appeared not more than ten rods south of us!* I looked, and, to my dismay, found that a crack or opening extended east and west to the land, distant about three miles! The gale had evidently set the sea in heavy motion somewhere, and its convulsive throbs were now at work underneath the ice close to and around us. It still blew very hard, but as yet the wind was easterly, and so far good, because, if a nearer disruption took place, we should be forced toward the land, but if it changed to north or northwest, away to sea we must go and perish!

Seriously alarmed, we consulted as to what was best to do— whether at once to hasten shoreward, or remain in the igloo and stand the chance. On shore, nothing but rugged precipices and steep mountains presented themselves; on the ice, we were in danger of our foundation giving way— that is, of being broken up, or else driven to sea. At length we decided to remain while the wind lasted in its present quarter, and, to guard as much as possible from any sudden movement taking us unawares, I kept within sight my delicately-poised needle, so that the slightest shifting of the ice on which we were encamped might be known.

In the evening the gale abated, and by 10 P.M. it was calm, but the heavy sea kept the ice cracking, screaming, and *thundering,* as it actually danced to and fro! It was to me a new but fearful sight. When I retired to bed I laid down with strange thoughts in my mind, but with a conviction that the same protecting hand would watch over me there as elsewhere.

The night passed away without alarm, and in the morning Koodloo made an opening with a snow-knife through the dome of the igloo for peering out at the weather. He reported all clear and safe, and, after a hot breakfast, we packed and started, though under great difficulty and hazard.

The ice had given way, and was on the move in every direction. The snow was also very deep— sometimes above our knees— and moreover very treacherous. We could hardly get along; and the poor dogs, which had been near starving since we had left the ship (Esquimaux dogs endure starvation, and yet work, amazingly), had to be assisted by us in pushing and hauling the sledge, while constant precaution was needed against falling through some snow-covered ice-crack. Every now and then we came to openings made by the gale and heaving sea. Some of these were so wide that our sledge could hardly bridge them, and a *detour* would be made for a better spot. At other places we had to overcome obstructions caused by high rugged ice that had been thrown up when masses had been crushed together by the tremendous power of the late storm.

To guard against and extricate ourselves from these dangers, yet find a track amid the hummocks around, each of us by turns took the lead, and in this manner we proceeded on our way; but it was evident we had hardly strength enough to persevere in reaching our destination that night. By 2 P.M. we were so exhausted that I deemed it best to make a halt, and use a little more of the slender stock of provisions I had with me, and which owing to our being so much longer on the way than expected, had become very low. Each of us, therefore, had a slice of *raw* salt pork and a quarter of a biscuit. This, however trifling, gave renewed strength, and again we pushed forward, hauling, scrambling, tumbling, and struggling almost for our lives.

It was dark ere we got near the locality where our next encampment was to be made, and where, in fact, we intended to remain a while for the purpose of hunting and sealing, and myself exploring.

At length we caught sight of an igloo which afterward proved to be Ugarng's, and soon as we saw it, fresh efforts were made to get nearer, but we found our passage more and more obstructed by the broken, upturned ice. Often the sledge was carried onward by making it leap over these impediments, sometimes from one point of ice to another, and at others down and up among the broken pieces. Finally we succeeded in reaching the shore ice, which we found all safe and sound, and in a short time more we were alongside of Ugarng's igloo, encamped on the southwest side of Roger's Island, overlooking Cornelius Grinnell Bay and the mountains surrounding it.

Immediately I ran into Ugarng's iglooo, and obtained some water to drink, for I must mention that all day long we had been famishing on account of thirst. The material to make water had been abundant around us— beneath our feet, here, there, and every where— but not a drop could be obtained, owing to our firelamp and equipments not being in use. Thus it was most thankfully I received the warmhearted welcome given me by Nikujar, family wife No. 1 of Ugarng, as she handed a cup of refreshing cold water. Then I remembered how, on one occasion at the ship, this same woman, with her infant, came and asked *me* for water which I gladly gave to her, with something else. Now *she* gave it to me.

I should mention that, in winter, water is most precious to the natives. It is made only by melting snow or ice over the ikkumer (fire-lamp), which is an expensive heat and light when oil and blubber become scarce; and in this case our materials for fuel were all expended.

While our own igloo was being erected, Ugarng and his second wife arrived from sealing, and, to the joy of all, brought with him a fine seal. He generously supplied us with what we wanted, and thus an excellent supper was added to cheerful light and genial warmth from the now well-fed lamp.

My fourth night in an igloo, on this journey, was spent more comfortably than the previous two had been, and on the following morning I rose greatly refreshed and strengthened. As I looked upon the expanse over which we had passed, I was startled to find the ice all gone out to sea. This was confirmed by a view shortly afterward obtained from the top of a mountain behind our igloos, and I felt truly grateful to HEAVEN for having so preserved us.

During the day I took a walk on shore, and the two Esquimaux went sealing. They returned at night with a fine prize, which made us an excellent feast; and, as my own stock of provisions was exhausted, except a trifle I reserved in case of sickness, this supply was most timely.

On the following day, January 15th, Ebierbing and Koodloo departed, with the sledge and dogs, on a hunting excursion, and I went away to examine the locality around. During my walk over the hills I came across numerous tracks of rabbits, and I also saw in the distance several prominent headlands that were familiar to me from noticing them when we first arrived here in the ship.

While rambling about, I fortunately preserved myself from a severe frostbite in the face by taking the precaution of carrying a small pocket mirror which belonged to Tookoolito. I had asked the loan of it, knowing how necessary it was, when one is alone in those regions, to have a detector of frostbites; and I found the use of a mirror in such a case equivalent to the companionship of another person.

That night I was alone with Tookoolito and Punnie; the latter Ugarng's third wife, she having come to our igloo to keep company with us until the husbands returned. It was very cold— the thermometer down to 57° below freezing point. Now my usual sleeping-place was between Ebierbing and Koodloo; but they being absent, I had to lay on the general bed, wrapped in my furs and blankets. During the early part of the night my feet were almost frozen. I tried all I could to keep them warm, but in vain. At last a smooth low voice reached my ear:

"Are you cold, Mr. Hall?"

I answered, "My feet are almost frozen. I can not get them comfortable."

Quick as thought, Tookoolito, who was distant from me just the space occupied by little Punnie (that is, Punnie slept in the middle), got down to the foot of her bed; thence she made passage for her hands directly across to my feet, seizing them and drawing them aslant to her side. My modesty, however, was quieted when she exclaimed,

"Your feet are like ice, and must be warmed *Innuit* fashion!"

Tookoolito then resumed her place beneath her tuktoo furs, intermingling her hot feet with the ice-cold ones of mine. Soon the same musical voice said,

"Do your feet feel better?"

I responded, "They do, and many thanks to you."

She then said, "Well, keep them where they are. Good-night again, sir."

My feet now were not only glowing warm, but *hot* through the remainder of the night. When I awoke in the morning, as near as I could *guess*, there were no less than three pairs of warm feet all woven and interwoven, so that some difficulty was experienced to tell which were my own.

Eibierbing and Koodloo did not return until the next evening, bringing with them some black skin and krang— all the success attending them— which was obtained from a *cache* made the previous fall by the natives when our ship was in the bay. The black skin was compelled to be our food, as nothing better could be had; and at supper I ate heartily of the *raw frozen whale hide.*

The following noon a very heavy snow-storm came on, and continued throughout the next and two following days, confining us almost entirely to the igloo, myself obliged to live on black skin, krang, and seal.

On Sunday, the 20th of January, ten days after leaving the ship, we found ourselves in a sad state from actual want of food. The weather continued so bad that it was impossible to procure any by hunting, and all we had hitherto obtained was now consumed, except a very small portion held in reserve. I had intended sending Koodloo back to the ship for supplies, but waited for more suitable weather. This morning, however, it was absolutely necessary an attempt should be made, and as Koodloo refused to go alone, I decided upon proceeding with him.

We expected to be obliged to make one night's encampment on the sea ice, now again, so far as we knew from that around us, compact, and we hoped to reach the ship on the following day. My only preparation was a sleeping bag and shawl, with a carpet sack of sundries, and half a pound of baked mutton, which I had carefully preserved to the present moment.

At 8 A.M. we were in readiness, with a sledge and team of 12 dogs, most of them nearly starved. Bidding adieu to Ebierbing and Tookoolito, Koodloo and I started on our journey.

At first, much hummocky ice impeded the way, but this we got through, and I anticipated a speedy trip. I was, however, disappointed. Soon, deep snow appeared; and though we struggled for some miles due south, it was at length evident that to go on like that would be impossible. Occasionally the sledge and dogs contrived to get forward pretty well, but often they were so buried as to be almost out of sight. Koodloo seemed to think of giving it up, and I was so weak as to be hardly capable of dragging myself along. While in this dilemma as to what we should do— go on, or return to the igloo— I perceived Ebierbing and Ugarng on their way toward us.

They had noticed my difficulty, and Ebierbing now came on snow-shoes to offer his services in going to the ship in my stead. I accepted the proposal, and he, with Koodloo, went forward, Ugarng going in another direction, seeking for seal-holes, while I, slowly and with difficulty, owing to my weakness, returned to the igloo. I was a long time getting back, and when I arrived there was obliged to throw myself on the snow platform quite exhausted.

Toward evening, the weather then being fine, I walked on to a hill that overlooked the bay, and with my glass saw Ebierbing and Koodloo slowly wending their way along near where our second igloo had been erected, the former leading. That night and the following day I was hardly able to move. My weak state, owing to want of food— all my daily fare being a small piece of black or whale skin— had become very serious.

In the evening I went to Ugarng's. He had just returned from sealing, having been out *two days and one night* over a seal-hole. All the reward he had, however, for his patient exertions was the seal coming up and giving a puff; then away it went, leaving Ugarng a disappointed Innuit. But he bore his disappointment very philosophically. He said, in his native tongue, "Away I go tomorrow morning again!"

The next morning, which was very fine, Ugarng and Jack went out sealing again, while I visited several portions of the island. The following day Ugarng returned once more unsuccessful, though he had remained all night over the seal-hole. This was very bad for the whole of us. We could not now have even a fire-light until another seal was captured; and when I called at Ugarng's, I found they were in the same condition. Nikujar (Polly) was alone, except her infant and Kookooyer, their daughter by George. They were without light. Her child was restless, and she said the cause was hunger. "Me got no milk— meat all gone— blubber too— nothing to eat— no more light— mo heat— must wait till get seal."

While I waited, the second wife came in and said Ugarng was still watching over a seal-hole. Jack soon afterward returned without success. Sad— very sad! My own state was bad enough, and I felt it severely; but I could not bear to witness the wants of the poor people around me, having no power to relieve them, unless Ebierbing should soon come back with some provisions from the ship. All that I had to eat was my piece of black skin, and this I relished. Indeed, I could have eaten any thing that would have gone toward keeping up the calories within me, and make bone and flesh.

One night I asked Tookoolito if I might try the taste of some blackened scraps that hung up. I knew that she had reserved these for the dogs, but nevertheless I had an uncontrollable longing for them. I was very hungry. Tookoolito replied that she could not think of my eating them— the idea made her almost sick; therefore I did not urge the matter more; but soon afterward I saw they were gone, Punnie (Ugarng's third wife) having taken them, and passed the whole into her own stomach!

Ugarng came in late again unsuccessful, and Tookoolito gave him a cup of tea, such as it was, for, owing to the absence of proper light and fuel, it could not be well made. Directly he had it, off he went once more to try for seal.

The next morning Ebierbing had not returned, and we were all at our wits' end to find something to eat. At length Tookoolito made out to cut off some of the white from a piece of black skin. From it she "tried" out sufficient oil to use for heating some snow-water, which, when warmed, was thickened with Indian meal, a few handfuls having been found remaining of the small quantity I had brought with me. The quantity of meal did not weigh above two ounces, yet it seemed to "*loom up*" as it was incorporated in the tepid water, and the incident strongly reminded me of the good woman and Elijah of Bible history. Tookoolito, with whom I shared the meal, thought the "pudding" excellent, and so did I. Indeed I shall not readily forget that breakfast, even— as I wrote at the time— "if I live to enjoy a thousand more dainty ones in my native home."

At this time, though I kept in general good health and spirits, I was fast losing flesh. But almost worse than want of food was the want of light and fuel.
On several occasions, the only way I had to keep myself from freezing was by
sitting in bed with plenty of tuktoo furs around me. The writing of my journal
was done with the thermometer +15° to less than 0, while outside it was from
−25° to −52°. During the day I several times went up the hill to look for
Ebierbing's reappearance from the vessel, but no signs of him met my eye, and
the night of January 24th (fourteen days from the ship) saw us with our last ration
of food, viz., a piece of "black skin" 1 ½ inch wide, 2 inches long, and ½ of an inch
thick. It was under these very "agreeable" circumstances I went to sleep, hoping to dream of better things, even if I could not partake of them. "Better
things" fortunately did arrive, and in a way that I *could* partake of them.

At midnight I heard footsteps within the passage-way to our igloo. Intuitively
I knew it was Jack with ooksook— seal-blubber. I sprang out of bed and drew
back the snow-block door. There *was* Jack, his spear covered with pierced seal-
blubber hanging in strips like string-dried apples. I had allowed my poor
starving dog "Merok" to sleep within the igloo that night, and, directly I had
opened the door, on his scenting the luscious fat, quicker than thought he gave
one leap— a desperate one, as if the strength of a dozen well-fed animals were
in him. In an instant I grappled with the dog, and made great efforts to save
the precious material; but, though I actually thrust my hands into his mouth,
and though Tookoolito and Punnie also battled with him, Merok conquered,
and instantly devoured that portion he had seized.

This misfortune, however, was not single. Before Jack could get his well-
loaded spear and himself into the igloo, all the other dogs about the place were
around him, fighting for a share of what was left. They succeeded in obtaining nearly all before we could drive them away, and thus the good portion
intended for us from what Jack had procured was lost *to us,* but not to the dogs!
Jack, who was of Ugarng's party, and had brought this as a present, returned
to his own igloo, and left us disconsolate to ours. "Better things," therefore,
in that case, were not for us; but, nevertheless, as I have said above, they did
arrive, and that speedily.

Not before 9 A.M. did I again leave my tuktoo bed and go outside the igloo
to look around. Naturally and longingly my first glance was in the direction
whence I expected Ebierbing. In a moment my eyes caught something black

upon the almost universal whiteness. I looked again and again. It moved, and immediately my heart leaped with joy as my tongue gave utterance in loud tones to Tookoolito within, "Ebierbing! Ebierbing! He is coming! he is coming!" The response was, "That is good;" and I— merely adding, "I go to meet him"— bounded away as fast as my enfeebled body would allow.

I soon found, however, that if progress was to be made toward him, I must do it by slow degrees and patient steps. "Black skin," in homoeopathic quantities, daily taken for food, had but kept my stomach in sufficient action to support life. All the strength I now had was mostly from the beefsteaks of dear Ohio, eaten and moulded into human fat, muscle, and bones before leaving my native home. But this remaining strength was very, very small, and thus my efforts to get on soon nearly exhausted me.

After a great struggle through the deep snow, I at last got within hailing distance, and sang out to know if it was really Ebierbing, as the party I had seen was no longer advancing. No reply came to my question, and I immediately hastened my feeble steps to see the cause. A moment or two more brought me near enough to be convinced. It *was* Ebierbing, with the sledge and dogs, but so exhausted with his labors that he had been obliged to throw himself down, completely overpowered. Soon I was by his side grasping his hand, and, with a grateful heart, thanking him for the really good deed he had performed in thus coming alone with the relief I saw before me.

In a short time the loaded sledge was examined, and I found a box of sundries sent from the ship, as also a *very fine seal, caught that morning by Ebierbing himself.* There was likewise a quantity of whale-meat, brought from Rescue Harbor for the use of our dogs.

Directly Ebierbing could renew his journey, we started together; but the dogs and both of use were hardly able to get the sledge along. Finally we reached the shore ice, and here we were so exhausted that not one inch farther could we drag the loaded sledge. Kunniu, wife No. 2 of Ugarng, seeing our condition, hastened to give assistance, and with her strong arms and our small help, the sledge was soon placed high on the shore by the side of the igloos.

Ebierbing's first and most earnest call was for "water." This was supplied to him, and then we commenced storing our new supplies. The seal was taken into the igloo— the usual place for a captured seal— and the sledge, with its contents, was properly attended to. Of course, the news of Ebierbing's arrival with a seal "spread like wildfire," and in our quiet little village, consisting of three igloos, all the inhabitants with exhausted stomachs— including my own— were prepared for wide distention.

The seal weighed, I should say, about 200 lbs., and was with young. According to Innuit custom, an immediate invitation was given by the successful hunter's family for every one to attend a "seal feast." This was speedily done, and our igloo was soon crowded. My station was on the dais, or bed-place, behind several Innuit women, but so that I could see over them and watch what was going on.

The first thing done was to consecrate the seal, the ceremony being to sprinkle water over it, when the stalwart host and his assistant proceeded to separate the "blanket"— that is, the blubber, with skin— from the solid meat and skeleton of the seal. The body was then opened and the blood *scooped* out. This blood is considered very precious, and forms an important *item* of the food largely consumed by Esquimaux. Next came the liver, which was cut into pieces and distributed all around, myself getting and eating a share. Of course *it was eaten raw*— for this was a raw-meat feast— its eating being accompanied by taking into the mouth at the same time a small portion of delicate white blubber, which answered the same as butter with bread. Then followed distributing the ribs of the seal for social picking. I joined in all this, doing as they did, and becoming quite an Innuit save in the *quantity* eaten. This I might challenge any *white man* to do. No human stomach but an Innuit's could possibly hold what I saw these men and women devour.

DURING HALL'S YEARS IN THE ARCTIC HE DID ACCOMPLISH PART OF *what he set out to do, finding not Franklin survivors but more Franklin relics, and he recovered more oral testimony from Eskimos in the region where Franklin's ships had vanished. He also discovered the remains of Martin Frobisher's expedition to Frobisher Bay—coal that Frobisher had left behind, including the trench Frobisher's miners had dug to extract what they hoped to be gold-bearing ore, and bits and pieces of glass, tile, and other artifacts. He also confirmed that Frobisher Bay was a bay and not a strait, and mapped its coastline. Over the years, it is worth noting, Hall became increasingly disenchanted with Eskimo life. He lived with natives and Joe and Hannah were his*

constant companions and friends, but he could not abide some of their customs, most especially their casual attitude toward marriage and fidelity, their indifference to Christianity and their persistent paganism. He was at bottom a difficult man, not only not good as a leader but not good with other people at all. In 1869 he mounted an expedition to King William Island, hiring five whalers to go with him, and wound up shooting and killing one because he thought he was threatening mutiny. The other four men deserted him as soon as they had the chance.

With his quest for Franklin survivors over, Hall turned to his other goal: the North Pole. He had established himself by now as the real thing, an Arctic explorer with a great deal of experience who knew how to survive Arctic winters. He lobbied Congress for funds to finance his next expedition, which would follow in the wake of Elisha Kent Kane through Smith Sound to the top of Ellesmere Island, and then to the Pole, and Congress voted the money. He left in 1871 with a contingent of two whaling captains, a one-time shipmate of Elisha Kent Kane's, a young German scientist and his German assistant, seven German crewmen and about the same number of Americans, and Joe and Hannah. They sailed on a Navy ship that had been refitted for Arctic service and renamed the Polaris aris.When they reached Greenland they picked up Hans Hendrik, who had by now sailed with Kane, and then with Isaac Hayes on his own unsuccessful expedition north.

By this time there was already, as with Kane, trouble on the ship. A naval officer on another ship in the area had to come aboard and remind all parties that they were under naval discipline, and that Hall was in charge. One of the whaling captains, a man named Budington, was hitting the liquor cabinet on the sly. Budington thought the entire expedition was foolish. The other whaling captain, George Tyson, thought Budington was incompetent. The German scientists looked down on Hall as an uneducated man. They were openly antagonistic, and so, as a result, were the German crewmembers.

Nevertheless the ship made it farther north than any other ship had made it, reaching more than 82 degrees north latitude in the narrow channel that separates the top of Greenland from the top of Ellesmere Island. It was the very edge of the Arctic Ocean—which was, of course, permanently frozen. In September Hall decided to winter a few miles south of his farthest north at a spot on the Greenland shore which he named Thank God Harbor. He would try for the Pole the following spring by sledge.

Within two months he was dead.

Who killed Hall? Suspicion has always centered on three men—Budington; the German scientist, whose name was Bessels; and the other German scientist, a man named Meyer. All three were glad to see him go. It is also possible that Hall killed himself, by accident, dosing himself out of his own medicine chest, which he was inclined to do. We shall never know for sure. The Navy board that was appointed to inquire into the circumstances decided that he died of a stroke. Only the exhumation of his body and the arsenic in his hair reversed this judgment.

But we do know that the ship fell apart after he died. Who was in charge? With two whaling captains on board, one of them a drunk and the other distrustful of the first, it was not a situation conducive to harmony. The Eskimos retreated to shore and built igloos to live in. The rest of the men spent a miserable winter on board. In August the following year the ice released the Polaris and they steamed south for three days until they ran into the pack. They spent the next two months adrift, attached to a floe, slowly moving south into Kane Basin. In mid-October the ice pinioned them against a huge iceberg that threatened to destroy the ship. Thinking it doomed, Budington, who was drunk at the time, ordered tons of supplies thrown overboard onto the surrounding ice, as well as the ship's two whaleboats. Some of the supplies were swept under the ship and lost. That night the crisis eased and George Tyson asked Budington to take him, the Eskimos, and the men on the floe, which was beginning to fall apart, back on board, but Budington ordered them to move the boats farther from the ship, along with the supplies. At that moment the ice gave way and it was too late. Tyson, the Eskimos, and a good part of the crew, a total of nineteen people, found themselves on the ice, with the Polaris rapidly drifting away. The Eskimos had their families with them. In a remarkably brief time the Polaris was lost to sight.

Thus began yet another of the Arctic's many amazing survival stories. The crew left on the Polaris looked for them the next day, but never saw them, even though Tyson could see the ship ten or twelve miles away and tried to signal. Nineteen people, five of them children, seven of them Germans armed with pistols who refused to follow orders from Tyson or anybody else, were stranded on an ice floe a mile across and five miles around thousands of miles from anywhere. Within a day one of the whaleboats, with 500 pounds of food aboard, was lost when the corner of the floe where it lay broke off. The Germans refused to get into the other boat and pursue it. They had to survive on what was left on the ice, which came to about 1,900 lbs. of food, and on what the Eskimos could hunt. The whaleboat with the lost food drifted back into reach within a week or so, but there was still not enough food for all those people. And they would drift for the next six months.

Those months were a nightmare. The Germans skulked in their tent like little toy Achilleses, refusing to help or participate, stealing more than their share of the food whenever they could. The Eskimos were convinced that they would kill them when food ran short, or if not them then their children, and eat the children. Tyson, unarmed, could exert no control over anyone. The Eskimos kept them alive, hunting seals and sharing their food. Joe Ebierbing, Hall's friend, did most of the successful hunting, going out in blizzards, the temperature at fifty below zero, to hunt. For the rest there was nothing to do, nothing at all. The Arctic winter and the Arctic night closed in on them. The ice floe might split up at any moment, without warning. When March came it did begin to fall apart. By the beginning of April it was no more than twenty yards across. We join them in April, just before they were rescued. The excerpt is from Tyson's account of the experience, written up by Euphemia Vale Blake.

EUPHEMIA VALE BLAKE

Arctic Experiences: Containing Capt. George E. Tyson's Wonderful Drift on the Ice-Floe

APRIL 13. I think this must be Easter-Sunday in civilized lands. Surely we have had more than a forty day's fast. May we have a glorious resurrection to peace and safety ere long!

"The ice opened again last night., but closed in the morning. It remained open but a few hours, slackening a little to-day. But we can neither travel over it nor use the boat; we can do nothing with it; we might as well be without volition. Our fate is not in our own hands.

'Last night, as I sat solitary, thinking over our desperate situation, the northern lights appeared in great splendor. I watched while they lasted, and there seemed to be something like the promise accompanying the first rainbow in their brilliant flashes. The auroras seem to me always like a sudden flashing out of the Divinity: a sort of reminder that God has not left off the active operations of his will. This, with my impression that it must be Easter-Sunday, has thrown a ray of hope over our otherwise desolate outlook.

"Saw some seals to-day, but the ice being in such a condition, we can not secure any. We should be very glad now of some of the meat we were obliged to abandon. Our latitude is 55° 23', approximate.

April 14. Wind, light, from the north. The pack still close. No chance of shifting our position for a better yet. See seals almost every day, but can not get them. We can neither go through the ice nor over it in its present condition. The weather is fine and the sea calm, or, rather, I should say, the *ice* is calm, for I see no water anywhere.

Our small piece of ice is wearing away very fast, and our provisions nearly finished. Things look very dark, starvation very near. Poor Meyers looks wretchedly; the loss of food tells on him worse than on the rest. He looks very weak. I have much sympathy for him, notwithstanding the trouble he has caused me. I trust in God to bring us all through. It does not seem possible that we should have been preserved through so many perils, and such long-continued suffering, only to perish at last.

April 15. Nearly calm; very light north wind. The ice still the same. No change except that it was much colder—8 to 10 degrees below zero. Snow is falling very thick, but without wind. Stopped snowing, and sun shining as bright as ever again—a spring 'spurt' of snow. This would be splendid weather to travel now; but are stayed and can not stir. Meyers looks very bad. Hunger and cold show their worst effects on him. Some of the men have dangerous looks; this hunger is disturbing their brains. I can not but fear that they contemplate crime. After what we have gone though, I hope this company may be preserved from any fatal wrong. We can and we must bear what God sends without crime. This party must not disgrace humanity by cannibalism.

April 16. One more day got over without a catastrophe. The ice is still the same. Some of the men's heads and faces are much swollen, but from what cause I can not discover. I know scurvy when I see it, and it is not that. We keep an hour-watch now through the night. The men are too weak to keep up long together. Some one has been at the pemmican. This is not the first time. I know the men; there are three of them. They have been the three principal pilferers of the party. One of them was caught at it on the 7th of this month. I should not blame them much for taking food, but of course all the others will have less in consequence. We have but a few days' provisions left. We came down still lower on our allowance this morning. Rather weakening work, but it must be done to save life in the end. The idea that cannibalism can be contemplated by any human being troubles me very much.

April 17. Light breeze; S.S.W. The ice the same; no opening yet. Lat 54° 27'.

April 18. Very light breeze from the north.

11A.M. Joe spied a small hole of water about half a mile off. He took his gun, and ventured over the loose ice. Joe is very small and light, and can go where an American can not. He had no sooner reached the spot than we heard the welcome sound of his rifle. He had shot a seal, and called loudly for the kayak, for the water was making rapidly. It took an hour to get the kayak there—an hour of intense anxiety, for we were afraid the seal would float away; but at last, with trouble and risk, it was accomplished, and a nice-sized seal, enough for three meals, rewarded our exertions. We shall have to eat it raw, but we are thankful to get that. It will save us from starving, perhaps worse.

The water is making quite a lead, and this morning at daylight the joyful sight of land greeted our eyes. It bore to the south-west. We saw it very plainly in the morning, but the weather has become so thick since that we have lost sight of it for the present. It is as if God had just raised the curtain of mist and showed us the promised land to encourage and keep us from despair. The seal, too, has put new life in us. We have only a few pounds of bread and pemmican left—enough for tonight. The lead had closed up again, but the 'pash' seems to slacken.

We had visitors today—a raven, some other land birds, and a large flock of ducks. I should think there was a hundred and fifty. I wish we could shoot some of them for a meal or two; but they keep off a mile or more. We have eaten up every scrap of that seal, every thing but the gall.

Poor Meyers, he is tall and very thin. He has on his hands a monstrous pair of deer-skin gloves, ever so much too large for him. It looked quite pitiable, though almost grotesquely amusing (if the case had not been so serious), to see him striving to gather up some bones, once abandoned, to pick at again for a scrap of meat. The gloves were so large, and his hands so cold, he could not feel when he had got hold of any thing; and as he would raise himself up, almost toppling over with weakness, he found time and again that he had grasped nothing. If Doré had wanted a model subject to stand for Famine, he might have drawn Meyers at that moment and made a success. He was the most wretched-looking object I ever saw.

Evening. It looks very threatening; breezing up from the north-east, and the swell increasing.

April 20. Blowing strong from the north-east. There is a very heavy swell under the ice.

At 9 PM, while resting in our tent, we were alarmed by hearing an outcry from the watch; and almost at the same moment a heavy sea swept across our piece, carrying away everything on it that was loose. This was but a foretaste of what was to follow; immediately we began shipping sea after sea, one after another, with only from five to ten minutes interval between each. Finally came a tremendous wave, carrying away our tent, skins, most all of our bed-cloth-ing, and leaving us destitute. Only a few things were saved, which we had man-aged to get into the boat; the women and children were already in the boat, or the little ones would certainly have been swept into watery graves. All we could do now, under this new flood of disaster, was to try and save *the boat*. So all hands were called to man the boat in a new fashion—namely, to hold on to it with might and main, to prevent its being washed away. Fortunately, we had preserved our boat warp, and had also another strong line, made out of strips of oogjook-skin, and with these we secured the boat, as well as we were able, to project-ing vertical points of ice; but having no grapnels or ice-anchors, these fastenings were frequently unloosed and broken, and the boat could not for one moment be trusted to their hold. All our additional strength was needed and we had to brace ourselves and hold on with all the strength we had.

As soon as possible I got the boat, with the assistance of the men, over to that edge of our ice where the seas first struck; for I knew if she remained toward the farther edge the gathered momentum of the waves as they rushed over the ice would more than master us, and the boat would go. It was well this pre-caution was taken, for, as it was, we were nearly carried off, boat and all, many times during this dreadful night. The heaviest seas came at intervals of fifteen or twenty minutes, and between these others that would have been thought very powerful if worse had not followed.

There we stood all night long, from 9 P.M. to 7 A.M., enduring what I should say few, if any, have ever gone through with and lived. Every little while one of these tremendous seas would come and lift the boat up bod-ily, and us with it, and carry it and us forward on the ice almost to the extreme opposite edge of our piece; and several times the boat got partly over, and was only hauled back by the superhuman strength which a knowledge of the desperate condition its loss would reduce us to gave us. Had the water been clear, it would have been hard enough. But the sea was full of loose ice, rolling about in blocks of all shapes and sizes, and with almost every sea would come an avalanche of these, striking us on our legs and bodies, and bowling us off our feet like so many pins in a bowling-alley. Some of these blocks were only a foot or two square; others were as large as an ordinary bureau, and others larger; in fact, all sorts and sizes. We all were black-and-blue for many a day after.

After each wave had spent its strength, sometimes near the farther edge and sometimes on it, we had then, whenever the boat had got unmoored, to push and pull and drag it back to its former position, and stand ready, bracing ourselves for the next sea, and the battery of the loose ice which we knew would accompany it. And so we stood, hour after hour, the sea as strong as ever, but we weakening from the fatigue, so that before morning we had to make Hannah and Hans's wife get out and help hold on too, I do not think Mr. Meyers had any strength from the first to assist in holding back the boat, but that by clinging to it he simply kept himself from being washed away; but this was a time in which all did their best, for on the preservation of the boat we knew that our lives depended. If we had but 'four anchors' as St. Paul describes in the account of his shipwreck, we could have 'awaited the day' with better hope; but 'when neither sun nor stars appeared, and no small tempest lay on us, all hopes that we should be saved was then taken away'—nearly all. That was the greatest fight for life we had yet had. Had it not been for the strength imparted to us by the last Providential gift of seal-meat, it does not seem possible that our strength would have sufficed for the night; and how we held out I know not. God must have given us the strength for the occasion. For twelve hours there was scarcely a sound uttered, save and except the crying of the children and my orders to 'hold on', 'bear down', 'put on all your weight', and the responsive ay ay sir; which for once came readily enough.

Daylight came at last, and I thankfully perceived a piece of ice riding quite easy, near to us, and I made up my mind that we must reach it. The sea was fearfully rough, and the men hesitated, thinking the boat could not live in such a heavy sea. But I knew that the piece of ice we were on was still more unsafe, and I told them they must risk it, and to 'launch away!' And away she went, the women and children being all snugly stowed in first; and the rest all succeeded in getting in safely but the cook, who went overboard, but, managing to cling hold of the gunwale of the boat, was dragged in and saved. Working carefully along, we succeeded in reaching the piece without other accident; and having eaten a morsel of food, we laid down on our new bit of floe, in our wet clothes, to rest. And we are all today well and sound, except the bruises we received from the blows and falls.

April 21.There are no dry clothes for any one to put on, for every sea washed over us, and there is not much sun to-day and but little drying in the air. We have taken off all we can spare to try and dry our clothes.

The men are now divided into two watches, and part sleep in the boat as best they can, stowing themselves here and there in all sorts of positions. The ice around us is very pashy and thick—we can not force the boat through it, and so must wait for a change. The sun showed himself just long enough to take an observation. Lat 53° 57'.

April; 22. The weather very bad again last night; snow-squalls, sleet, and rain; raining until twelve noon. The ice is closing around us. What we want most now is food. We begin to feel, more than at first, the exhousting effects of our over-strained efforts on the night of the 19th-20th.

Now as I recall the details, it seems as if we were through the whole of that night the sport and jest of the elements. They played with us and our boat as if we were shuttlecocks. Man can never believe, nor pen describe, the scene we passed through, nor can I myself believe that any other party have weathered such a night and lived. Surely we are saved by the will of God alone, and I suppose for some good purpose of his own. The more I think of it, the more I wonder that we were not all washed into the sea together, and ground up in the raging and crushing ice. Yet here we are, children and all, even the baby, sound and well—except the bruises. Half-drowned we are, and cold enough in our wet clothes, without shelter, and not sun enough to dry us even on the outside. We have nothing to eat; every thing is finished and gone, The prospect looks bad enough; but we can not have been saved through such a night to be starved now. God will send us some food.

Afernoon. If something does not come along soon, I do not know what will become of us. Fearful thoughts career through my brain as I look at these eighteen souls with not a mouthful to eat. Meyers is actually starving. He can not last long in this state. Joe has been off on the soft ice a little way, but can not see any thing. We ate some dried skin this morning that was tanned and saved for clothing, and which we had thrown into the boat when the storm first came on—tough, and difficult to sever with the teeth. Joe ventured off for the fourth time, and, after looking a while from the top of a hummock saw a bear coming slowly toward us! Joe returned as fast as possible for his gun, all hope and anxiety lest the creature should turn another way. All the party were ordered to lie down (in imitation of seals), and keep perfectly still, while Joe climbed to the top and Hans secreted himself behind the hummock, both with their rifles ready. It was a period of intense, anxious excitement. Food seemed within our reach now, but it might yet escape. The bear came slowly on, thinking, undoubtedly, that we were seals, and expecting to make a good dinner upon us. A few stops more, and he was within range of the rifles; both fired, killing him instantly. We arose with a shout. The dread uncertainty was over. We all rushed to the spot, and bending on a line, dragged him, in grateful triumph, over broken ice to camp—'camp' meaning now our boat and the point of ice where we 'most do congregate.' Poor Polar! He meant to dine on us, but we shall dine on him. God has sent us food.

The blood of the bear was exceedingly acceptable; for though we had more water than enough on the outside, we had nothing to drink, and were very thirsty. This bear was farther to the south than Arctic bears usually come. His stomach was empty, and he was quite thin; but his flesh was all the better for that. When permeated with fat, it is gross feeding, and very strong. We had no hope of seeing a bear in this latitude.

April 23. Wind east north-east, and later in the day north north-east, where I hope it will remain. The weather is still disagreeably full of rain, squally and cloudy. We are now living entire on raw bear-meat. Every thing wet still, but looking for brighter days. This can not last long at this time of the year; but we are still surrounded by this miserable pash, and can not get free. All well. Mr. Myers recuperated since refreshed by the bear meat.

April 24. Wind still north-north-east, sometimes backing to the north; raining all last night, and still continuing; every thing wet through for several days now; no possible means of drying.

Saw a large flock of ducks this morning, and another later in the day. Can not be far from land, of which we get glimpses now and then, when the falling weather holds up a little, and then again, we seem to be driven from the coast.

There was a fine lead of water last night, and I thought we were going to have a chance to take the boat and get to the shore, but it soon closed up again. Another lead to-day, but farther off.

April 25. Wind increased to a gale last night from the northeast; raining all night and all day. If it was not for the bear meat we should be chilled to death—that keeps some heat in us; but it is not equal to seal-meat for that, though it is tender and good. Now and then, for variety, we have a snow-squall. We launched our boat this morning about five o'clock, determined to try and get to land, though the attempt was dangerous in the extreme; for the boat was badly damaged, with her struggle on the ice and other hard usage. She was scratched and patched, but we have no means now of putting her in repair. It seemed like putting to sea in a cracked bowl. But what were we to do?

The piece of ice we were on had wasted away so much that we knew it could never ride out the gale. The danger was very great either way. The light, overladen, damaged boat looked as if she would founder; but the ice certainly would before long, if not founder, be broken up into pash, affording us not even a foothold.

So, with this crippled, overloaded boat, we start, the wind blowing a gale, and a fearful sea running, full of small ice as sharp as knives. But thank God we came safe through it, and, after eight hours' fruitless labor at the oars—for we made no westing—hauled up on a piece of floe, and prepared to camp for the night. It snowed all night and this forenoon; it stopped snowing in the afternoon. We see plenty of water some distance off, but can not get to it. Can take no observation, the sun being absent, and know not how far we have drifted, the weather being too thick for me to recognize the coast. We are all well.

April 28. A gale of wind has sprung up from the westward, and a heavy sea is running. Water again washing over our little bit of floe. Had to stand 'all ready' by the boat again all night. Not quite so bad as the other night, but had snow-squalls all the time, and the following forenoon. The ice seeming unsafe from the effects of the gale, we again launched our boat at daylight, but could get nowhere for the smaller ice, a heavy sea, and a head wind blowing a gale right in our teeth. Had to haul up in a piece of ice, after an hour's exhausting but use-less effort. Laid down and had a few hours' sleep on the ice.

3:10 P.M. Threatened by some heavy bergs to be smashed to pieces. These bergs were having quite a battle among themselves, and bearing all the time right for us. The gale has set every thing that can float moving—a grand and awful sight. The sounds accompanying these collisions are frightful, combined with the roar of the waves, and the actual danger to such frail supports as either our bit of floe or slender boat. Seeing they were coming too near, I called the watch, and launched the boat to try and get out of the way of these approaching hostile bergs. We left our floe at one o'clock in the afternoon, the ice very slack, and more water than I have seen for a long time.

Joe shot three young bladder-nose seals as we were coming along, and, not being very large, we took them into the boat. Hope soon to see whalers.

★

THE POLARIS, IN THE MEANWHILE, HAD DRIFTED FOR ONLY ONE MORE *day before the crew remaining on board abandoned ship to spend the winter on the Greenland shore. They were eventually rescued and testified to the Navy's board of inquiry, which uncovered the dissension on board. Budington's career was over. Years later, in an interesting sidelight to Tyson's drift, Hans Hendrik wrote his memoirs in his native language and one Henry Rink translated and published them in London in 1878. He devotes about eight pages to the drift on the ice floe and his slant on the experience is remarkably different from Tyson's. He says there was no shortage of meat. It always turned up when they most needed it. He did not think the drift especially adventurous. This is what life is like in the north. There were seals, and they ate. Sometimes they were short of food, but Eskimos are used to being short of food. In the end things worked out. Nobody died. He treats the experience in the most matter-of-fact way. He was thankful his children survived. Nothing out of the ordinary took place*

WOULD HALL HAVE MADE IT TO THE POLE IF HE HAD LIVED? PROBABLY not. *The Pole was not so easy a prize to win, as the British were about to find out. It had taken a generation for those few Englishmen still committed to the Arctic to persuade their countrymen to spring for a try at the Pole. The memory of Franklin's fate stayed fresh in the British mind. Two ships had been lost, and 130 men. The Northwest Passage was impassable. Many millions of dollars in today's money had been spent to find out what had happened. Enough was enough.*

In the end, though, appeals to patriotism changed people's minds. The British attitude, here as at the South Pole, was that they were the polar explorers and the polar regions somehow belonged to them. Other countries besides the United States were in the field. The Austrians had sent an expedition north and had discovered a new archipelago above the Siberian coast of Russia. They named it Franz Josef Land after the Habsburg emperor then in power. The Scandinavians were beginning to look north and would shortly produce the best of all the polar explorers, Nansen and Amundsen. In the late 1870s, then, more than thirty years after Franklin had set out for the Canadian archipelago, the English sent yet another expedition north, a naval expedition under the command of George Nares. Behind the expedition was the forceful and influential Clements Markham, then an honorary secretary of the Royal Geographical Society and later its president. Markham would become famous as the eminence grise behind

British Antarctic exploration. Robert Falcon Scott was his personal choice to lead two expeditions to Antarctica, on the second of which Scott died. He was an advocate of manhauling sledges in polar exploration, rather than using dogs. He thought using dogs cruel. To the dogs.

The British turned out to have learned very little from their previous polar experience. Two ships bulled north up the channels between Ellesmere Island and Greenland, reaching approximately the same latitude Hall had reached, a little higher than 82 degrees north. Beyond that lay the Arctic Ocean, frozen solid as far as the eye could see. Once more the open polar sea proved to be a myth. There was no choice, really, but to sledge to the Pole, using men, of course, to haul the sledges. As soon as he could, Nares sent sledging parties north to lay depots. They were an instant disaster. Second in command on the expedition was Albert Markham, Clements' cousin. He came back from his trip with a third of his men suffering from frostbite. Three men lost fingers and toes to frostbite. In an early sledging party in March one man lost both his feet to frostbite and later died. That party covered only sixteen miles in four days.

In April, nevertheless, the sledging began in earnest. The excerpt we are using comes mostly from the journal of Albert Markham, who led one of the parties north toward the Pole, hauling two boats on two sledges north along with three other sledges loaded with supplies. His second in command was Lieutenant Alfred Parr. They were hauling loads of more than 240 pounds per man. They did not wear furs. They did not use dogs. They did not hunt for fresh meat. They did not build igloos, but slept in light tents. One is reminded of what the Cheyenne woman said when she punctured the eardrum of the dead George Armstrong Custer on the battlefield at the Little Big Horn. It was a lesson to him, she said, because he would not listen.

GEORGE STRONG NARES

Narrative of a Voyage to the Polar Sea During 1875-6 in H.M. Ships ALERT and DISCOVERY

ON THE EVENING OF THE 8TH, LIEUTENANT PARR MADE HIS APPEARANCE on board the *Alert*. As he crossed the quarter-deck, silently nodding to the one or two who chanced to meet him, his grave and weary expression was unmistakable, and in a very few moments the certainty that some sore calamity had occurred had spread throughout the ship. So travel-stained was he on entering my cabin that I mistook him for his more swarthy friend Beaumont, then on the Greenland coast, and therefore anxiously questioned his totally unexpected return.

I then received the distressing intelligence that nearly the whole of Commander Markham's men were attacked with scurvy and in want of immediate assistance. Markham and the few men who were able to work had succeeded in conveying the invalids to the neighbourhood of Cape Joseph Henry, twenty-seven miles distant from the ship, and were still advancing slowly; but each day was rapidly adding to the intensity of the disease and the number of the sick.

Under these circumstances Parr nobly volunteered to bring me the news and so obtain relief for his companions.

Starting with only an alpenstock and a small allowance of provisions, at the end of twenty miles he arrived at a shooting tent in Dumbell Bay, where he hastily made himself a cup of tea; pushing on, he completed his long and solitary walk within twenty-four hours.

Arrangements were at once made to proceed to Commander Markham's assistance, and by midnight two strong parties of officers and men had started; Lieutenant May, and Dr. Moss who wore snow-shoes, pushing on before us, with the dog-sledge laden with appropriate medical stores. By making a forced march they reached Markam's camp within fifty hours of Parr's departure.

Their arrival had naturally a most exhilarating effect on the stricken men; but to our great regret they were unfortunately too late to save the life of George Porter, who only a few hours previously had expired: he was buried in the floe by the wayside.

Early on the following day I joined them with the main relief party, when the hope and tryst which had never deserted them was quickened to the utmost; even the prostrate men losing the depression of spirits induced by the disease that had attacked them, and which in their case was much intensified by the recent loss of their comrade.

It is difficult for a stranger to the surrounding circumstances and scenery to realize the condition and appearance of these men, who in spite of their truly pitiable state were yet making slow progress towards the ship.

On my first meeting them Markham and five men were dragging two sledges, three hands at each; each sledge being freighted with two invalids and as much of the tent furniture as was requisite to keep them warm and to form as comfortable a couch as the circumstances and the rough road permitted. Lying on the top of the third sledge, which was laden with the rest of the baggage and the provisions, and left about half a mile in the rear, was the fifth invalid.

Struggling along over the uneven, snow covered, ice as best they could, were four other men whose limbs becoming daily more cramped foretold that they must shortly succumb; they were gallantly holding out to the last in order not to increase by their weight, a moment sooner than could be avoided, the already haevy loads being dragged by their very slightly stronger companions.

These poor fellows were in the habit of starting off each morning before the main party, knowing that if they experienced a bad fall or came to an unusually deep snow-drift they could not recover themselves without help. Frequently the sledge party overtook them lying helpless on the ice; but once raised on their legs, with a smile and some happy cheerful expression, again they would start on their painful and weary journey.

With the exception of Markham, who dragged to the very last, and in addition had to pioneer a way for the sledges before the daily start, the others remaining on the drag-ropes were in a great measure dependent on the leaders, John Radmore and Thomas Jollife. Although these two men were the most vigorous of the sledge crews, they were greatly enfeebled; yet rather than resign the post of honour as leaders, which entailed the extra labour of treading down a pathway through the snow, they journeyed along supporting each other arm-in-arm, and by keeping the drag-rope taut afforded a means of support for their more disabled companions in the rear.

The prevailing good-humour and dutiful submission of one and all of these men to the severe labour demanded of them, their manful and determined struggle along the roughest road imaginable, is far beyond all praise. After seeing their condition there is no difficulty in realizing the statement concerning Sir John Franklin's men, as made by the Eskimo to Sir Leopold McClintock, 'They fell down and died as they walked along.'

Early on the morning of the 12th the whole party encamped on the shore at Cape Richardson; exchanging the dreary prospect of icy desolation afforded by the confused disarray of ice hummocks, which had so frequently bounded their view for nearly sixty days, for the agreeable sight of the newly-sprouting but sparse vegetation on the sides of the familiar and well-known hills, now becoming partially cleared of snow. Equally inspiriting was the change, from the intense solitude of the inanimate pack, affforded by the frequent sweet song of snow-buntings collected confidingly near the tent, the sharp call of some knots which were flying about in flocks of ten or a dozen, and the occasional deep notes of some geese which had opportunely just arrived from the southward and were looking for a resting-place.

This total change of circumstances, together with the anxious and unremitting care of Dr. Moss, the alteration of diet, and a plentiful supply of fresh game and limejuice arrested the disease, and at once produced a marked improvement in the appearance of all.

The following is an abridged account of this memorable sledge journey which is published in the parliamentary Blue Books, c. 1636, of 1877.

In addressing the crews of the two sledges previous to their departure I made the following statement:—

The work before you, although not more perilous than Arctic journeys usually are, will undoubtedly be a very arduous and irksome one, and monotonous in the extreme. The daily advance will necessarily be slow; for you must always journey over the same road twice, and frequently far oftener. You therefore cannot hope for the exhilarating spur accompanying quick progress which others will feel; but are called on to show that we possess the high quality of resolute perseverance to overcome whatever obstacles are before us.

The only journey to be likened in any way to yours is the similar attempt of Sir Edward Parry to reach a high northern latitude, with much the same equipment, and absent for the same number of days. We all hope that with God's blessing you will at all events be as successful.

Extracts from my orders to Commander Markham; dated 3rd of April, 1876:—

Taking command of the sledges 'Marco Polo' Victoria, Bull-dog, Alexandra, and Blood-hound, you will proceed to the neighbourhood of Cape Parry, and from thence force your way to the northward over the ice, with the two boats which have been equipped for that purpose, and provisioned for an absence of about seventy days.

The object of your journey is to attain the highest northern latitude possible; and to ascertain the possibilty of a more fully equipped expedition reaching the North Pole.

At present we know little or nothing concerning the movement of the ice in the offing. The journey on which you are about to engage is therefore a far more arduous one than Arctic journeys usually are. The heavy nature of the ice across which you have to travel has hitherto baffled all attempts made to cross it, and the formidable obstacles it presents at present, while stationary, must be considerably increased when once it is in motion. Even during the summer, with occasional lanes of navigable water between the floes, Parry and Ross could scarcely average a daily journey of three miles.

Therefore, while, with the full confidence in your ability and discretion, I leave you entirely free as to the carrying out of your journey in all its details, I must direct your most serious consideration—first, to the extreme hazard of attempting an advance beyond the time when half your provisions will be expended; and, secondly, to the danger of separating your party or of leaving depots of provisions on a road which it is impossible to mark, and which will probably break-up in your rear. It is true that your men on the return journey will be dragging diminished loads; but towards the end of the season the ice will probably be in motion, and one of your chief enemies, the misty weather, will be more continuous. Over stationary ice, however rough, there is a choice of roads; once it is in motion, no choice is left.

During your absence should you, contrary to my present expectations, experience a general break-up of the ice, or, arriving at the edge of the firm ice, find the outer pack broken up, you are to consider the position you will then have attained as the limit of your advance; and, after making what observations are practicable, you are to retreat to the ship.

Extracts from Commander Markham's oifficial journal:—

3rd—Left the ship at 11 A.M. The western division, under the command of Lieutenant Aldrich, in company. The travelling by no means good; snow deep, and the sledges dragging very heavily. This being our first march, and the men showing signs of fatigue, a halt was called at 5:30, and the tents pitched on the eastern side of the neck of land connecting Mushroom Point with the main. Men in capital spirits. Distance made good six miles.

4th—Commenced the march at 7:30 A.M. Double-banked all the sledges over the land, which fortunately for us had a good covering of snow; nevertheless, we found it hard work with our heavy sledges; the travelling round and beyond Harley Spit excessively heavy and laborious, Men getting tired, halted at 4:45, and camped. Everything frozen perfectly hard. To use Admiral Richardson's simile, our sleeping-bags resembled sheet-iron whilst the currie paste, as our cook observed, was exactly like a piece of brass, and was equally hard. We were all hungry enough to eat our full allowance of pemmican at supper, and enjoyed it. Distance marched ten miles; made good six miles. Temperature minus 35.

5th—Although the temperature inside our tent last night was minus 25, we all slept a little more comfortably, or rather a little less uncomfortably, though deprived of all feeling in our feet. Travelling much the same as yesterday, therefore compelled to advance in the same manner—that is, sledges double-banked. The men appear a little stiff, and complain of having suffered a good deal last night from pain in their limbs, and are to-day suffering from great thirst.

A wolf's track, seen each day since we left the ship, has been the only vestige of animal life observed. Encamped on the floe a short distance from Simmon's Island. The travelling has not improved, and the temperature has been as low as minus 45. Everything very cold and uncomfortable. Distance marched twelve miles; made good four miles.

6th—Another cold sleepless night over. A beautifully sunny day, but with a temperature at 35 below zero. Everything frosen stiff and hard. Dressing by no means an easy operation. Sledges double-banked as before. Progression slow. Reached a stream of young ice extending to Depot Point, the traveling on which being good, enabled us to single-bank the crews, and to arrive at Depot Point at 5:30; off which we camped on the floe.

7th—The sledge Blood-hound having fulfilled the duties entrusted to her, she was despatched to the ship at 8a.m. Gave her three cheers on parting. A beautiful day, but *very* cold. A few slight frostbites were sustained yesterday, but quickly restored. The travelling today is a foretaste of what we are to expect; heavy floes fringed with hummocks, through and over which the sledges have to be dragged. Dr. Moss was fortunate enough to shoot a hare on Depot Point, which is to be reserved as a *bonne bouche* for us when we attain our highest latitude. Land very much distorted by mirage. Camped for the night on a floe off Cape Hercules. Temperature remains extraordinarily low: minus 41. Distance marched fourteen miles; made good four and a half.

8th.—A charming day, although the temperature persists in remaining low. Care has to be taken in selecting the road so as to avoid the hummocks as much as possible; occasionally we are brought to a standstill by a belt of more than ordinarily large ones, through which we have to cut a road with pickaxes and shovels. Sledges double-banked as before. The large sledge, on which is the twenty-foot ice boat, drags very heavily. This is caused by the overhanging weight at the two extremities. Glare from the sun has been very oppressive; the snow in places resembles coarse sand, and appears more crystallised than usual. A few of the party, including Parr and myself, suffering from snow-blindness. Distance marched ten miles. Temperature minus 30.

9th—Same system of double-banking the sledges continues. Parr's snow-blindness is no better, mine no worse. The snow goggles are worn by all, and certainly afford relief to the eyes. Moss is rendering valuable service by assisting me in the selection of a road—no easy task whilst going through hummocks. Although the temperature is minus 30, the sun has sufficient influence to dry our blanket wrappers and other gear; the yards of the boats being very convenient for the purpose of tricing up our robes, etc. The snow is still very deep on the floes and between the hummocks, materially retarding our progress. Halted at seven, and encamped on a heavy floe. From its north-western edge the depot at Cape Jospeh Henry was plainly visible; a great relief to our minds, as thoughts of its being buried in deep snow-drift would frequently occur to us. Distance marched thirteen miles; made good four.

10th—Leaving the tents pitched, we started with an empty sledge for the depot, distant about two miles. We experienced heavy work in cutting a road through the line of shore hummocks that girt the coast, and did not succeed in reaching the depot until eleven o'clock. Sending the party back to camp, Aldrich, Giffard, Moss and I ascended View Hill (650 feet), whence we obtained a good look-out. The prospect was anything but cheering. To the northward was an irregular sea of ice, composed of small floes and large hummocks. Our anticipations of slow travelling and heavy work seem about to be realized. The sun was so powerful that the snow was thawing, and the water trickling down on the southern side of the hill. We shall start to-morrow morning with pro-visions complete for sixty-three days. Thus loaded, the sledges will drag uncom-monly heavy, and over the rough hummocks we are certain to encounter our only mode of advancing will be by a system of double-banking, which simply means one mile made good for every five actually marched. If we accomplish two miles a day it will be a fair day's work. On shore we observed numerous traces of hares and ptarmigan, but although Dr. Moss followed up the trails of the former, his attempts to obtain any were not crowned with success.

11th—A dull, overcast day, Snow falling. I was again greatly indebted to Moss for his efficient aid in assisting me to choose a road for the sledges, Parr being still laid up with snow-blindness, and my sight 'not quite the thing.' Aldrich has very wisely determined to return to the land and try his luck through the Snow valley, instead of rounding Cape Joseph Henry. At one o'clock, dis-played all colours, and parted company with Aldrich's division and our two sup-porting sledges amid much cheering. They were soon lost sight of amongst the hummocks. Parr in advance with half a dozen men cutting a road with pick-axes and shovels, the remainder of the men dragging up the sledges singly. Got on to a heavy flow and then in amongst a mass of heavy hummocks, through which appeared no road or outlet; but the steady and persevering exertions of Parr and his road-makers performed wonders, and the sledges were soon trav-eling over a road that had before looked impenetrable and impassable. The floes are small, but very heavy. It is difficult to estimate their thickness, but it must be very considerable. They appear to have had a terrible conflict with one another, the result being what we are now encountering, namely, a great expanse of hummocks varying in height from twenty feet to small round nobbly pieces over which we stagger and fall. Between these hummocks the snow-drifts are very deep, and we are continually floundering up to our waists, but the men struggle bravely on. Possibly when we leave the vicinity of Cape Joseph Henry, and get well clear of the land, we may experience better travelling, larger flows, and less snow. One thing is pretty certain, we cannot have much worse, and this is a consolation. Encamped amongst the hummocks, after a very hard and weary day's work. The men appear a good deal done up. The road-making was incessant the whole afternoon. Distance marched ten miles; made good two and a quarter.

12th—An unexpected but most gratifying change of temperature caused us to pass a comparatively comfortable night; temperature inside our tent as high as 16, and during supper rose as high as 22. After breakfast, commenced with half a dozen road-makers cutting a road through the hummocks, leaving the remainder of the party to strike the tents, pack, and bring up the sledges one by one as far as the road was practicable. Being a beautifully bright sunny day, the tent robes and other gear were triced up to the masts and yards to dry. Parr's cysts are improving, and he now works like a slave with pickaxe and shovel, working with and superintending the labours of the road-makers.

After lunch emerged from the hummocks on to a small floe, and then through another mass of hummocks, having only made about half a mile during the afternoon.

The surface snow on the floes sparkles and glitters with the most beautiful iridescent colours, the ground on which we walk appearing as if strewn with bright and lustrous gems; diamonds, rubies, emeralds, and sapphires being the most prominent. At 3 P.M. observed the fresh traces of a lemming. It is strange the little creature should wander so far from the land, the nearest point being quite three miles off. Crossed over some streams of young ice, and through a long fringe of hummocks leading on to a large floe of "ancient lineage" presenting an undulating surface, and having on it diminutive ice mountains, or frozen snow-drifts, from fifteen to twenty feet in height. Halted at the edge of a belt of hummocks, through which a road was cut whilst the tents were being pitched. Camped for the night, the men being rather fatigued, having had a hard day's work. We are all suffering from cracked skin, the combined action of sun and frost, our lips, cheeks, and noses being especially very sore. The temperature all day had been delightful, ranging from minus 8 to minus 20. Travelling through hummocks is most unsatisfactory work; it is a succession of standing pulls—one, two, three, haul! And very little result. Distance marched nine miles; made good one and-a-half.

13th—Passed through a fringe of hummocks about 200 yards in breadth, then arrived on a fine large floe that afforded us capital travelling for about a mile due north, and then on to another long fringe of large and troublesome hummocks, until we were completely brought up by enormous masses of ice, piled up, piece on piece, to the height of over twenty feet. Through this we resolved to cut a passage, although foreseeing it would be a long and tedious job; however, there appeared no other alternative, so immediately after lunch the road-makers, always supervised and headed by Parr, who is not only a first-rate engineer but also a most indefatigable labourer, set to work to cut a road. This by 6 P.M.—with such resolution did they work—was completed, the sledges dragged through and on to another old floe, girt by more hummocks which were in their turn attacked by Parr and his gang, and we had the satisfaction of halting and encamping on a fine large floe, which promises to give us a good lead for some way to the north to-morrow. Parr, I am happy to say, has quite recovered from his snow-blindness.

14th—Crossed an old floe, having a deep incrustation of frozen snow on its surface, rendering the dragging very laborious, then through a belt of small hummocks on to another fair-sized floe. These belts, or cordons, of hummocks vary in breadth from 50 and 100 yards to as much as a quarter and half-a-mile. As a rule round the larger floes appear the heavier hummocks. We have been assailed by an unpleasant nipping breeze from the northward, our faces being constantly touched up by Jack Frost. Temperature minus 28. We were employed, during the afternoon, in making a road through a more than ordinary broad hedge of hummocks, and pulling the sledges through, we made in consequence little head-way. The wind freshening and the weather becoming very thick, we halted earlier than we otherwise would have done. Many frost-bites about the face. John Shirley complaining of pain in his ankle and knee was duly treated. Distance marched eight miles; made good one and three quarters.

15th—Blowing a north-westerly gale, with the temperature 35 below zero, and a considerable drift which rendered travelling quite out of the question. Extreme wretchedness and almost abject misery was our lot to-day. We derived no heat from our robes, they were frozen so hard, the temperature inside our tent being minus 22. It is rather remarkable that we have this day experienced, during a gale of wind, a lower temperature than we have had during any gale the whole winter, which leads one to the conclusion that it is evident there can be no open water existing either to the northward or the westward of us.

The wind this morning was still blowing fresh, though it had moderated considerably; it was, however, so cutting and piercing, and the drift was so dense, making it almost impossible for us to see our way through the hummocks, that it was deemed more prudent and advisable to remain encamped, however unpleasant and disagreeable such a course was to all concerned. We unanimously came to the conclusion that it was the most wretched and miserable Easter Sunday that any one of us had ever passed. Forty-eight hours in a bag, in a gale of wind off Cape Joseph Henry, with a temperature of 67 below freezing point, is not a delightful way of passing the time—sleep was almost out of the question. In spite of the cold we did not omit the usual Saturday night's toast last evening; and as it was also the first anniversary of the Ships' commissioning we gave three cheers; this was taken up by the "Victoria," and then we commenced to cheer each other, by way of keeping up our spirits.

At five struck the tents and commenced the march. Shirley being unable to walk, we were obliged to place him on one of the sledges, keeping him in his sleeping bag, and wrapping him well up in the coverlet and lower robe. This increases our weight to be dragged, besides diminishing our strength. Crossed the floe on which we were encamped, and cut our way through a hedge of hummocks, about one-third of a mile in breadth, on to another floe of apparently great thickness. These floes, although of stupendous size regarding their thickness, are unfortunately for us of no very great superficial extent, varying only from a quarter of a mile to a mile in north and south direction. The recent strong wind, blowing the snow from off the land to the floes, has made the travelling rather heavier than it was before. Between some of the large floes we occasionally meet small patches of young ice along which the sledges run smoothly; but, alas!

They are never more than a few yards in extent. Encamped for the night on a large floe. Men appearing more done up, after lying so long idle in their bags, than if they had had a hard day's dragging. Beyond Cape Parry, which is at present the most distant land visible to the westward, can e seen two cloud-like objects that may be Aldrich's "Cooper Key Mountains"; but again they may be clouds or mirage. Distance marched seven miles; made good one and a quarter.

17th—Commenced the march at 7 A.M. Shirley has again to be put on the sledge. Porter is rendered *hors de combat*, and is suffering a good deal of pain, He is just able to hobble after us. Our force is much weakened by the loss of these two men. A beautiful sunny day with the temperature as high as minus 24. The men are taking kindly to their goggles, rarely taking them off whilst on the march, and quite willing to put up with a little inconvenience rather than be afflicted with snow-blindness. The snow being deep, we found the travelling on the floes very heavy indeed; the large boat comes along very slowly, and it is seldom we can advance many paces without resorting to standing pulls. Arrived at the edge of a broad belt of hummocks, through which a road had to be cut, then on to a small floe, then through more hummocks, which again had to succumb before the strenuous exertions of Parr and his untiring road-makers; then more small floes and more hummocks, and so it goes on.

Some of the floes are thicker than others, and it is of no infrequent occurrence that we have to lower the ledges a distance of six or seven feet from the top of one to the surface of another, or vice versa. After lunch, George Porter, being unable to walk any farther, had to be carried on the sledge. This is sad work; it makes our progress very slow and tedious. Distance marched nine miles; made good one and a quarter.

18th—Having made a slight alteration in our weights by lessening those on the heavy sledge, we resumed the march at noon. Shirley had slightly improved, and is able to walk slowly in our rear. So hard were our sleeping-bags frozen last night, that the operation of getting into them was positively painful; the night, however, was comparatively warm, and we slept pretty comfortably. Our travelling during the early part of the day was across floes of an uneven surface, and between hummocks, through which, however, there was no necessity of cutting a road; but the deep snow rendered the dragging exceedingly heavy. These floes, or the majority of them, are all massed together, squeezed one against the other, but with few huge piled-up masses we had to content with nearing the shore. After lunch, the description of ice over which we were travelling underwent great change, and it appeared that we had at length arrived on the veritable ' paleo crystic' floes. We seem to have quite got away from the smooth level floes surrounded by dense hummocks, and have reached those of gigantic thickness with a most uneven surface, and covered with deep snow. The travelling has been rough and heavy. The *Victoria* capsized, but was quickly righted without damage to either sledge or boat, and without even giving the invalid, who was securely wrapped up inside the boat, a shaking. The foremost batten of the "Marco Pole" was also carried away. A southeasterly breeze sprang up at 5 P.M., sending the temperature down sharply to minus 33, and we had to be cautious about frost-bites. Distance marched ten miles; made good one mile.

19th—A fine clear day. Our sleeping-bags last night were rendered a little more habitable from having been exposed during the day to the heat of the sun, which had the effect of extracting from them the greater part of the moisture. The helmet worsted caps so kindly and considerately presented to the Expedition by the Empress, are very warm and comfortable for sleeping in, and are much appreciated by the men, who call them Eugenies.

Experienced great difficulty in getting from one floe on to another, some of them being, with the snow on their surface, as much as eight and nine feet above the others. After labouring and toiling for three-and-a-half hours, standing pulls nearly the whole time , during which period we had barely advanced 300 yards, I came to the determination of abandoning the twenty-foot ice-boat. I did not arrive at this decision until after very mature deliberation, and from my own conviction that amongst such ice as we were then encountering, should a disruption occur, the boats would be of little avail to us, except to be used as a ferry from one floe to another. For this purpose the smaller boat will suffice. At 7 P.M. we arrived on some young ice, between the floes and amongst hummocks, that afforded us capital travelling. On this we rattled gaily along, accomplishing half a mile in something like a couple of hours—good work for us. 10:15 P.M. pitched our tents on a regular paleocryistic floe, having rounded hillocks on its surface from twenty-five to thirty feet high. Distance marched eight miles; made good one mile.

*

THE RESCUE TEAMS MADE IT IN TIME TO SAVE MOST OF THE MEN, BUT ONE man had died and all but three had lost the use of their feet. They were riddled with scurvy. Scurvy then attacked the men left on the ships. They used dynamite to blow themselves out of the trap the ice had set for them and fled south. A sledging party that ventured into Greenland fared even worse than Markham's. Two men died on that one. Nares and his ships barely made it out of the ice before being frozen in again.

When it was over Albert Markham summed it up: "I feel it is impossible for my pen to depict with accuracy, and yet not be accused of exaggeration, the numerous drawbacks that impeded our progress. One point, however, in my opinion is most definitely settled, and that is, the utter impracticability of reaching the North Pole over the floe in this locality; and in this opinion my able colleague, Lieutenant Parr, entirely concurs. I am convinced that with the very lightest equipped sledges, carrying no boats, and with all the resources of the ship concentrated in the one direction, and also supposing that perfect health might be maintained, the latitude obtained by the party I had the honour and pleasure of commanding would not be exceeded by many miles, certainly not by a degree.' Markham had reached 83 degrees north, 400 miles south of the Pole. On one particularly bad day he and his men had taken an entire day to drag their sledges a mere 100 yards. The British gave up. They would not send explorers north again until the 1930s.

But other countries were not discouraged. The Germans had sent an expedition to the east coast of Greenland. Some of them had also suffered through a drift on an ice floe, shorter but no less dramatic than Tyson's. In 1878 a Swedish explorer named Nils Nordenskjold had navigated the Northeast Passage. He was the first to do so. And the Americans continued to have faith in polar expeditions, even to believe, against all the evidence, in the theory of an open polar sea. In 1879 the wealthy, flamboyant press magnate James Gordon Bennett got behind an attempt at the Pole through the Bering Strait. The German scientist who was the main, and only surviving, advocate of an open polar sea had persuaded Bennett that it was just a matter of penetrating the pack. Beyond it lay not more ice, but water. Bennett saw the potential for news in an expedition and bought a ship, the Jeannette, persuaded Congress to pay for refitting it for Arctic service, and hired Commander George De Long, a navy officer, to lead the expedition.

De Long took with him the usual mix of people with Arctic experience, whom he recruited himself, various naval personnel, and people recruited on the docks. He also took a navigator, foisted on him by Bennett, who was syphilitic, had poor eyesight, and had only recently emerged from a mental hospital after suffering a nervous breakdown. Bennett forced him to take the New York Herald's weatherman as well. The Herald was Bennett's paper. De Long left San Francisco for the Arctic in July 1879. He had provisions aboard for three years.

August found him sailing through Bering Strait into the Bering Sea. He steered to the northwest, hoping to reach Wrangel Island, which had never been properly explored. One hundred miles away, he got stopped by the pack. He tried then to reach Herald Island 50 miles to the east. He could not reach that, either. Then the ice took over his ship, freezing him in at an angle, heeling the ship over so that no one could stand up straight and plates slid off tables and keeping coffee in your mug was a problem. The ice began to press slowly on the reinforced sides of the ship. The navigator began to go blind in one eye from the syphilis he had not told De Long that he had. The Herald's meteorologist had failed to bring the chemicals to develop photograph plates, so although they had the camera and the plates, they could not develop the pictures. The ship drifted in an erratic pattern, at the mercy of currents they could not see. When the ship sprang leaks from the pressure of the ice they ran low on fuel keeping the pumps operating. They spent the winter in this way, keeping the ship afloat as best they could, hoping to get out that summer.

Summer came, and the ship remained trapped. The ice refused, as ice—living by its own rules—will do, to release them. They were far from land. The next winter came and they were still there. Back in the United States, no one thought to rescue them. No one believed they were in trouble. We would have heard from them if they were in trouble, was the general consensus. No one bothered to wonder exactly how they might have gotten the message out that they needed help.

In June 1881, nearly two years after they had left San Francisco, the ice sank the ship in less than a day. Now they were stranded on the frozen ocean 200 miles from the coast of Siberia. They numbered 33 men, of whom 22 were fit. They had five sledges of supplies, three boats mounted on sledges, and enough food. They had made themselves sealskin clothing. De Long kept them on short rations, not knowing how long it would take to reach the coast. Much longer, as it happened, than he hoped. Here the ice does not drift south, as it does above the Canadian archipelago. Here, ever malevolent, it drifts north. After a few days De Long found that they were 26 miles farther north than where they had started from. They were going backward.

De Long changed direction, crossing the current, traveling southwest instead of south, and they did begin to make progress. As they got closer to land the leads opened and they were able to use the boats more. Eventually they abandoned the sledges altogether, divided the party into three boat crews, and headed for the delta of the Lena River. Almost at once a storm hit and scattered the boats. One of them, with eight men aboard, vanished forever. The two others made the delta, but widely separated. And the delta is a maze 260 miles wide. Just figuring out which of its hundreds of waterways is the main one is, to someone not familiar with it, pure guesswork. One of the two boat crews, under the command of George Melville, got lucky. They found a village and survived. The other, under De Long, was not so fortunate. We take our excerpt from the end of De Long's journal, which is all the more moving for its understatement, as he chronicles, obviously with great difficulty, their last days. The journal was found by his body, as if the last thing he had done was to make an entry before he died. The two men of his party he had sent out to look for help survived. No one else in De Long's whaleboat did.

GEORGE W. DELONG

The Voyage of the JEANNETTE: *The Ship and Ice Journals of George W. DeLong, Ed: By His Wife, Emma De Long*

Chapter XVIII.
The Fatal Month.
October, 1881.

October 1st, Saturday. —One hundred and eleventh day, and a new month. Called all hands as soon as the cook announced boiling water, and at 6.:45 had our breakfast; one half pound of deer meat and tea. Sent Nindemann and Alexey to examine the main river, other men to collect wood. The doctor resumed the cutting away of poor Ericksen's toes this morning. No doubt it will have to continue until half his feet are gone, unless death ensues, or we get to some settlement. Only one toe left now. Temperature 18°.

At 7:30 Nindemann and Alexey were seen to have crossed, and I immediately sent men to carry one load over.

Left the following record:—

Fourteen of the officers and men of the U.S. Arctic Steamer *Jeannette* reached this hut on Wednesday, September 28th, and having been forced to wait for the river to freeze over, are proceeding to cross to the west side this A.M. on their journey to reach some settlement on the Lena River. We thus far to get game in our pressing needs, we have no fear for the future.

Our party are all well, except one man, Ericksen, whose toes have been amputated in consequence of frost-bite. Other records will be found in several huts on the east side of this river, along which we have come from the northward.

George W. De Long,
Lieutenant U.S. Navy, Commanding Expedition.

At 8.30 we made the final trip, and got our sick man over in safety. From there we proceeded until 11.20, dragging our man on the sled. Halted for dinner; one half pound meat and tea each. At one went ahead again until 5.05.

Actually under way: 8.30 to 9.15, 9.30 to 10.20, 10.30 to 11.20, 1.00 to 1.40, 1.50 to 2.10, 2.20 to 2.40, 3.00 to 3.25, 3.35 to 4.00, 4.15 to 4.35, 4.45 to 5.05. Total, 5 h. 15 m. At least two miles an hour. Distance made good ten to twelve miles.

And where are we? I think at the beginning of the Lena River at last. "Sagastyr" has been to us a myth. We saw two old huts at a distance, and that was all, but they were out of our reach, and the day not half gone. Kept on ice all the way, and therefore I think we were over water, but the stream was so narrow and so crooked that it never could have been a navigable water. My chart is simply useless. I must go on plodding to the southward, trusting in God to guide me to a settlement, for I have long since realized that we are powerless to help ourselves.

A bright, calm, beautiful day. Bright sunshine to cheer us up, an icy road, and one day's rations yet. Boots frozen, of course, and balled up. No hut in sight, and we halt on a bluff to spend a cold and comfortless night. Supper one half pound meat and tea. Made a rousing fire, built a log bed, set a watch (two hours each) to keep the fire going, and at eight P.M. crawled into our blankets.

October 2d, Sunday— I think we all slept fairly well until midnight; but from that time it was so cold and uncomfortable that sleep was out of the question. At 4.30 we were all out and in front of the fire, daylight just appearing. Ericksen kept talking in his sleep all night, and effectually kept those awake who were not already wakened by the cold.

Breakfast five A.M. One half pound meat and tea. Bright, cloudless morning. Light N. airs. At seven went ahead, following frozen water wherever we could find it, and at 9.20 I feel quite sure we have gone some distance on the main river. I think our gait was at least two miles an hour, and our time under way two hours four minutes. I call our forenoon work at least six miles: 7:00

to 7.35, 7.45 to 8.05, 8.15 to 8.30, 8.40 to 8.50, 9.20 to 9.40, 9.50 to 10.12, 10.22 to 10.40, 10.55 to 11.15. Dinner camp. 1.00 to 1.30, 1.40 to 2.00, 2.15 to 2.35, 2.45 to 3.00, 3.20 to 3.40, 3.50 to 4.05, 4.15 to 4.20.

Divine service before dinner. Dinner one half pound meat and tea. Started ahead at one P.M., and by 4.15 had completed two marching hours and made four miles. I was much bewildered by the frequent narrowing of the river to a small vein of ice, and the irregular rambling way in which it ran. Frequently it led us into a sand bank or deep snow, and our floundering around was both exhaustive of energy and consumptive of time. There is no use denying it, we are pretty weak. Our food is not enough to keep up our strength, and when we lose a night's sleep we feel it keenly. I had several bad falls on the ice this afternoon which shook me up pretty badly. A freshening N.E. wind had blown the efflorescence off the ice, and left smooth, clear spots as clear as glass. Frozen boots are but poor foot gear, and besides cramping the feet, are like boots of iron in walking. Slip, slide, and down you are on your back.

At 4.05 P.M. I saw more wood than we had sighted since our dinner camp, and but little ahead. I therefore called a halt and "camped," i.e., sat down, made a fire and got supper. Then we stood by for a second cold and wretched night. There was so much wind that we had to put our tent halves up for a screen, and sit shivering in our half blankets.

October 3d, Monday.—One hundred and thirteenth day. At midnight it was so fearfully cold and wretched that I served out tea to all hands, and on that we managed to struggle along until five A.M., when we ate our last deer meat and had more tea. Our remaining food now consists of four fourteenths pounds pemmican each, and a half-starved dog. May God again incline unto our aid. How much farther we have to go before reaching a shelter or a settlement, He alone knows.

Brisk wind. Ericksen seems failing. He is weak and tremulous, and the moment he closes his eyes talks incessantly in Danish, German, and English. No one could sleep even if our other surroundings permitted.

For some cause my watch stopped at 10.45 last night while one of the men on watch had it. I set it as near as I could come to the time by guessing, and we must run by that until I can do better. Sun rose yesterday morning at 6.40 by the watch when running all right: 7.05 to 7.40 (35 m.), 7.50 to 8.20 (30 m.), 8.30 to 9.00 (30 m.), 9.15 to 9.35 (20 m.), 10.25 to 10.40 (15 m.), 11.00 to 11.20,

11.30 to 11.50, 11.50 dinner- 1 h. 55 m. –2 h. 35 m., say five miles.

Our forenoon's walk I put as about at five miles. Some time and distance was lost by crossing the river upon seeing numerous fox-traps. A man's track was also seen in the snow, bound south, and we followed it until it crossed the river to the west bank again. Here we were obliged to go back in our tracks, for the river was open in places, and we could not follow the man's track direct. Another of the dozen shoals which infest the river swung us off to the eastward, too, and I hastened to get on the west bank again, reaching there at 11.50 for dinner. Our last four fourteenths pound pemmican.

At 1.40 got under way again and made a long fleet until 2.20. While at the other side of the river Alexey said he saw a hut, and during our dinner camp he again saw it. Under our circumstances my desire was to get to it as speedily as possible. As Alexey pointed out it was on the left bank of the river of which we were now on the right side looking south. But a sand bank gave us excellent walking for a mile, until we took to the river ice and got across it diagonally. Here, at 2.20, I called a rest, and Alexey mounted the bluff to take a look again. He now announced that he saw a second hut about one and a quarter miles back from the coast, the first hut being about the same distance south and on the edge of the bluff. The heavy dragging across country of a sick man on a sled made me incline to the hut on the shore, since as the distance was about the same, we could get over the ice in one third of the time. Nindemann, who climbed the bluff, while he saw that the object inland was a hut, was not so confident about the one on the shore. Alexey, however, was quite positive, and not seeing very well myself I unfortunately took his eyes as best and ordered an advance along the river to the southward. Away we went, Nindeman and Alexey leading, and had progressed about a mile when, splash! in I went through the ice up to my shoulders before my knapsack brought me up. While I was crawling out, in went Gortz to his neck about fifty yards behind me, and behind him in went Mr. Collins to his waist. Here was a time. The moment we came out of the water we were one sheet of ice, and danger of frostbite was imminent. Along we hobbled, however, until we came, at 3.45, abreast the point on which the hut was seen. Here Nindemann climbed the bluff, followed by the doctor. At first the cry was, "All right, come ahead," but no sooner were we all up than Nindemann shouted, "There is no hut here." To my dismay and alarm nothing but a large mound of earth was to be seen, which, from its regular shape and singular position would seem to have been built artificially for a beacon; so sure was Nindemann that it was a hut that he went all around it looking for a door, and then climbed on top to look for a hole in the roof. But of no avail. It was nothing but a mound of earth. Sick at heart I ordered a camp to be made in a hole in the bluff face, and soon before a roaring fire we were drying (and burning) our clothes, while the cold wind ate into our backs.

And now for supper! Nothing remained but the dog. I therefore ordered him killed and dressed by Iversen, and soon after a kind of stew was made of such parts as could not be carried, of which everybody except the doctor and myself eagerly partook. To us two it was a nauseating mess and—but why go on with such a disagreeable subject. I had the remainder weighed, and I am quite sure we had twenty-seven pounds. The animal was fat and—as he had been fed on pemmican—presumably clean, but—

Immediately upon halting I had sent off Alexey with his gun toward the hut inland, to determine whether that was a myth like our present one. He returned about dark, certain that it was a large hut, for he had been inside of it, and had found some deer meat, scraps, and bones. For a moment I was tempted to start everybody for it, but Alexey was by no means sure he could find it in the dark, and if we lost our way we should be worse off than before. We accordingly prepared to make the best of it where we were.

We three wet people were burning and steaming before the fire. Collins and Gortz had taken some alcohol, but I could not get it down. Cold, wet, with a raw N.W. wind impossible to avoid or screen, our future was a wretched, dreary night. Ericksen soon became delirious, and his talking was a horrible accompaniment to the wretchedness of our surroundings. Warm we could not get, and getting dry seemed out of the question. Nearly everybody seemed dazed and stupefied, and I feared that some of us would perish during the night. How cold it was I do not know, for my last thermometer was broken in my many falls on the ice, but I think it must have been below zero. A watch was set to keep the fire going and we huddled around it, and thus our third night without sleep was passed. If Alexey had not wrapped his sealskin around me and sat down alongside of me to keep me warm by the heat of his body, I think I should have frozen to death. As it was I steamed, and shivered, and shook. Ericksen's groans and rambling talk rang out in the night air, and such a dreary, wretched night I hope I shall never see again.

October 4th, Tuesday.—One hundred and fourteen day. At the first approach of daylight we all began to move around, and the cook was set to work making tea. The doctor now made the unpleasant discovery that during the night Ericksen had got his gloves off and that now his hands were frozen. Men were at once set to work rubbing them, and by six A.M. we had so far restored circulation as to risk moving the man. Each one had hastily swallowed a cup of tea, and got his load in readiness. Ericksen was quite unconscious, and we lashed him on the sled. A S.W. gale was blowing, and the sensation of cold was intense; but as six A.M. we started, made a forced fleet of it, and at eight A M. had got the man and ourselves, thank God, under the cover of a hut large enough to hold us. Here we at once made a fire, and for the first time since Saturday morning last got warm.

The doctor at once examined Ericksen and found him very low indeed. His pulse was very feeble, he was quite unconscious, and under the shock of the exposure of the past night he was sinking very fast. Fears were entertained that he might not last many hours, and I therefore called upon every one to join with me in reading the prayers for a sick person before we sought any rest for ourselves. This was done in a quiet, and reverent manner, though I fear my broken utterances made but little of the service audible. Then setting a watch we all, except Alexey, laid down to sleep at ten A.M. Alexey went off to hunt, but returned at noon wet, having broken through the ice and fallen in the river.

At six P.M. all roused up, and I considered it necessary to think of some food for my party. Half a pound of dog was fried for each one and a cup of tea given, and that constituted our day's food. But we were so grateful that we were not exposed to the merciless S.W. gale that tore around us that we did not mind short rations.

October 5th, Wednesday—One hundred and fifteenth day. The cook commenced at 7.30 to get tea, made from yesterday's tea leaves. Nothing can be served out to eat until evening. One half pound dog per day is our food until some relief is afforded us. Alexey went off hunting again at nine, and I set the men to work collecting light sticks enough to make a flooring for the house, for the frozen ground thawing under everybody has kept them damp and wet and robbed them of much sleep.

S.W. gale continues. Mortification has set in in Ericksen's leg and he is sinking. Amputation would be of no use, for he would probably die under the operation. He is partially conscious. At twelve Alexey came back, having seen nothing. He crossed the river this time, but unable longer to face the cold gale was obliged to return.

I am of the opinion that we are on Tit Ary Island, on its eastern side, and about twenty-five miles from the Ku Mark Surka, which I take to be a settlement. This is a last hope, for our Sagastyr has long since faded away. The hut in which we are is quite new, and clearly not the astronomical station marked on my chart. In fact this hut is not finished, having no door and no porch. It may be intended for a summer hut, though the numerous set fox-traps would lead me to suppose that it would occasionally be visited at other times. Upon this last chance and one other seem to rest all our hopes of escape, for I can see nothing more to be done. As soon as this gale abates I shall send Nindemann and one other man to make a forced march to Ku Mark Surka for relief. At six P.M. served out one half pound of dog meat and second-hand tea, and then went to sleep.

October 6th, Thursday.—One hundred and sixteenth day. Called all hands at 7.30. Had a cup of third-hand tea with one half ounce of alcohol in it. Everybody very weak. Gale moderating somewhat. Sent Alexey out to hunt. Shall start Nindemann and Noros at noon to make the forced march to Ku Mark Surka. At 8.45 A.M. our messmate Ericksen departed this life. Addressed a few words of cheer and comfort to the men. Alexey came back empty-handed. Too much drifting snow. What in God's name is going to become of us,—fourteen pounds of dog meat left, and twenty-five miles to a possible settlement? As to burying Ericksen, I cannot dig a grave, for the ground is frozen and we have nothing to dig with. There is nothing to do but to bury him in the river. Sewed him up in the flaps of the tent, and covered him with my flag. Got tea ready, and with one half ounce alcohol will try to make out to bury him. But we are all so weak that I do not see how we are going to move.

At 12.40 P.M. read the burial service and carried our departed shipmate's body down to the river, where, a hole having been cut in the ice, he was buried; three volleys from our two Remingtons being fired over him as a funeral honor.

A board was prepared with this cut on it:—
In Memory
H.H. ERICKSEN,
Oct. 6, 1881.
U.S.S. *Jeanette.*
and this will be stuck in the river bank abreast his grave.

His clothing was divided up among his messmates. Iversen has his Bible and a lock of his hair. Kaack has a lock of his hair.

Supper at five P.M.— one half pound dog meat and tea.

October 7th, Friday.—One hundred and seventeenth day. Breakfast, consisting of our last one half pound dog meat and tea. Our last grain of tea was put in the kettle this morning, and we are now about to undertake our journey of twenty-five miles with some old tea-leaves and two quarts alcohol. However, I trust in God, and I believe that He who has fed us thus far will not suffer us to die of want now.

Commenced preparations for departure at 7.10. Our Winchester rifle being out of order is, with one hundred and sixty-one round ammunition, left behind. We have with us two Remmingtons and two hundred and forty-three round ammunition. Left the following record in the hut:—

Friday, October 7, 1881.

The undermentioned officers and men of the late U.S. Steamer *Jeannette* are leaving here this morning to make a forced march to Ku Mark Surka, or some other settlement on the Lena River. We reached here on Tuesday, October 4th, with a disabled comrade, H.H. Ericksen (seamen), who died yesterday morning, and was buried in the river at noon. His death resulted from frost-bite and exhaustion, due to consequent exposure. The rest of us are well, but have no provisions left— having eaten our last this morning.

Under way at 8.30 and proceeded until 11.20, by which time we had made about three miles. Here we were all pretty well done up, and, moreover, seemed to be wandering in a labyrinth. A large lump of wood swept in by an eddy seemed to be a likely place to get hot water, and I halted the party. For dinner we had one ounce alcohol in a pot of tea. Then went ahead, and soon struck what seemed like the river again. Here four of us broke through the ice in trying to cross, and fearing frost-bite I had a fire built on the west bank to dry us. Sent Alexey off meanwhile to look for food, directing him not to go far nor to stay long; but at 3.30 he had not returned, nor was he in sight. Light S.W. breeze, hazy; mountains in sight to southward.

At 5.30 Alexey returned with one ptarmigan, of which we made soup, and with one half ounce of alcohol had our supper. Then crawled under our blankets for a sleep. Light W. breeze; full moon; starlight. Not very cold. Alexey saw a river a mile wide with no ice in it.

October 8th, Saturday.— One hundred and eighteenth day. Called all hands at 5.30. Breakfast, one ounce alcohol in a pint of hot water. Doctor's note: Alcohol provides a great advantage; keeps off craving for food, preventing gnawing at stomach, and has kept up the strength of the men, as given, —three ounces per day as estimated, and in accordance with Dr. Anstie's experiments.

Went ahead until 10.30; one ounce alcohol 6.30 to 10.30; five miles; struck big river; 11.30 ahead again; sand bank. Meet small river. Have to turn back. Halt at five. Only made advance one mile more. Hard luck. Snow; S.S. E. wind. Cold camp; but little wood; one half ounce alcohol.

October 9th, Sunday.— One hundred and nineteenth day. All hands at 4.30 one ounce alcohol. Read divine service. Send Nindemann and Noros ahead for relief; they carry their blankets, one rifle, forty rounds ammunition, two ounces alcohol. Orders to keep west bank of river until they reach settlement. They started at seven; cheered them. Under way at eight. Crossed creek. Broke through ice. All wet up to knees. Stopped and built fires. Dried clothes. Under way again at 10.30. Lee breaking down. At one strike river bank. Halt for dinner,— one ounce alcohol. Alexey shot three ptarmigans. Made soup. We are following Nindemann's track, though he is long since out of sight. Under way at 3.30. High bluff. Ice running rapidly to northward in river. Halt at 4.40 upon coming to wood. Find canoe. Lay our heads on it and go to sleep; one half ounce alcohol for supper.

October 10th, Monday.— One hundred and twentieth day. Last half ounce alcohol at 5.30; at 6.30 send Alexey off to look for ptarmigan. Eat deerskin scraps. Yesterday morning ate my deerskin foot-nips. Light S.S.E. airs. Not very cold. Under way at eight. In crossing creek three of us got wet. Built fire and dried out. Ahead again until eleven. Used up. Built fire. Made a drink out of the tea-leaves from alcohol bottle. On again at noon. Fresh S.S.W. wind, drifting snow, very hard going. Lee begging to be left. Some little beach, and then long stretches of high bank. Ptarmigan tracks plentiful. Following Nindemann's tracks. At three halted, used up; crawled into a hole in the bank, collected wood and built fire. Alexey away in quest of game. Nothing for supper except a spoonful of glycerine. All hands weak and feeble, but cheerful. God help us.

October 11th, Tuesday.- One hundred and twenty-first day. S.W. gale with snow. Unable to move. No game. One spoonful glycerine and hot water for food. No more wood in our vicinity.

October 12th, Wednesday.— One hundred and twenty-second day. Breakfast;

last spoonful glycerine and hot water. For dinner we tried a couple of handfuls
of Arctic willow in a pot of water and drank the infusion. Everybody getting
weaker and weaker. Hardly strength to get fire-wood. S.W. gale with snow.

October 13th, Thursday.— One hundred and twenty-third day. Willow tea.
Strong S.W. wind. No news from Nindemann. We are in the hands of God, and
unless He intervenes we are lost. We cannot move against the wind, and staying here means starvation. Afternoon went ahead for a mile, crossing either
another river or a bend in the big one. After crossing, missed Lee. Went down
in a hole in the bank and camped. Sent back for Lee. He had turned back, lain
down, and was waiting to die. All united in saying Lord's Prayer and Creed after
supper. Living gale of wind. Horrible night.

October 14th, Friday.— One hundred and twenty-fourth day. Breakfast, willow tea. Dinner, one half teaspoonful sweet oil and willow tea. Alexey shot one
ptarmigan. Had soup. S.W. wind, moderating.

October 15th, Saturday.— One hundred and twenty-fifth day. Breakfast, willow tea and two old boots. Conclude to move at sunrise. Alexey breaks down,
also Lee. Come to empty grain raft. Halt and camp. Signs of smoke at twilight
to southward.

October 16th, Sunday.—One hundred and twenty-sixth day. Alexey broke
down. Divine service.

October 17th, Monday.— One hundred and twenty-seventh day. Alexey dying.
Doctor baptized him. Read prayers for sick. Mr. Collins' birthday— forty years
old. About sunset Alexey died. Exhaustion from starvation. Covered him with
ensign and laid him in the crib.

October 18th, Tuesday.— One hundred and twenty-eighth day. Calm and
mild, snow falling. Buried Alexey in the afternoon. Laid him on the ice of the
river, and covered him over with slabs of ice.

October 19th, Wednesday.— One hundred and twenty-ninth day. Cutting up
tent to make foot gear. Doctor went ahead to find new camp. Shifted by dark.

October 20th, Thursday.— One hundred and thirtieth day. Bright and
sunny but very cold. Lee and Kaack done up.

October 21st, Friday.—One hundred and thirty-first day. Kaack was found dead
about midnight between the doctor and myself. Lee died about noon. Read
prayers for the sick when we found he was going.

October 22d, Saturday.— One hundred and thirty-second day. Too weak to carry the bodies of Lee and Kaack out on the ice. The doctor, Collins, and I carried them around the corner out of sight. Then my eye closed up.

October 23d, Sunday.— One hundred and thirty-third day. Everybody pretty weak. Slept or rested all day, and then managed to get enough wood in before dark. Read part of the divine service. Suffering in our feet. No foot gear.

October 24th, Monday.— One hundred and thirty-fourth day. A hard night.

October 25th, Tuesday.— One hundred and thirty-fifth day.

October 26th, Wednesday.— One hundred and thirty-sixth day.

October 27th, Thursday.— One hundred and thirty-seventh day. Iversen broken down.

October 28th, Friday.— One hundred and thirty-eighth day. Iversen died during early morning.

October 29th, Saturday.— One hundred and thirty-ninth day. Dressler died during night.

October 30th, Sunday.— One hundred and fortieth day. Boyd and Gortz died during night. Mr. Collins dying.

EVENTUALLY THE COUNTRY DID REMEMBER THE JEANNETTE AND SENT *ships north to rescue De Long and his men. It was much too late—and nobody knew where they were. One ship looked for them near Spitzbergen. Another caught fire and sank. Its crew were themselves then stranded in Russia. The third ship, the* Corwin, *steamed through Bering Strait, investigated the seas from northern Siberia to northern Alaska, and found nothing. Aboard, however, was John Muir. He had come less to rescue the Jeannette's crew than to study his first love, glaciation, and to report on the search for the* San Francisco Evening Bulletin. *These reports, and Muir's journal entries for the trip, were woven in 1917, after Muir's death, into a book titled* The Cruise of the Corwin *and our next selection comes from this book. It is a small gem of a piece on an encounter with the Chukchi and a sigh of light-hearted relief after the heartbreak of De Long's final struggle with starvation and exhaustion.*

JOHN MUIR

The Cruise of the Corwin

A CHUKCHI ORATOR

Steamer Corwin
St. Lawrence Bay, Siberia, June 6, 1881.

Yesterday morning at half-past one o'clock, when we were within twenty-five miles of Plover Bay, where we hoped to be able to repair our rudder, we found that the ice-pack was crowding us closer and closer inshore, and that in our partly disabled condition it would not be safe to proceed farther. Accordingly we turned back and put into St. Lawrence Bay, to await some favorable movement in the ice.

We dropped anchor at half-past seven in the morning opposite a small Chukchi settlement. In a few hours the wind began to blow fresh from the north, steadily increasing in force, until at eight in the evening it was blowing a gale, and we were glad that we were in a good harbor instead of being out at sea, slashing and tumbling about with a broken rudder among the wind-driven ice. It also rained and snowed most of the afternoon, the blue and gray sleet mingling in grand uproar with the white scud swept from the crests of the waves, making about as stormy and gloomy an atmosphere as I ever had the fortune to breathe. Now and then the clouds broke and lifted their ragged edges high enough to allow the mountains along the sides and round the head of the bay to be dimly seen, not so dimly, however, as to hide the traces of the heavy glaciation to which they have been subjected. This long bay, as shown by its trends, its relation to the ice-fountains at its head and the sculpture of its walls, is a glacial fiord that only a short time ago was the channel of a glacier that poured a deep and broad flood into Bering Sea, in company with a thousand others north and south along the Siberian coast. The more I see of this region the more I am inclined to believe that all of Bering Sea and Strait is a glacial excavation.

In a party of natives that came aboard soon after we had dropped anchor, we discovered the remarkable Chukchi orator, Jaroochah, whose acquaintance we made at the settlement on the other side of the bay, during our first visit, and who had so vividly depicted the condition of the lost whaler *Vigilant*. To-day, after taking up a favorable position in the pilot-house, he far surpassed his previous efforts, pouring forth Chukchi in overwhelming torrents, utterly oblivious of the presence of his rival, the howling gale.

During a sudden pause in the midst of his volcanic eloquence he inquired whether we had rum to trade for walrus ivory, whereupon we explained, in total abstinence phrase, that rum was very bad stuff for Chukchis, and by way of illustration related its sad effects upon the Eskimo natives of St. Lawrence Island. Nearly all the natives we have thus far met admitted very readily that whiskey was not good for them. But Jaroochah was not to be so easily silenced, for he at once began an anti-temperance argument in saloon-and-moderate-drinker style, explaining with vehement gestures that some whiskey was good, some bad; that he sometimes drank five cupfuls of the good article in quick succession, the effect of which was greatly to augment his happiness, while out of a small bottle of the bad one, a small glass made him sick. And as for whiskey or rum causing people to die, he knew, he said, that that was a lie, for he had drunk much himself, and he had a brother who had enjoyed a great deal of whiskey on board of whalers for many years, and that though now a gray old man he was still alive and happy.

This speech was warmly applauded by his listening companions, indicating a public opinion that offers but little hope of success for the efforts of temperance societies among the Chukchis. Captain Hooper, the surgeon, and myself undertook to sketch the orator, who, when he had gravely examined our efforts, laughed boisterously at one of them, which, in truth, was a slanderous caricature of even *his* countenance, villainous as it was.

In trading his ivory for supplies of some sort, other than alcohol, he tried to extract some trifling article above what had been agreed on, when the trader threatened to have nothing further to do with him on account of the trouble he was making. This set the old chief on his dignity, and he made haste to declare that he was a good and honorable man, and that in case the trade was stopped he would give back all he had received and go home, leaving his ivory on the deck heedless of what became of it. The woman of the party, perhaps eighteen years of age, merry and good-looking, went among the sailors and danced, sang, and joked with them.

The gale increased in violence up to noon to-day, when it began to abate slightly, and this evening it is still blowing hard. The *Corwin* commenced to drag her anchor shortly after midnight, when another that was kept in readiness was let go with plenty of chain, which held, so that we rode out the gale in safety. The whalers *Francis Palmer* and *Hidalgo* came into the bay last evening from Bering Strait and anchored near us. This morning the *Hidalgo* had vanished, having probably parted her cable.

Last evening a second party of natives came aboard, having made their way around the head of the bay or over the ice. Both parties remained on board all night as they were unable to reach the shore in their light skin boats against the wind. Being curious to see how they were enduring the cold, I went on deck early. They seemed scarcely to feel it at all, for I found most of them lying on the deck amid the sludge and sleeping soundly in the clothes they wore during the day. Three of them were sleeping on the broken rudder, swept by the icy wind and sprinkled with snow and fragments of ice that were falling from the rigging, their heads and necks being nearly bare.

I inquired why their reindeer parkas were made without hoods, while those of the Eskimos of St. Lawrence Island had them; observing that they seemed far more comfortable in stormy weather, because they kept the head and neck warm and dry. They replied that they had to hunt hard and look quick all about them for a living, therefore it was necessary to keep their heads free; while the St. Lawrence Eskimos were lazy, and could indulge in effeminate habits. They gave the same reason for cutting off most of the hair close to the scalps, while the women wear the hair long.

One of their number was very dirty, and Captain Hooper, who is becoming interested in glacial studies, declared that he had discovered two terminal moraines in his ears. When asked why he did not wash himself, our interpreter replied, "Because he is an old fellow, and it is too much work to wash." This was given with an air of having explained the matter beyond further question. Considering the necessities of the lives they lead, most of these people seem remarkably clean and well-dressed and well-behaved.

The old orator poured forth his noisy eloquence late and early, like a perennial mountain spring, some of his deep chest tones sounding in the storm like the roar of a lion. He rolled his wolfish eyes and tossed his brown skinny limbs in a frantic storm of gestures, now suddenly foreshortening himself to less than half his height, then shooting aloft with jack-in-the-box rapidity, while his people looked on and listened, apparently half in fear, half in admiration. We directed the interpreter to tell him that we thought him a good man, and were, therefore, concerned lest some accident might befall him from so much hard speaking. The Chukchis, as well as the Eskimos we have seen, are keenly sensitive to ridicule, and this suggestion disconcerted him for a moment and made a sudden pause. However, he quickly recovered and got under way again, like a wave withdrawing on a shelving shore, only to advance and break again with gathered force.

The chief man of the second party from the other side of the bay is owner of a herd of reindeer, which he said were now feeding among the mountains at a distance of one sleep—a day's journey—from the head of a bay to the south of here. He readily indicated the position on a map that we spread before him, and offered to take us to see them on a sled drawn by a reindeer, and to sell us as many skins and as much meat as we cared to buy. When we asked how many reindeer he had, all who heard the question laughed at the idea of counting so many. "They cover a big mountain," he said proudly, "and nobody can count them." He brought a lot of ivory to trade for tobacco, but said nothing about it until the afternoon. Then he signified his readiness for business after awakening from a sound sleep on the wet icy deck.

Shortly after we had breakfasted, the reindeer chief having intimated that he and his friends were hungry, the Captain ordered a large pot of tea, with hardtack, sugar and molasses, to be served to them in the pilot-house. They ate with dignified deliberation, showing no unseemly haste, but eating rather like people accustomed to abundance. Jaroochah, who could hardly stem his eloquence even while eating, was particular about having his son invited in to share the meal; also, two boys about eight years old, giving as a reason, "they are little ones." We also called in a young woman, perhaps about eighteen years old, but none of the men present seemed to care whether she shared with them or not, and when we inquired the cause of this neglect, telling them that white men always served the ladies first, Jaroochah said that while girls were "little fellows" their parents looked after them, but when they grew big they went away from their parents with "some other fellow," and were of no more use to them and could look out for themselves.

Those who were not invited to this meal did not seem to mind it much, for they had brought with them plenty of what the whalers call "black skin" —the skin of the right whale—which is about an inch thick, and usually has from half and inch to an inch of blubber attached. This I saw them eating raw with hearty relish, snow and sludge the only sauce, cutting off angular blocks of it with butcher-knives, while one end of the tough black rubber-like mass was being held in the left hand, the other between their teeth. Long practice enables them to cut off mouthfuls in this way without cutting their lips, although they saw their long knives back and forth, close to their faces, as if playing the violin. They get the whale skin from the whalers, excepting the little they procure themselves. They hunt the whale now with lances and gear of every kind bought from the whalers, and sometimes succeed in killing a good many. They eat the carcass, and save the bone to trade to the whalers, who are eager to get it.

After the old orator left the steamer, the reindeer man accused him of being "a bad fellow, like a dog." He evidently was afraid that we were being fooled by his overwhelming eloquence into believing that he was a great man, while the precious truth to be impressed upon us was, that he, the reindeer man, whose herd covers a big mountain, was the true chief. I asked his son, who speaks a little English, why he did not make a trip to San Francisco, to see the white man's big town. He replied, as many a civilized man does under similar circumstances, that he had a little boy, too little to be left, and too little to leave home, but that soon he would be a big fellow, so high, indicating the hoped-for stature with his hand, then he would go to San Francisco on some whale-ship, to see where all the big ships and good whiskey came from.

These [Chukchis] also had heard the story of the *Vigilant*. The reindeer man's son is going with us to Plover Bay to look after some of his father's debtors. He has been supplying them with tobacco and other goods on credit, and he thought it was time they were paying up. His little boy, he told us, was sick—had a hot, sore head that throbbed, showing with his hand how it beat in aching pulses, and asked for medicine, which the surgeon gave him with necessary directions, greatly to his relief of mind, it seemed.

Around the shore opposite our anchorage the ground is rather low, where the ancient glacier that filled the bay swept over in smooth curves, breaking off near the shore, an abrupt wall from seventy to a hundred feet high. Against this wall the prevailing north winds have piled heavy drifts of snow that curve over the bluff at the top and slope out over the fixed ice along the shore from the base. The gale has been loosening and driving out past the vessel, without doing us any harm, large masses of the ice, capped with the edge of the drift. One large piece drifted close past the steamer and immediately in front of a large skin canoe capable of carrying thirty men. The canoe, which was tied to the stern of the ship, we thought was doomed to be carried away. The owners looked wistfully over the stern, watching her fate, while the sailors seemed glad of the bit of excitement caused by the hope of an accident that would cost them nothing. Greatly to our surprise, however, when the berg, rough and craggy, ten or twelve feet high, struck her bow, she climbed up over the top of it, and, dipping on the other side, glided down with a graceful, launching swoop into the water, like a living thing, wholly uninjured. The sealskin buffer, fixed in front of inflated like a bladder, no doubt greatly facilitated her rise. She was tied by a line of walrus hide.

Now that the wind is abating, we hope to get away from here to-morrow morning, and expect to find most of the ice that stopped our progress yesterday broken up and driven southward far enough to enable us to reach Plover Bay without further difficulty.

TWENTY OF THE THIRTY-PLUS MEN WHO SAILED ON THE JEANNETTE DIED. *For the Greely expedition the percentages were worse. Of the twenty-five men who went with Greely to the upper reaches of Ellesmere Island, in the same general area where Hall and Kane had wintered, only six came back.*

The Greely expedition was ostensibly scientific in nature, inspired by the first International Polar Year, 1882-83. Eleven nations agreed to establish polar stations in both the Arctic and the Antarctic to conduct scientific research. The United States agreed to set up their station in the same place George Nares had spent the winter six years before, and it put a U. S. Army officer, Capt. Adolphus W. Greely, in charge. This was, in fact, an Army operation. Greely was a polar addict and wanted the post badly. While science was the ostensible reason for the expedition, Greely also hoped to reach the Pole.

Greely went north in the summer of 1881, built a hut he named Fort Conger at Lady Franklin Bay on Ellesmere Island, and prepared for the winter. That fall Greely sent out the usual preliminary sledge parties to the north and then they all settled in—and began the bickering that nearly every expedition toward the North Pole encountered. The difficulty this time arose between Greely, who was a military man through and through and believed in military discipline, and the expedition's doctor, Octave Pavy, who felt himself above discipline and, as a scientist, looked down on Greely. He had an ally in one of the other officers, who disliked Greely as much as Pavy did and had tried to resign from the expedition at the last minute, just as their supply ship was leaving, but missed, as they say, the bus.

When spring came two sledging parties left to try for the Pole. One, led by Dr. Pavy, got only as far as the first open water above Ellesmere Island. The other traced the north coast of Greenland and reached Cape Britannia. They continued from there, two men and an Eskimo dog driver, another hundred miles, and attained a new farthest north, reaching latitude 83 degrees, 24 minutes, four miles farther than Albert Markham had reached with the Nares expedition, but still hundreds of miles, of course, from the Pole. And their supply ship could not reach them that summer. The channels had iced up 200 miles to the south. They had nothing to do and the only books in the hut were books about the Arctic. The enlisted men got along, but the officers did not, and Pavy did not get along with anybody.

Next spring sledging parties set off again, and two Americans and an Eskimo set new records: a farthest north, a farthest east, a farthest west. The scientific work went less well—at least the work under Pavy's care. Pavy had not preserved his specimens properly or even organized them. His only real interest in the North was in setting geographical records himself. Meanwhile they waited for the relief ship once again. Once again it did not come. Greely had left orders that if they could not reach them, they should at least leave depots on the eastern coast of Ellesmere Island at set intervals so that they could leave Fort Conger and move south. Greely had set up depots himself on his way north. He had every reason to believe that there were plenty of supplies along the way, should he be forced to abandon Fort Conger. Early in August of 1883, Greely decided to do just that. They left on August 9.

Relief ships, meanwhile, were struggling with the ice in Smith Sound and Kane Basin. They could not reach Greely and, in a fatal combination of errors of judgment, inexperience and incompetence, they did not deposit the supplies they were supposed to deposit. The principal depot was to be at Cape Sabine, toward the bottom of Kane Basin. The relief ship stopped at Kane Basin but the officer in charge, a cavalry officer who had never been to the Arctic, was so anxious to take advantage of what he saw as an open lead to the north that he did not take the time to leave supplies there. Instead he took the ship, a sealer, against the advice of the ship's captain, who did know the Arctic, into Smith Sound, where the ice promptly sank it. The sealers and the soldiers fled in small boats. When Greely got to Cape Sabine he would find provisions enough to last three weeks. And no more. The men in the small boats all survived, but the relief mission had been a disaster. Greely had left Fort Conger, where there was a building, provisions, and plenty of game, for Cape Sabine, where he would have a tent, three weeks' worth of supplies to last him yet another winter, and where game was exceedingly scarce.

We take our next excerpt from Greely's account of his Arctic experiences, specifically from the chapter that covers November, when the Arctic winter gets serious. It is a grim example of what it is like to live when all your thoughts are on food and every single crumb of it is meaningful to you.

ADOLPHUS W. GREELY

Three Years of Arctic Service: An Account of the Lady Franklin Bay Expedition, 1881–84

THE FIRST DAYS OF NOVEMBER GAVE US A REALIZING SENSE OF THE HORRORS and miseries to be expected from a sunless winter of nearly four months' duration under existing conditions. Nearly half of the party were unfit for duty, by reason of frostbite or injuries received during our arduous autumn work. Our sleeping-bags and clothing were already frozen to the ground, and their interiors were thawed only by the heat of our bodies, and froze solidly on quitting them. The roofs and walls speedily gathered frost and ice, as did every other article in our wretched hut. It appears better to me that the story of our life that terrible winter should be set forth in the language of our journals, and should not be elaborated now in the comforts of civilization. While cleaving to stern facts, I have occasionally modified the sharpness of my comments. The reader is asked to bear in mind that the entries quoted were written by men patient in hardships, and always inclined to underrate, as a matter of pride, their great discomforts.

"November 1st.—We have on hand at this date the following stores: Lemons, 150; pemmican, 228 lbs.; bacon, 232 lbs.; beef, 410 lbs.; seal, 115 lbs.; potatoes, 76 lbs.; butter, 93 lbs.; lard, 50 lbs.; rice, 18 lbs.; raisins, 40 lbs.; tea, 73 lbs.; extract of coffee, 82 lbs.; extract of chocolate, 76 lbs.; onion-pickles, 10 gals.; milk, 38 lbs.; sugar, 15 lbs.; salt, 2 lbs.; onion-powder, 2 lbs.; pepper, 12 ozs.; bread, 1, 395 lbs.; dog-biscuit, 152 lbs.; extract of beef, 34 cans; soup, 48 cans; tomatoes, 24 cans; corn, 24 cans; peas, 27 cans; carrots, 13 cans; cloudberries, 46 cans; seal-blubber, 200 lbs.

"The quantity of bread is uncertain, being partly estimated. The dog-biscuits, English bread, English chocolate, and some other small stores are in bad condition, but must of necessity be eaten. We commenced to-day on a ration declared by the doctor to be insufficient for the support of life, but which has been adopted by me, after mature deliberation, as being our only chance of safety.

"It is as follows: Meat, 4 ozs.; extract of beef, 0.26 oz.; evaporated potatoes, 0.4 oz.; soup, 0.6 oz.; tomatoes, 0.3 oz.; peas, 0.2 oz.; corn, 0.2 oz.; carrots, 0.1 oz.; bread, 6 ozs.; dog-biscuits, 0.8 oz.; butter, 0.5 oz.; lard, 0.26 oz.; rice, 0.1 oz.; raisins, 0.16 oz.; tea, 0.3 oz.; extract of coffee, 0.44 oz.; extract of chocolate, 0.3 oz.; pickled onions, 0.4 oz.; milk, 0.2 oz.; and mulberries, 0.2 oz.

"Lieutenant Kislingbury is suffering very much, and fainted twice this evening, from his injury received while sledging, which the doctor reports to be rupture. Schneider killed a white fox weighing five and a quarter pounds, all of which, except the skin, is to be eaten. It is a great disappointment to find that the English potatoes cached in Payer Harbor are mouldy and almost uneatable. They are packed, however, in paper, which accounts for the deterioration. Bender has made a stove from the sheet-iron with which the whaleboat was sheathed. It is a truncated cone in shape, and answers its purpose admirably. The barrels in which the food was cached, a small quantity of birch-wood, and the broken-up whaleboat is the scanty fuel, which supplements the English stearine and our own alcohol. In order to insure perfect combustion, and to derive the greatest heat from the fuel, the wood is cut up into pieces not much longer than matches."

"November 2d.—The doctor informs me that Lieutenant Kislingbury's rupture, from which he has suffered very much, is very serious, and may prove fatal. Ralston killed a white fox weighing four and a half pounds, and Brainard shot a blue one weighing three pounds. Our first meal cooked with wood in stoves made by Bender was eaten to-night. The stoves work very well; and, in order to economize fuel, I determined that the cooking should be done hereafter on one stove. There was a great deal of adverse criticism in regard to this decision, as, the party being divided into two messes, it will be necessary for one mess to wait until the cooking for the other is done. This is certainly trying to hungry men, but fuel is very scarce, and must be utilized to the utmost extent. Brainard discovered that a quarter of the English tobacco from Payer Harbor cache is missing. We were unable to determine whether it was never packed, or if it has been taken by some one. The former I prefer believing at present."

"November 3d.—Long came from Rice Strait for further rations. He brought me the joyful news that he has killed an harbor-seal, which he thinks will weigh one hundred and fifty pounds gross. The foxes have been very troublesome at Rice Strait; no matter what precautions are taken, the foxes manage to make their way into the tent and levy contribution on the meat there. Lieutenant Kislingbury is fortunately better. Colorless auroral streamers were visible from 3 p.m. until after 7 p.m., the curtain formation showing at times, and the auroral light was seen in all quarters except the north. Sergeant Israel observed Vega to-night. The temperature sank to -13° (-25° C.). Fresh bear-tracks were seen by Long near Cocked Hat Island, the animal coming from and returning toward Bache Island. The hunters have hopes of Master Bruin some day. The men are hopeful and cheerful, bearing well the cold, and short rations, and entire absence of light in the hut, except such as is afforded by the bit of rag dipped in seal-oil."

"November 4th.—Long left this morning, taking provisions to include Thursday. Brainard reports that the temporary commissary storehouse was entered last night. He suspects one of the party, who has been known to eat hard bread in his sleeping-bag. I am pushing work on the storehouse to avoid such dangers in the future. I decided to dispose of the foxes that we may kill as follows: They are to be issued as extra meat; the first fox being for the present week, the second fox for the last week in February, the third for the next week, the fourth for the third week in February, etc. Under this rule, we ate to-day the fox killed by Bender, weighing three and three-fourths pounds. It is the first fox ever tasted by me, or, indeed, by any of the men, except, perhaps, the Eskimos. We pronounced it extraordinarily good, seasoned as it is with ravenous hunger. We are troubled much by smoke from the stoves. Issued a pound of blubber extra to-day for food, and another pound for light. Reading in the evening as usual, including the Psalms for to-day. The temperature down to -25.7° (-32.1° C.); terribly cold for our hunters and the unprotected travellers in Baird Inlet. With the rum, this evening, I issued a quarter of a lemon, which we unanimously declared to be the most delicious fruit ever tasted."

"November 5th.—Commissary-house finished, but not covered. A chimney was inserted in the bottom of the boat, which forms part of the roof of our house. It was made from several tomato-cans, and affords great relief from the intolerable smoke. The doctor reports that Henry's foot was frozen more badly than he had thought. I have ordered that the mouldy bread, rotten biscuit, and other damaged stores be issued now, while our systems will best assimilate them, so that the best and strongest food shall come later, and so be an increase in nutrition though not in quantity."

"November 6th.—The stores were moved into the commissary-house to-day, and I feel somewhat relieved, although I cannot consider them safe until a frame and door, with lock and key, which we fortunately have, are arranged. Brainard overhauled the English sugar and tea; of the former but a few pounds remain, and the latter is quite worthless. If those articles only had been replaced, what comfort to us!"

"November 7th.—Strong westerly wind in the morning, with the temperature down to -20.3° (-29.1° C.). It sent down the temperature of our hut very much, and must be almost unendurable for the *Isabella* party. I cannot sleep much for thinking of them. Christiansen came in from Rice Strait, and reports that Long wants a sledge to-morrow to bring in his meat and camp equipage. Unfortunately they have not been able to kill anything since last week. Brainard's report that the seal-blubber overruns some ninety pounds, by his improvised scales, encourages the party greatly. I am doubtful as to the accuracy of the scales, but maintain silence, knowing Brainard's integrity and impartiality; and realizing, too, the importance of adding or seeming to add a half ounce of blubber to our ration."

"November 8th.—The temperature still falling, being at -31.5° (-35.3° C.) this morning. It was necessary, however, to send Lieutenant Lockwood, Dr. Pavy, Brainard, and five others to Rice Strait to bring in Long's equipage and meat. On their return I issued an allowance of rum to them. Private Schneider, owing to Brainard's exhausted condition, being charged with portioning out the rum, took for himself a quantity without authority, and was visibly affected by it. He left the hut while the supper was cooking – he being the cook – and, not returning at once, search was made for him, and he was detected coming out of the commissary storehouse. The general sentiment is that Schneider has been implicated in the thefts which have been made therefrom. I am in doubt as to whether he entered the storehouse in a responsible condition mentally, but his taking the liquor is as bad as the food. I issued an order forbidding any one from entering the storehouse except the issuing sergeant, and took Schneider to task most severely for his misconduct."

"November 9th.—Lieutenant Lockwood discovered an opened but full can of milk hidden away. It had evidently been concealed by some one, who, surprised, had been unable to eat it after opening."

It appeared from the marks that the can was opened by a knife broken in a peculiar manner. It was afterward ascertained that the knife belonged to Henry, but he claimed to have lent it to Schneider.

"November 13th.—The minimum temperature last night was -34° (-36.7° C.). Elison's condition is much better than could have been reasonably hoped for. Dr. Pavy thinks it barely possible that amputation may not be necessary. Bierderbick shot a white fox to-day, which weighed five and a half pounds. Biederbick is devoting himself particularly to the care of Elison. He spends sixteen hours daily watching him and changing his bandages. Dr. Pavy, who has moved to the side of Elison to facilitate his attention, cares for the sick man the remainder of the day. I have given him (Elison) my mattress, which has been used to this time by Gardiner."

"November 14th.—Elison very bad all day; he suffers excruciating pain in his hands and feet. The men are slowly recovering from their exhaustion on the late severe trip."

"November 16th.—Strong wind last night; tide to-day the highest yet known; high water at 12:05 P.M. (Washington mean time)."

"November 17th.—The canvas roof was put on the vestibule to-day, which substantially finishes out-door work. I have been able to do but little of this. The men have shown an excellent spirit in this respect. Some of them have requested that I should do no work at all, thinking that my mental responsibility, as commander, is enough for me at this time. I, however, have done, as far as my physical condition would permit, the same manual labor as the others. My feet, which have been badly cracked from frost-bite, have prevented me from exposing myself without there should be some pressing demand.

"I have been casting about for some means to amuse and divert the party during the weary time now upon us. The entire work of the party does not require more than an hour's labor from two or three, and the remainder, by choice or necessity, remain almost continually in the sleeping-bags. As we have fairly entered upon an Arctic night of nearly four months' duration, it is an absolute necessity that the spirits of the men should not be allowed to flag.

"After much thought and some consultation, I have decided to give, daily, a lecture, of from one to two hours in length, upon the physical geography and the resources of the United States in general; followed later by similar talks on each State and Territory in particular. I commence to-day by talking on the physical geography of the United States, particularly with reference to its mountain and river systems. Lieutenant Kislingbury is much better of his rupture. He has suffered a great deal of pain from it, and once fainted under the doctor's hands."

"November 18th.—I talked for an hour or more to-day, regarding the peculiarities of climate and the various products, etc., of the United States. In the evening I read the Psalms for the day. Rum was issued, except to those who drew in advance on their return from their last trip to Long Point. There was some dissatisfaction among those who had drawn in advance, and I mentally resolved I would not permit advance rations to be again issued, except in extreme cases. I received no rum, having given my allowance, a couple of days since, to the nurses on watch over Elison. Brainard to-day put up a signal pole on the adjoining cliffs, which should be seen by any party travelling along the coast. I have not the faintest expectation of such a party this winter, but some of the rest have, and I am unwilling to depress their spirits by destroying any hopes they may nourish."

"November 19th.—Long shot a blue fox weighing four and a quarter pounds; Jens shot one weighing three and seven-eighths, which has much encouraged us. The entrails of the foxes killed go alternately to the messes, being used as an addition to, or flavor for, the stew. Talked for an hour or two on the grain and fruit products of the United States. Last evening there was reading from 'Pickwick,' by Jewell; 'Two on a Tower,' by Rice; 'A History of Our Own Times,' first by Lieutenant Lockwood, and later by Henry."

"November 20th.—I have been obliged to order reduction of meat and bread a fraction of an ounce, so that hereafter we have four ounces of meat daily and six ounces of bread. This reduction has been made necessary to provide extra rations for Elison. The doctor urged a very large increase, but I finally compromised the matter by giving him four ounces extra of bread and four ounces of meat. It seems to me that this, together with the extract of beef in the medical department, should be sufficient. The reduction was, of course, made on my own responsibility, but it was exceedingly gratifying to note that no one in the party in any way expressed his dissent from or dissatisfaction with my action. I believe the feeling to be general that the party realize that Elison's helpless condition has arisen from a spirit of self-sacrifice on his part in our behalf, and that in consequence we should be willing to deny ourselves, each a little, in his interest."

"November 21st.—Elison has improved a great deal, and the doctor thinks that he will recover without an operation. On the doctor's representations, I have set aside all the lard (fifty pounds) for medical purposes. I hardly think it can all be necessary for Elison's wounds, but I am glad to indorse anything which seems to show forethought for the future. The reduction of lard and meat will be in a slight degree replaced by an inconsiderable amount of seal-blubber, which can be spared from our stock of oil. I gave an hour to the mineral productions of the United States. It was interesting to note the lack of interest shown by the party regarding the production of gold and silver. Several have spoken on the subject of money, and there are but few men who would not willingly sacrifice their entire pecuniary fortunes, if by so doing they could guarantee the successful return of the expedition to the United States."

"November 22d.—Long shot a blue fox weighing three and one-half pounds, and later Christiansen shot another, also blue, which weighed the same as Long's. I gave another hour to the United States in general; treating particularly of its geographical subdivisions, as I intend commencing on the States in detail to-morrow."

"November 23d.—Talked for nearly two hours to-day on the State of Maine, touching on its climate, its vegetable and mineral products, its river system, mountain ranges, principal cities, its most important resources and manufactures, its history, and the famous men who have come from the State; and also as to its inducements to emigrants to settle within its limits. The same line of discussion will be followed regarding the other States. Subsequently I called upon Jewell, who has lived in Maine, to supplement my statements by any additional information he might possess; and, later, invited questions from any of the party on mooted or neglected points."

"November 24th.—Talked for a couple of hours on New Hampshire; my remarks being supplemented by Jewell by an account of life on Mount Washington, which he contrasted very favorably with our present deplorable condition. Instead of the customary reading from the Bible, Dickens, and the Army Regulations, this evening was given up to reminiscences pertaining to the past lives and domestic surroundings of the men."

"November 25th.—Sunday celebrated as usual by a 'sun-of-a-gun' for breakfast. This dish consists of a mixture of hard bread, raisins, milk, and as much seal-blubber as can be properly spared for the purpose. Several of my mess united with me in contributing our lemon-peel, in order to give it a flavor, and with the hope that the entire party will do so hereafter. Christiansen shot a blue fox, which weighed four and one-fourth pounds, and Long saw another, but too far distant to be fired at."

"November 26th.—The temperature was down almost to freezing mercury this morning, with a clear sky. Jens reports that there are dense water-clouds to the north, but that toward Greenland the sky is entirely clear. I infer from this that the straits are freezing over.

"Bender complained to-day of unfair treatment toward himself, as to the amount of bed-clothing assigned him; claiming that he did not receive his due proportion. Such an accusation is extremely annoying to the whole party, as everybody realizes the fact of Bender's having received a much larger share than he is entitled to. Every consideration has been shown him by me, owing to his delicate condition on leaving Conger. I sometime since stripped the blanket from my own bag, much to the annoyance of Sergeants Jewell and Israel, who are occupying it in common with me. The result of Bender's complaint was that part of a blanket was transferred to him by other parties, who needed it as much as he. In addition, he has been given, for his personal use, a buffalo overcoat found here at the wreck cache."

"November 27th.—The temperature was down to -43.5° (-41.9° C.) last night, and went down to nearly 20° (-6.7° C.) inside the hut. I talked for awhile on Vermont to-day."

"November 28th.—Strong wind and drifting snow, which makes our quarters much more uncomfortable than yesterday, although the outside temperature has risen to 11° (-23.9° C.). A fox was fired at, but unfortunately missed."

"November 29th.—The last Thursday in the month, and so set aside by me as a day of thanksgiving and praise, in order that we might act in accord with those we have left behind. The day has been looked forward to for weeks; and with a view of properly celebrating it, six pounds of rice, five pounds of raisins, two pounds each of extract of coffee and chocolate, and two pounds of milk were reserved from the general stock when an inventory was made. It seemed to me then that making this a great and happy day would so break in on our wretchedness and misery as to give us new courage and determination. I am convinced that the idea was a most wise one. To-day we have been *almost* happy, and had *almost* enough to eat.

"I doubt if any other men in the world have been more thankful for their health, strength, and comparative happiness than we. An extra half gill of rum and a few lemons, under skilful manipulation, gave us the most delicious punch we had ever tasted. Songs, stories and merriment in general kept us all amused and cheerful until midnight. It seemed to me that the Psalms of the day made a deeper impression than I have ever before noted."

"November 30th.—A stormy day, with the temperature at 3° (-16.1° C.); the first time it has been observed above zero (-17.8° C.) this month. The month ends comparatively well, with Elison in much better condition than any one had hoped for. The party in general are in good health, although a number suffer much from constipation."

"December 1st.—An easterly storm of great violence set in, and made us very uncomfortable by drifting snow entering through the roof, and lowering the temperature within the hut. The evening was given up to personal reminiscences; and, when those failed, to discussing future prospects, which were looked on hopefully by most."

"December 2d.—The storm, which was exceedingly violent, continued until noon. It required several hours' work on the part of three men to clear out the entrance to the house, which had been entirely filled with snow. We find that the storm unroofed the passage-way, blew away some of our wood and also the minimum thermometer. The cooks prepared breakfast under great difficulties. There was about eight inches of snow in the passage-way and on the bottoms of the sleeping-bags, which had to be cleared out as well as possible before anything could be done. Afterward the heat from the cooking-lamps melted the snow remaining, and in consequence the cooks were wet through by moisture from above and below."

"December 3d.—As much as possible of the wood was gathered up and brought within the house or the passage-way. Gave a couple of hours to-day to the State of New York."

"December 4th.—During last night some one, without doubt, took bread from Corporal Elison's bread-can. I was awake, and plainly heard it done."

In this entry of the most unfortunate experience of the month the name of Dr. Pavy was omitted. I was shocked that the surgeon of the expedition should so fail in his duty to the men and his commanding officer, and this discovery gave me great anxiety. Realizing that an open charge would result in a denial and bitter discussion, I committed my knowledge of this fact only to Lieutenant Lockwood, as my successor in command, and to Sergeant Brainard, who doled out the provisions. The importance of the doctor's services to us at that time was manifest to the entire party; nearly every one but myself had been treated medically since reaching Sabine, and the demand for medical treatment was constantly increasing. Whether right or wrong, I felt the necessity of pursuing conciliatory methods entirely.

"December 5th.—Another violent easterly gale set in last night, which changed to the west this morning, filling with snow the passage-way and commissary storehouse. The frequency of these late storms is trying to us, not only from the physical discomforts experienced, but because the straits must necessarily remain open during the prevalence of such high winds. Our reading in the evening, which is apart from my lectures upon the various States, generally consists of a chapter or two from the Bible, by Gardiner; the Army Regulations, by myself; and a chapter of 'Pickwick,' by Jewell."

"December 6th.—Long shot a blue fox; weight three pounds. Gave an hour or more to Pennsylvania to-day. Reports from parties who have been on the hill indicate that the straits are open at present."

"December 7th.—A new water-hole was dug in the lake with great difficulty, as there were no proper tools for the work and the ice is nearly four feet thick."

"December 8th.—Brainard happily shot two blue foxes which together weighed seven and three-fourths pounds. Gardiner relieved me by talking an hour or more regarding Philadelphia. In cleaning out the snow from the vestibule the can of alcohol was unfortunately struck, and a small quantity (perhaps a pint) was lost. The careless man was soundly berated by the community at large."

"December 9th.—Two blue foxes were shot to-day, weighing over five pounds; one by Long and one by Brainard. The large number of foxes killed lately encourages us to hope that the supply may continue. One of the foxes shot was but half blue; all others have been distinctly blue or white, the blue species being invariably the smaller. Rice gave a glowing account of a year spent in one of the tropical islands of the Gulf of Mexico. The contrast to our present situation was so great that it added to the force of his graphic descriptions."

"December 10th.—A strong westerly gale, with drifting snow. Temperature, -27° (-32.8° C.). Dr. Pavy informs me that Elison's feet will be saved. Part of one hand must be eventually lost, but no amputation will be made in our present camp. The patient is cheerful, talks much, and his face has healed to such an extent that he enjoys smoking."

"December 11th.—Bierderbick, who does not agree with the doctor, told Lieutenant Lockwood that Elison would lose his feet and part of his hands, as the line of demarcation is quite plain, being just below the ankle in the feet, and through the fingers of the hands.

"Brainard overworking himself again, and was faint and dizzy this evening. I was obliged to remonstrate with him for doing other work than issuing, as I have forbidden it; but when he points out the apathy of the party, and the necessity, I am silenced. Every one does the best he can, and I regret bitterly that I have only the ability to kill time, and am unable to do besides the hard physical labor."

"December 13th.—Trouble in Lieutenant Kislingbury's mess to-day; they accuse Frederick of unfairness in dividing the rations. Dr Pavy, Henry, and Whisler stated they had plotted to catch Frederick dealing unfairly. At my request, Lieutenant Kislingbury listened to all the members of his mess had to say upon the subject. After hearing all the testimony, to which I also listened, Lieutenant Kislingbury decided that the complaints were unfounded, and he desired that Frederick should remain on duty as their cook. I concurred in Lieutenant Kislingbury's opinion; but, in order to prevent any recurrence of such a suspicion, directed that hereafter the bread should be brought in by Sergeant Brainard, that its division should be made openly in the presence of the party by Frederick into the mess-pans, and that these portions should be hereafter distributed to that mess by the different members in turn, it being understood that the cook should receive the one which was left. We have so far avoided following the rule in the 'Investigator,' where the carver took the portion remaining after each man had helped himself. One bit of flame, affording about as much light as a poor tallow candle, suffices for the entire hut. The steam and smoke which are produced in cooking are so dense that but few of the party are able to even sit up in their bags while cooking is going on, and only on favorable occasions can a man see the face of his neighbor touching him. In the midst of these dense clouds of smoke and steam, without any additional light, the cooks are obliged to divide the stews, tea, and other food. I do not believe that either cook has intentionally shown partiality to any member of the mess, or retained an extra quantity for himself. The ravenous, irritable condition in which the entire party are at present cannot but have the effect of making most men morbid and suspicious. Sergeant Gardiner lately said to me that he objected very decidedly to passing Rice's ration to him, if it could be avoided. He declared that he realized the fairness of the cooks, but that, in allowing a cup of tea or a plate of stew to pass through his hands, he could not prevent himself from mentally weighing the food as it passed, by comparing it to the portion which came to himself. Such a comparison he knew was small and petty, but his starving condition must explain and excuse it. I readily understood his feelings, as I myself have avoided handing another man's portion for similar reasons.

"Discouraging weather—high winds, with a temperature of -25° (-31.7° C.), which makes our hut even colder than usual."

Looking back on those days, when an ounce of food was worth far more than its weight in gold, I wonder only that our two cooks, Long and Frederick, aggravated and excited by the odor of their dishes, came so blameless from the ordeal of a long winter night, where all eyes watched as far as possible their every motion and action.

ONE OF THE STRONGEST OF GREELY'S MEN WAS DAVID L. BRAINARD. *He kept a journal, too, and our next excerpt continues the story in the following April, after the winter's long, slow, terrible starvation.*

BESSIE ROWLAND JAMES

Six Came Back: The Arctic Adventure of

David L. Brainard

X
DEATH

April 2nd [1884].
Rice and Fredericks remained at the fishing grounds seven hours, returning with thirty-two pounds of shrimps.

Eskimo Fred's ration has been increased to the same amount received by the hunters. Fred does not improve. In face, he is failing rapidly. He is now sulky and angry because he is not given more food. He has always been so faithful and devoted that I cannot complain of him now when it is hunger and not the man who speaks....

April 5th.
Eskimo Fred died at 9 A.M. Although not altogether unexpected, his death was very sudden. He was outdoors during the night and ate his breakfast only two hours before he died. He then passed away quietly and without pain. The exposure incident to his trip with Long to Mount Carey last month is the immediate cause of Fred's death. Really, though, he slowly starved to death. His remains were interred on Cemetery Ridge at 2 P.M. and a salute fired over his grave.

Jens did not display the stoicism usually attributed to the people of his race, but exhibited signs of deep and heart-felt emotion. Nevertheless, Jens speaks hope-fully of the future and recommends Eskimo Point as an excellent hunting ground. To keep up his spirit at this time when his countryman has passed away, the Commanding Officer has ordered double rations for Jens until further orders.

No game was seen by the hunters today although they worked faithfully.

I worked nearly all day getting Rice and Fredericks ready for the field. They start for Baird Inlet tomorrow.

I am afraid that Lieut. Lockwood and Linn will soon follow the faithful Eskimo who has just died. They cannot, or will not, eat the shrimps any longer. Although they are given an extra allowance of dovekie, it is not suffi-cient to restore their depleted strength. Heaven help them!

Sunday, April 6th.

Linn, our comrade and trusted friend, passed away quietly at 7 P.M. During the winter Linn had been rather petulant and irritable. This was not his natural disposition. His mind was weakened during those awful two days and nights that he and Fredericks spent in the sleeping bag with Elison.

Whatever irritation Linn exhibited, it was quickly forgiven and forgotten by all of us. At Fort Conger in good health he was a noble, generous-hearted, faithful fellow and this is how we always will remember him.

Death in our midst has ceased to rouse our emotions. How indifferently we look on anything of this kind now! After Linn's death, Rice and Ralston slept soundly in the same bag with the corpse which we hope to have strength enough to prepare for burial tomorrow.

As contemplated, Rice and Fredericks departed on their hazardous mission to Baird Inlet at 9:15 P.M. Earlier in the day Lieut. Kislingbury, Ellis and I hauled their travelling equipment on the small sledge to the summit of the island, thus saving their strength somewhat. I do not believe that anyone has ever until today really appreciated the full extent of our weakness. We had to ascend the gla-cier near the shrimping grounds. Four hours and ten minutes were required to reach the summit and one hour and thirty minutes to return. This trial has fully convinced us of the utter hopelessness of escape to Littleton Island.

Our farewells to Rice and Fredericks were uttered with husky voices and tremulous lips. The silent prayers of those who remained went with them and eyes, to which tears were strangers, were dimmed with the love and fear we felt for these two brave souls. Weak and despondent, they go out alone in the bleak wastes of an Arctic desert, taking their lives in their hands, to bring food to their starving companions. Before them lie famine, indescribable cold, torture to their minds and then, perhaps, failure. And in the hut we must wait for the end of the story.

April 7th.
Snow has been falling heavily all day. Temperature at 6 A.M. −8.7°.

Poor Linn was buried at 10 A.M. Lieut. Lislingbury scooped out a grave for him on Cemetery Ridge which was only six inches deep. It was all eight of us could do to haul the body to the ridge on the large sledge, although Linn was literally a skeleton.

I shot two ptarmigan this morning with one shot.

Biederbick diluted a quantity of alcohol and, with some slight flavoring, made an excellent moonshine drink which imparted warmth and life to the poor fellows for a short time.

Lieut. Lockwood and Jewell will soon follow Linn. They are very weak. Jens is in good spirits and continues to predict success to the hunters with warm weather.

Several of the party are writing their wills, as well as letters to their friends.

April 8th.
All last night and throughout the day, snow has fallen and high winds prevailed. The drift was at times terrific. Rice and Fredericks must be suffering greatly in this storm.

Diluted alcohol was again issued with a most satisfactory effect.

Salor said that he was no longer able to walk to the shrimping grounds, and I have relieved him. After dinner I went down through the howling storm and returned at 9 P.M. with 15 pounds of shrimps.

April 9th.
Lieut. Lockwood became unconscious early this morning and at 4:20 P.M. breathed his last. This will be a sad blow to his family who evidently idolized him. To me it is also a sorrowful event. He had been my companion during long and eventful excursions, and my feeling toward him was akin to that of a brother. Biederbick and myself straightened his limbs and prepared his remains for burial. This was the saddest duty I have ever yet been called upon to perform.

Moonshine was again issued today.

The order of August, 1881, relieving Lieut. Kislingbury from duty with the expedition, was revoked today and that officer once more restored to duty. Lieut. Greely eulogized him from Fort Conger, and expressed a wish that their future intercourse might be of the most agreeable nature. The reinstatement was made to provide a second in command, since Lieut. Lockwood is dead.

Ellis was again detected eating a stearine and, as a punishment, his dinner was denied him. He wept and begged in the most abject manner for a remission of his sentence, and Lieut. Greely finally modified it so that only half a cup of tea was taken from him.

I took an inventory of provisions this morning, with the following result: Meat of all kinds, 156 pounds; bread, 70 pounds. And on this we expect to prolong life another month until May 10th. The future is dark and gloomy. I think that Arctic clouds are seldom seen with a silver lining.

[After the death of his first officer, Lieutenant Greely took out the map that Lockwood and Barinard had charted on their dash along Greenland's northern coast. Beside a tiny dot at the Farthest North, he wrote, "Mary Murray Island," giving it the name of the favorite sister of whom Lieutenant Lockwood talked unceasingly as his end drew near.]

April 10th.

The storm, which has been raging for four days, abated about 8 P.M. What can have been the fate of Rice and Fredericks in the snow and wind? I have thought of them every moment, of what they must be suffering and wondered whether they could endure and survive.

Jewell is endeavoring to rally, but the attempt is a feeble one. He does not relish the shrimps and his death by starvation seems inevitable.

The last, sad rites were performed over the remains of Lockwood, and he was interred with the others on Cemetery Ridge.

Although Biederbick is quite ill, he continues in wonderful spirits and does all in his power to cheer his more dependent companions. Gardiner is gradually drooping, and Connell and Ellis are beginning to feel to a marked degree the effects of this horrible life.

Jens is feeling far from well. What could we do without his assitance?

The alcoholic drink was again issued and pleasant results followed. I used the last of the bird skins for shrimp bait this evening.

Whistler made a most startling statement to both the Commanding Officer and myself regarding the disloyal conduct of Dr. Pavy during the autumn of 1881, when they were traveling toward Cape Joseph Henry.

[The original diary does not give the particulars of Whisler's statement. Some years later Brainard inserted the following between the pages of the manuscript:

Fort Bidewell, Cal.,
February 3rd, 1890.

The "disloyal conduct" as stated by Whisler, was to this effect. In October 1881, he (Dr. Pavy) left Fort Conger with party of Private Whisler and Jens, Eskimo dog driver, taking a dog team and sledge with provisions for a journey to Cape Joseph Henry. While on this journey, Whisler states that Dr. Pavy tried to induce him to join in an expedition to the north the following year, with the intention of making the highest latitude ever attained, and, further, that Whisler should join him in stealing the only remaining dog team at the station so that the North Greenland Party (Lieutenant Lockwood and Sergeant Brainard) could not travel so far, while the Doctor's party would be enabled to go much farther north. Whisler says that on his refusal to aid the Doctor in such a scheme, the latter became angry and abusive, whereupon W. drew a revolver.

D.L.B.

April 11th.

The most beautiful day that we have had this month. Clear and a temperature of −23° at 4 A.M. and the sun shining all day. What more could we ask?

Long and Jens went down to the open water, but saw nothing except a walrus, which they could not reach. Long narrowly escaped being carried away this morning. A piece of the floe on which he was standing at the water's edge broke from the main body of ice and drifted out to sea. From a distance Jens saw Long's situation and paddled out to him in his kayak. Long urged him in vain to return to the fast ice and save himself. The faithful fellow refused to obey and explained in his simple way, "You go, me go too." Fortunately the turning tide wafted them back to the fast ice.

Israel broke down completely this morning. Jewell does not rally, except under the influence of stimulants. Late in the evening he became delirious.

Owing to my heavy duties, Lieut. Greely ordered me to issue myself two ounces of pemmican daily. He also directed that the rations of Jewell and Israel be increased four ounces each daily. We are all once more making imaginary bills of fare, and partaking of sumptuous repasts.

Whisler volunteered to relieve me at the shrimp fishery this morning. He went down at four o'clock, returning with about three pounds. At 11:30 A.M., having fished three hours, I brought in about eight pounds. After dinner I went down again. While waiting for the tardy little crustaceans to collect, I walked up and down to keep from freezing, my mind occupied with thoughts of our deplorable situation and then again with dishes of which I would like to partake.

Chancing to glance in the direction of Beebe Point, I saw a medium-sized bear about two hundred yards away approaching at a shambling gait. My first impulse was to hide behind a hummock and attack with the hatchet and seaweed spear. These, however, did not strike me as particularly devastating weapons for an encounter with a hungry bear, especially when wielded by one whose strength scarcely equals that of a child's. Taking the five pounds of shrimps which I had collected (I could not afford to lose both the shrimps and the bear), I moved away as quickly as I could toward the hut. It seemed ages while I was crawling over Cemetery Ridge. I feared the bear might get away before I could reach the hunters and I feared, too, that he might overtake me. Near the house I abandoned my heavy mittens and shrimp bucket to increase my speed.

Crawling on my hands and knees, I pushed open the door with my head and fell into the hut, yelling, "Bear!!!"

I was too exhausted to say more. A quantity of diluted alcohol was poured down my throat and in a moment I was able to tell Long and Jens where I had seen the bear. They started out immediately. Lieut. Kislingbury also went out but, having run to Cemetery Ridge, he broke down.

At 9:50 P.M. we heard the hunters returning. From the time we heard their footsteps until they entered the hut, the suspense was terrible. Our lives were hanging in the balance and the chances for life or death were equal. And then they came and announced their success. The bear was lying dead within a few feet of the open water about three miles away.

Everything was at once excitement and animation. Within twenty minutes the large sledge was ready and Dr. Pavy, Long, Schneider, Henry, Whisler, Ralston, Salor, Ellis and myself went down to the open water. Before starting three ounces of bacon were issued each that our strength might be maintained.

The open water was reached at midnight and with considerable difficulty the heavy animal loaded and fastened to the sledge. The blood which had flowed from the bullet holes over the ice was chopped out with a hatchet and saved.

This is Good Friday. We hope it is the last fast day we will experience in these regions.

April 12th.
We started back from the open water after midnight, reaching the hut at 2:20 A.M. We had made a most remarkable trip, considering our weak condition. Ellis accompanied us half a mile when his strength was exhausted and he turned back.

Amid feeble cheers, our still more feeble men hauled the glorious prize into the middle of the hut where he was skinned and dressed by Bender and Biederbick. Everything will be utilized—intestines, lungs, heart, head, etc. The liver, wind-pipe, feet and stomach (which was nearly empty) have been set aside for shrimp bait. The blood will thicken our stews.

This fellow is our salvation. Without him Ellis, Connell, Bender, Biederbick, Israel, Gardiner, Salor and Kislingbury would have been in their graves in two weeks. No words can express the rejoicing in our little party today. For days and weeks we had been expecting death at any time, and its approach had been robbed of all its terrors by our sufferings. Life had seemed to us a vague something in the misty distance which was beyond our power to reach or control. Now, to believe that we will be enabled to reach our homes, was sufficient cause for tears.

Jewell died at 10 A.M. without a struggle. Biederbick and myself closed his eyes and straightened his thin limbs. At 2 P.M. he was placed beside the others on Cemetery Ridge. Poor fellow! Had the bear been killed twenty-four hours earlier, he might have been saved.

Lieut. Greely was kind enough to transfer me to the Signal Corps with the rank of sergeant, subject to the approval of the Hon. Secretary of War.

Meat ration has been increased to eight ounces per day. The hunters and shrimper (Long, Jens and myself) will receive eight ounces extra meat daily. Ellison also receives the same.

The hunters rested today and Bender repaired their guns.

Sunday, April 13th.

After two days of joy over the bear, gloom settled down over the party today with the arrival of Fredericks who reported the death of our beloved friend and comrade, Rice, at Baird Inlet on April 9th, during the progress of a severe storm. They had reached Eskimo Point where they abandoned everything except their sledge, rum, fuel and a few rations. They then proceeded out on the floe of the inlet in search of the meat. No trace of it could be found during the driving storm. Rice at last (3 P.M.) broke down from exhaustion and weakness and at 7:45 P.M. breathed his last. With cheering words and stimulants, Fredericks tried to revive him, but all in vain.

Can anyone conceive a sadder picture than the distracted survivor lying on a sledge with his dead companion in his arms, miles from any human being, and no power on earth to assist him? The storm howled about Fredericks and blinding drift added to his sufferings. He scooped a shallow grave in the snow and in it placed the body of his friend. A heap of broken ice is all that marks the resting place of the bravest and noblest of this expedition.

Fredericks brought back all their effects on the sledge as far as Cocked Hat Island where he abandoned them. He performed his duty nobly and this trip in which he and Rice participated will ever be conspicuous as one of the most heroic efforts made by men in these regions. Although utterly worn out and weakened by his various trials, Fredericks brought back untouched Rice's remaining rations to be returned to the common larder.

Long shot a small seal at noon and Whisler and I hauled him in. He will weigh about sixty pounds, in addition to twenty-five pounds of blubber.

Lieut. Greely increased our meat ration to one pound daily to offset the sad news of Rice's death and our disappointment in losing the English meat.

Elison was promoted and transferred to the Signal Corps to fill the vacancy left by Rice.

[In the files of the War Department, written in his own hand, is Sergeant Frederick's report of the death of the "bravest and noblest of this expedition":

"I discovered about 4 P.M. that Rice was weakening. I therefore reminded him of the agreement made before leaving Camp Clay, that in case either of us should show signs of exhaustion his comrade should tell him, in order that necessary steps might be taken to prevent disaster, and

I again urged upon Rice the necessity of returning to the sleeping bag for rest and shelter.

"But he said that he was only a little tired, and would soon recover by traveling a little slow. After a short time, however, I could plainly see that Rice was weakening rapidly, and observing an iceberg about 1,000 yards to the west of us, I urged upon Rice to reach it in order to obtain at least a partial shelter. We fortunately accomplished this. By this time he was almost completely exhausted. I gave him some brandy and spirits of ammonia, which seemed to revive him. I now lighted the lamp and prepared some warm food for him; after having eaten it and drunk a cup of warm tea I endeavored to start him, in order to keep him from freezing, but it was all in vain. His condition was becoming alarming. He was too weak to stand up, and his mind seemed to be taken up with recollections of his relatives and friends at home, of whom he spoke, and he also kept talking of the different meals he would eat when he should have reached home....We remained here on this desolate piece of ice, with the wind blowing a hurricane, for two hours or more, after which time my poor heroic companion lost consciousness. I did everything for him that my limited means permitted. I wrapped him up in my *temiak* in order to keep him as warm as possible, and remained on the sledge amidst the drifting snow with my unconscious friend in my arms until 7:45 P.M., when poor Rice passed away. My situation can be easier imagined than described. Here I was left alone with the body of my friend in an icebound region, out of reach of help or assistance. The death of my companion under these circumstances made a deeper impression on my mind than any experience my whole life. As here I stood, completely exhausted, by the remains of poor Rice, shivering with the cold, unable to bury the remains, hardly able to move, I knew that my chances to reach Eskimo Point, which was about 7 miles to the north, were small indeed. I was completely disheartened; I felt more like remaining here and perishing by the side of my companion than to make another effort, but the sense of the duty which I owed to my country and my companions and to my dead comrade to bear back the sad tidings of the disaster, sustained me in this trial. I stopped and kissed the remains of my dead companion and left them there for the wild winds of the Arctic to sweep over.

"I traveled to the north, and after 7 hours of hard travel I reached the sleeping bag completely exhausted. I found the bag frozen stiff as a piece of cordwood, and in my weak condition I was unable to unroll it, and I thought surely that I should have to perish here; but, as fortune would have it, I found in my pocket a small vial which contained a few drops of ammonia, which I took. This revived me so that it enabled me to get into the bag, where I lay until the following morning. I then hustled out about 8 A.M.; got some warm food, and started back to bury the remains of my companion.... When I reached the gloomy spot where lay the remains of poor Rice, thinking that he might have something on his person which ought to be returned to his relatives, I searched his clothing, and found several small articles....

"I then began the difficult task of digging a grave for the remains of my poor friend, which was accomplished after hard labor of several hours. I had no shovel, only an ax, and the loose ice I had to remove with my hands, and it is here, on a paleocrystic floe, that I laid the remains of one who was so dear to me. Here, in this icy grave, I leave my comrade, and will endeavor to carry back the sad news to our companions. After a few hours I again reached Eskimo Point where I camped for the night...."

✳

THE SEVEN SURVIVORS WERE RESCUED ON JUNE 22 OF THAT YEAR. *One more died almost immediately. The editor of Brainard's account notes that on the day they were rescued, when Brainard tried to make another entry in his journal, he was too weak to hold his pencil.*

The American public soured on Arctic exploration after the De Long and Greely disasters. The Arctic was a starving ground. If you did not starve you died of the cold, or the terrible labor of trying to cross the corrugated ice of the Arctic Ocean. You could not win in the Arctic; you could not beat it. You struggled across the ice, making a few miles a day, and the drift took you farther south than you had hauled north. Rescue was difficult if not impossible. In the summer the ice that enclosed your ship might or might not melt. The winter darkness drove you mad. Men seemed helpless in the face of this overwhelming place—nature extreme, indifferent, huge. Men bickered with each other, came to hate each other, in their confined spaces. The smallest error killed you.

But the North Pole had still to be conquered, and if Americans weren't eager to try for it, the Scandinavians were. They came at it, furthermore, with the built-in experience of living in subArctic conditions. They were born knowing how to ski, they were used to long winters and winter darkness, they were acclimatized. Nordenskjold had already made the Northeast Passage look easy, and he had become a national hero. The great Swedish explorer Sven Hedin remembered as a child watching the celebrations when Nordenskjold returned to Stockholm on his ship, the Vega. For Hedin that was all the inspiration he needed. He decided on the spot that he wanted that kind of acclaim.

A similar acclaim was to await the Norwegian Fridtjof Nansen. Nansen was not only an explorer, he was a neuroscientist, highly respected in his field. After his triumphs as an explorer he became involved in the negotiations that led to Norway's independence from Sweden. After World War I he attended the Peace Conference at Versailles and was asked in 1920 to head a commission to provide relief to the hundreds of thousands of people, most of them prisoners of war, that the War had displaced all across Europe, and get them home. He invented the so-called Nansen passport to facilitate the process, he led a famine relief program to Greece, and when it was all over, in 1922, the Swedes gave him the Nobel Peace Prize.

Nansen first demonstrated his prowess when he skied across the Greenland ice cap in 1888, starting on the uninhabited east coast so that he could not turn back to rescue, and, six weeks later, reaching the west coast and safety. This was a first and it made Nansen's name. His next idea was much more interesting. He had become intrigued when in 1884 wreckage and debris from the Jeannette, which foundered off the coast of Siberia, turned up on the coast of Greenland. Other pieces of Siberian origin—native throwing sticks, driftwood that could be identified as from tree species native to Siberia— also turned up. Only ocean currents could do this, so there must be a current that crossed the Arctic Ocean near the Pole. If you could construct a ship that could ride the ice, you might simply drift to the North Pole and wind up somewhere near Greenland. All you needed was a proper ship.

It took nine years and the Greenland crossing, which gave him the status to raise the funds, but in 1893 he set out in a ship called the Fram whose rounded sides made it ride up onto the ice when it was frozen in. The ship was more or less indestructible. The only danger, he realized, was from boredom. Once they were frozen into the ice the drift might take years, and who could endure it? Norwegians. He took only thirteen men with him, all of them Norwegians, all hand-picked, not only for their ability but for their patience. Patience was essential in a voyage such as this. Fergus Fleming in Ninety Degrees North quotes him as saying that "two Norwegians, alone of all other nationals, could sit face to face on a cake of ice for three years without hating each other." He also abolished all rank on board the ship. They all shared the work, and they would all share equally in the glory if they lived.

It was Nansen himself who finally got too bored to stay with the ship on its drift. The Fram steamed from Vardo at the northern tip of Norway across the top of Russia to the New Siberian Islands, and then into the pack. By late September 1893, the ship was frozen in. Over the ensuing year it followed a zigzag course in the Laptev Sea, trending north, but not far enough to reach the Pole; the ship never got much higher than 85 degrees north latitude. Late in 1894 Nansen decided to try for the Pole by sledge, taking one man with him, leaving the rest of his shipmates to drift home. His companion was a man named Hjalmar Johansen. They traveled with three sledges, three kayaks, 28 dogs, and food for 100 days. They left on March 14, 1895. We join them on that day. We leave them when they reach their farthest north, which was the farthest north any human being had ever been.

FRIDTJOF NANSEN

Farthest North: The Exploration of the Fram, 1893-96

II
WE SAY GOODBYE TO THE Fram

AT LAST BY MIDDAY, ON MARCH 14, WE FINALLY LEFT THE Fram, TO THE noise of a thundering salute. For the third time farewells and mutual good wishes were exhcanged. Some of our comrades came a little way with us, but Sverdrup soon turned back in order to be on board for dinner at 1 o'clock. It was on the top of a hummock that we two said goodbye to each other; the Fram was lying behind us, and I can remember how I stood watching him as her strode easily homewards on his snowshoes. I half wished I could turn back with him and find myself in the warm saloon; I knew only too well that a life of toil lay before us, and that it would be many a long day before we should again sleep and eat under a comfortable roof; but that that time was going to be so long as it really proved to be, none of us then had any idea. We all thought that either the expedition would succeed, and that we should return home that same year, or- that it would not succeed.

A little while after Sverdrup had left us, Mogstad also found it necessary to turn back. He had thought of going with us till the next day, but his heavy wolf-skin trousers were, as he un-euphemistically expressed it, 'almost full of sweat, and he must go back to the fire on board to get dry.' Hansen, Henriksen, and

Pettersen were then the only ones left, and they laboured along each with his load on his back. It was difficult for them to keep up with us on the flat ice, so quickly did we go; but when we came to pressure-ridges we were brought to a standstill and the sledges had to be helped over. At one place the ridge was so bad that we had to carry the sledges a long way. When, after considerable trouble, we had managed to get over it, Peter shook his head reflectively, and said to Johansen that we should meet plenty more of the same kind, and have enough hard work before we had eaten sufficient of the loads to make the sledges run lightly. Just here we came upon a long stretch of bad ice, and Peter became more and more concerned for our future; but towards evening matters improved, and we advanced more rapidly. When we stopped at 6 o'clock the odometer registered a good 7 miles, which was not so bad for a first day's work. We had a cheerful evening in our tent, which was just about big enough to hold all five. Pettersen, who had exerted himself and become over-heated on the way, shivered and groaned while the dogs were being tied up and fed, and the tent pitched.

He, however, found existence considerably brighter when he sat inside it, in his warm wolfskin clothes, with a pot of smoking chocolate before him, a big lump of butter in one hand and a biscuit in the other, and exclaimed, 'Now I am living like a prince.' He thereafter discoursed at length on the exalting thought that he was sitting in a tent in the middle of the Polar Sea. Poor fellow, he had begged and prayed to be allowed to come with us on this expedition; he would cook for us and make himself generally useful, both as a tin and blacksmith; and then, he said, three would be company. I regretted that I could not take more than one companion, and he had been in the depths of woe for several days, but now found comfort in the fact that he had, at any rate, come part of the way with us, and was out on this great desert sea, for, as he said, 'not many people have done that.'

The others had no sleeping-bag with them, so they made themselves a cosy little hut of snow, into which they crawled in their wolfskin garments, and had a tolerably good night. I was awake early the next morning; but when I crept out of the tent I found that somebody else was on his legs before me, and this was Pettersen, who, awakened by the cold, was now walking up and down to warm his stiffened limbs. He had tried it now, he said; he never should have thought it possible to sleep in the snow, but it had not been half bad. He would not quite admit that he had been cold, and that was the reason why he had turned out so early. Then we had our last pleasant breakfast together, got the sledges ready, harnessed the dogs, shook hands with our companions, and, without many words being uttered on either side, started out in solitude. Peter shook his head sorrowfully as we went off. I turned round when we had gone some little way, and saw his figure on the top of the hummock; he was still looking after us. His thoughts were probably sad; perhaps he believed that he had spoken to us for the last time.

We found large expanses of flat ice, and covered the ground quickly, farther and farther away from our comrades, into the unknown, where we two alone and the dogs were to wander for months. The *Fram's* rigging had disappeared long ago behind the margin of the ice. We often came on piled-up ridges and uneven ice, where the sledges had to be helped and sometimes carried over. It often happened, too, that they capsized altogether, and it was only by dint of strenuous hauling that we righted them again. Somewhat exhausted by all this hard work, we stopped finally at 6 o'clock in the evening, and had then gone about 9 miles during the day. They were not quite the marches I had reckoned on, but we hoped that by degrees the sledges would become lighter, and the ice better to travel over. The latter, too, seems to have been the case at first. On Sunday, March 17, I say in my diary: 'The ice appears to be more even the farther north we get; came across a lane, however, yesterday which necessitated a long detour.[1] At half past six we had done about 9 miles. As we had just reached a good camping-ground, and the dogs were tired, we stopped. Lowest temperature last night, -45° F (-42.3° C.)'

The ice continued to become more even during the following days, and our marches often amounted to 14 miles or more in the day. Now and then a misfortune might happen which detained us, as, for instance, one day a sharp spike of ice which was standing up cut a hole in a sack of fish-flour, and all the delicious food ran out. It took us more than an hour to collect it all again, and repair

---

[1] It was not advisable for many reasons to cross the lanes in the kayaks, now that the temperature was so low. Even if the water in the lanes had not nearly always been covered with a more or less thick layer of ice, the kayaks would have become much heavier from the immediate freezing of the water which would have entered them, for they proved to be not absolutely impervious; and this ice we had then no means of dislodging.

the damages. Then the odometer got broken through process of lashing. But on we went northwards, often over great, wide ice-plains which seemed as if they must stretch right to the Pole. Sometimes it happened that we passed through places where the ice was 'unusually massive, with high hummocks, so that it looked like undulating country covered with snow.' This was undoubtedly very old ice, which had drifted in the Polar Sea for a long time on its way from the Siberian Sea to the east coast of Greenland, and must have been subjected year after year to severe pressure. High hummocks and mounds are thus formed, which summer after summer are partially melted by the rays of the sun, and again in the winters covered with great drifts of snow, so that they assume forms which resemble ice-hills, rather than piles of sea-ice resulting from upheaval. *Wednesday, March 20,* my diary says:

Beautiful weather for travelling in, with fine sunsets; but somewhat cold, particularly in the bag, at nights (it was −41.8° and −43.6°F, for −41° and −42°C). The ice appears to be getting more even the farther we advance, and in some places it is like travelling over 'inland ice'. If this goes on the whole thing will be done in no time. That day we lost our odometer, and as we did not find it out till some time afterwards, and I did not know how far we might have to go back, I thought it was not worth while to return and look for. It was the cause, however, of our only being able subsequently to guess approximately at the distance we had gone during the day. We had another mishap, too, that day. This was that one of the dogs (it was Livjaegeren) had become so ill that he could not be driven any longer, and we had to let him go loose. It was late in the day before we discovered that he was not with us; he had stopped behind at our camping ground when we broke up in the morning, and I had to go back after him on snowshoes, which caused a long delay.

Thursday, March 21. Nine in the morning −43.6°F, or −42°C. (Minimum in the night, -47.2° F, or −44° C). Clear, as it has been every day. Beautiful, bright weather; glorious for travelling in, but somewhat cold at nights, with the quicksilver continually frozen. Patching Finn-shoes in this temperature inside the tent, with one's nose slowly freezing away, is not all pure enjoyment.

Friday, March 22. Splendid ice for getting over; things go better and better. Wide expanses, with a few pressure-ridges now and then, but passable everywhere. Kept at it yesterday from about half past eleven in the morning to half past eight at night, did a good 21 miles, I hope. We should be in about latitude

85°. The only disagreeable thing to face now is the cold. Our clothes are transformed more and more into a cuirass of ice during the day, and wet bandages at night. The blankets likewise. The sleeping-bags get heavier and heavier from the moisture which freezes on the hair inside. The same clear settled weather every day. We are both longing now for a change; a few clouds and a little more mildness would be welcome.

The temperature in the night, -44.8° F (-42.7° C). By an observation which I took later in the forenoon, our latitude that day proved to be 85° 9'N.

Saturday, March 23. On account of observation, lashing the loads on the sledges, patching bags, and other occupations of a like kind, which are no joke in this low temperature, we did not manage to get off yesterday before 3 o'clock in the afternoon. We stuck to it till nine in the evening, when we stopped in some of the worst ice we have seen lately. Our day's march, however, had lain across several large tracts of level ice, so I think that we made 14 miles or so all the same. We have the same brilliant sunshine; but yesterday afternoon the wind from the north-east, which we have had for the last few days, increased, and made it rather raw.

We passed over a large frozen pool yesterday evening; it looked almost like a large lake.

It could not have been long since this was formed, as the ice on it was still quite thin. It is wonderful that these pools can form up there at that time of the year.

From this time forward there was an end of the flat ice, which it had been simple enjoyment to travel over; and now we had often great difficulties to cope with. On *Sunday, March 24,* I write:

Ice not so good; yesterday was a hard day, but we made a few miles, not more, though, than seven, I am afraid. This continual lifting of the heavily loaded sledge is calculated to break one's back; but better times are coming, perhaps. The cold is also appreciable, always the same; but yesterday it was increased by the admixture of considerable wind from the north-east. We halted about half past nine in the evening. It is perceptible how the days lengthen, and how much later the sun sets; in a few days' time we shall have the midnight sun.

We killed Livaegeren yesterday evening, and hard work it was skinning him.

This was the first dog which had to be killed; but many came afterwards, and it was some of the most disagreeable work we had on the journey, particularly now at the beginning when it was so cold. When the first dog was dismembered and given to the other, many of them went supperless the whole night in preference to touching the meat. But as the days went by and they became more worn-out, they learned to appreciate dog's flesh, and later on we were not even so considerate as to skin the butchered animal, but served it hair and all.

The following day the ice was occasionally somewhat better; but as a rule it was bad, and we became more and more worn-out with the never ending work of helping the dogs, righting the sledges every time they capsized, and hauling, or carrying them bodily over hummocks and inequalities of the ground. Sometimes we were so sleepy in the evenings that our eyes shut and we fell asleep as we went along. My head would drop, and I would be awakened by suddenly falling forward on my snowshoes. Then we would stop, after having found a camping ground behind a hummock ridge of ice, where there was some shelter from the wind. While Johansen looked after the dogs, it generally fell to my lot to pitch the tent, fill the cooker with ice, light the burner and start the supper as quickly as possible. This generally consisted of *lobscouse* one day, made of pemmican and dried potatoes; another day of a sort of fish rissole substance known as *fiskegratin* in Norway, and in this case composed of fish-meal, flour, and butter. A third day it would be pea, bean, or lentil soup, with bread and pemmican. Johansen preferred the *lobscouse,* while I had a weakness for the *fiskegratin.* As time went by, however, he came over to my way of thinking, and the *fiskegratin* took precedence of everything else.

As soon as Johansen had finished with the dogs, and the different receptacles containing the ingredients and eatables for breakfast and supper were brought in, as well as our bags with private necessities; the sleeping-bags were spread out, the tent door carefully shut, and we crept into the bag to thaw our clothes. This was not very agreeable work. During the course of the day the damp exhaltions of the body had little by little become condensed in our outer garments, which were now a mass of ice and transformed into complete suits of ice-armour. They were so hard and stiff that if we had only been able to get them off they could have stood by themselves, and they crackled audibly every time we moved. These clothes were so stiff that the sleeve of my coat actually rubbed deep sores in my wrists during our marches; one of these sores— the one on the right hand—got frostbitten, the wound grew deeper and deeper, and nearly reached the bone. I tried to protect it with bandages, but not until late in the summer did it heal, and I shall probably have the scar for life. When we got into our sleeping-bags in the evening, our clothes began to thaw slowly, and on this process a considerable amount of physical heat was expended. We packed ourselves tight into the bag, and lay with our teeth chattering for an hour, or an hour and a half, before we became aware of a little warmth in our bodies which we sorely needed. At last our clothes became wet and pliant only to freeze again in a few minutes after we had turned out of the bag in the morning There was no question of getting these clothes dried on the journey so long as the cold lasted, as more and more moisture from the body collected in them.

How cold we were as we lay there shivering in the bag, waiting for the supper to be ready! I, who was cook, was obliged to keep myself more or less awake to see to the culinary operations, and sometimes I succeeded. At last the supper was ready, was portioned out and, as always, tasted delicious. These occasions were the supreme moments of our existence, moments to which we looked forward the whole day long. But sometimes we were so weary that our eyes closed, and we fell asleep with the food on its way to our mouths. Our hands would fall back inanimate with the spoons in them and the food fly out on the bag. After supper we generally permitted ourselves the luxury of a little extra drink, consisting of water, as hot as we could swallow it, in which whey-powder had been dissolved. It tasted something like boiled milk, and we thought it wonderfully comforting; it seemed to warm us to the very ends of our toes. Then we would creep down into the bag again, buckle the flap carefully over our heads, lie close together, and soon sleep the sleep of the just. But even in our dreams we went on ceaselessly, grinding at the sledges and driving the dogs, always northwards, and I was often awakened by hearing Johansen calling in his sleep to Pan, or Barrabas, or Klapperslangen: 'Get on, you devil, you! Go on, you brutes! Sass, sass![2] Now the whole thing is going over!' and execrations less fit for reproduction, until I went to sleep again.

In the morning, as cook, I was obliged to turn out to prepare the breakfast, which took an hour's time. As a rule, it consisted one morning of chocolate, bread, butter, and pemmican; another of oatmeal porridge, or a compound of flour, water, and butter, in imitation of our 'butter-porridge' at home. This was

[2] Used by the Lapps to their dogs.

washed down with milk, made of whey-powder and water. The breakfast ready, Johanasen was roused; we sat up in the sleeping-bag, one of the blankets was spread out as a tablecloth, and we fell to work. We had a comfortable breakfast, wrote up our diaries, and then had to think about starting. But how tired we sometimes were, and how often would I not have given anything to be able to creep to the bottom of the bag again and sleep the clock round. It seemed to me as if this must be the greatest pleasure in life, but our business was to fight our way northwards, always northwards. We performed our toilets, and then came the going out into the cold to get the sledges ready, disentangle the dogs' traces, harness the animals, and get off as quickly as possible. I went first to find the way through the uneven ice, then came the sledge with my kayak. The dogs soon learned to follow, but at every unevenness of the ground they stopped, and if one could not get them all to start again at the same time by a shout, and so pull the sledge over the difficulty, one had to go back to beat or help them, according as circumstances necessitated. Then came Johansen with the two other sledges, always shouting to the dogs to pull harder, always beating them, and himself hauling to get the sledges over the terrible ridges of ice. It was undeniable cruelty to the poor animals from first to last, and one must often look back on it with horror. It makes me shudder even now when I think of how we beat them mercilessly with thick ash sticks when, hardly able to move, they stopped from sheer exhaustion. It made one's heart bleed to see them, but we turned our eyes away and hardened ourselves. It was necessary; forward we must go, and to this end everything else must give place. It is the sad part of expeditions of this kind that one systematically kills all better feelings, until only hard-hearted egoism remains. When I think of all those splendid animals, toiling for us without a murmur, as long as they could strain a muscle, never getting any thanks or even so much as a kind word, daily writhing under the lash until the time came when they could do no more and death freed them from their pangs—when I think of how they were left behind, one by one, up there on those desolate ice-fields, which had been witness to their faithfulness and devotion, I have moments of bitter self-reproach.

It took us two alone such a long time to pitch the tent, feed the dogs, cook, etc., in the evening, and then break up again and get ready in the morning, that the days never seemed long enough if we were to do proper day's marches, and, besides, get the sleep we required at night. But when the nights became so light, it was not so necessary to keep regular hours any longer, and we started when we pleased, whether it was night or day. We stopped, too, when it suited us, and took the sleep which might be necessary for ourselves and the dogs. I tried to make it a rule that our marches were to be of nine or ten hours' duration. In the middle of the day we generally had a rest and something to eat; as a rule bread and butter, with a little pemmican or liver paté. These dinners were a bitter trial. We used to try and find a good sheltered place, and sometimes even rolled ourselves up in our blankets, but all the same the wind cut right through us as we sat on the sledges eating our meal. Sometimes, again, we spread the sleeping-bag out on the ice, took our food with us, and crept well in, but even then did not succeed in thawing either it or our clothes. When this was too much for us we walked up and down to keep ourselves warm, and ate our food as we walked. Then came the no less bitter task of disentangling the dogs' traces, and we were glad when we could get off again. In the afternoon, as a rule, we each had a piece of meat—chocolate.

Most Arctic travellers who have gone on sledge journeys have complained of the so-called Arctic thirst, and it has been considered an almost unavoidable evil in connection with a long journey across wastes of snow. It is often increased, too, by the eating of snow. I had prepared myself for this thirst, from which we had also suffered severely when crossing Greenland, and had taken with me a couple of india-rubber flasks, which we filled with water every morning from the cooker, and by carrying in the breast were able to protect from the cold. To my great astonishment, however, I soon discovered that the whole day would often pass by without my as much as tasting the water in my flask. As time went by, the less need did I feel to drink during the day, and at last I gave up taking water with me altogether. If a passing feeling of thirst made itself felt, a piece of fresh ice, of which, as a rule, there was always some to be found, was sufficient to dispel it.[3] The reason why we were spared this suffering which has been one of the greatest hardships of many sledge expeditions, must be attributed in a great measure to our admirable cooking apparatus. By the

---

[3] Whereas eating snow may increase the above-mentioned feeling of thirst, and have disagreeable consequences in other ways, sucking a piece of ice, which will soon quench it, may safely be resorted to, particularly if it be held in the hand a little while before putting it to the mouth. Many travellers have, no doubt, had the same experience.

help of this we were able, with the consumption of a minimal of fuel, to melt and boil so much water every morning that we could drink all we wished. There was even some left over, as a rule, which had to be thrown away. The same thing was generally the case in the evening.

Friday, March 29. We are grinding on, but very slowly. The ice is only tolerable, and not what I expected from the beginning. There are often great ridges of piled up ice of dismal aspect, which take up a great deal of time, as one must go on ahead to find a way, and, as a rule, make a greater or less detour to get over them. In addition, the dogs are growing rather slow and slack, and it is almost impossible to get them on. And then this endless disentangling of the haul-ing-ropes, with their infernal twists and knots which get worse and worse to undo! The dogs jump over, and in between one another incessantly, and no sooner has one carefully cleared the hauling-ropes, than they are twisted into a veritable skein again. Then one of the sledges is stopped by a block of ice. The dogs howl impatiently to follow their companions in front; then one bites through a trace and starts off on his own account, perhaps followed by one or two others, and these must be caught, and the traces knotted; there is no time to splice them properly, nor would it be a very congenial task in this cold. So we go on when the ice is uneven, and every hour and a half, at least, have to stop and disentangles the traces.

We started yesterday about half past eight in the morning, and stopped about five in the afternoon. After dinner the north-easterly wind, which we have had the whole time, suddenly became stronger, and the sky overcast. We wel-comed it with joy, for we saw in it the sign of a probable change of weather and an end to this perpetual cold and brightness. I do not think we deceived our-selves either. Yesterday evening the temperature had risen to −29.2° F (-34°C), and we had the best night in the bag we have had for a long time. Just now, as I am getting the breakfast ready, I see that it is clear again, and the sun is shining through the tent wall.

The ice we are now travelling over seems, on the whole, to be old; but some-times we come across tracts, of considerable width, of uneven new ice, which must have been pressed up a considerable time. I cannot account for it in any other way than by supposing it to be ice from great open pools which must have formed here at one time. We have traversed pools of this description, with level ice on them several times.

That day I took a meridian observation, which, however, did not make us farther north than 85° 30'. I could not understand this; thought that we must be in latitude 86°, and, therefore, supposed there must be something wrong with the observation.

Saturday, March 30. Yesterday was Tycho Brahe's day. At first we found much uneven ice and had to strike a devious route to get through it, so that our day's march did not amount to much, although we kept at it a long time. At the end of it, however and after considerable toil, we found ourselves on splendid flat ice, more level than it had been for a long time. At last, then, we had come on some more of the good old kind, and could not complain of some rubble and snow drifts here and there but then we were stopped by some ugly pressure-ridges, of the worst kind, formed by the packing of enormous blocks. The last ridges was the worst of all, and before it yawned a crack in the thick ice, about 12 feet deep. When the first sledge was going over all the dogs fell in and had to be hauled up again. One of them—Klapperslangen—slipped his harness and ran away. As the next sledge was going over it fell in bodily, but happily was not smashed to atoms, as it might have been. We had to unload it entirely in order to get it up again, and then reload, all of which took up a great deal of time. Then, too, the dogs had to be thrown down and dragged up on the other side. With the third sledge we managed better, and after we had gone a little way farther the runaway dog came back. At last we reached camping ground, pitched our tent, and found that the thermometer showed –45.4° F (-43° C). Disentangling dog-traces in this temperature, with one's bare, frost-bitten, almost skinless hands is desperate work. But finally we were in our dear bags with the Primus singing cosily, when, to crown our misfortunes, I discovered that it would not burn. I examined it everywhere but could find nothing wrong. Johansen had to turn out and go and fetch the tools and a reserve burner, while I studied the cooker. At last I discovered that some ice had got in under the lid, and this had caused a leakage. Finally we got it to light, and at 5 o'clock in the morning the pea soup was ready, and very good it was. At three in the afternoon I was up again cooking. Thank Heaven, it is warm and comfortable in the bag, or this sort of life would be intolerable.

Sunday, March 31. Yesterday, at last, came the long-wished-for change of weather, with southerly wind and rising temperature. Early this morning the thermometer showed –22° F (-30° C), regular summer weather, in fact. It was, therefore, with lightened hearts that we set off over good ice, and with the wind at our backs. On we went at a very fair pace, and everything was going well, when a lane suddenly opened just in front of our first sledge. We managed to get over this by the skin of our teeth; but just as we were going to cross the lane again after the other sledges a large piece of ice broke under Johansen, and he fell in, wetting both legs, a deplorable incident. While the lane was gradually opening more and more, I went up and down it to find a way over, but without success. Here we were, with one man and a sledge on one side, two sledges and a wet man on the other, with an ever widening lane between. The kayaks could not be launched, as, through the frequent capsizing of the sledges they had got holes in them, and for the time being were useless. This was a cheerful prospect for the night; I on one side with the tent, Johansen, probably frozen stiff, on the other. At last, after a long detour, I found a way over; and the sledges were conveyed across. It was out of the question, however, to attempt to go on, as Johansen's nether extremities were a mass of ice and his overalls so torn that extensive repairs were necessary.

12
A HARD STRUGGLE

Tuesday, April 2. There are many different kinds of difficulty to overcome on this journey, but the worst of all, perhaps, is getting all the trifles done and starting off. In spite of my being up by 7 o'clock on Monday evening to do the cooking, it was nearly two this morning before we got clear of our camping ground. The load on Johansen's sledge had to be relashed, as the contents of one grip had been eaten up, and we had to put a sack of bread in its place. Another grip had to be sewn together, as it was leaking pemmican. Then the sledge from which the bread sack had been taken had to be lashed secure again, and while we had the ropes undone it was just as well to get out a supply of potatoes.[4] During this operation we discovered that there was a hole in the fish-flour sack, which we tied up, but no sooner had we done so, than we found another

[4] We always kept a supply of our various provisions in small bags inside the kayaks, so that we could get out whatever we wanted for our daily consumption without undoing the big sacks, which were sewn up or securely fastened in other ways.

large one which required sewing. When we came to pack the potato sack this too had a hole in it, which we tied up, and so on, Then the dogs' traces had to be disentangled; the whole thing was in an inextricable muddle, and the knots and twists in the icy, frozen rope got worse and worse to deal with. Johansen made haste and patched his trousers before breakfast. The south wind had become what on board the *Fram* we should have called a 'mill breeze' (i.e. 19 to 23 feet in the second); and, with this at our back, we started off in driving snow. Everything went splendidly at first, but then came one pressure-ridge after another, and each one was worse than the last. We had a long halt for dinner at eight or nine in the morning, after having chosen ourselves a sheltered place in the lee of a ridge. We spread out the sleeping-bag, crept down into it with our food, and so tired was I that I went to sleep with it in my hand. I dreamed I was in Norway, and on a visit to some people I had seen once in my life before. It was Christmas Day, and I was shown into a great empty room, where we were intended to dine. The room was very cold, and I shivered, but there were already some hot dishes steaming on the table, a beautiful fat goose. How unspeakably did I look forward to that goose. Then some other visitors began to arrive; I could see them through the window, and was just going out to meet them when I stumbled in deep snow. How it all happened, in the middle of the dining-room floor, I know not. The host laughed in an amused way, and—I woke up and found myself shivering in a sleeping-bag on the drift-ice in the far north Oh, how miserable I felt! We got up, packed our things silently together, and started off. Not until 4 o'clock that afternoon did we stop, but everything was dull and cheerless, and it was long before I got over my disappointment. What would I not have given for that dinner, or for one hour in the room, cold as it was?

The ridges and the lanes which had frozen together again, with rubble on either side, became worse and worse. Making one's way through these new ridges is desperate work One cannot use snowshoes—as there is too little snow between the piled-up blocks of ice, and one must wade along without them. It is also impossible to see anything in this thick weather—everything is white— irregularities and holes; and the spaces between the blocks are covered with a thin, deceptive layer of snow, which lets one crashing through into cracks and pitfalls, so that one is lucky to get off without a broken leg. It is necessary to go long distances on ahead in order to find a way; sometimes one must search in one direction, sometimes in another, and then back again to fetch the sledges, with the result that the same ground is gone over many times. Yesterday, when we stopped, I really was done. The worst of it all, though, was that when we finally came to a standstill we had been on the move so long that it was too late to wind up our watches. Johansen's had stopped altogether; mine was ticking, and happily still going when I wound it up, so I hope that it is all right. Twelve midday, -24.6° F (-31.5° C). Clear weather, south-easterly wind (13 feet in the second).

The ice seems to be getting worse and worse, and I am beginning to have doubts as to the wisdom of keeping northwards too long.

Wednesday, April 3. Got under way yesterday about three in the afternoon. The snow was in first- rate condition after the south-east wind, which continued blowing till late in the day. The ice was tolerably passable, and everything looked more promising; the weather was fine, and we made good progress. But after several level tracts with old humpy ice, came some very uneven ones, intersected by lanes and pressure-ridges as usual. Matters did not grow any better as time went on, and at midnight or soon after we were stopped by some bad ice and a newly frozen lane which would not bear. As we should have had to make a long detour, we encamped, and Russen was killed (this was the second dog to go). The meat was divided into 26 portions, but eight dogs refused it, and had to be given pemmican. The ice ahead does not look inviting. These ridges are enough to make one despair, and there seems to be no prospect of things bettering. I turned out at midday and took a meridian observation, which makes us in 85° 59' N. It is astonishing that we have not got farther; we seem to toil all we can, but without much progress. Beginning to doubt seriously of the advisability of continuing northwards much longer. It is three times as far to Franz Josef Land as the distance we have now come. How may the ice be in that direction? We can hardly count on its being better than here, or our progress quicker. Then, too, the shape and extent of Franz Josef Land are unknown, and may cause us considerable delay, and perhaps we shall not be able to find any game just at once. I have long seen that it is impossible to reach the Pole itself or its immediate vicinity over such ice as this, and with these dogs. If only we had more of them! What would I not give now to have the Olenek dogs? We must turn sooner or later. But as it is only a question of time, could we not turn it to better account in Franz Josef Land than by travelling over this ice-drift, which we have now had a good opportunity of learning to know? In all probability it will be exactly the same right to the Pole. We cannot hope to reach any considerable distance higher before time compels us to turn. We certainly ought not to wait much longer. Twelve midday, -20.8° F (-29.4° C), clear weather, 3 feet wind from east; twelve midnight, -29.2° F (-34° C) clear and still.

It became more and more of a riddle to me that we did not make greater progress northwards. I kept on calculating and adding up our marches as we went along, but always with the same result; that is to say, provided only the ice were still, we must be far above the eighty-sixth parallel. It was becoming only too clear to me, however, that the ice was moving southwards, and that in its capricious drift at the mercy of wind and current, we had our worst enemy to combat.

Friday, April 5. Began our march at three yesterday morning. The ice, however, was bad, with lanes and ridges, so that our progress was but little. These lanes, with rubble thrown up on each side, are our despair. It is like driving over a tract of rocks, and delays us terribly. First I must go on ahead to find a way, and then get my sledge through; then, perhaps, by way of a change, one falls into the water: yesterday I fell through twice. If I work hard in finding a way and guiding my sledge over rough places, Johansen is no better off, with his two sledges to look after. It is a tough job to get even one of them over the rubble, to say nothing of the ridges; but he is a plucky fellow, and no mistake, and never gives in. Yesterday he fell into the water again in crossing a lane, and got wet up to his knees. I had gone over on my snowshoes shortly before, and did not notice that the ice was weak. He came afterwards without snowshoes walking beside one of the sledges, when suddenly the ice gave, and he fell through. Happily he managed to catch hold of the sledge, and the dogs, which did not stop, pulled him up again. These baths are not an unmixed pleasure now that there is no possibility of drying or changing one's clothes, and one must wear a chain mail of ice until they thaw and dry on the body, which takes some time in this temperature. I took an observation for longitude and a magnetic observation yesterday was 86° 2.8' N. This is very little, but what can we do when the ice is what it is? And these dogs cannot work harder than they do, poor things. I sigh for the sledge-dogs from the Olenek daily now. The longitude for yesterday was 98° 47.15", variation 44.4°.

I begin to think more and more that we ought to turn back before the time we originally fixed.[5] It is probably 350 miles or so to Petermann's Land (in point of fact it was about 450 miles to Cape Fligely); but it will probably take us all we know to get over them. The question resolves itself into this: Ought we not, at any rate, to reach 87° N? But I doubt whether we can manage it, if the ice does not improve.

Saturday, April 6. Two A.M., -11.4° F (-24.2° C). The ice grew worse and worse. Yesterday it brought me to the verge of despair, and when we stopped this morning I had almost decided to turn back. I will go on one day longer, however, to see if the ice is really as bad farther northwards as it appears from the ridge, 30 feet in height, where we are encamped. We hardly made 4 miles yesterday. Lanes, ridges, and endless rough ice, it looks like an endless moraine of iceblocks; and this continual lifting of sledges over every irregularity is enough to tire out giants. Curious, this rubble-ice. For the most part it is not so very massive, and seems as if it had been forced up somewhat recently, for it is incompletely covered with thin, loose snow, through which one falls suddenly up to one's middle. And thus it extends mile after mile northwards, while every now and then there are old floes, with mounds that have been rounded off by the action of the sun in the summer—often very massive ice.

I am rapidly coming to the conclusion that we are not doing any good here. We shall not be able to get much farther north, and it will be slow work indeed if there be much more of this sort of ice towards Franz Josef Land. On the other hand, we should be able to make much better use of our time there, if we should have any over. 8.30 P.M., -29.2° F (-34° C).

Monday, April 8. No, the ice grew worse and worse, and we got no way. Ridge after ridge, and nothing but rubble to travel over. We made a start at two o'clock or so this morning, and kept at it as long as we could, lifting the sledges all the time; but it grew too bad at last. I went on a good way ahead on snowshoes, but saw no reasonable prospect of advance, and from the highest hummocks only the same kind of ice was to be seen. It was a veritable chaos of ice-blocks, stretching as far as the horizon. There is not much sense in keeping on longer; we are sacrificing valuable time and doing little. If there be much

[5] When I left the ship I had purposed to travel northwards for 50 days, for which time we had taken provender for the dogs.

more such ice between here and Franz Josef Land, we shall, indeed, want all the time we have.

I therefore determined to stop, and shape our course for Cape Fligely.

On this northernmost camping ground we indulged in a banquet, consisting of *lobscouse*, bread and butter, dry chocolate, stewed *tytlebaer*, or red whortleberries, and our hot whey drink, and then, with a delightful and unfamiliar feeling of reple-tion, crept into the dear bag, our best friend. I took a meridian observation yes-terday, by which I see that we should be in latitude 86° 10' N., or thereabouts.[6] This morning I took an observation for longitude. At 8.30 A.M., -25.6° F (-32° C).

NANSEN'S ADVENTURE WAS NOT OVER, TO BE SURE, JUST BECAUSE HE *turned around. He had no idea where the Fram was by this time, and finding it would have required a miracle. Nansen and Johansen headed instead for Franz Josef Land, which was more than 400 miles south. They traveled through the rest of April, through May, into June, and they did not know where they were. They should have reached Franz Josef Land, but they had not. Slushy snow delayed them. Open leads required them to launch their kayaks repeatedly, load the sledges on them, cross the leads, then unload and put the kayaks back on the sledges. They had to shoot and eat their dogs, and when they finally did reach Franz Josef Land in late July the season was too late for them to go any farther. They had food now, polar bears, walrus, seals, but no shelter. They made one out of a pit in the ground, covering it with walrus skins. They endured a miserable winter in this fashion, two men alone amidst this waste of ice and stone, talked out, with little to do. In May they headed south again, hoping to find a way across the stretch of ocean between Franz Josef Land and Spitzbergen.*

In June the miracle occurred after all. Having reached one of the islands on the south side of Franz Josef Land, one morning Nansen heard a dog barking. Then more dogs. The owner was an English explorer named Frederick Jackson who was exploring Franz Josef Land to see whether it might not constitute a land route to the North Pole. Nansen could assure him it was not. Jackson took the two men

[6] This was the latitude I got by a rough estimation, but on further calculation it proved to be 86° 13.6' N.; the longitude was about 95° E.

aboard his ship and Nansen arrived back in Norway just a week before the Fram got there. No one had died. No one had starved to death. For an Arctic expedition, it was a stunning success.

But God did not create all Scandinavians with equal polar smarts. If Nansen was a brilliant explorer, Salomon Andree was one of God's fools. Andree was a Swede with a strong career in the sciences. Born in 1854, by 1885 he was chief engineer at the Swedish patent office with an enthusiasm for balloons that had been encouraged by meetings with John Wise, the great American balloonist. He had a little experience in the Arctic. As part of the International Polar Year of 1881-82, he had done some electrical experiments in a tethered balloon in Spitzbergen. In 1895 he announced his plans to fly to the North Pole in a balloon. He had worked it all out. He knew the wind patterns over Spitzbergen, he had designed a kind of sail with which he thought he could steer the balloon and a system of trailing drag lines that were supposed to help it tack, and he had financial backing. No less a person than Alfred Nobel, who established the Nobel Prizes, put up half the money. More came from the King of Sweden.

Andree's enthusiasm was contagious. His project, harebrained on the face of it, was also adventurous, romantic, a crowd pleaser. Think of it. A mere thirty days to the Pole, skimming comfortably above the surface of the ice, and then on to Alaska. For the public it was great drama.

Calmer, saner sorts tried to talk him out of it. Adolphus W. Greely was one. Fridtjof Nansen was another. Nansen told him that the wind patterns over the Arctic Ocean were against him, and no one knew better than Nansen what those patterns were. The weather was also problematic. But Andree persisted. He had made plans, he had announced his intentions, he had thought it all out. He was a scientist out of the mold of Mary Shelley's Dr. Frankenstein, bold, experimental, sure of himself—and doomed. After an aborted start in 1896 he returned to Spitzbergen in 1897 with his balloon, which he named the Eagle, and two companions willing to go with him: a young scientist named Nils Strindberg, and an athlete named Knut Frankel. In July they inflated the balloon with hydrogen, creating it on the spot from tons of iron filings, sulfuric acid, and water, stocking the gondola that hung below the balloon with provisions for four months, a sled for crossing the ice if they should come down, a collapsible boat, and a cookstove that hung on wires below the gondola so that, while cooking, it would not start a fire. They soared out of Spitzbergen on July 11. A downdraft from the mountains drove the gondola toward the water and they lost the guide ropes when they caught on rocks. But then they slowly gained altitude and, after an hour or two, drifted out of sight over the Arctic Ocean.

They had taken thirty carrier pigeons with them to send messages back. One of them showed up.

In 1900 a woman found a buoy on the coast of Norway that Andree had dropped with a message in it dated the day they left and noting that all was well.

Then in 1930 the mystery was solved. A Norwegian sealer stopped at White Island, a barren, glacier-covered rock that lay halfway between Spitzbergen and Franz Josef Land, to let some scientists on board poke around and take geological samples. There they lay— three skeletons, the collapsible boat, and the expedition's journals. One of the men had been buried, Arctic fashion, under loose stones. Another lay on the ground. What they took to be Andree's skeleton leaned against the rocks in a sitting position. The last journal entry was dated October 7. They had reached White Island on October 4. They had lacked the strength to do more than pull the boat up on the beach. They hadn't been able to unload the little that was left of their supplies.

The journals told the story. Andree, who thought he had worked out all the variables, had neglected the water vapor in the air. In sunlight the Eagle floated high and free. When the air was moist it condensed on the balloon and weighed it down, so far down that the gondola sometimes nearly touched the water. They could cast out ballast and did, but eventually—within three days—the balloon gondola started bouncing along the ice like a kangaroo, and it soon came to a complete stop. They had no choice but to abandon it.

What followed was a three-month trek across difficult, slushy summer ice toward Franz Josef Land, the drift taking them west from their objective to White Island. Our excerpt is from Andree's recovered journal, covering the days of early August, when their spirits were still high. It makes an interesting contrast with Nansen's account of his own trek across the ice. Andree, ever the scientist, cannot forbear taking notes on the animal life, the nature of the ice, and everything else he sees. You grow fond of him on this hopeless journey. You come to wish he had lived.

SALOMAN ANDREE

Andree's Story: The Complete Record of His Polar Flight

LA T. 82° 22' LONG 29° 12'

BOTH OF THEM GOOD DETERMINATIONS.

These values show that we have driven westwards quicker than we have walked eastwards. This is not encouraging but we shall continue our course to the east sometime more, as long as there is a bit of sense in doing so. Red-breasted gull[1] visible. Clay in quantities, in the shape of small grains up to the size of a walnut (rare). We arrived at a lofty pyramidal mass of ice but from it could see neither land nor sea. Half-frozen and snow-covered little pools very treacherous. Humour and spirits good. Out on the ice one cannot at all notice that it is in movement except that at our resting-places the leads change while we are sleeping. Towards the evening we followed a fresh track after a large bear. He had gone down in the soup[2] a couple of times so that not even he is above making mistakes in this regard. During the last few days we have seen no other birds than the one mentioned above and an ivory gull and a few fulmars. The water is [filled] with sponge-like masses.

[1] The red-breasted gull often mentioned by Andree is the Ross's gull. -Trans

[2] Andree hardly ever uses the word "water" even when he means "drinking-water." He employs the term "*soup*" instead. This makes it difficult to know the character of the waters in the pools and leads, etc., and to know whether the water be clear, or sludgy, etc.

We started on Aug 1 Sunday 8.30 o'cl. after I had mended the sleeping-sack with bear-skin. We had excellent good ice until midday but then we had an hour's hard work after which the ice again became good. Our distance was probably 7 kilom. [4.2 mile] at least. Three red-breasted gulls seen and two of them fairly unafraid unlike what has previously been the case.

The ice seems to have become of a more favourable character, perhaps because we are approaching the edge of the great ice-stream and our territory lies to leeward of the tide-water under Franz Jos' Land. Today, for instance, we have not needed to use the boat once for crossing lanes, these having been narrow and very often with even edges etc. Fulmars and seals were often seen. Two fresh bear-tracks have been crossed and we are longing for bears for the meat is finished. This evening we have seen the back of a new animal which looked like a long snake 10-12 metre [33-39 ft.] long of a dirty yellow colour and, in my opinion, with black stripes running from the back for some distance down the sides. It breathed heavily almost like a whale which I suppose it really was.

Stockings are dried best by putting them on over the wool-and-hair stockings [*raggsockor*] on the feet. At our mealtimes the seats consist of 1 medicine-chest, 1 photographic apparatus and 1 case of matches. For some days back I have greased my hands with bear-fat and in that way keep them soft.

Aug. 2 we awakened 9.30 o'cl. more tired than usual. It seems as if good country were more fatiguing than half-good.

Aug. 2 at 12 o'cl. midd. we broke camp. The last bear-meat was cut into small pieces so that it might at least *look like* being a lot. Thickness of ice 1. 2 m. [3.96 ft.]. Scarcely an hour after breaking camp we got a new bear. It was an old worn-out male animal with rotten teeth. I brought it down by a shot in the chest at a distance of 38 m [125 ft.] S-g and Fr-l both fired outers. Clear calm and hot the whole day but the country extraordinarily difficult. I do not think we made 2 km. [2200 yds.] in 10 hours. Axe destroyed. 1 skua visible and 2 gulls circling around the body of the bear. We did not get into our berths before 2 a.m. Aug. 3. I washed my face for the first time since July 11 and in the evening I mended a stocking. We hope that one bear will be enticed to follow us by the remains of the one shot, and so on so that we shall always have fresh meet at our heels. This time we took from the one we shot the fillet too (close in to the back) and the kidneys- 1 ? kilo. [3 ⅓ lbs]—and the tongue and ribs. Aug. 3 at 12 o'cl. we rose after being much plagued by the heat in the tent. We have determined to "lie outdoors" today. We photographed the story of the evolution of our forks. It is so warm that we do the pulling without any coats on. The ice horrible. Clothes-drying on a large scale. I made a fork for Fraenkel. The forks photographed.

Aug. 3 4.45. Driftwood on the ice 1.1 m. [43 in.] ong. Towards the water it is seen that the air is filled with a fine rain of water or particles of snow.

Freshwater-floe thickn. 1.4 m [54.6 in.]

"Is it easy to get across?" "Yes, it is easy with difficulty." Extremely difficult ice small floes much pressure and new ice in the leads. The only advantage of the cold is that the edges hold better. Yesterday and today the course has been more S E than E. for that course is usually impossible. A skua was observed and a gull. A red-breasted gull visible. Much joking about my old bear which E declared the oldest bear in the Polar regions. Tough as leather galoshes. He believed it was an escaped menagerie-bear. We have passed tracks of 1 bear with 2 cubs. 2 A.M. Aug. 4, with the field-glass and in extremely clear air I looked N-E-SE for land or water without being able to notice either. Only ice and very difficult ice visible in all directions. In consequence we determined to abandon our efforts to move eastwards.

(Long. 29° 43' and probably lat. 82° 17' Decl. 0.8° west)

We can surmount neither the current nor the ice and have absolutely no prospect of doing anything by continuing our tramp to E. We have therefore decided to begin our next next march in the direction of the Seven Islands which we hope to reach in 6-7 weeks. At 4 A.M. Aug. 4 we turned in. Bread and biscuits etc. wet through. N.B. that the movement of an ice-floe in one direction made the stomach feel empty. The great stream that Nansen has shown to exist thus produces perhaps quite other directions of currents in the neighbourhood.

Aug. 4 3.30 P.M. break camp. Alga sample (no.3) on ice-foot (green ice-foot but not at a depth of more than 0.5 m. [19 in.] below surface of water). Thickness of ice 1.05 [41 in.]. Often the most practicable crossings lie at the ugliest hummock, the edges of the leads being nearest each other there. Of course these bridges are terrible but still they are bridges. In a lead running N 40° W we saw a hummock direct towards the channel. Wide leads free from floes but with piled-up edges all around are the very devil. But as long as there is no fog we can get along.

Invent. of provisions.

Aee	Aee
front basket	rear basket

Coc. powder extract 4 tins		3 Snowflake[3]	
coffee	1 "	2 mellin's food	
butter	5 "	5 biscuits	
milk	8 "	2 bottles	
lact ser [dired milk?] 4			4 butter
bread	4 "		1 pastry
sardines	5	2 salt	
bird paste	1	2 soup tablets	
cheese	—	1 flour	
		1 lactoser.	

Alga-sample No. 4 was frozen into the new ice in an opening.

Stock-taking of provisions Aug. 5 in morning.

	12.1 [Kgms.]	[26.4 lbs.]	
Hardtack.........11 b. [oxes] of 1.1 [2.4 lbs].			
12 biscuits.........12 b. of	15.5	34.1	
+5 Mellins' food	15.00	3	3
butter.............17 b. of 900 [2 lbs.]	15.3	3	4
Chocolate powder.........9 b. of 1 [2.2 lbs.] extr.	9.00	2	0
milk...........10 b. of 250 [½ lb.]	2.5	5	
Lact ser.........10 b. of	2.5	5	
Pemmican	3.0	6 . 5	
Sugar	5.00	1	1
1 tin Stauffer prep	4.5	1	0
Coffee	2.00	4 . 5	
1 tin chocolate			
3 b. Lime-juice tablets			
Whortleberry jam	1.00	2 . 2	
9 tins sardines			

[3] Paraffin used as fuel for the stove.

3 tins paste

Soup tablets 3 tins

2 bottles syrup

1 bottle port-wine

6 Snowflake

flour   1.   2.2]

This stock-taking shows that we must be careful, especially with the bread.

Temp. falling still lower and each degree makes us creep deeper down into the sleeping-stack. Bad day today the first with course N 40° W = Seven Islands.

The 5th 8.30 P.M. start. Course S 40° W. Thickness of ice (fresh-) 1.2 m. [47 in]. Some drops of rain fell. On all fours today as in the spring of our youth. "Glassy ice flop" or "flop-flop." The ice much divided. A rafting of more than 1 km. [1100 yds.] 4 hours. Thickness of ice 0.7 m. [27 in.] Thickness of ice 1.1 and 1.2 m. [43-47 in.]. Great seal on the ice. Many bear-tracks. Fulmars. 1 red gull. The ice after rafting first fairly and afterwards extremely good. At 6.30 a.m. Aug. 6 we stopped. Lat. 10 a.m. G.M.T. 82° 10'7". Short ribs of bear and tongue. Paradise. Large level ice-floes with fresh-water pools full of syrup and water and here and there a young Polar bear with tender meat.

The 6th 11 P.M. Start. Ice 1.6 m. [5.28 ft.] mild. 2 red-breasted gulls. Shy. Visit once and then fly. Ice exc. favourable large level floes and many but easy crossings. What joy when the needle pointed across a level— some hundred metres.

1 pressure-line lead N 25° W. When we [and] the sledges made the worst somersaults F. remarked that the journey once more could not be called altogether hopeless.4 Powdered-sugar ice and ice-gravel. Greatest distance of all probably at least 3 minutes but the wind is almost right against us and has probably driven us just as far back.

Two red-breasted gulls. The bear-meat is very good when it has become old. The snow difficult so-called powdered-sugar snow. One's feet glide and one easily slips, while the sledges cut deep into the snow. We are very tired now as we go to our berths at 12 midday of the 7. The wind is S 55° W and our course is S 40° W. New difficulty: the leads altering while we are crossing them. At 10.30 P.M. of the 7 we wakened at last and felt ourselves fully rested. The wind

---

4 In Swedish a passable pun: hop-less. –Trans.

was still fresh but had swung round more from the west (S 75° W). A *little* rein-deer-hair in the food is recommended for while taking it out one is prevented from eating too quickly and greedily. 2 A.M. the 8 break camp. Ice 1.45 m. [4.75 ft.] Pretty good ice. Ice-humps and leads but large floes. The wind right in our noses but it is cooling. The ice has been about the same almost for the last three days. I do not use spectacles excepting in bright sunshine. I squint instead. Two little auks visible in the water. They made a sound I have not heard before. If the wind fr. S W. does what it has done before, i.e. closes up the leads, then it can keep on for a week or two. I wish I had a summer jacket. It is warm work pulling the sledge. 2 red-breasted gulls. For a change we have come into a dread-ful country with fresh water (photogr.) but E who otherwise complains of the want of change, did not like what was offered him. All three of us have our noses running constantly. A permanent catarrh. The fresh-water pools are often more difficult to pass than the salt-water channels for their edges are eaten away below and the depths are so slight that the boat cannot be used.

Aug. 9 at 2.20 a.m. we began to get up in the tent.

3.00 *primus started*
3.18 the steak ready and the coffee-maker begun
3.29 the steak eaten
3.48 the coffee made
4.00 the coffee drunk
5.30 broke camp

The state of the country is dreadful. The country consists of ice-humps blocks and hills with snow-drifts between and this is difficult for the pullers but for the sledges the going is not difficult for the snow supports them.

At 7.30 I saw an ice-hump formed in a lane which was at right angles to the direc-tion of the wind which led to a hummock. The country consists of large uneven fields full of brown ice small ice-hums with snow-sludge and waterpools but not many large sea-leads. It is extremely tiring. E has diarrhoea for the 2nd time and there does not seem much left of his morale. The sweet-water leads were often not so very "sweet" to cross. A black guillemot visible. A fine beautiful bear approached us but fled before we had a chance to shoot. This was great grief for us and a pity too for soon we shall have no bear's-meat left. S. and E went after him but in vain. We were tired out and E was ill. I gave him opium for the diarrhoea. Afterwards we had several hours' work getting S's gun in order. Its mechanism is dreadfully carelessly constructed. We have been awake and busy for 18 hours when at 8 P.M. we creep into the sleeping-sack. The course always S 40° W. The 10th at 6.10 A.M. all up.

Load on my sledge

1 small sack	3.5 [kgms.]	[7.7 lbs.]
1 front basket	37.1	81.7
1 rear "	37.3	82.0
1 private sack	15.5	34
1 medicine chest	9.00	20.0
1 tent	9.0	20.0
2 tentp.	1.5	3.3
meat	5.0	11
	117.9	259.7
1 gun	1.6	3.5
	119.5	263.2
1 b. ammunition	6.5	14.3
	126.0 kilo	277.5
1 sext	2.2	4.8
1 sack	6.0 photog.	13.2
	134.2	295.5]

Fraenkel's sledge.

Boat	63.00	[138.6 lbs]		107.5	[236.8]
1 sack private	17.00	37.	1 sack books	3.0	6.6
1 hose	3.5	7.7	2 oars	4.5	10.0
3 pieces wood	2.0	4.4	3 poles	2.0	4.4
1 ammunit.	3.5	7.7	1 gun	2.0	4.4
1 univers.	3.0	6.6	1 sack shoe-hay	1.0	2.2
2 field-glass	2.0	4.4			

3 blankets	4.5	10.0		120	264
1 sleep. sack	9.0	20.0			
	107.5	[236.8]			

cook. app. food etc			120	[264	
8 boxes of matches			12.0	26.4 lbs	
1 sextant		3.00		6.6	
1 aner.		0.5		1.1	4.6	10.1
1 psychr.		3.1		6.8	
1 change-sack		1		2.2	
spirit service etc.					8.00	17.6
2 cushions, gun case					1.7	3.7
& cleaning-box						
1 drift-wood					2.0	4.4
1 tarpaulin					2.5	5.5
					153.8	338.4

Long. 29° 5

Lat. 81° 56′ 5

Ordinary gull visible. The ground extraordinarily difficult. Absolutely untrafficable sludge-pools encountered today. They consist of broad channels filled with small lumps of ice and snow. Neither sledge nor boat can be moved forward there. In consequence of the place—determination given above the course was altered to S 50° W. (to the Seven Islands). It is remarkable that we have travelled so far in latitude in spite of the wind having been right against us for several days. In consequence of our having come below 82° we have today had a feast with sardines for dinner and a Stauffer cake for supper. The going today has been good although the road is bad. We assume that we have gone 3 kilometers [1.8 mile] or possib. 2 minutes. Today I found for the first time small stones and leaves etc. on the ice. The character of the locality was as follows. Aug. 10 4 P.M. (No. 5) The ice hard, uneven, with hollows yellow and greyish, little covered by snow. The depth of the ice below the water close to the place: 1.05, 1.05, 1.35, 1.35, 1.35, 1.05 m. [41, 41, 52.6, 52.6, 52.6, 41 in.]. The find lay on a large floe in a hollow, 20 cm.

[8 in.] deep and abt. 50 cm. [10 in.] in diameter. This find should make it possible to determine where this great amount of brown and hard ice which we constantly see has its place of origin. Up till now I have not found anything on the brown-yellow ice other than fine clay and now I find on the same ice a whole consignment of plants, sand, small stones, etc.

Today there came a slight rain and then snow. We have gone into our tent after only 7 hours' march but it was so dreadfully fatiguing. Now S. is sitting mending trousers in "the seat" and F. is oiling guns. F.s stomach pains are now over.

Aug. 11 was a regular Tycho Brahe day.[5] First thing in the morning I got into the water and so did my sledge so that nearly everything became wet through. S. ran into F.s sledge and broke the boat with the grapnel. All the sledges turned somersaults repeatedly during the course of the day. Mine was twice turned completely upside down. The going was good but the country terrible. All imaginable difficulties happened and when the evening came we were not at all happy. Something else happened, however. F. shot an ivory gull. It was snow-white with black legs and feet. The legs had white stripes right across them and the feet (the webs) were chequered with white stripes. Three toes with web and a toe (short) behind. At the outer edge of the wings there were some small feathers with grey patches. The beak had a yellow point but was otherwise yellowish-white with black longitudinal shadings. The birds landed quite near us.

Thickness of ice 1.45 m. [4.8 ft.] I think I can assert with certainty that today I have seen a couple of blocks of glacier ice. One block contained 7 layers of dirt-stripes with white snow or ice between. The thickness of the block was 1.05 m [3.5 ft.] and the layers were nearly of even thickness and were parallel. A peculiar incident happened on crossing a lead. We stood quite at a loss what to do for the edges of the ice were wretched and the channel so shallow that the boat could not float. Our ordinary methods failed us altogehter. Then while we were talking it over the ice-floe beneath Fraenkel broke and so we obtained a bit of ice of considerable size and with the assistance of this piece we then made the crossing quite neatly. We have not been able to keep the course but have been obliged to go both to the north and to the east but endeavour to go S 50° W. Our distance today probably did not exceed 3.5 km. [2.1 miles].

5 Unlucky day.- Trans

At 4.30 P.M. our longitude was 30° E. At midday our latitude was 81° 54' 7. E thought he saw land and it was really so like land that we changed the course in that direction but it was found to be merely a peculiarly shaped large ice-hump.

Aug. 12. Sounding 320 m. [176 fathoms]. No bottom. Thickn. of ice 1.2 [4 ft.]. Sample 8 came up on the sounding-line when 200 m. [110 fathoms] had been sounded. At the close of the day's march we at last got better country after having had extremely difficult going for several days. Our distance today amounted probably to 2.5 minutes although the marching-time was shorter than usual.

The course has been S 50° W and we are now so near Gillis Land that we might well expect to catch a glimpse of it. But neither that nor any other land is visible. Today we have eaten ivory gull without any other preparation than ordinary frying and found it tasted excellent. We tried to get at a seal as now we have not more than one meal of bear-meat left. My shoes begin to be so cut to pieces that I am afraid their fate will soon be sealed. Now it is raining on the tent when we go to bed at 3.30 A.M. Aug. 13. I make preparations for manufacturing a waterproof. The instant after we had gone to bed we again heard a whale but could not catch sight of it.

Aug. 13 at 5 P.M. start. Tried in vain to get a seal. The ice reasonably good. In a fissure found a little fish which was hardly frightened at all and seemed astonished to see us. I killed him with the shovel. It had a length of 7.5 cm. [3 in.]. Grey-green, dark prickly back, red-violet sides and white belly. Black pupil surrounded by eyeball of 5.5 mm. [.2 in.] diam. Three dorsal fins, 1 caudal fin, 2 anal fins, 1 pair ventral fins beneath the head, 1 pair lateral fins behind the head. Just when we had passed the fissure S-g cried: "Three bears!" We were at once in motion and full of excited expectation. Warned by our previous disappointments we now went to work carefully. We concealed ourselves behind a hummock and waited, but no bears came. Then I chose myself as bait and crept forward along the level, whistling softly. The she-bear became attentive, came forward winding me but turned round again and lay down. At last it was too cold for me to lie still in the snow and I called out to the others that we should rush up to the bears. We did so. Then the she-bear came towards me but was met by a shot which missed. I sprang up however and shot again while the bears which were running away stopped for a moment. Then the she-bear was wounded at a distance of 80 paces but ran a little way whereupon I dropped her on the spot at 94 paces. My 4th shot dropped one cub. Then the third one ran but was wounded by Fraenkel and dropped by Strindberg who had had a longer way to go and so could not come up as quickly as I. There was a great joy in the caravan and we cut our bears in pieces with pleasure and loaded our sledges with not less than 42 kilograms [92.5 lbs.] fresh meat, enough for 23 days. Among our experiments as to the value of the parts of the bear it may be mentioned that we found the heart, brain, and kidneys very palatable. The tongue too is well worth taking. The meat on the ribs is excellent. In the evening I shot an ivory gull. The work of cutting up the bears, etc., gave us so much to do that we did not travel far this day. The wind has now swung round to SE so that we hope to drift westwards. Today the weather has been extremely beautiful and that is a good thing for otherwise the work would have been ticklish. When a bear is hit he gives a roar and tries to run away as quick as he can. We have been butchers the whole day. I have been trying the business of tanning in order to get skin to mend the sleeping-sack with. The skin of the fore-legs seems to be the most suitable being the lightest. With fairly clear air today we have not seen land in any direction. The 14th at 6.30 A.M. we went to our berths after having washed our hands and eaten ourselves chock full. The she-bear stiffened in a very little while, but the cubs were soft a long time. The she-bear had bitten her tongue right through. The ivory gull has three cries: 1 piyrrr with four soft and trilling r's; 2. pyot-pyot; 3. resembling the croaking of the crow. The 15th at 12 o'cl. midd. we found our berths after having lain still on account of the rain and for repairs. I had manufactured a waterproof. The sleeping-sack mended, the knives sharpened. Coats mended. Spectacles ditto. One or two ivory gulls came to the remains of the bears. We have had rain for almost 24 hours and the wind from SE. Diarrhoea attacks S-g and Aée. Strindberg bandaged all over with cotton-wool and bindings for a cut in the hand and a boil on the upper lip. Washing with sublimate solution. Eating masses of meat.

The [?] at 4 a.m. start amid wind and snow. The skin-vest and "bashlik" taken out but were hardly needed. The country very bad but the going good. We crossed bear-tracks. I think that practically all the ice is pressure-ice. Even on level floes we see parallel lines which point to the floe containing pieces standing on edge. I have seen the same thing today in various places in the old yellow floes. All the hilly country consists undoubtedly of old hummocks and here most of the country is hilly. Our long. today 31° E and probably latitude 81° 50'. We shall therefore change our course tomorrow to S 60° W. Pretty clear now for a while out no land visible. August 17, 10.40 A.M. a Ross's gull and two black guillemot or little auks. Our journey today has been terrible. We have not advance 1000 meters [1100 yds.] but with the greatest difficulty have dodged on from foe to floe. The ice here is fearfully pressed together and shattered into small floes. A fairly reliable latitude determination gave 81° 47'. Bear-heart (fried) tastes a little bitter. Bear-meat in Stauffer's soup tasted very good. The ration of bear-meat per meal is from tomorrow morning to be increased to 1.1 kilo [2.4 lbs] per person.

Aug. 18 at 1.40 P M. start. During the night the ice had altered very much. The wind had turned more northerly. The weather beautiful. The going extremely troublesome, we ferried 5 times before midday, i.e., in 4 ¾ hours and had to begin again as soon as we had eaten. The ice is much divided into small floes. Many seals in the large open waters between the floes. A black guillemot visible. The sight of F's gun had dropped off but was found again. We must be near the sea, the ice being so divided. The horizon almost perfectly clear towards Gillis Land but we did not see any land in that direction. I believe that unpressed ice is found only near the egress of the Polar stream into the open sea [and is] formed by the freezing of the sludgy water. In the afternoon we had 3 ferryings and 1 rafting. With all this work we have hardly come 1 kilometer [1100 yds.] on our course, I suppose Thick. of ice 1.2 and 1.7 m [3.9 and 5.6 ft.]. A little auk visible. While we were sitting inside the tent and S. & F. were getting the supper ready and I was mending my pants I heard a noise outside the tent and when I looked through the crack in the opening I saw a bear close to my nose. I did not leave off sewing but merely said: "Look, there's another bear for us," whereupon F. took hold of one of the guns (which by chance had been taken into the tent for cleaning) and crept out. The bear then stood a few steps from him and...in order to attack but was met by a ball that brought him down dead after he had gone a few paces. We continued our work and our supper before we even looked at the carcass. But afterwards when we inspected the animal we found it was a large he-bear, undoubtedly the finest of all we had shot. We took out the brain, kidneys, tongue, and some pieces along the back, altogether abt. 10 kilo [22 lbs.] in order to supplement our supply of fresh meat. Strindberg took the lunar distance to check the chronometers and determined our position. He also set out some tackle for night fishing baited with meat (bear). The wind is now easterly and we are happy. Now too the horizon towards Gillis Land has been fairly clear but we have not seen anything of it. The difficulties in ferrying and rafting are constantly increased by the formation of new ice and the lively moments of the floes, which during the last twenty-four hours has been greater than we have noticed on any other occasion.

The 19th at 8 P.M. Start. Attempt at frying with bear-fat and F. said: "What a treat if we can make sandwiches." Of the bear we took only the brain, kidneys, and the best pieces, altogether abt. 8 kilo [17.5 lbs]. We have done a good day's work probably 5 kilom. [3 miles]. Leads large but regular and with large [strips] between. The terrain exceedingly tiring, the new snow preventing us from seeing the irregularities which constantly give the sledges unexpected jerks. The fresh-water pools, not yet frozen, force us to detour a lot. I am quite worn out by the day's work. The recconnoitrings are carried out by me and are very troublesome. I often have to go a long way among hummocks and over pools and along the leads. The worst are the fresh-water pools which turn in innumerable windings, real labyrinths, and which are united by means of wide fissures that do not become visible before one is close to them. I almost always throw my gun over my shoulder when I go off reconnoitring. S and F sit waiting and shivering. Sometimes they reconnoitre in one direction and I in the other. The reconnoitring for a route in the uneven country is almost as trying.

WE have encountered an immense lead running N 20° E. Exciting crossings must often be made. The sledges capsize or remain hanging over an abyss while the puller tumbles down. Then comes the order "lie still" and there he lies a long while holding up the sledge until the others can come to his help. The sledges must often be pulled at a great speed at one part of the crossing and slowly during another part. They must often be swung round on a point or in the middle of a pass. The axe and the spade must often be used to make a road. Tracks for one or both of the runners must be hewn. Perhaps the sledges have to be unloaded entirely or else they are balanced across the boat. A line at each end of the boat makes it possible to pull it forwards or backwards. The quays break just when the weight of the sledge rests on them. The sledge with its valuable cargo is in a position of the greatest danger.

Aug. 21, 12.10 A.M. start. Red-breast. Magnificent day. Air light. Faint north wind but the half frozen leads and pools of water have caused us an immense loss of time. A single ferrying took 2 hours. I believe that we have not hitherto had such a large tract of ice so hummocky and so broken. Sample No. 10 was attached frozen and fast and half dry (grey) to the fractured surface of a piece of ice pressed up by a lead. This evening on my proposal we tasted what raw meat was like. Raw bear with salt tastes like oysters and we hardly wanted to fry it. Raw brain is also very good and the bear's meat was easily eaten raw. Just as we were pitching our tent three bears came to attack us. We took up a position near a hummock. S-g shot the old one with one bullet. F. shot the other with two. I fired four shots at the other cub and made hits with all but his wounds were not so serious but that he could manage to get away among the fissures and pools. We took the best bits, i.e., ⅔ of the tongue, the kidneys and the brains. We also took the blood and F. was instructed to make blood-pancake (my suggestion). He did this by using oatmeal and frying in butter after which it was eaten with butter and found to be quite excellent. Of the bear-cubs one was rather big, the other (a female) was smaller. All the cubs we have seen have been young ones from the previous year. Experiment with alga-soup and Mellin's food-cake (water with yeast-powder) gave exc. result. The alga-soup (green) was proposed by S. and should be considered as a fairly important discovery for travellers in these tracts. Aug. 22, 5 A.M. Start. Young ivory gull, weight 475 gr [1 lb.] (full grown) was shot by me. It had black tips to the big tail and wing feathers as well as to the short cover-feathers. On the upper side and the sides of the neck there were some feathers with grey tips. The head was grey-black around the root of the beak, the eyes, and the front part of the head, the beak black. It seems to be the young ones that give the cry "pyot-pyot" noted under Aug. 14 as that of the ivory gull. When the mother is anxious or gives a warning she makes the cry piyrrr (see Aug. 14) but then with sharp r and in close succession. The young bird was white underneath. But the feet were marked as stated for the older [birds]. The terrain today has been terrible and I repeat what I wrote yesterday that we have not previously had such a large tract with ice so hummocky. Scarcely two square metres of ice can be found which does not present evident traces of pressure, the entire country consisting of a boundless field of large and small hummocks. One cannot speak of any regularity among them.

★

WHEN THE AGE OF THE DIRIGIBLE DAWNED IN THE 1920s, MEN WOULD *try again to reach the North Pole with a lighter-than-air machine, but for the time* being Andree's disappearance scotched the idea. But the Pole still beckoned. It was a matter of national pride for some, personal pride for others, a challenge in either case, and human beings are programmed to accept challenges. For one man in particular, the American naval officer Robert Peary, the challenge was to become the raison d'e-tre of his life. For Dr. Frederick Cook, his bête noire, it was something else, not so much a challenge as an afterthought—or so he claimed; but he made many claims—to his own ambitions, which centered around making his name however he could. Take them together and you have a drama that Eugene Ionesco might have written, a theater of the absurd in which it is hard to find much meaning and everything ends badly for all concerned.

Cook is in some ways the most interesting of the two, and certainly the more unexpected. The son of a German immigrant doctor, he was adventurous as a child. He once jumped into a swimming hole knowing he could not swim and learned on the spot. His father died when he was five and the family was poor, so he worked his way through medical school in New York, delivering milk from one to seven in the morning, then attending classes. He first shows up on the polar scene in 1891, having answered a newspaper ad asking for a surgeon to join an expedition to northern Greenland. The leader of the expedition was Lt. Robert E. Peary. Peary, reportedly, rather liked him. Cook said of Peary that he was a "thoroughly decent fellow."

Opinions on both sides of this equation would change soon enough. In 1894 Cook returned to Greenland at the head of his own expedition. He had learned a great deal about Eskimos and their way of life while on Peary's first expedition and had made himself enough of an expert to lecture widely on the subject when he came back to the United States. After turning down Peary's offer to accompany him on a second expedition, a Yale professor named James Hoppin financed Cook's own expedition to Greenland, on condition that Cook take Hoppin's son with him. Cook and Peary were now rivals. And Cook was now as passionate about the Arctic as Peary was.

Cook accomplished nothing with this expedition, which did little more than touch upon the Greenland coast here and there, except to enhance his own fame. He brought back some Eskimos with him and put them on public display, giving lectures about them and earning more money than his medical practice had ever paid. He made a third trip to Greenland, this time financing it by persuading students to fork over $500 for the trip. This voyage did not go well. His ship struck an iceberg, then went aground off the Greenland coast. All hands had to be rescued. The failure put paid to his chances at finding the funds for another expedition, so Cook turned south, signing on as the physician on a Belgian expedition to Antarctica. The ship was the Belgica and it had an international crew that spoke seven languages. The first mate was a young man named Roald Amundsen. The Belgica was frozen into the ice off the west coast of the Antarctic Peninsula and spent the winter there. On this occasion Cook behaved heroically. Amundsen not only praised him for his medical skills but gave him credit for keeping up the morale of the depressed, bored, light-starved crew, indeed for saving at least one of them from going mad. Amundsen and Cook would remain friends for the rest of Amundsen's life.

In 1901 Peary and Cook would meet again. Peary had disappeared into northern Greenland and the Peary Arctic Club asked Cook to help in the search. Cook joined the rescue expedition, which sailed to Etah, the Eskimo settlement where John Ross had so long before found the Arctic Highlanders who thought they were the only people on earth. Peary was there, exhausted and half-starved. Cook nursed him back to health.

By this time Peary was focused on reaching the North Pole and had made it, in effect, his life's work. Peary had backing, furthermore, the wealthy friends who formed the Peary Arctic Club. Cook had no backing. Cook was more the free-lance explorer, picking up financing wherever, however he could. He, too, wanted the Pole but it was not at all obvious where the money for it would come from. He needed a dramatic achievement to attract patrons and the idea for it came from an article in NATIONAL GEOGRAPHIC about Mt. McKinley in Alaska, the highest mountain in North America. No one had climbed it yet. If he could be the first up the mountain, Cook reasoned, money for a North Pole expedition would be easy to find. Cook had done a little climbing, but nothing that would prepare him for such a mountain, one of the most dangerous in the world. Cook was able to scrounge enough money for the Alaska expedition, and in 1903 he made the trip and came at the mountain from the north. It proved impossible. He and his party did manage the extremely difficult feat of circling the mountain, but they did not climb it.

Cook had established his reputation as an explorer, however, and no one yet had any reason to doubt his willingness to tell the truth. In 1905 he became one of the founders of the Explorers Club and in 1906 he was elected its president. Another founder was Robert Peary. The two men remained on friendly terms, although Peary never believed that Cook was his equal, either in social status or as an explorer. In 1906 Cook made his second attempt on Mt. McKinley. Herschel Parker, a wealthy mountaineer and professor of physics at Columbia University, provided most of the funds, on the condition that he could go. They took Belmore Browne along, a young climber recently graduated from Harvard. Browne and Parker were friends and it was they who would ultimately conquer Mt. McKinley—but in 1912, not 1906.

It was the 1906 expedition that was the beginning of Dr. Frederick Cook's undoing. Cook must have known that he could not climb the mountain, but he also knew that if he failed a second time, money for an attempt on the Pole would be impossible to find. When the party reached Mt. McKinley they looked for routes up but found nothing promising once again. Late in August, as they began to split up and go their separate ways, Cook said he was returning to the mountain to explore in the foothills and look for a route there he could pursue the following year. Belmore Browne asked to go with him, but Cook declined. He took instead a man named Ed Barrill, a blacksmith from Montana who had been brought along to help with the packhorses. On September 22, Cook and Barrill emerged from the McKinley foothills and Cook claimed to have climbed the mountain.

It has long since been demonstrated that Cook never reached the top, or even came close to it. The photograph he supposedly took from the top was actually taken at a spot some 7,000 feet up the mountain. Belmore Browne doubted Cook's story right away. There were too many discrepancies. Nevertheless the world accepted Cook's claim, at least at first, and it got him what he wanted—a hero's welcome. He gave lectures, was elected president of the Explorers Club (replacing Adolphus W. Greely), and spoke at the annual dinner of the National Geographic Society in Washington, where the guest of honor was— Robert E. Peary. Cook's "achievement," needless to say, stole Peary's thunder. He was not amused. That winter a wealthy sportsman named John Bradley gave Cook $10,000 to finance a hunting trip to Greenland the next summer. From Greenland, Cook told Bradley, he intended to try for the North Pole.

Perhaps no polar explorer except John Rae has ever traveled as lightly in the Arctic as Frederick Cook did on his dash to the north. Cook spent the winter at an Eskimo encampment some miles above Etah at the southern edge of Kane Basin. He left in February 1908 with nine Eskimo companions and a man named Rudolph Franke, who had been Bradley's steward on the yacht that brought them north. They crossed Ellesmere Island to Axel Heiberg Island to the west of it, which Norwegian explorer Otto Sverdrup had discovered and explored a couple of years earlier. Cook planned to jump off for the Pole from the northern coast of Axel Heiberg. He set out on March 18. He took two sledges, 28 dogs, half a ton of food and two Eskimos, young hunters named Etukishcok and Ahwelah. He left Rudolph Franke and the other Eskimos behind; they headed back to Greenland. Neither of the two men he took with him could speak English, and neither of them knew a sextant from a thermometer. The question of whether he reached the Pole or not would depend entirely on Cook's own testimony.

We catch up to Dr. Cook at a particularly dramatic moment in his race to the Pole, five days into it.

DR. FREDERICK A. COOK

My Attainment of the Pole

Crossing Moving Seas of Ice
XV
THE FIRST STEPS OVER THE GRINDING CENTRAL PACK

ILL AT EASE AND SHIVERING, WE ROSE FROM OUR CRYSTAL BERTHS ON March 23 and peeped out of a pole-punched porthole. A feeble glow of mystic color came from everywhere at once. Outside, toward a sky of dull purple, columns of steam-like vapor rose from open ice water, resembling vapors from huge boiling cauldrons. We sank with chattering teeth to our cheerless beds and quivered with the ghostly unreality of this great vibrating unknown.

Long before the suppressed incandescent night changed to the prism sparkle of day we were out seeking a way over the miles of insecure young ice separating us from the central pack. On our snowshoes, with an easy tread, spread feet and with long life lines tied to each other, we ventured to the opposite shores of that dangerous spread of young ice. Beyond, the central pack glittered in moving lines and color, like quicksilver shot with rainbow hues.

The Big Lead was mottled and tawny colored, like the skin of a great constrictor. As we stood and looked over its broad expanse to the solid floes, two miles off, there came premonitions to me of impending danger. Would the ice bear us? If it broke, and the life line was not quickly jerked, our fate would almost certainly be sure death. Sontag, the astronomer of Dr. Hay's Expedition, thus lost his life. Many others have in like manner gone to the bottomless deep. On two occasions during the previous winter I had thus gone through, but the life line had saved me. What would be our fate here? But, whatever the luck, we must cross. I knew delay was fatal, for at any time a very light wind or a change in the drift might break the new ice and delay us long enough to set the doom of failure upon our entire venture.

Every precaution was taken to safeguard our lives. The most important problem was to distribute the weight so that all of it would not be brought to bear on a small area. We separated our dog teams from the sleds, holding to long lines which were fastened about our bodies and also to the sleds. The sleds were hitched to each other by another long line.

With bated breath and my heart thumping, I advanced at the end of a long line which was attached to the first sled, and picked my way through the crushed and difficult ice along shore. With the life-saving line fastened to each one of us, we were insured against possible dangers as well as forethought could provide. Running from sled to sled, from dog to dog, and man to man, it would afford a pulling chance for life should anyone break through the ice. It seemed unlikely that the ice along the entire chain would break at once, but its cracking under the step of one of us seemed probable.

I knew, as I gently placed my foot upon the thin yellowish surface, that at any moment I might sink into an icy grave. Yet a spirit of bravado thrilled my heart. I felt the grip of danger, and also that thrill of exultation which accompanies its terror.

Gently testing the ice before me with the end of my axe, with spread legs, on snowshoes, with long, sliding steps, I slowly advanced.

A dangerous cracking sound pealed in every direction under my feet. The Eskimos followed. With every tread the thin sheet ice perceptibly sank under me, and waved, in small billows like a sheet of rubber.

Stealthily, as though we were trying to filch some victory, we crept forward. We rocked on the heaving ice as a boat on waves of water. Now and then we stepped upon sheets of thicker ice, and hastily went forward with secure footing. None of us spoke during the dangerous crossing. I heard distinctly the panting of the dogs and the patter of their feet. We covered the two miles safely, yet our snail-like progress seemed to cover many anxious years.

I cannot describe the exultation which filled me when the crossing was accomplished. It seemed as though my goal itself were stretching toward me. I experienced a sense of unbounded victory. I could have cheered with joy. Intoxicated with it, I and my companions leaped forward, new cheer quickening our steps. The dangers to come seemed less formidable now, and as we journeyed onward it was the mastering of these, as did our accomplishment in crossing the Big Lead, which gave us a daily incentive to continue our way and ever to apply brain and muscle to the subduing of even greater difficulties with zest.

It was in doing this that the real thrill, the real victory—the only thrill and victory, indeed—of reaching the North Pole lay. The attaining of this mythical spot did not then, and does not now, seem in itself to mean anything; I did not then, and do not now, consider it the treasure-house of any great scientific secrets. The only thing to be gained from reaching the Pole, the triumph of it, the lesson in the accomplishment, is that man, by brain power and muscle energy, can subdue the most terrific forces of a blind nature if he is determined enough, courageous enough, and undauntedly persistent despite failure.

On my journey northward I felt the ever constant presence of those who had died in trying to reach the goal before me. There were times when I felt a startling nearness to them—a sense like that one has of the proximity of living beings in an adjoining room. I felt the goad of their hopes within me; I felt the steps of their unfailing determination revive me when I was tempted to turn back in the days of inhuman suffering that were to come. I felt that I, the last man to essay this goal, must for them justify humanity; that I must crown three centuries of human effort with success.

With the perilous Big Lead behind us, a bounding course was set to reach the eighty-fifth parallel on the ninety-seventh meridian. What little movement was noted on the ice had been easterly. To allow for this drift we aimed to keep a line slightly west of the Pole.

We bounded northward joyously. Under our speeding feet the ice reverberated and rumbled with the echo of far-away splitting and crashing.

The sun sank into a haze like mother-of-pearl. Our pathway glowed with purple and orange. We paused only when the pale purple blue of night darkened the pack.

Starting forward in the afternoon of March 24, we crossed many small floes with low-pressure lines separated by narrow belts of new ice. Our speed increased. At times we could hardly keep pace with our dogs. The temperature rose to forty-one below zero. The western sky cleared slightly. Along the horizon remained misty appearances resembling land. This low-lying fog continued during our entire second hundred miles over the Polar basin. Under it we daily expected to see new land.

But Nature did not satisfy our curiosity for a long time. Both Ah-we-lah and E-tuk-I-shook were sure of a constant nearness to land. Because of the native panic out of its reassuring sight, I encouraged this belief, as I did concerning every other possible sign of land further northward. I knew that only by encouraging a delusion of nearness to land could I urge them ever farther in the face of the hardships that must inevitably come.

An altitude of the sun at noon on March 24 gave our position as latitude 83° 31'. The longitude was estimated at 96° 27'. The land clouds of Grant Land were still visible. The low bank of mist in the west occasionally brightened. For a while I believed this to be an indication of Crocker Land.

Until midday I took observations and endeavored to study the appearances of land. Our dogs sniffed the air as if scenting game. After a diligent search, one seal blow-hole was located, and later we saw an old bear track. No algae or other small life was detected in the water between the ice crevices. At the Big Lead a few algae had been gathered. But here the sea seemed sterile. Signs of seal and bear, however, were encouraging to us as possible future food supply. In returning, I calculated the season would be more advanced, and it was possible that life might move northward, thus permitting an extension of the time allowance of our rations.

Although the heat of the sun was barely felt, its rays began to pierce our eyes with painful effects. Reflected from the spotless surface of the storm-driven snows, the bright light could not long be endured without some protection, even by the Eskimos. Now came the time to test a simple expedient that had occurred to me at Annoatok. Amber-colored goggles, darkened or smoked glasses and ordinary automobile goggles had all been tried with indifferent results. They failed for one reason or another, mostly because of an insufficient range of vision or because of a faulty construction that made it impossible to proceed more than a few minutes without removing the accumulated condensation within them. At Annoatok I had made amber-colored goggles from the glass of my photographic supplies. By adjusting them I soon found they were a priceless discovery. They entirely eliminated one of the greatest torments of Arctic travel.

While effectually screening the active rays that would have injured the eye, these amber glasses at the same time possessed the inestimable advantage of not interfering with the range of vision.

Relieved of the snow glare, the eye was better enabled to see distant objects than through field glasses. It is frequently extremely difficult to detect icy surface irregularities on cloudy days. The amber glass dispelled this trouble perfectly, enabling the eye to search carefully every nook and crevice through the vague incandescence which blinds the observer in hazy weather. The glasses did not reduce the *quantity* of light, as do smoked glasses, but the *quality*; the actinic rays, which do the greatest harm, were eliminated. We were not only relieved of the pain and fatigue of eye strain, but the color imparted a touch of cheer and warmth to our chilled blue horizon. The usual snow goggles add to the ugly gray-blue of the frozen seas, which alone sends frosty waves through the nervous fibers.

So thoroughly delighted were we with the goggles that later we wore them even in igloos while asleep, with the double object of screening the strong light which passes through the eyelids and of keeping the forehead warm.

On our march in the early part of the afternoon of the 24th the weather proved good. The ice, though newly crevassed, improved as we advanced. The late start spread our day's work close to the chill of midnight. When we started the wind blew kindly. With glad hearts we forged forward without delays. On the ice I heard the soft patter of swift dog feet and the dashing, cutting progress of the sleds. As a scene viewed from a carousel, the field of ice swept around me in our dizzy, twisting progress. We swept resistlessly onward for twenty-three miles. As we had taken a zigzag course to follow smooth ice, I therefore recorded only eighteen miles to our credit.

The night was beautiful. The sun sank into a purple haze. Soon, in the magic of the atmosphere, appeared three suns of prismatic colors. These settled slowly into the frozen sea and disappeared behind that persistent haze of obscuring mist which always rests over the pack when the sun is low. During the night a narrow band of orange was flung like a ribbon across the northern skies. The pack surface glowed with varying shades of violet, lilac, and pale purplish blue. Many such splendid sights are to be constantly seen in the Arctic.

Although I reveled in it now, the time was soon to come when weariness and hunger numbed my faculties into a dreary torpor in which the splendor was not seen.

Signs appeared of a gale from the west before we were quite ready to camp. Little sooty clouds with ragged edges suddenly began to cover the sky, scurrying at an alarming pace Beyond us a huge smoky volume of cloud blackened the pearly glitter.

Suitable camping ice was sought. In the course of an hour we built an igloo. We made the structure stronger than usual on account of the threatening storm. We constructed double tiers of snow blocks to the windward. A little water was thrown over the top to cement the block. We fastened the dogs to the lee of hummocks. The sleds were securely lashed and fastened to the ice.

We expected a hurricane, and had not to wait to taste its fury. Before we were at rest in our bags the wind lashed the snows with a force inconceivable. With rushing drift, the air thickened. Dogs and sleds in a few minutes were buried under banks of snow and great drifts encircled the igloo. The cemented blocks of our dome withstood the sweep of the blast well. Yet, now and then, small holes were burrowed through the snow wall by the sharp wind. Drift entered and covered us. I lay awake for hours. I felt the terrible oppression of that raging, life-sucking vampire force sweeping over the desolate world. Disembodied things—the souls of those, perhaps, who had perished here— seemed frenziedly calling me in the wind. I felt under me the surge of the sweeping, awful sea. I felt the desolation of this stormy world within my shuddering soul; but, withal, I throbbed with a determination to assert the supremacy of living man over these blind, insensate forces; to prove that the living brain and palpitating muscle of a finite though conscious creature could vanquish a hostile Nature which creates to kill. I burned to justify those who had died here; to fulfill by proxy their hopes; to set their calling souls at rest. The storm waked in me an angry, challenging, determination.

Early in the morning of the 25th the storm ceased as suddenly as it had come. A stillness followed which was appalling. It seemed as if the storm had heard my thoughts and paused to contemplate some more dreadful onslaught. The dogs began to howl desperately, as if attacked by a bear. We rushed out of our igloo, seeking guns. There were no approaching creatures. It was, however, a signal of serious distress that we had heard. The dogs were in acute misery. The storm-driven snows had buried and bound them in unyielding ice. They had partly uncovered themselves. United by trace and harness, they were imprisoned in frozen masses. Few of them could even rise and stretch. They were in severe torment.

We hurriedly freed their traces and beat the cemented snows from their furs with sticks. Released, they leaped about gladly, their cries, curling tails and pointed noses telling of gratitude. While we danced about, stretching our limbs and rubbing our hands to get up circulation, the sun rose over the northern blue, flushing the newly driven snows with warm tones. The temperature during the storm had risen to only 26° below, but soon the thermometer sank rapidly below −40°. The west was still smoky and the weather did not seem quite settled. As it was still too early to start, we again slipped into the bags and sought quiet slumber.

As yet the dreadful insomnia which was to rob me of rest on my journey had not come, and I slept with the blissful soundness of a child. I must have been asleep several hours, when, of a sudden, I opened my eyes.

Terror gripped my heart. Loud explosive noises reverberated under my head. It seemed as though bombs were torn asunder in the depths of the cold sea beneath me. I lay still, wondering if I were dreaming. The sounds echoingly died away. Looking about the igloo, I detected nothing unusual. I saw Ah-we-lah and E-tuk-I-shook staring at me with wide-open frightened eyes. I arose and peeped through the eye port. The fields of ice without reflected the warm light of the rising sun in running waves of tawny color. The ice was undisturbed. An unearthly quiet prevailed. Concluding that the ice was merely cracking under the sudden change of temperature, in quite the usual harmless manner, I turned over again, reassuring my companions, and promptly fell asleep.

Out of the blankets of sleep I suddenly wakened again. Half-dazed, I heard beneath me a series of echoing, thundering noises. I felt the ice floor on which I lay quivering. I experienced the sudden giddiness one feels on a tossing ship at sea. In the flash of a second I saw Ah-we-lah leap to his feet. In the same dizzy instant I saw the dome of the snowhouse open above me; I caught a vision of the gold-streaked sky. My instinct at the moment was to leap. I think I tried to rise, when suddenly everything seemed lifted from under me; I experienced the suffocating sense of falling, and next, with a spasm of indescribable horror, felt about my body a terrific tightening pressure like that of a chilled and closing shell of steel, driving the life and breath from me.

In an instant it was clear what had happened. A crevasse had suddenly opened through our igloo, directly under the spot whereupon I slept; and I, as helpless creature in a sleeping bag, with tumbling snow blocks and ice and snow crashing about and crushing me, with the temperature 48° below zero, was floundering in the opening sea!

Land Discovered
XVI

I THINK I WAS ABOUT TO SWOON WHEN I FELT HANDS BENEATH MY armpits and heard laughter in my ears. With an adroitness such as only these natives possess, my two companions were dragging me from the water. And while I lay panting on the ice, recovering from my fright, I saw them expeditiously rescue our possessions.

It seemed that all this happened so quickly that I had really been in the water only a few moments. My two companions saw the humor of the episode and laughed heartily. Although I had been in the water only a brief time, a sheet of ice surrounded my sleeping bag. Fortunately, however, the reindeer skin was found to be quite dry when the ice was beaten off. The experience, while momentarily terrifying, was instructive, for it taught us the danger of spreading ice, especially in calms following storms.

Gratitude filled my heart. I fully realized how narrow had been the escape of all of us. Had we slept a few seconds longer we should all have disappeared in the opening crevasse. The hungry Northland would again have claimed its human sacrifice.

The ice about was much disturbed. Numerous black lines of water opened on every side; from these oozed jets of frosty, smoke-colored vapor. The difference between the temperature of the sea and that of the air was 76°. With this contrast, the open spots of ice-water appeared to be boiling.

Anxious to move along, away from the troubled angle of ice, our usual breakfast was simplified. Melting some snow, we drank the icy liquid as an eye-opener, and began our ration of a half-pound boulder of pemmican. But with cold fingers, blue lips and no possible shelter, the stuff was unusually hard. To warm up, we prepared the sleds. Under our lashes the dogs jumped into harness with a bound. The pemmican, which we really found too hard to eat, had to be first broken into pieces with an axe. We ground it slowly with our molars as we trudged along. Our teeth chattered while the stomach was thus being fired with durable fuel.

✳

Did Cook reach the Pole? He claimed to have reached it in a little over a month, on April 21. On the way he saw, or said he saw, a sizable body of land that he named Bradley Island, after his patron. There is no land where he said that he found it. His account of reaching the Pole itself is full of measurements, but he was the only one capable of making them. In his book he draws shadow dials and explains them. He writes about temperature variations. He prints the photographs he took at the Pole. But was he there? Could a man who gave up at 7,000 feet on Mt. McKinley while claiming to have reached the summit be truthful about a claim to have traveled over the ice nearly six hundred miles in a month, a rate of nineteen miles a day? When no other Arctic explorer (except Peary) has ever made such good time?

We leave the question for now. What we do know about Cook is that the rest of his trip was one of the most remarkable in the annals of Arctic travel. For it was one thing to go to the Pole. It was something else to make it back alive. The three men backtracked south, but west of their track north. Cook hoped to explore his new island. He couldn't find it. He pushed farther south, once again at an unbelievable rate even though they were on half rations and totally exhausted. Cook is vague about the details. Late in May they found themselves to the west of Axel Heiberg Island and fresh game was available. But they were running out of ammunition. Their pemmican had run out.

They reached the northern shore of Devon Island in September with four rounds of ammunition among the three of them, matches, knives, the remains of their sled, and their collapsible boat. It was too late in the season to make it back to Etah. They had no choice but to find shelter and figure out a way to survive. Our next selection from Cook's account describes how they did that, reverting to Stone Age conditions, using spears they made themselves as weapons. No one questions this part of the story.

Bull Fights With thee Musk Ox
XXVI
To the Winter Camp at Cape Sparbo

As we crossed the big bay to the east of Cape Sparbo, our eyes were fixed on the two huge Archaen rocks which made remarkable landmarks, rising suddenly to an altitude of about eighteen thousand feet. They appear like two mountainous islands lifted out of the water. On closer approach, however, we found the islands connected with the mainland by low grassy plains, forming a peninsula. The grassy lands seemed like promising grounds for caribou and musk ox. The off-lying sea, we also found, was shallow. In this, I calculated, would be food to attract the seal and walrus.

In our slow movement over the land swell of the crystal waters, it did not take long to discover that our conjecture was correct.

Pulling up to a great herd of walrus, we prepared for battle. But the sea suddenly rose, the wind increased, and we were forced to abandon the chase and seek shelter on the nearest land.

We reached Cape Sparbo, on the shores of Jones Sound, early in September. Our dogs were gone. Our ammunition, except four cartridges which I had secreted for use in a last emergency, was gone. Our equipment consisted of a half sledge, a canvas boat, a torn silk tent, a few camp kettles, tin plates, knives, and matches. Our clothing was splitting to shreds.

Cape Sparbo, with its huge walls of granite, was to the leeward. A little bay was noted where we might gain the rocks in quiet water. Above the rocks was a small green patch where we hoped to find a soft resting place for the boat, so that we might place our furs in it and secure shelter from the bitter wind.

When we landed we found to our surprise that it was the site of an old Eskimo village. There was a line of old igloos partly below water, indicating a very ancient time of settlement, for since the departure of the builders of these igloos the coast must have settled at least fifteen feet. Above were a few other ruins.

Shortly after arriving we sought an auspicious place, protected from the wind and cold, where later we might build a winter shelter. Our search disclosed a cave-like hole, part of which was dug from the earth, and over which, with stones and bones, had been constructed a roof which now was fallen in.

The long winter was approaching. We were over three hundred miles from Annoatok, and the coming of the long night made it necessary for us to halt here. We must have food and clothing. We now came upon musk oxen and tried to fell them with boulders, and bows and arrows made of the hickory of our sledge. Day after day the pursuit was vainly followed. Had it not been for occasional ducks caught with looped lines and sling shots, we should have been absolutely without any food.

By the middle of September, snow and frost came with such frequency that we omitted hunting for a day to dig out the ruins in the cave and cut sod before permanent frost made such work impossible. Bone implements were shaped from skeletons found on shore for the digging. Blown drifts of sand and gravel, with some moss and grass, were slowly removed from the pit. We found under this, to our great joy, just the underground arrangement which we desired; a raised platform, about six feet long and eight feet wide with suitable wings for the lamp, and footspace, lay ready for us. The pit had evidently been designed for a small family. The walls, which were about two feet high, required little alteration. Another foot was added, which leveled the structure with the ground. A good deal of sod was cut and allowed to dry in the sun for use as a roof.

While engaged in taking out the stones and cleaning the dungeon-like excavation, I suddenly experienced a heart-depressing chill when, lifting some debris, I saw staring at me from the black earth a hollow-eyed human skull. The message of death which the weird thing leeringly conveyed was singularly unpleasant; the omen was not good. Yet the fact that at this forsaken spot human hands had once built shelter, or for this thing had constructed a grave, gave me a certain companionable thrill.

On the shore not far away we secured additional whale ribs and with these made a framework for a roof. This was later constructed of moss and blocks of sod. We built a rock wall about the shelter to protect ourselves from storms and bears. Then our winter home was ready. Food was now an immediate necessity. Game was found around us in abundance. Most of it was large. On land there were bear and musk ox, in the sea the walrus and the whale. But what could we do without either dogs or rifles?

The first weapon that we now devised was the bow and arrow, for with this we could at least secure some small game. We had in our sledge available hickory wood of the best quality, than which no wood could be better; we had sinews and seal lashings for strings, but there was no metal for tips. We tried bone, horn and ivory, but all proved ineffective.

One day, however, E-tuk-I-shook examined his pocket knife and suggested taking the blades for arrow tips. This was done, and the blade with its spring was set in a bone handle. Two arrows were thus tipped. The weapons complete, the Eskimo boys went out on the chase. They returned in the course of a few hours with a hare and an eider-duck. Joy reigned in camp as we divided the meat and disposed of it without the process of cooking.

A day later, two musk oxen were seen grazing along the moraine of a wasting glacier. Now the musk ox is a peace-loving animal and avoids strife, but when forced into fight it is one of the most desperate and dangerous of all the fighters of the wilderness. It can and does give the most fatal thrust of all the horned animals. No Spanish bull of the pampas, no buffalo of the plains, has either the slant of horn or the intelligence to gore its enemies as has this inoffensive-looking bull of the ice world. The intelligence, indeed, is an important factor, for after watching musk oxen for a time under varied conditions, one comes to admire their almost human intellect as well as their superhuman power of delivering self-made force.

Our only means of attack was with the bow and arrow. The boys crept up behind rocks until within a few yards of the unsuspecting creatures. They bent the bows, and the arrows sped with the force and accuracy as only a hungry savage can master. But the beasts' pelts were too strong. Each arrow, as it came, was broken into splints by the feet and the teeth.

When the arrows were all used a still more primitive weapon was tried, for the sling shot was brought into use, with large stones. These missiles the musk oxen took good naturedly, merely advancing a few steps to a granite boulder, upon which they sharpened their horn points and awaited further developments. No serious injury had been inflicted and they made no effort to escape.

Then came a change. When we started to give up the chase they turned upon us with a fierce rush. Fortunately, many big boulders were about, and we dodged around these with large stones in hand to deliver at close range. In a wild rush a musk ox cannot easily turn, and so can readily be dodged. Among the rocks two legs were better than four. The trick of evading the musk ox I had learned from the dogs. It saved our lives.

After a while the animals wearied, and we beat a hasty retreat, with new lessons in our book of hunting adventures. The bow and arrow was evidently not the weapon with which to secure musk oxen.

The musk ox of Jones Sound, unlike his brother farther north, is ever ready for battle. He is often compelled to meet the bear and the wolf in vicious contests, and his tactics are as thoroughly developed as his emergencies require. Seldom does he fall the victim of his enemies. We were a long time in learning completely his methods of warfare, and if, in the meantime, we had not secured other game our fate would have been unfortunate.

Harpoons and lances were next finally completed, and with them we hastened to retrieve our honor in the "ah-ming-ma" chase. For, after all, the musk ox alone could supply our wants. Winter storms were coming fast. We were not only without food and fuel, but without clothing. In our desperate effort to get out of the regions of famine to the Atlantic, we had left behind all our winter furs, including the sleeping bags; and our summer garments were worn out. We required the fuel and the sinew, the fat and the horn.

One day we saw a herd of twenty-one musk oxen quietly grazing on a misty meadow, like cattle on the western plains. It was a beautiful sight to watch them, divided as they were into families and in small groups. The males were in fur slightly brown, while the females and the young ones were arrayed in magnificent black pelts.

To get any of them seemed hopeless, but our appalling necessities forced us onward. There were no boulders near, but each of us gathered an armful of stones, the object being to make a sudden bombardment and compel them to retreat in disorder and scatter among the rocks.

We approached under cover of a small grassy hummock. When we were detected, a bull gave a loud snort and rushed toward his nearest companions, whereupon the entire herd gathered into a circle, with the young in the center.

We made our sham rush and hurled the stones. The oxen remained almost motionless, with their heads down, giving little snorts and stamping a little when hit, but quickly resuming their immobile position of watchfulness. After our stones were exhausted, the animals began to shift positions slightly. We interpreted this as a move for action. So we gave up the effort and withdrew.

The days were long and the nights still light enough to continue operations as long as we could keep our eyes open. The whip of hunger made rest impossible. So we determined to seek a less formidable group of oxen in a position more favorable. The search was continued until the sinking glimmer of the sun in the north marked the time of midnight—for with us at that time the compass was the timepiece.

When E-tuk-I-shook secured a hare with the bow and arrow, we ascended a rocky eminence and sat down to appease the calling stomach without a camp fire. From here we detected a family of four musk oxen asleep not far from another group of rocks.

This was a call to battle. We were not long in planning our tactics. The wind was in our favor, permitting an attack from the side opposite the rocks to which we aimed to force a retreat. We also found small stones in abundance, these being now a necessary part of our armament. Our first effort was based on the supposition of their remaining asleep. They were simply chewing their cud, however, and rose to form a ring of defence as we advanced. We stormed them with stones and they took to the shelter of the rocks. We continued to advance slowly upon them, throwing stones occasionally to obviate a possible assault from them before we could also seek the shelter of the rocks.

Besides the bow and arrow and the stones, we now had lances and these we threw as they rushed to attack us. Two lances were crushed to small fragments before they could be withdrawn by the light line attached. They inflicted wounds, but not severe ones.

Noting the immense strength of the animals, we at first thought it imprudent to risk the harpoon with its precious line, for if we lost it we could not replace it. But the destruction of the two lances left us no alternative.

Ah-we-lah threw the harpoon. It hit a rib, glanced to a rock, and was destroyed. Fortunately we had a duplicate point, which was quickly fastened. Then we moved about to encourage another onslaught.

Two came at once, an old bull and a young one. E-tuk-I-shook threw the harpoon at the young one, and it entered. The line had previously been fastened to a rock, and the animal ran back to its associates, apparently not severely hurt, leaving the line slack. One of the others immediately attacked the line with horns, hoofs and teeth, but did not succeed in breaking it.

Our problem now was to get rid of the other three while we dealt with the one at the end of the line. Our only resource was a sudden fusilade of stones. This proved effective. The three scattered and ascended the boulder-strewn foreland of a cliff, where the oldest bull remained to watch our movements. The young bull made violent efforts to escape but the line of sealskin was strong and elastic. A lucky throw of a lance at close range ended the strife. Then we advanced on the old bull, who was alone in a good position for us.

We gathered stones and advanced, throwing them at the creature's body. This, we found, did not enrage him, but it prevented his making an attack. As we gained ground he gradually backed up to the edge of the cliff, snorting viciously but making no effort whatever either to escape along a lateral bench or to attack.

His big brown eyes were upon us; his sharp horns were pointed at us. He evidently was planning a desperate lunge and was backing to gain time and room, but each of us kept within a few yards of a good-sized rock.

Suddenly we made a combined rush into the open, hurling stones, and keeping a long rock in a line for retreat. Our storming of stones had the desired effect. The bull, annoyed and losing its presence of mind, stepped impatiently one step too far backwards and fell suddenly over the cliff, landing on a rocky ledge below. Looking over we saw he had broken a fore leg. The cliff was not more than fifteen feet high. From it the lance was used to put the poor creature out of suffering. We were rich now and could afford to spread out our stomachs, contracted by long spells of famine. The bull dressed about three hundred pounds of meat and one hundred pounds of tallow.

We took the tallow and as much meat as we could carry on our backs, and started for the position of our prospective winter camp, ten miles away. The meat left was carefully covered with heavy stones to protect it from bears, wolves and foxes. On the following day we returned with the canvas boat, making a landing about four miles from the battlefield. As we neared the caches we found to our dismay numerous bear and fox tracks. The bears had opened the caches and removed our hard-earned game, while the foxes and the ravens had cleared up the very fragments and destroyed even the skins. Here was cause for vengeance on the bear and the fox. The fox paid his skin later, but the bear outgeneraled us in nearly every maneuvre.

We came prepared to continue the chase but had abandoned the use of the harpoon. Our main hope for fuel was the blubber of the walrus, and if the harpoon should be destroyed or lost we could not hope to attack so powerful a brute as a walrus with any other device. In landing we had seen a small herd of musk oxen at some distance to the east, but they got our wind and vanished. We decided to follow them up. One day we found them among a series of rolling hills, where the receding glaciers had left many erratic boulders. They lined up in their ring of defence as usual when we were detected. There were seven of them; all large creatures with huge horns. A bitter wind was blowing, driving some snow, which made our task more difficult.

The opening of the fight with stones was now a regular feature which we never abandoned in our later developments of the art, but the manner in which we delivered the stones depended upon the effect which we wished to produce. If we wished the musk oxen to retreat, we would make a combined rush, hurling the stones at the herd. If we wished them to remain in position and discourage their attack, we advanced slowly and threw stones desultorily, more or less at random. If we wanted to encourage attacks, one man advanced and delivered a large rock as best he could at the head. This was cheap ammunition and it was very effective.

In this case the game was in a good position for us and we advanced accordingly. They allowed us to take positions within about fifteen feet, but no nearer. The lances were repeatedly tried without effect, and after a while two of these were again broken.

Having tried bow and arrow, stones, the lance and the harpoon, we now tried another weapon. We threw the lasso—but not successfully, owing to the bushy hair about the head and the roundness of the hump of the neck. Then we tried to entangle their feet with slip loops just as we trapped gulls. This also failed. We next extended the loop idea to the horns. The bull's habit of rushing at things hurled at him caused us to think of this plan.

A large slip loop was now made in the center of the line, and the two natives took up positions on opposite sides of the animal. They threw the rope, with its loop, on the ground in front of the creature, while I encouraged an attack from the front. As the head was slightly elevated the loop was raised, and the bull put his horns in it, one after the other. The rope was now rapidly fastened to stones and the bull tightened the loop by his efforts to advance or retreat. With every opportunity the slack was taken up, until no play was allowed the animal. During this struggle all the other oxen retreated except one female, and she was inoffensive. A few stones at close range drove her off. Then we had the bull where we could reach him with the lance at arm's length, and plunge it into his vitals. He soon fell over, the first victim to our new art of musk ox capture.

The others did not run far away. Indeed, they were too fat to run, and two more were soon secured in the same way. This time we took all the meat we could with us to the camp and left a man on guard. When all was removed to the bay we found the load too heavy for our boat, so, in two loads, we transported the meat and fat and skins to our camp, where we built caches which we believed to be impregnable to the bear, although the thieving creatures actually opened them later.

Our lances repaired, we started out for another adventure a few days later.

It was a beautiful day. Our methods of attack were not efficient, but we wished to avoid the risk of the last plunge of the lance, for our lives were in the balance every time if the line should break, and with every lunge of the animal we expected it to snap. In such case, we knew, the assailant would surely be gored.

We were sufficiently independent now to proceed more cautiously. With the bull's willingness to put his head into the loop, I asked myself whether the line loop could not be slipped beyond the horns and about the neck, thus shutting off the air. So the line was lengthened with this effort in view.

Of the many groups of oxen which we saw we picked those in the positions most to our advantage, although rather distant. Our new plan was tried with success on a female. A bull horned her vigorously when she gasped for breath, and which aided our efforts. A storming of stones scattered the others of the group, and we were left to deal with our catch with the knife.

Our art of musk ox fighting was now completely developed. In the course of a few weeks we secured enough to assure comfort and ease during the long night. By our own efforts we were lifted suddenly from famine to luxury. But it had been the stomach with its chronic emptiness which had lashed the mind and body to desperate efforts with sufficient courage to face the danger. Hunger, as I have found, is more potent as a stimulant than barrels of whiskey. Beginning with the bow and arrow we had tried everything which we could devise, but now our most important acquisition was our intimate knowledge of the animal's own means of offence and defense.

We knew by a kind of instinct when an attack upon us was about to be made, because the animal made a forward move, and we never failed in our efforts to force a retreat. The rocks which the animals sought for an easy defense were equally useful to us, and later we forced them into deep waters and also deep snow with similar success. By the use of stones and utilizing the creatures' own tactics we placed them where we wished. And then again, by the animal's own efforts, we forced it to strangle itself, which, after all, was the most humane method of slaughter. Three human lives were thus saved by the invention of a new art of chase. This gave us courage to attack those more vicious but less dangerous animals, the bear and walrus.

The musk ox now supplied many wants in our "Robinson Crusoe" life. From the bone we made harpoon points, arrow pieces, knife handles, fox traps and sledge repairs. The skin, with its remarkable fur, made our bed and roofed our igloo. Of it we made all kinds of garments, but its greatest use was for coats with hoods, stockings and mittens. From the skin, with the fur removed, we made boots, patched punctures in our boat, and cut lashings. The hair and wool which were removed from the skins made pads for our palms in the mittens and cushions for the soles of our feet in lieu of the grass formerly used.

The meat became our staple food for seven months without change. It was a delicious product. It has a flavor slightly sweet, like that of horseflesh, but still distinctly pleasing. It possesses an odor unlike musk but equally unlike anything that I know of. The live creatures exhale the scent of domestic cattle. Just why this odd creature is called "musk" ox is a mystery, for it is neither an ox, nor does it smell of musk. The Eskimo name of "ah-ming-wa" would fit it much better. The bones were used as fuel for outside fires, and the fat as both fuel and food.

At first our wealth of food came with surprise and delight to us, for, in the absence of sweet or starchy foods, man craves fat. Sugar and starch are most readily converted into fat by the animal laboratory, and fat is one of the prime factors in the development and maintenance of the human system. It is the confectionery of aboriginal man, and we had taken up the lot of the most primitive aborigines, living and thriving solely on the product of the chase without a morsel of civilized or vegetable food. Under these circumstances we especially delighted in the musk ox tallow, and more especially in the marrow, which we sucked from the bone with the eagerness with which a child jubilantly manages a stick of candy.

COOK REACHED THE ESKIMO SETTLEMENT HE HAD LEFT IN GREENLAND *fourteen months after he had left. The trek back from their winter home on Devon Island was as harrowing as the winter itself had been. They were forced to eat rotten seals, to chew on their boots, to starve. That they made it at all is one of the Arctic's miracles, and a truly epic feat. It's a pity it was mixed up with Cook's claims about reaching the Pole.*

PEARY HAD BEEN TO THE ESKIMO SETTLEMENT WHILE COOK WAS GONE. *It was now 1909 and Peary was making his own attempt at the Pole, the one he announced would be his last. For Peary it was now or never.*

He had his own problems with credibility. He was a civil engineer with a Navy commission and, having read Elisha Kent Kane's books about the Arctic as a youth, he had been obsessed with reaching the Pole for many years. He had a tendency to boast and to make claims about discoveries that turned out not to be true. Land that he said he had seen—like Cook with Bradley Land—did not exist. He made his first trip north in 1886 to explore, on his mother's money, western Greenland and worked his way 100 miles inland. He wanted very badly to be famous, wanted it perhaps worse than Cook wanted it. He needed to feel superior to those around him. He became furious when Nansen beat him to the crossing of Greenland, accusing him of stealing his idea, even though Nansen had planned the trip four years before Peary even thought of it. His obsession with the Pole, and with his fame, took him over. It made him imperious, driven, unpleasant to be around.

Peary returned to Greenland in 1891, this time to cross it to its northeast corner. This is the trip that Cook accompanied him on. He brought his wife with him, too, and his servant, a black man named Matthew Henson. Henson always went on his expeditions. In April 1892 Peary and another man, a Norwegian named Astrup, set out across Greenland and got as far as one of the fjords that penetrate into the northeast coast of the island. It was a remarkable feat, most notable for its speed. He had covered 1,100 miles there and back in 85 days, a rate twice Nansen's. He had also shown that Greenland was an island. He had come to the end of it.

Or almost. Looking from the top of a cliff at this end of the world, staring out over what he called Peary Channel, he had seen more land. Peary Channel was in fact another fjord, and the land he saw on the other side of it was simply another piece of Greenland. But no one knew that then and the world hailed him as a great Arctic explorer. When he returned to the United States he wrote the usual book and went on the usual lecture tour, making as much as $2,000 a day, a princely sum in 1892, for his appearances.

In 1893 he went back. From his first expedition only Peary's wife, now pregnant, and Astrup accompanied him, because only they could stand him. Peary insisted on his own way no matter what. He forced everyone to sign contracts that they would not write about their experiences until a year after he had published his own account. This trip was not so successful, coming close, indeed, to disaster when a tidal wave created when a nearby glacier calved swept away his shoreline camp. When the supply ship returned the following summer Peary stayed in Greenland with Henson and one other man—but not Astrup. He had had enough now, too. The rest of the team, and Peary's wife, left for home.

When spring came he repeated his trip across Greenland to the same destination. They left on that trip with 42 dogs; they came back with one. They were close to starvation. Peary had made the trip, but it accomplished nothing. His only accomplishment, if it can be called that, was to take back to the United States two of the three meteorites that the northern Eskimos he had been living with had used for centuries as their source of iron—really their source of survival. These meteorites had supplied this tribe with the metal tools that Sir John Ross had seen when he first discovered them in 1817.

Later he came back for the third meteorite.

To our minds the act is unforgivable. For Peary it was another triumph. The public was enthralled. The Smithsonian bought them for $40,000. They're still there. He also brought back living Eskimos for scientists to study. Like most Eskimos moved to warmer climates, they soon died.

By now Peary had some very powerful friends, powerful enough not just to finance his expeditions but to quiet the Navy, which would have liked him to be of some use to them, since he was a naval officer. In 1898 he went north again, with the President of the United States, Theodore Roosevelt, clearing the way for him. Nobody liked an explorer more than Roosevelt. This time he was headed for the Pole. He planned to launch the attack from Adolphus Greely's old station, Fort Conger. To get there he trekked north for eighteen days from where his ship had left him and endured cold so terrible that when he reached the Fort his feet were completely white and without feeling. Several toes from each foot snapped off when his boots were removed. With him were Henson and Dr. Tom Dedrick. When Dedrick asked him why he hadn't told him his feet were numb, Peary replied, "A few toes aren't much to give to achieve the Pole." In the end he lost eight of them.

He pressed on regardless, making his way up the northern coast of Greenland to the end this time, to Cape Jessup, which he named after his chief patron, Morris Jessup. As they always did in the Arctic, especially in a Peary camp, relations among the members of the team deteriorated. He fired Dedrick and Dedrick left, not the Arctic but Fort Conger; he went across to the Eskimos and worked with them as a doctor. Peary's wife showed up with the supply ship. This was awkward, as Peary had acquired an Eskimo consort and had fathered a child on her. Peary walked with a limp now, and clumsily, thanks to the loss of his toes, but he still planned to try for the Pole. In March 1902 he did, making his way up the east coast of Ellesmere Island to the Arctic Ocean, then attempting the crossing. Even grim determination did not serve. The drift was to the west here, and swept him off his path. He came to the Big Lead and could go no farther. He had spent four years in the Arctic to no purpose. He was missing eight toes. His wife had discovered his Eskimo consort and his half-Eskimo child. Anyone else might have given up. Peary did not give up.

He was back on the hunt in 1906, this time not traveling light but with a large team of Eskimos in support, some of them leading the way across the notoriously uneven ice, making a reasonably level trail by cutting through ridges and hummocks. The Big Lead stopped them for a week until it froze over. Then they crossed it, but a storm stopped them for another week. He was moving too slowly, he recognized, to make the Pole. He got to 87 degrees north, or said that he did. He was trying to break the record set by the Duke of the Abruzzi several years before. To reach this latitude he had suddenly been able, after moving an average of only seven miles a day, to ratchet his speed up to eighteen miles a day. Remarkable. As would be true three years later, he was the only man on this dash who had the instruments, and the knowledge of how to use them, to verify his claims. Peary was in the same position as Frederick Cook. He needed achievements to raise money to come back and try again. So he achieved things, a farthest north. Or said he did. Nobody had any evidence to challenge him with. Everything depended on his veracity.

On that account, Peary also "discovered" on this expedition a piece of land that he saw breaking the northwest horizon in the distance from the top of Axel Heiberg Island. He named it Crocker Land, after yet another of his sponsors. Like Frederick Cook's Bradley Land, it was a chimera. There is no land where Peary places it.

Did Peary reach the Pole in 1909? Can we trust the achievements a man so needy of achievements claimed for himself?

Once again, everything depends on his veracity. Once again he took a large team with him to blaze the trail—133 dogs pulling nineteen sledges and 24 men. They left on the first of March. They lost a week waiting for the Big Lead to freeze over. By the end of March Peary had reached nearly 88 degrees north latitude, 133 miles from the Pole. He had with him on this last dash to the Pole a man named Robert Bartlett, and it was Bartlett who recorded this reading. But Bartlett was not destined to go to the Pole with Peary. Peary had promised him he would be his companion, but then Peary changed his mind. His black servant, Matthew Henson, would go with him instead. Bartlett was bitterly disappointed, although he hid it well. Henson, Peary told Bartlett, was a better traveler, better with the dogs, better with the Eskimos. What he neglected to add was that Henson did not know how to use navigational equipment. Bartlett, of course, did.

We take our next excerpt from Henson's account. In some ways Peary's choice of Henson was entirely just. Henson had traveled with him in the past under terrible conditions, risked his life, been faithful to his employer through it all—even though Peary was something of a racist. If Peary did reach the Pole, Henson, from Peary's own testimony, was actually the first of the two to get there. We take from Henson's book the chapter where he describes Bartlett's turning back, and the next phase of the trip north.

MATTHEW A. HENSON

A Negro Exploration at The North Pole

Leaving the Commander and Marvin at the igloos, my party took up the Captain's trail northward. It was expected that Peary would follow in an hour and that at the same time Marvin would start his return march. After a few minutes' going, we came to young ice of this season, broken up and frozen solid, not difficult to negotiate, but requiring constant pulling; leaving this, we came to an open lead which caused us to make a detour to the westward for four miles. We crossed on ice so thin that one of the sledgerunners broke through, and a little beyond one of the dogs fell in so completely that it was a precarious effort to rescue him; but we made it and, doglike, he shook the water out of his fur and a little later, when his fur froze, I gave him a thorough beating; not for falling in the water, but in order to loosen the ice-particles, so that he could shake them off. Poor brute, it was no use, and in a short while he commenced to develop symptoms of the dread piblokto, so in mercy he was killed. One of the Esquimo boys did the killing.

Dangerous as the crossing was, it was the only place possible, and we succeeded far better than we had anticipated. Beyond the lead we came to an old floe and, beyond that, young ice of one season's formation, similar to that which had been encountered earlier in the day. Before us lay a heavy, old floe, covered with soft, deep snow in which we sank continually; but it was only five P.M. when we reached the Captain's igloo. Anticipating the arrival of the

Commander, we built another igloo, and about an hour and a half later the Commander and his party came in.

March 28: Exactly 40° below zero when we pushed the sledges up to the curled-up dogs and started them off over rough ice covered with deep soft snow. It was like walking in loose granulated sugar. Indeed I might compare the snow of the Arctic to the granules of sugar, without their saccharine sweetness, but with freezing cold instead; you can not make snowballs of it, for it is too thoroughly congealed, and when it is packed by the wind it is almost as solid as ice. It is from the packed snow that the blocks used to from the igloo-walls are cut.

At the end of four hours, we came to the igloo where the Captain and his boys were sleeping the sleep of utter exhaustion. In order not to interrupt the Captain's rest, we built another igloo and unloaded his sledge, and distributed the greater part of the load among the sledges of the party. The Captain, on awakening, told us that the journey we had completed on that day had been made by him under the most trying conditions, and that it had taken him fourteen hours to do it. We were able to make better time because we had his trail to follow, and, therefore, the necessity of finding the easiest way was avoided. That was the object of the scout of pioneer party and Captain Bartlett had done practically all of it up to the time he turned back at 87° 48' north.

March 29: You have undoubtedly taken into consideration the pangs of hunger and of cold that you know assailed us, going Pole-ward; but have you ever considered that we were thirsty for water to drink or hungry for fat? To eat snow to quench our thirst would have been the height of folly, and as well as being thirsty, we were continuously assailed by the pangs of a hunger that called for the fat, good, rich, oily, juicy fat that our systems craved and demanded.

Had we succumbed to the temptations of thirst and eaten the snow, we would not be able to tell the tale of the conquest of the Pole; for the result of eating snow is death. True, the dogs licked up enough moisture to quench their thirsts, but we were not made of such stern stuff as they. Snow would have reduced our temperatures and we would quickly have fallen by the way. We had to wait until camp was made and the fire of alcohol started before we had a chance, and it was with hot tea that we quenched our thirsts. The hunger for fat was not appeased; a dog or two was killed, but his carcass went to the Esquimos and the entrails were fed to the rest of the pack. We ate no dogs on this trip, for various reasons, mainly, that the eating of dog is only a last resort, and we had plenty of food, and raw dog is flavorless and very tough. The killing of a dog is such a horrible matter that I will not describe it, and it is permitted only when all other exigencies have been exhausted. An Esquimo does not permit one drop of blood to escape.

The morning of the 29th of March, 1909, a heavy and dense fog of frost spicules overhung the camp. At four A.M., the Captain left camp to make as far a northing as possible. I with my Esquimos followed later. On our way we passed over very rough ice alternating with small floes, young ice of a few months' duration, and one old floe. We were now beside a lead of over three hundred feet in width, which we were unable to cross at that time because the ice was running steadily, though to the Northward. Following the trail of the Captain, which carried us a little to the westward of the lead, within one hundred feet of the Captain's igloo, the order to camp was given, as going forward was impossible. The whole party was together farther north than had ever been made by any other human beings, and in perfectly good condition; but the time was quickly coming when the little party would have to be made smaller and some part of it sent back. We were too fatigued to argue the question.

We turned in for a rest and sleep, but soon turned out again in pandemonium incomprehensible; the ice moving in all directions, our igloos wrecked, and every instant our very lives in danger. With eyes dazed by sleep, we tried to guide the terror-stricken dogs and push the sledges to safety, but rapidly we saw the party being separated and the black water begin to appear amid the roar of the breaking ice floes.

To the westward of our igloo, stood the Captain's igloo, on an island of ice, which revolved, while swiftly drifting to the eastward. On one occasion the floe happened to strike the main floe. The Captain, intently watching his opportunity, quickly crossed with his Esquimos. He had scarcely set foot on the opposite floe when the floe on which he had been previously isolated swung off, and rapidly disappeared.

Once more the parties were together. Thoroughly exhausted, we turned in and fell asleep, myself and the Esquimos too dumb for utterance, and Commander Peary and Bartlett too full of the realization of our escape to have much to say.

The dogs were in very good condition, taking everything into consideration.

When we woke up it was the morning of another day, March 30, and we found open water all about us. We could not go on until either the lead had frozen or until it had rafted shut. Temperature 35° below zero, and the weather clear and calm with no visible motion of the ice. We spent the day industriously in camp, mending foot-gear, harness, clothing, and looking after the dogs and their traces. This was work enough, especially untangling the traces of the bewildered dogs. The traces, snarled and entangled, besides being frozen to the consistency of wire, gave us the hardest work; and, owing to the activity of the dogs in leaping and bounding over each other, we had the most *unideal* conditions possible to contend with, and we were handicapped by having to use mitted instead of ungloved fingers to untangle the snarls of knots. Unlike Alexander the Great, we dared not cut the "Gordian Knots," but we did get them untangled.

About five o'clock in the afternoon, the temperature had fallen to 43° below zero, and at the same time the ice began to move again. Owing to the attraction of the moon, the mighty flanks of the earth were being drawn by her invisible force, and we were commencing again to crack and be rent asunder.

We loaded up hurriedly and all three parties left the camp and crossed over the place where recently had been the open lead, and beyond for more than five miles, until we reached the heavier and solid ice of the large floes. Northward our way led, and we kept on in that direction accordingly, at times crossing young ice so thin that the motion of the sledges would cause the ice to undulate. Over old floes of the blue, hummocky kind, on which the snow had fallen and become packed solid, the rest of this day's journey was completed. We staggered into camp like drunken men, and built our igloos by force of habit rather than with the intelligence of human beings.

It was continuously daylight, but such a light as never was on land or sea.

The next day was April 1, and the Farthest North of Barlett. I knew at this time that he was to go back, and that I was to continue, so I had no misgivings and neither had he. He was ready and anxious to take the backtrail. His five marches were up and he was glad of it, and he was told that in the morning he must turn back and knit the trail together, so that the main column could return over a beaten path.

Before going to sleep, Peary and he (Captain Bartlett) had figured out the reckoning of the distance, and, to insure the Captain's making at least 88° north, Peary let him have another go, for a short distance northward, and at noon on the day of his return, the observations showed that Captain Bartlett had made 87° 47' North Latitude, or practically 88° north. "Why, Peary," he said, "it is just like every day," and so it was, with the exception, like every day in the Arctic, but with all of every day's chances and hazards. The lion-like month of March had passed. Captain Bartlett bade us all farewell. He turned back from the Farthest North that had ever been reached by any one, to insure the safe return of him who was to go still Farther North, the very top of the world, the Pole itself.

While waiting for Bartlett to return from his forced march, the main party had been at work, assorting dogs (by this time without much trouble, as only one was found utterly unfit to make progress), and rearranging loads, for the Captain had almost three hundred miles of sea-ice to negotiate before he would reach *terra firma,* and he had to have his food-supply arranged so that it would carry him to the land and back to the ship, and dogs in good enough condition to pull the loads, as well as enough sledges to bear his equipment. When he did come back to our camp, before parting, he was perfectly satisfied, and with the same old confidence he swept his little party together and at three P.M., with a cheery "Good-by! Good Luck!" he was off. His Esquimo boys, attempting in English, too, gave us their "Good-bys." The least emotional of all our partings; and this brave man, who had borne the brunt of all of the hardships, like the true-blue, dead-game, unconquerable hero that he was, set out to do the work that was left for him to do; to knit the broken strands of our upward trail together, so that we who were at his rear could follow in safety.

I have never heard the story of the return of Captain Bartlett in detail; his Esquimo boys were incapable of telling it, and Captain Bartlett is altogether too modest.

✳

AND NOW WE COMPLETE THE STORY, WITH THE TRIUMPHANT CLIMACTIC *thirty-second chapter of Peary's own book, in which he describes reaching the Pole on April 6, 1909, four days after leaving Bartlett behind 133 miles to the south. If Peary is telling the truth, after leaving Bartlett they traveled at the astonishing rate of more than 30 miles a day. Believe it or not.*

ROBERT E. PEARY

The North Pole

THE POLE IS MINE

THE LAST MARCH NORTHWARD ENDED AT TEN O'CLOCK OF THE FORENOON
of April 6. I had now made the five marches planned from the point at which
Bartlett turned back, and my reckoning showed that we were in the immediate neighbourhood of the goal of all our striving. After the usual arrangement for going into camp, at approximate local noon, on the Columbia
meridian, I made the first observation at our polar camp. It indicated our
position as 89° 5′7″.

We were now at the end of the last long march of the upward journey. Yet
with the Pole actually in sight I was too weary to take the last few steps. The
accumulated weariness of all those days and nights of forced marches and insufficient sleep, constant peril and anxiety, seemed to roll across me all at once.
I was actually too exhausted to realize at the moment that my life's purpose had
been achieved. As soon as our igloos had been completed, and we had eaten
our dinner and double-rationed the dogs, I turned in for a few hours of
absolutely necessary sleep, Henson and the Eskimos having unloaded the
sledges and got them in readiness for such repairs as were necessary. But,
weary though I was, I could not sleep long. It was, therefore, only a few hours
later when I woke. The first thing I did after awaking was to write these
words in my diary: "The Pole at last. The prize of three centuries. My dream
and goal for twenty years. Mine at last! I cannot bring myself to realize it. It
seems all so simple and commonplace."

Everything was in readiness for an observation at 6 P.M., Columbia meridian time, in case the sky should be clear, but at that hour it was, unfortunately, still overcast. But as there were indications that it would clear before long, two of the Eskimos and myself made ready a light sledge carrying only the instruments, a tin of pemmican, and one or two skins; and drawn by a double team of dogs, we pushed on an estimated distance of ten miles. While we travelled, the sky cleared, and at the end of the journey, I was able to get a satisfactory series of observations at Columbia meridian midnight. These observations indicated that our position was then beyond the Pole.

Nearly everything in the circumstances which then surrounded us seemed too strange to be thoroughly realized, but one of the strangest of those circumstances seemed to me to be the fact that, in a march of only a few hours, I had passed from the western to the eastern hemisphere and had verified my position at the summit of the world. It was hard to realize that, on the first miles of this brief march, we had been travelling due north, while on the last few miles of the same march, we had been travelling south, although we had all the time been travelling precisely in the same direction. It would be difficult to imagine a better illustration of the fact that most things are relative. Again, please consider the uncommon circumstance that, in order to return to our camp, it now became necessary to turn and go north again for a few miles and then to go directly south, all the time travelling in the same direction.

As we passed back along the trail which none had ever seen before or would ever see again, certain reflections intruded themselves which, I think, may fairly be called unique. East, west, and north had disappeared for us. Only one direction remained and that was south. Every breeze which could possibly blow upon us, no matter from what point of the horizon, must be a south wind. Where we were, one day and one night constituted a year, a hundred such days and nights constituted a century. Had we stood in that spot during the six months of the Arctic winter night, we should have seen every star of the northern hemisphere circling the sky at the same distance from the horizon, with Polaris (the North Star) practically in the zenith.

All during our march back to camp the sun was swinging around in its ever-moving circle. At six o'clock on the morning of April 7, having again arrived at Camp Jesup, I took another series of observations. These indicated our position as being four or five miles from the Pole, toward Behring Strait.

Therefore, with a double team of dogs and a light sledge, I travelled directly towards the sun an estimated distance of eight miles. Again I returned to the camp in time for a final and completely satisfactory series of observations on April 7 at noon, Columbia meridian time. These observations gave results essentially the same as those made at the same spot twenty-four hours before.

I had now taken in all thirteen single, or six and one-half double, altitudes of the sun, at two different stations, in three different directions, at four different times. All were under satisfactory conditions, except for the first single altitude on the sixth. The temperature during these observations, had been from minus 11° Fahrenheit to minus 30° Fahrenheit, with clear sky and calm weather (except as already noted for the single observation on the sixth.)

In traversing the ice in these various directions as I had done, I had allowed approximately ten miles for possible errors in my observations, and at some moment during these marches and countermarches, I had passed over or very near the point where north and south and east and west blend into one.

Of course there were some more or less informal ceremonies connected with our arrival at our difficult destination, but they were not of a very elaborate character. We planted five flags at the top of the world. The first one was a silk American flag which Mrs. Peary gave me fifteen year ago. That flag has done more travelling in high latitudes than any other ever made. I carried it wrapped about my body on every one of my expeditions northward after it came into my possession, and I left a fragment of it at each of my successive "farthest norths": Cape Morris K. Jesup, the nothernmost point of land in the known point of Jesup Land, west of Grant land; Cape Columbia, the northenrmost point of North American lands; and my farthest north in 1906, latitude 87° 6' in the ice of the polar sea. By the time it actually reached the Pole, therefore, it was somewhat worn and discoloured.

A broad diagonal section of the ensign would now mark the farthest goal of earth—the place where I and my dusky companions stood.

It was also considered appropriate to raise the colours of the Delta Kappa Epsilon fraternity, in which I was initiated a member while an undergraduate student at Bowdoin College, the "World's Ensign of Liberty and Peace," with its red, white, and blue, in a field of white; the Navy League flag, and the Red Cross flag.

After I had planted the American flag in the ice, I told Henson to time the Eskimos for three rousing cheers, which they gave with the greatest enthusiasm. Thereupon, I shook hands with each member of the party—surely a sufficiently unceremonious affair to meet with the approval of the most democratic. The Eskimos were childishly delighted with our success. While, of course, they did not realize its importance fully, or its world-wide significance, they did understand that it meant the final achievement of a task upon which they had seen me engaged for many years.

Then, in a space between the ice blocks of a pressure ridge, I deposited a glass bottle containing a diagonal strip of my flag and records of which the following is a copy:

90 N. Lat., North Pole,
April 6, 1909.

Arrived here to-day, 27 marches from C. Columbia.

I have with me 5 men, Matthew Henson, coloured, Oo-tah, E-ging-wah, Seegloo, and Oo-ke-ah, Eskimos; 5 sledges and 38 dogs. My ship, the S.S. *Roosevelt*, is in winter quarters at C. Sheridan, 90 miles east of Columbia.

The expedition under my command which has succeeded in reaching the Pole, is under the auspices of the Peary Arctic Club of New York City, and has been fitted out and sent north by the members and friends of the club for the purpose of securing the geographical prize, if possible, for the honour and prestige of the United States of America.

The officers of the club are Thomas H. Hubbard, of New York, President; Zenas Crane of Mass., Vice-President; Herbert L. Bridgman, of New York, Secretary and Treasurer.

I start back for Cape Columbia to-morrow.

Robert E. Peary,
United States Navy.

90 N. Lat., North Pole.
April 6, 1909.

I have to-day hoisted the national ensign of the United States of America at this place, which my observation indicates to be the North Polar axis of the earth, and have formally taken possession of the entire region, and adjacent, for and in the name of the President of the United States of America.

I leave this record and United States flag in possession.

Robert E. Peary,
United States Navy.

If it were possible for a man to arrive at 90° north latitude without being utterly exhausted, body and brain, he would doubtless enjoy a series of unique sensations and reflections. But the attainment of the Pole was the culmination of days and weeks of forced marches, physical discomfort, insufficient sleep, and racking anxiety. It is a wise provision of nature that the human consciousness can grasp only such degree of intense feeling as the brain can endure, and the grim guardians of earth's remotest spot will accept no man as guest until he has been tried and tested by the severest ordeal.

Perhaps it ought not to have been so, but when I knew for a certainty that we had reached the goal, there was not a thing in the world I wanted but sleep. But after I had a few hours of it, there succeeded a condition of mental exaltation which made further rest impossible. For more than a score of years that point on the earth's surface had been the object of my every effort. To attain it my whole being, physical, mental, and moral, had been dedicated. Many times my own life and the lives of those with me had been devoted to this object. This journey was my eighth into the Arctic wilderness. In that wilderness I had spent nearly twelve years out of the twenty-three between my thirtieth and my fifty-third year, and the intervening time spent in civilized communities during that period had been mainly occupied with preparations for returning to the wilderness. The determination to reach the Pole had become so much a part of my being that, strange as it may seem, I long ago ceased to think of myself save as an instrument for the attainment of that end. To the layman this may seem strange, but an inventor can understand it, or an artist, or any one who has devoted himself for years upon years to the service of an idea.

But though my mind was busy at intervals during those thirty hours spent at the Pole with the exhilarating thought that my dream had come true, there was one recollection of other times that, now and then, intruded itself with startling distinctness. It was the recollecting of a day three years before, April 12, 1906, when after making a fight with ice, open water, and storms, the expedition which I commanded had been forced to turn back from 87° 6′ north latitude because our supply of food would carry us no further. And the contrast between the terrible depression of that day and the exaltation of the present moment was not the least pleasant feature of our brief stay at the Pole. During the dark moments of that return journey in 1906, I had told myself that I was only one in a long list of Arctic explorers, dating back through the centuries, all the way from Henry Hudson to the Duke of the Abruzzi, and including Franklin, Kane, and Melville. A long list of valiant men who had striven and failed. I told myself that I had only succeeded at the price of the best years of my life in adding a few links to the chain that led from the parallels of civilization towards the polar centre, but that, after all, at the end the only word I had to write was failure.

But now, while quartering the ice in various directions from our camp, I tried to realize that, after twenty-three years of struggles and discouragement, I had at last succeeded in placing the flag of my country at the goal of the world's desire. It is not easy to write about such a thing, but I knew that we were going back to civilization with the last of the great adventure stories—a story the world had been weaiting to hear for nearly four hundred years, a story which was to be told at last under the folds of the Stars and Stripes, the flag that during a lonely and isolated life had come to be for me the symbol of home and everything I loved—and might never see again.

The thirty hours at the Pole, what with my marchings and counter-marchings, together with the observations and records, were pretty well crowded. I found time, however, to write to Mrs. Peary on a United States postal card which I had found on the ship during the winter. It had been my custom at various important stages of the journey northward to write such a note in order that, if anything serious happened to me, these brief communications might ultimately reach her at the hands of survivors. This was the card, which later reached Mrs. Peary at Sydney:

90 North Latitude, April 7th
My dear Jo,

I have won out at last. Have been here a day. I start for home and you in an hour. Love to the "kidsies."
Bert.

In the afternoon of the 7th, after flying our flags and taking our photographs, we went into our igloos and tried to sleep a little, before starting south again.

I could not sleep and my two Eskimos, Seegloo and Egingwah, who occupied the igloo with me, seemed equally restless. They turned from side to side, and when they were quiet I could tell from their uneven breathing that they were not asleep. Though they had not been specially excited the day before when I told them that we had reached the goal, yet they also seemed to be under the same exhilarating influence which made sleep impossible for me.

Finally I rose, and telling my men and the three men in the other igloo, who were equally wakeful, that we would try to make our last camp, some thirty miles to the south, before we slept, I gave orders to hitch up the dogs and be off. It seemed unwise to waste such perfect travelling weather in tossing about on the sleeping platforms of our igloos.

Neither Henson nor the Eskimos required any urging to take to the trail again. They were naturally anxious to get back to the land as soon as possible—now that our work was done. And about four o'clock in the afternoon of the 7th of April we turned our backs upon the camp at the North Pole.

Though intensely conscious of what I was leaving, I did not wait for any lingering farewell of my life's goal. The event of human beings standing at the hitherto inaccessible summit of the earth was accomplished, and my work now lay to the south, where four hundred and thirteen nautical miles of ice floes and possibly open leads still lay between us and the north coast of Grand Land. One backward glance I gave—then turned my face toward the south and toward the future.

THE AFTERMATH WAS EXTREMELY UNPLEASANT FOR FREDERICK COOK. *Peary found out on his return that Cook was claiming the Pole, that he had, indeed, reached it, or so he said, a year before Peary. Cook had strangely left his journals and papers back in Greenland, however, so he had no written evidence of his claims. He said he had spent that remarkable winter in the cave on Devon Island with his two Eskimo friends writing, he said, in a tiny script, in his own personal shorthand, with four pencils he kept constantly sharpened, on a prescription pad and in two small booklets, no fewer than 150,000 words. If this record actually existed, he never showed it to anyone. From Greenland he went to Europe rather than America. He consented to have his claim examined at the University of Copenhagen. The Danes at first feted him. When he showed them what he had in the way of proof, a typescript account he prepared while in Europe, they said it wasn't enough. "Not proven" was their verdict.*

Peary called him a fraud. Peary attacked him at every opportunity. Peary arranged for the two Eskimos who accompanied Cook through the Arctic to be interrogated on board Peary's ship. They spoke no English and the interrogators were only marginally capable in their language, but according to them the two men, who were interrogated separately, said that Cook had never left the sight of land. Oddly, two men on board the ship did speak Eskimo fluently, but they were not asked to join the interrogation. The press became heavily involved in the controversy, at first leaning toward Cook, then toward Peary. Peary submitted to examination of his claims by a committee of the National Geographic Society. He knew most of the members of this committee personally. The examination was perfunctory. Since no one but Peary had taken measurements at the Pole, it was a matter of accepting Peary's word or rejecting it. They chose to accept it. How had he been able to jack up his rate of speed to more than thirty miles a day? Henson had noted open leads, where there are leads there is moving ice, where the ice moves it creates ridges. How had he negotiated the leads, the ridges, with such sudden rapidity? He was exhausted at the end, said Henson, dead weight. The questions went unanswered.

So they remain. Inevitably it was Peary who got the credit for reaching the North Pole, and the honors. It is his name in the record books. Dr. Cook's later career included imprisonment for mail fraud. But the fact is that we do not know for sure who made it to the North Pole first. There are reasons to believe, and disbelieve, both men. If Cook had not left the sight of land, for example, why hadn't he retraced his steps to the caches he had set up crossing Ellesmere and Axel Heiberg Islands? Why starve himself and his two companions for an entire year, lost in the high Arctic? Why didn't Peary take Bartlett, who could have confirmed his sun sightings, instead of Henson? But then why would he lie, if he was only 133 miles south of the Pole? If he hadn't actually reached it on April 6 he could certainly have taken a few more days to get there.

The consensus of opinion among Arctic historians is that neither Cook nor Peary reached the Pole. At least one of the explorers who have been to the Pole since Peary, however, himself recorded high speeds over flat ice near the Pole. This was Will Steger, who set out in March, 1986, to reach the Pole the traditional way, by dog team, carrying their supplies on sledges, entirely unsupported from the air. One of Steger's goals was to test whether Peary might have reached the Pole in the time claimed. Steger's early rates are quite slow. For a full month his team never made more than nine miles a day north. But later they begin to speed up. On the last days, as they neared the Pole, he was making up to 32 miles a day over flat ice. Steger thinks Peary may have told the truth. It was possible.

But Fergus Fleming argues that it was not. Peary said that he made 133 miles in four days. He also said, notes Fleming, that he made the same 133 miles back in just two. "The distances," says Fleming, "of almost sixty miles per day which he claimed for the southern journey are fantastical." He and Henson and his Eskimo companions would have had to be supermen.

We must leave it at that.

EPILOGUE

BECAUSE THE WORLD MOSTLY ACCEPTED PEARY'S CLAIM THAT HE HAD reached the North Pole, interest in it languished after 1910. Not until the 1920s, when aviation and its possibilities were beginning to excite the public, did adventurers once more turn their attention north, this time with the intention of being the first to fly over the Pole.

Roald Amundsen was the first to make the attempt. In 1925 he bought two Dornier flying boats from Germany and raised money for the flight from Lincoln Ellsworth, the well-to-do American, who would later fly across Antarctica. They took off from Spitzbergen in May 1925 and landed on an open lead well short of the Pole when one of the planes developed engine trouble. The lead froze up within hours of their landing, stranding them on the ice with about three weeks worth of food, if they reduced their rations. It took them three weeks of exhausting labor to construct a runway from which the remaining Dornier could take off on skis. They just made it into the air.

Amundsen tried again in 1926, this time in a dirigible named the Norge with the Italian pilot Umberto Nobile at the controls. In this machine the two men reached the Pole and circled it several times, then flew on to Alaska. But the U. S. Navy officer Richard E. Byrd seemed to have beaten them to it. Two days before the Norge left Spitzbergen, on May 9, 1926, Byrd and his pilot, Floyd Bennett, took off in a Fokker trimotor and returned fifteen hours and thirty minutes later. They claimed that they had reached the Pole. Byrd's claim was accepted at the time and he became a new American hero, eclipsed in the 1920s only, perhaps, by Charles Lindbergh. But did he indeed make the

Pole? Most critics think not. The Fokker he was flying had a top speed of 85 miles an hour. Byrd would have had to average 98 miles an hour to have made the Pole and back in the time he was in the air. Floyd Bennett later told a friend that they had not reached the Pole, only flown about in the area. Byrd himself many years later told someone else that they had gotten no closer to the Pole than 150 miles. So Amundsen and Nobile were almost certainly the first to fly to the North Pole.

However this accomplishment, too, was a bitter fruit. Amundsen and Nobile had argued, in print, about who deserved the credit for their feat, and when Nobile disappeared on another flight to the Pole in 1928, the Italian government specifically forbade Amundsen from joining in the search. Amundsen flew north anyway and was never seen again.

Since then the Pole has been reached many times. In 1937 Russians flew to the Pole, landed there, and set up manned scientific drift stations to monitor the weather and the movements of the ice. They were the first human beings known for sure to have set foot on the frozen ocean that covers the Pole, at the exact spot where it would emerge from the ice were it, as the Eskimos imagined it, a Big Nail. In 1958 the American nuclear submarine U. S. S. Nautilus cruised over the Pole under the ice that covers it. An Electrician's Mate named James Sordelet became the first man ever to re-enlist in the Navy at the North Pole. In 1967 an American insurance salesman named Ralph Plaisted, sitting in a restaurant with some friends, decided on a whim to organize an expedition to the North Pole over the ice on snowmobiles. Defeated the first time out, Plaisted succeeded in 1968. He thereby became the first person known for certain, beyond a doubt, to have reached the Pole over the ice. A year later the English adventurer Wally Herbert reached the Pole via dog sledge. He and his companions were the first human beings to cross the Arctic Ocean on the ice from one continent to the other, the Pole being a subsidiary goal. It took Herbert over a year to make the trip. He was resupplied from the air, however, as Plaisted had been. The first person to reach the Pole via dog sledge but without being resupplied by air—traveling, in other words, as Robert E. Peary had traveled—was Will Steger in 1986. It took Steger and his team 55 days. They were flown out.

It is unlikely there will be much more of this sort of Arctic adventuring. The Arctic has become the stage for another kind of human drama, the drama of global warming. Already the average thickness of the Arctic ice pack is half what it was a century ago. The permafrost in the Canadian high Arctic is melting to a greater depth every summer. Bogs in northern Sweden that have been frozen for 10,000 years are melting and releasing huge quantities of methane, which is 25 times more effective as a greenhouse gas than carbon dioxide. The Northwest Passage is now ice-free most summers. Some scientists predict that the Arctic ice pack will melt completely every summer by the end of this century. The concomitant melting of the Greenland ice cap will raise sea levels worldwide by nearly twenty-five feet.

If these developments are not to have a profoundly tragic ending, human beings must find in themselves a different kind of courage, the courage to make radical changes in their way of life, indeed in the very idea of what the earth is for and what we are doing on it. Most of us will not be here to see the outcome of this particular drama, yet it is our responsibility to make a beginning, to find the courage to rethink the human adventure and give it a viable future.

Suggested Readings

No one book exists that covers all Arctic exploration, from the beginning to the present, except for A Fabulous Kingdom, by Charles Officer and Jake Page. It is, however, a short book and only an introduction. The best book on the voyage of Pytheas and its context is Barry Cunliffe's The Voyage of Pytheas the Greek. Ann Savours, The Search for the Northwest Passage, is useful as an introduction to the Elizabethan and Jacobean voyages of the sixteenth and early seventeenth centuries. It is less helpful for later voyages. Glyn Williams is an expert on early exploration and his book, Voyages of Delusion, covers the eighteenth-century voyages in Hudson Bay in great detail. For the nineteenth century three books are indispensable: Pierre Berton, Arctic Grail; Fergus Fleming, Barrow's Boys; and Fergus Fleming again, Ninety Degrees North.

For particular voyagers the literature can be very extensive, while on others it is virtually nonexistent. Frobisher, for example, has been written about frequently. The best book on him is James McDermott's Martin Frobisher: Elizabethan Privateer, an exhaustive new biography. On Davis, Hudson, and Barents it is another story. Practically the only sources are the introductions to the nineteenth-century Hakluyt Society editions of their works, which are very difficult to find. Samuel Eliot Morison's The European Discovery of America: The Northern Voyages is some help, but the Savours book mentioned above is the most useful.

For Arctic whaling, Richard Ellis's comprehensive history of whaling, Men and Whales, is authoritative. On the Rosses, John and James, on Parry, and on English Arctic explorers of the nineteenth century generally, the Fergus Fleming books above are pretty good, although he makes small mistakes in dating and the like. On John Ross the best recent source is Ray Edinger, Fury Beach. For John Franklin, whom the English generally still regard with respect, the literature is much broader. There have been a number of biographies, the latest being Martyn Beardsley's Deadly Winter. Other books detail the search for Franklin, including Leslie H. Neatby, Search for Franklin, and Roderic Owen, The Fate of Franklin, while John Rae has his own well-deserved biography, Fatal Passage, by Ken McGoogan.

For a man who was once so famous, Elisha Kent Kane has been strangely neglected. The only recent biography is by George W. Corner, Doctor Kane of the Arctic Seas, and it dates from 1972. Kane could use a fresh biography, and Kane's papers are available. As in so many cases in the history of exploration, what Kane published differs considerably from his manuscript diaries and journals of his expeditions.

Charles Francis Hall is another story. The story of his expedition, his murder, and the drift south on the ice floe that George Tyson detailed in his selection in this anthology, is so dramatic that a number of books are available. The best is Chauncey Loomis, Weird and Tragic Shores. On the Greely expedition consult Leonard F. Guttridge, Ghosts of Cape Sabine, and Alden Todd, Abandoned.

Contemporary literature on Cook and Peary is, unfortunately, not abundant. Peary's personality seems to have put off biographers. Bradford Washburn and Peter Cherici took apart Cook's claim to have climbed Mt. McKinley in their recent book, The Dishonorable Dr. Cook. An even more recent book by Bruce Henderson, True North, on the other hand, takes a more sympathetic view of Cook's claims to have reached the North Pole. The final word on that controversy is unlikely ever to be written.

As for global warming, the situation gets worse with every study. The recent book by Charles Wohlforth, The Whale and the Supercomputer, is already a bit out of date, but it is an excellent introduction to the whole subject of climate change and its effects on the Arctic. As for the native people who are already feeling its effects, their most persistent champion is the French anthropologist Jean Malaurie, whose quirky, passionate Ultima Thule is a fascinating look at the relationships all these explorers had—from John Ross to Cook and Peary and beyond—with the native peoples who so often saved them from the cold and starvation and death.

NATIONAL GEOGRAPHIC
ADVENTURE CLASSICS

20 HRS., 40 MIN.: OUR FLIGHT IN THE *FRIENDSHIP*
Amelia Earhart
ISBN: 0-7922-3376-X
$14.00 U.S./$22.00 Canada

Amelia Earhart's high-spirited account of her *first* crossing of the Atlantic by airplane in 1928, as a co-pilot aboard the *Friendship*, rich with autobiographical information and a discussion on the future of flight—including the important role she expected women to play.

THE ADVENTURES OF CAPTAIN BONNEVILLE
Washington Irving
ISBN: 0-7922-3743-9
$15.00 U.S./$24.00 Canada

Captain Benjamin Louis Eulalie de Bonneville, United States Army, explorer, fur trapper, and trader was one of the most colorful figures in the history of the American West and an irresistible subject to Washington Irving, who purchased the Captain's journals and wrote this engaging, historical account of Bonneville's death-defying experiences across the American West.

THE CRUISE OF THE *SNARK*
Jack London
ISBN: 0-7922-6244-I
$13.00 U.S./$21.00 Canada

In 1907 the author of *The Call of the Wild* and *The Sea Wolf* decided to undertake his own grand adventure: a seven year, round-the-world cruise aboard the *Snark*. From Hawaii to the Marquesas to the Solomons to Bora Bora the story of the voyage is one of excitement and spirit, occasional leaks, and London's own hilarious attempts to understand the mysteries of navigation.

THE EXPLORATION OF THE
COLORADO RIVER AND ITS CANYONS
John Wesley Powell
ISBN: 0-7922-6636-6
$14.00 U.S./$21.50 Canada/£8.99 U.K.

John Wesley Powell, the legendary one-armed pioneer lead the first expedition down the Colorado River into the Grand Canyon. Powell and his crew faced forbidding rapids and scarce food, all of which are documented in thrilling detail in this harrowing saga of strength, determination, and perseverance.

INCA LAND
Hiram Bingham
ISBN: 0-7922-6194-I
$14.00 U.S./$22.00 Canada

In 1911, Yale University Scholar Hiram Bingham set off for Peru with the goal of climbing Peru's highest peak.Along the way discovered Machu Picchu, an ancient Inca stronghold high in the mountains. Bingham's wonderfully literate account of the extraordinary find is preceded by an engaging description of his own freewheeling adventures in Peru.

THE JOURNALS OF LEWIS AND CLARK
Meriwether Lewis and William Clark
ISBN: 0-7922-6921-7
$16.00 U.S./$25.00 Canada/£9.99 U.K.

This newly abridged and edited edition of Meriwether Lewis and William

Clark's unprecedented a two-year, 5,000 mile journey through the heart of the unknown American West to the Pacific Ocean includes a modern English "translation" that corrects the duo's famously poor spelling and grammar, making for a truly readable account of the journey.

MY LIFE AS AN EXPLORER
Sven Anders Hedin
ISBN: 0-7922-6987-X
$16.00 U.S./$25.00 Canada/£9.99 U.K.
An adventurer with a capital "A," Sven Hedin explored the parts of Asia marked "unknown" on the maps of the 19th and early 20th centuries. His delightful memoir is filled with dangerous situations, the discovery of lost cities, and exotic lands and people, all brilliantly illustrated by the author.

THE OREGON TRAIL
Francis Parkman
ISBN: 0-7922-6640-4
$14.00 U.S./$21.00 Canada/£8.99 U.K.
The first historian of the American frontier left his home in Boston in 1846 to travel west with the Conestoga wagons along the Oregon Trail. Parkman encountered a truly wild land fraught with danger, starvation, and marauding Indians, all of which he recorded in the classic account of America's move west.

SAILING ALONE AROUND THE WORLD AND
THE VOYAGE OF THE *LIBERDADE*
Joshua Slocum
ISBN: 0-7922-6556-4
$13.00 U.S./$21.00 Canada
Joshua Slocum's 1899 account of the first solo voyage around the world has been treasured by sailors for more than 100 years. This Adventure Classics edition of Slocum's thrilling chronicle of raging storms, threatening pirates, and treacherous reefs includes another harrowing tale of hardships along the coast of South America: *The Voyage of the Liberdade*.

SCRAMBLES AMONGST THE ALPS
Edward Whymper
ISBN: 0-7922-6923-3
$14.00 U.S./$22.00 Canada/£8.99 U.K.

Before thermal clothing, even before reliable ropes, Edward Whymper braved the Alps with energy and determination as he pioneered modern mountaineering. This classic account of his adventures recounts Whymper's many attempts to climb the Matterhorn and the shocking tragedy that befell his companions when they finally achieved their goal.

THE SILENT WORLD
Jacques Cousteau
ISBN: 0-7922-6796-6
$13.00 U.S./$19.50 Canada

This 50th anniversary edition of Jacques Cousteau's thrilling memoir includes his charming story of the invention of S.C.U.B.A. from spare automobile parts in the 1940s and details the adventures that followed as he and his team tested the limits of endurance as they pioneered ocean exploration.

THE SOUTH POLE: A HISTORY
OF THE EXPLORATION OF ANTARCTICA
Featuring Shackleton, Byrd, Scott, Amundsen, and more
ISBN: 0-7922-6797-4
$15.00 U.S./$22.50 Canada

Through the words of the famous—and not so famous—explorers the challenges and hardships of reaching and exploring the South Pole are documented through journals, ship's logs, and personal accounts that tell the extraordinary story of the exploration of the frozen continent.

THE TOMB OF TUTANKHAMUN
Howard Carter
ISBN 0-7922-6890-3
$14.00 U.S./$22.00 Canada

The 1922 discovery of the undisturbed tomb of an Egyptian pharaoh gave the world its first glimpse into the splendor of ancient Egypt. Carter's account, published for the first time as a single volume, deftly conveys his own amazement as he uncovers priceless treasures, including the pharaoh's intact mummy.

TRAVELS IN WEST AFRICA
Mary Kingsley
ISBN: 0-7922-6638-2
$14.00 U.S./$21.50 Canada/£8.99 U.K.

Defying Victorian conventions, Mary Kingsley traveled alone to West Africa in 1893. Kingsley was often the first European to enter remote villages, but she made fast friends with the tribes she encountered while collecting priceless samples of flora and fauna. Kingsley's engaging book records numerous obstacles and challenges, including a hilarious encounter with a panther. She faced each one head-on, and always dressed as a lady!

VOYAGE OF THE *BEAGLE*
Charles Darwin
ISBN: 0-7922-6559-9
$13.00 U.S./$21.00 Canada

Charles Darwin's 1845 account of a 5-year journey to South America as the naturalist aboard the HMS *Beagle* is a wonderfully told tale of a marvelous journey, rich with vivid descriptions of the natural world, the observations of which would lead to the publication of the *Origin of Species*.

THE WORST JOURNEY IN THE WORLD
Apsley Cherry-Garrard
ISBN: 0-7922-6634-X
$16.00 U.S./$25.00 Canada/£9.99 U.K.

While Robert Falcon Scott and his party set off on an attempt to be the first men to reach the South Pole, Cherry-Garrard and companions set off in search of the never-before-seen breeding grounds of the Emperor Penguin, a miserable assignment that the author dubbed "the worst journey in the world"— until he returned and discovered the shocking fate of his expedition's leader.

TO ORDER NATIONAL GEOGRAPHIC ADVENTURE CLASSICS
VISIT YOUR LOCAL BOOKSTORE OR LOG ON TO:
HTTP://WWW.NATIONALGEOGRAPHIC.COM/BOOKS.

INTRODUCTION
TO
ELECTRICAL
ENERGY SYSTEMS